CHARTER SCHOOLS

CHARTER SCHOOLS

Hope or Hype?

Jack Buckley and Mark Schneider

PRINCETON UNIVERSITY PRESS

PRINCETON AND OXFORD

Second printing, and first paperback printing, 2009
Paperback ISBN: 978-0-691-14319-4

The Library of Congress has cataloged the cloth edition of this book as follows

Buckley, Jack, 1972–
Charter schools : hope or hype? / Jack Buckley and Mark Schneider.
p.   cm.
Includes bibliographical references and index.
ISBN-13: 978-0-691-12985-3 (cl : alk. paper)—ISBN-10: 0-691-12985-1 (cl : alk. paper)
1. Charter schools—United States. I. Schneider, Mark, 1946– II. Title.
LB2806.36.B82 2007
371.01—dc22   2006049706

British Library Cataloging-in-Publication Data is available

This book has been composed in Sabon and Univers

Printed on acid-free paper. ∞

press.princeton.edu

Printed in the United States of America

3   5   7   9   10   8   6   4   2

Whereas boosters and advocates, myself included, once supposed that charter schools would almost always turn out to be good schools, reality shows that some are fantastic, some are abysmal, and many are hard to distinguish from the district schools to which they're meant to be alternatives. Merely hanging a "charter" sign over a schoolhouse door frees it to be different but doesn't assure quality—or even differentness. Those running the school need to know what they're doing—and be good at doing it. Too many well-meaning (or, sometimes, greedy) folks set out to create charter schools that they aren't competent to run.

—*Chester E. Finn, Jr.*, National Review,
October 9, 2006

CONTENTS

FIGURES

TABLES

ACKNOWLEDGMENTS

THE WORK REPORTED in this book has been helped by a number of people and organizations. First, we would like to acknowledge support from the Political Science Program at the National Science Foundation, grant number SES-0314656. As are many other political scientists, we are particularly appreciative of the support (and droll sense of humor) displayed by Frank Scioli, the program director at the NSF. We would also like to thank the Smith Richardson Foundation for its support, particularly the inspirational Phoebe Cottingham, who was the program officer at the foundation when the award was made.

We would like to acknowledge the contribution of Elif Calki, in particular for her work on developing more detailed information about specific charter schools. Erin Cassese, who is a coauthor of chapter 2, also provided feedback on many other chapters. Robert Cane, Executive Director of Friends of Choice in Urban Schools, and Michael Peabody, chair of FOCUS, provided entry into the world of charter schools (without their help, we would never have been able to develop the list of charter school parents that made this study possible). Mary Filardo, Executive Director of the 21st Century School Fund, also provided entry to the world of Washington, D.C. schools. Yi Shang, a Ph.D. student at the Lynch School of Education at Boston College, provided invaluable research support in both gathering and analyzing the data. At Stony Brook, Simona Kucsova, who is now an assistant professor at Grand Valley State University, played a similar role. Melissa Marschall, as always, provided helpful suggestions, as did Jeff Henig, Ken Wong, William Howell, and Chris Berry.

Greg Elacqua, Professor at the School of Government at the Universidad Adolfo Ibáñez in Chile and senior adviser to the Minister of Education, helped at many points in the development of this book and in particular provided a valuable cross-national perspective to some of the arguments. Ed Metz provided very constructive feedback on chapter 12, in which we study the role of charter schools in providing civic education and helping to develop democratic citizenship.

Gary King and Jonathan Wand patiently helped us employ the CHOPIT model used in chapter 9. Finally, we would like to thank Hank Levin, of Teachers College, and the National Center for the Study of the Privatization of Education he directs, for providing a forum for early versions of much of this work as well a whole set of constructive comments and criticisms.

CHARTER SCHOOLS

1

Introduction

IN THE UNITED STATES TODAY, many different education reforms compete for the attention of political leaders, policy makers, parents, and school officials. Charter schools constitute one of the most widespread and important of these. Since Minnesota passed the first charter-school law in 1991, forty-two states, including the District of Columbia, have passed similar legislation, and thirty-seven of these have operating charter schools (WestEd 2003, 1). As of April 2006, there were over 3,500 charter schools serving over 1 million students nationwide (Center for Education Reform 2006),[1] up from only 100 schools in 1995 (Research Policy Practice International 2001).

There are many excellent explorations of the history and the politics of the charter-school "movement," and there is no need for us to repeat that information in detail here.[2] But there is a series of fundamental questions and definitions that we need to address before moving on to the core of our analysis. First, there is the question of exactly what a charter school is. One interesting characteristic of most extant definitions is that, while they identify the core characteristics of charter schools, they almost always include language about not only what charter schools *are* but also glowing language about what they *will do*—that is, they often portray the hope of charter schools, while adding a bit of hype. For example, according to the U.S. Department of Education's Office of Innovation and Improvement:

> The promise charter schools hold for public school innovation and reform lies in an unprecedented combination of freedom and accountability. Underwritten with public funds but run independently, charter schools are free from a range of state laws and district policies stipulating what and how they teach, where they can spend their money, and who they can hire and fire. In return, they are held strictly accountable for their academic and financial performance. (U. S. Department of Education 2004, 1)

Putting aside the value-laden aspects of this description, this excerpt helps to identify the key structural characteristics of charter schools. Broadly defined, charter schools are publicly funded schools that are granted significant autonomy in curriculum and governance in return for greater accountability. In addition, the charter establishing a school is, ideally, a performance contract that details the school's mission, its program and goals, the population served, and ways to assess success (or failure). Charters are granted for fixed lengths of time (usually three to five years), at which time the body that authorized the charter reviews the performance of the school and decides whether or not to renew it.[3] We should note that almost every aspect of the legislation governing charter schools—such as the length of charters, who can apply for charters, and the like—can and does vary widely from state to state, so there are exceptions to almost every general statement describing charter schools (Kucsova and Buckley 2004).

While there are many perspectives on charter schools and while specific practices may vary widely across the nation, it is important to note that there is general agreement about what charter schools are supposed to do. The theoretical or intellectual basis for these expectations stems from the pro-market orientation that has helped to shape education policy reform in the United States for the last fifteen or so years. From this perspective, charter schools are expected to generate competition among schools, a competition in which poorly performing schools disappear and good ones prosper. Moreover, by reducing the level of bureaucratic regulation and control, charter schools should be free to innovate and create more effective and efficient programs that serve their clientele better. According to the U.S. Charter Schools web site,[4] charter schools are designed to:

- Increase opportunities for learning and access to quality education for all students;
- Create choice for parents and students within the public school system;
- Provide a system of accountability for results in public education;
- Encourage innovative teaching practices;
- Create new professional opportunities for teachers;
- Encourage community and parent involvement in public education;
- Leverage improved public education broadly.

Or, once again according to the Department of Education's Office of Innovation and Improvement, charter schools are free to:

lengthen the school day, mix grades, require dress codes, put teachers on their school boards, double up instruction in core subject areas like math or reading, make parents genuine partners in family-style school cultures, adopt any instructional practice that will help achieve their missions—free, in short, to do whatever it takes to build the skills, knowledge, and character traits their students need to succeed in today's world.

By allowing citizens to start new public schools with this kind of autonomy, making them available tuition-free to any student, and holding them accountable for results and family satisfaction, proponents hope that this new mix of choice and accountability will not only provide students stronger learning programs than local alternatives, but will also stimulate improvement of the existing public education system. With charter schools, it is accountability that makes freedom promising. No charter is permanent; it must be re-newed—or revoked—at regular intervals. Continued funding, which is tied to student enrollment, also depends on educational results. (2004, 1)

Note that in this vision, the charter schools themselves are not only better schools, they also "stimulate improvement of the existing public educa-tion system." To the extent that these processes—innovation, competi-tion, leverage, accountability—work, charter schools help create a "mar-ket" for schools that produces better schools and increases "productive efficiency."[5]

The theory behind charter schools holds another promise: charter schools should also increase "consumer" satisfaction. By being more re-sponsive to the needs of parents, students, and the community at large, and by allowing parents and students to choose schools that deliver the type of education that they feel best meets their needs, charter schools can improve the match between what schools offer and what "parent/consumers" prefer. We can think of this tighter match as improving "allo-cative efficiency" (see Schneider, Teske, and Marschall 2000).

While charter schools have found fertile ground in the market approach to policy reform, support for charter schools as a form of school choice has also grown for political reasons. In the competition between vouchers and charter schools, two contending ideas that use choice as a means to reform schools, state legislators have usually chosen to adopt charter schools. As Henig et al. (2002) explain, "[F]rustrated with the poor per-formance of public schools, but unable to advance more radical notions of privatization, such as vouchers, advocates saw charter schools as the most effective means of building market incentives." (Also see Mintrom 1997. For more on the difference between charter schools and voucher schools see Hassel 1999.)

Despite the strong forces propelling them forward and a historically high growth rate, charter schools appear to be moving from the growth spurt of adolescence to a more sedate adulthood. Nationwide, there are signs that, while the number of charter schools is still growing, this expan-sion is now occurring at a decreasing rate. This may show that charter schools are reaching the normal maturation point of the typical sigmoid curve describing the diffusion of many innovations (Porter 1980; Schnei-der, Teske, and Mintrom 1995, chap. 4). For charter schools, this pattern may be driven by a variety of factors, such as the depletion of the popula-tion of reformers with the skills and energy needed to pioneer charter schools (Wells 2002, 1–2). It may also be driven by a particular temporal sequence: charter schools in some states have now been operating for five or more years, and there is growing pressure for a critical assessment of their academic and financial performance, perhaps slowing down their continued expansion. For example, in Massachusetts, where charter schools have existed since 1995, the state legislature in 2004 threatened a moratorium on further charter expansion, reversing itself only after reducing state funding for the schools (Greenberger 2004a, 2004b). In Washington, D.C., the Board of Education, one of the two chartering authorities in the city, has been approving less than 20 percent of applications before it in the last few years, while in the early years of the city's charter-school experience it approved all applications (see chapter 2).

THE RATIONALE(S) FOR CHARTER SCHOOLS

Despite this slowdown in the rate of expansion, charter schools are clearly a popular policy. But are they a good one?

Charles Lindblom once wrote that the test of a good policy is that diverse actors can agree on it even if they cannot agree on why (Lindblom 1959). By this criterion, charter schools seem to be good policy; indeed, there sometimes seems to be as many arguments in favor of charter schools as there are schools themselves. Amy Stuart Wells (2002) argues that this collection of rationales can be boiled down into three main categories: standards-based or systemic reform, local autonomy, and neoliberal market-based reform.

Systemic Reform

Central to the appeal of charter schools for the proponents of systemic reform is the promise of increased accountability (Miron and Nelson 2000). In theory, charter schools, in exchange for the ability to operate relatively unencumbered by the policies of the local school district, are held accountable for improving the academic performance of their students. Thus charter schools can be seen as part of the broader trend in the last decade to reconstruct educational policy centered on measures of academic outcomes (Elmore, Abelmann, and Fuhrman 1996, 65–98)—a trend that is perhaps best exemplified by the provisions of the national No Child Left Behind Act of 2001, which has affected educational practices throughout the United States.

In reality, however, this autonomy-for-accountability trade-off can be problematic, as administrators find themselves in the ambiguous position of holding schools accountable while not directly supervising them (Wells et al. 2002, 29–53). In addition, charter schools have clear incentives to seek a continuing stay of evaluation or to obfuscate evidence of poor performance (Henig 1994, 234). Moreover, state rules and regulations governing the release of school performance data are often lax, and this has allowed charter schools (and, to be sure, other schools of choice) far too much latitude regarding the disclosure of the information parents and students need to make choices and policy makers need to evaluate the schools. In a recent report on charter schools in Ohio, for example, the Legislative Office on Educational Oversight found that many charter schools "are not reporting data that allow them to be compared to their contracts" (Legislative Office Of Education Oversight 2003, 26). Consider, too, Van Dunk and Dickman's analysis of schools of choice in Milwaukee:

> There is no question that there are good private voucher schools here, just as there are good public schools. Unfortunately, however, no accountability data exist to prove this, much less to prove that these schools' high performance was spurred by competition. . . . We have found that, overall, parental knowledge of specific schools tends to be low, and that parents face considerable barriers in their efforts to obtain information about schools. Thus parents are unable, by themselves, to hold schools fully accountable. (2004, 52)[6]

While Van Dunk and Dickman were specifically referring to voucher schools, there is no question that the same problems exist in connection with charter schools and other forms of school choice (see chapter 6; also see Schneider, Teske, and Marschall 2000).

Local Autonomy

The ability of charter schools to provide a space for locally autonomous, community-centered education is another reason charter schools enjoy broad support from diverse constituencies. Charter schools can provide a means for parents and students who perceive themselves as marginalized or disenfranchised to seek shelter from an indifferent or even hostile public school system. Groups as diverse as right-wing Christians in California (Huerta 2000, 177–202) to Afrocentrists in Michigan (Yancey 2000, 66–97) have taken advantage of charter-school laws to create schools catering to their particular interests. Charter-school operators and their founding parent communities frequently use a broad set of strategies, including selective recruitment and explicit parent contracts, to create and maintain their distinctive identity (Lopez, Wells, and Holme 2002, 129–58). Insofar as they are successful, charter schools of this type may nurture and protect their constituent community, but some worry that by so doing they can exacerbate racial, ethnic, religious, and cultural segregation and inequalities (Fuller 2000a).

While many critics of choice fear the fragmentation of education and extol the virtues of the "common school,"[7] others argue that homogeneity within schools coupled with a diversity across schools *increases* the opportunity for parents to become involved in their schools and learn more directly about the benefits (and costs) of participation in the provision of public goods and services. Moreover, many researchers have argued that parental involvement in schools is essential for improving academic performance and that the more supportive homogeneous environment of charter schools coupled with their commitment to parental involvement increases the chances for academic success. This argument is intimately tied into the idea of building what have been called "effective schools" (Coleman and Hoffer 1987; Henderson 1987; Bryk and Schneider 2002) and also to the idea of "coproduction" of public goods and services (Levine 1984; Marschall 2004)—points we explore in depth in chapter 11.

The Market for Schools

The third rationale for charter schools and school choice more broadly, and the framework in which both the most compelling and the most contentious arguments for and against such reforms are now framed, is found in the neoliberal theories of the market.[8]

The closing decades of the twentieth century saw a profound transformation in American public policy—the privatization of services once thought to be the exclusive province of the state. In the area of education, this was not a new idea: Milton Friedman (1955) proposed educational vouchers in the 1950s, and the intellectual history of the idea can be traced back to the political philosophies of John Stuart Mill and Thomas Paine (Walberg and Bast 2003), but the changing intellectual climate among policy makers and analysts moved such plans to the forefront in the 1990s.

While the idea of vouchers had been around for decades, instrumental in bringing the idea of educational privatization to a broader audience was John Chubb and Terry Moe's *Politics, Markets, and America's Schools*, a book that provoked fierce debate by proposing that government-run schools were destined to fail because of the very mechanisms of American democracy itself. According to Chubb and Moe, "the specific kinds of democratic institutions by which American public education has been governed for the last half century appear to be incompatible with effective schooling" (1990, 2). More specifically, the authors believe that in the American education system, where interest groups have easy and continual entry into the policy-making process, many entrenched organizations, particularly teacher unions, exercise too much control over decisions—and they skew decisions in favor of their own needs rather than the needs of students. Making the point even more explicit, they argue that poor academic performance is "one of the prices Americans pay for choosing to exercise direct democratic control over their schools" (2). Their solution was a market for education in which parents would be free to choose their child's school and where choice "is a self-contained reform with its own rationale and justification." For Chubb and Moe, choice "has the capacity *all by itself* to bring about the kind of transformation that, for years, reformers have been seeking to engineer in myriad other ways" (217).

Critics of school privatization were quick to point out that a system of school vouchers (or "scholarships" in the language of Chubb and Moe) was theoretically quite a distance away from the ideal market of neoclassical economics, and that transactions in such a "quasi market" were rife with unintended and possibly pernicious consequences, such as increased stratification across socioeconomic groups or further weakening of already struggling public schools. Henig (1994) suggests that the "market" in this case is better understood as a metaphor than as social reality, and a misleading metaphor at that (also see Fiske and Ladd 2000; Smith and Meier 1995; cf. Walberg and Bast 2003, 210–21).[9] But despite these criticisms, Chubb and Moe succeeded in redefining vouchers from a conservative, esoteric microeconomic theory into a broad-based practical approach to fixing the ills of urban education that became an integral (if contested) item on many agendas for educational reform.

The central idea of a market (metaphorical or otherwise) for education is that once the government's monopoly on public schooling is broken and parents and students become "consumers," a host of new suppliers of education will enter the market and compete with existing schools and among themselves to provide educational programs that better meet the demands of parents and students than does the current monopoly provision of education. One key underlying assumption is that parents and students know what they want—and what they want is academically strong schools. Another key assumption is that schools (or some other organization) will provide information about their programs and quality and that parents will be able to find this information and use it to make choices and to hold schools accountable (Schneider, Teske, and Marschall 2000). In this idealized system of choice, programs and curricula will align with consumer preferences, and efficiency and academic outcomes will improve. Schools that do not improve or do not meet parental and student needs will lose students and be forced to reform or close.

Note that, according to proponents, not all these outcomes need be present for a market-based reform to be viewed as a success. For example, even if academic achievement (in today's environment, almost always defined by standardized test scores) remains constant, but costs go down, this higher productivity would still be a victory for market-based policy

(Hoxby 2003, 287–341). Similarly, an improvement in consumer satisfaction or the utility of parents, even without gains in achievement or productivity, would still represent a net gain in social welfare.

Different systems of school choice approach the ideal of this neoliberal model in various degrees. Clearly voucher programs are most closely tied to the precepts of the model—and given recent court decisions, the expansion of voucher programs to include parochial schools will increase the number and range of providers dramatically. However, even school voucher programs still fall short of the ideal market, and charter schools are arguably even further from this ideal. At best, according to education economist Henry Levin, charter schools "simulate some of the dynamics of a market by increasing the supply of alternatives to parents and by competing with existing public schools" (Levin and Belfield 2003, 10). Nevertheless, according to Levin, "as long as there is some choice and competition it is believed that outcomes will be better than when there are no choices at all" (15).

Or will they? Although proponents of privatization and other market-based reforms do not often acknowledge it, a theoretical result in welfare economics, the "general theory of second best" (Lipsey and Lancaster 1956, 11–32), holds that "if any aspects of the free-market ideal are fundamentally unattainable (as is of course the case), then incremental movement toward that ideal is not necessarily a welfare improvement" (Ackerman 2004, 2–7). In a complex system like education, partial or even full privatization may turn out to *increase* costs and *reduce* benefits (Sclar 2000).

To ensure a net increase in social welfare in the real world of imperfect markets, the task of the policy maker is to meet all the sufficient conditions for such an increase, not merely a few necessary ones piecemeal. Unfortunately, identifying the sufficient conditions for a successful market for education is still an elusive goal. And, without the identification (and satisfaction) of such conditions, the "magic of the market" may, like many magic tricks, go up in smoke, leaving the evaluation of charter schools (and schools of choice more generally) much more difficult.

What Limits the Market for Education?

Economists and public policy analysts frequently evaluate policy options with reference to the *Pareto criterion* (named for Italian economist Vilfredo Pareto, 1848–1923). This standard holds that a policy choice is preferred if it makes at least one person better off and no one worse off. The attraction of the market as a mechanism for the allocation of goods and services is that, under ideal conditions, through voluntary transactions the market will yield a *Pareto optimum*, a point at which no one can be made better off without making another worse off.[10]

What the theory of second best simply points out is that, under less than perfect market conditions, a Pareto optimum is no longer guaranteed—and getting closer to the ideal market in some dimension does not, a priori, predict an overall increase in social welfare. To return to the context at hand, two important questions should be posed: How might the implementation of a charter-school reform differ in the "real world" from implementing charter schools in an ideal one? And, after we take into account these differences, have we met enough of the sufficient conditions to increase social welfare?

Another critical issue in the evaluation of the "market" for education is the extent to which education generates *externalities*—social costs or benefits to a market transaction that are not properly accounted for by the price mechanism. The presence of externalities can lead to the wrong level of a good or service being produced, and the existence of externalities is one of the prime justifications for the public provision of public education. The example most often presented of externalities in education highlights the difference between the individual and the collective (societal) benefits of education. Put simply, when an individual invests in her own education, many of the benefits of that education accrue directly to her in terms of a better career and higher wages. But her community and the nation as a whole get an added benefit from having a more highly educated workforce—there is a positive externality to education that spills over from the individual to society.

Left strictly to individuals to decide, the level of education in a society will not reflect this "added" payoff, and all the societal benefits of education will not be reaped. The traditional economic solution calls for the public provision of education to reduce its cost to the individual consumer.[11] In turn, this lower cost will make people willing to "buy" more education, and the public subsidy helps society reach the optimum level of education for the community and the nation.

According to Levin and Belfield, "[p]robably the greatest challenge to the view of market efficiency in education is created by the presence of externalities" (2003, 16). But, and this is crucial, the externalities Levin and Belfield have in mind are broader than the standard case of externalities presented above. Specifically, they link the provision of education to the very functioning of democratic society: "It has long been held that one of the central purposes of schools is to improve the cohesion and stability of society through the provision of a common experience that prepares the young for adult roles and responsibilities. Schools are expected not only to educate students as individuals, but also to contribute to the overall effectiveness of society through creating competent adult citizens. . . . The larger question is how to reconcile the private choices of families with the public requirements of education for democratic knowledge and values" (16).

Political theorist Amy Gutmann uses a similar argument based on the presence of externalities to build a case against elite private schools. She argues that while parents are choosing to spend their own money to boost their child's chances at lifetime success, there is a social cost in that the public schools will be rendered less capable of fulfilling their purpose of perpetuating democracy through the loss of socioeconomically elite students and politically powerful parents. This cost is a *negative externality* flowing from individual choices and transactions in the market for private education (1987, 115–18).[12]

Not all externalities are bad, however. As we discuss in chapter 12, parents may choose a charter school in order to improve their child's chances of academic success, but this individually motivated choice may help create a stronger, school-centered community. Or, returning again to theories of democratic education, parents enrolling their children in Catholic schools may find that they emerge better trained for the duties of citizenship (Bryk, Lee, and Holland 1993; Coleman, Hoffer, and Kilgore 1982), helping to improve their communities and society as whole. In short, some school-generated externalities can have important positive effects on civil society—but to achieve them may require action by government that transcends strictly market-based rationales.

Closely related to the idea of externalities is the fact that some, perhaps a large, part of education can be considered a *public good*. Once again using the case of democratic education, if there is little obvious return to individual students from civic education and engagement, and since such areas of a curriculum have both a real cost (the cost of teacher time, for example) and an opportunity cost (that is, a cost in terms of lost opportunity to cover other subjects or activities), in a competitive market we should expect democratic education to be driven out of the curriculum by lack of demand. If, however, society as a whole desires the production of good citizens through democratic education, then either traditional, government-run public schools subsidizing the provision of democratic education or else some regulation or limit on the market will be required.

The Flow of Information

Markets also fail to function optimally if participants make transactions under conditions of *information asymmetry*. As the term suggests, this sort of market failure occurs when one party in a transaction knows more about the quality of goods or services than the other.

There are at least two types of asymmetries that we need to consider. First, in the public policy and economics literature, there is the traditional difference in the quantity or quality of information between buyers and sellers—here between parents and students, the consumers who are "shopping" for schools, and the schools themselves, which almost certainly have more information about the true quality and nature of educational service provided. Levin and Belfield note, "[T]here has been considerable debate over whether school quality can be easily codified and quantified (or even manipulated), leading to the possibility that parents will be making choices based on false information" (2003, 15). Schneider and various coauthors have shown that many parents know very little about the range of schooling available to them (Schneider et al. 1997; Schneider et al. 1998). This asymmetry may be exacerbated by false advertising (Lubienski 2003; also see Kane and Staiger, 2002) or through the spread of bad information through low quality social networks (Schneider et al. 1999). The current drive to release test-score data may do nothing to solve this problem. Ladd argues that measures of average levels of performance provide misleading information to parents about how much the school is likely to add to student learning. Instead, average test scores provide information about the socioeconomic status of the average student at the school. Ladd notes: "While that information is not irrelevant to parents (and could be very important to some), it differs from information about the contribution of the school to student learning" (2001, 391).

The second asymmetry stems from differences among parents themselves. To ask a question familiar in the school-choice literature: "Who chooses and who loses?" While it may be possible in a given market for education that a small number of well-informed or "marginal" consumers increase social welfare for all through their shopping behavior and the response of providers (Schneider, Teske, and Marschall 2000), it is also possible that this information differential may exacerbate existing socioeconomic inequalities (Henig 1996).

To add an additional layer of complexity to the problem of information, schooling is an "experience good," the quality of which can not necessarily be evaluated until the student has been enrolled for some period (or perhaps even a "postexperience good" that cannot be evaluated until many years after consumption).[13] Thus parents may be more satisfied in the short run with a charter school's focus on athletics, but ultimately regret the decision when their child gets his first paycheck.

Entry Barriers

Yet another way in which a market for education could fail is through imperfect competition. For example, there may be high entry barriers limiting the number of providers who step forward to create new schools. Finn, Manno, and Vanourek (2001) identify a host of such barriers, including political opposition from state or local boards of education; school district resistance or excessive regulations; state education department resistance; union or bargaining unit collective bargaining agreements; and trouble with federal regulations (also see Research Policy Practice International 2001, 44). Finn et al. (1997) also cite financial difficulties, including lack of capital financing, especially for facilities;[14] little or no start-up money; inadequate per-pupil operating funds; and uneven cash flow. And finally, they highlight what they call "policy problems" embedded in "weak" charter laws (see also Kucsova and Buckley 2004).

Among the provisions of weak laws that can inhibit the creation of new charter schools are the following:

- Narrow eligibility. For example, existing schools may "convert" to charter status, but new schools may not be started;
- Too many rules and regulations restricting the school's autonomy;
- Severe restrictions on how many charters may be issued or how many students may enroll in them;
- Granting school boards sole authority for issuing charters (see Teske, Schneider, and Cassese 2005).

There can be other "supply side" problems in the market as well. For example, small providers who run a single charter school may be unable to compete with larger "educational maintenance organizations" (EMOs) due to economies of scale or the ability of large educational conglomerates to expend substantial amounts in political lobbying at the local, state, and federal levels. This could lead to the creation of an oligopoly in which the education market is made up of only a handful of large providers, possibly restricting consumer choice or charging high per-pupil fees from the district, state, or even parents, even if they are not producing higher achievement scores or increasing parental satisfaction.[15]

Additionally, one of the prime justifications for charter schools is their role as "laboratories of reform," that are free from the bureaucratic restrictions placed on traditional public schools by teacher unions and administrators (Nathan 1996; Kolderie 1990). However, empirical research has found little evidence of this (Rofes 1998; Teske et al. 2001) and the structure of real charter-school markets may actually act to inhibit programmatic competition (Lubienski 2003). Ironically, it may be that parents are risk-averse when it comes to their children's education—they may choose schools that emphasize traditional values and educational approaches rather than "buy" innovative programs with a high degree of risk. This is quite reasonable from a parent perspective, but may create systemic problems in a system of schools that is designed both to innovate and to respond to parental preferences.

EVALUATING CHARTER-SCHOOL REFORM

Obviously, the study of charter schools is complicated. Although a strong neoliberal, pro-market theoretical foundation propels much of the discussion in the literature, there are many signs that mapping the logic of the market onto the real world of charter schools is less than perfect. Even assuming that we want more consumer choice and more competition among suppliers, we have no strong guidance as to whether these alone are sufficient conditions to create markets for schools that actually improve overall social welfare. We also know that since schools have a strong public good dimension and they generate many externalities, their nonmarket dimensions are as important as their more narrowly defined efficiency.

As if explicating these "big ideas" is not enough of a task, there is yet another challenge. As empirical social scientists, we must find a way to translate these ideas into questions that are tractable for analysis. To lay out a way of doing this, in the next section we rearrange these issues concerning the market for schools into five dimensions around which we structure the analysis we present in this book.

Five Dimensions for Evaluating Charter Schools

We argue that the ongoing debate over charter schools can be thought of as encompassing five dimensions, which we use to organize our study. These include "three C's:"

- *Competition,*
- *Choice,*
- *Community,*

and "two A's":

- *Accountability,*
- *Achievement.*

Several of these dimensions map onto those identified by Levin (2002; Levin and Belfield 2003, 19–20) and Gill and his colleagues (Gill et al. 2001), but, we believe, our specification is more tractable for empirical analysis. In the next few pages, we begin to explore each of these criteria. We then describe the structure of the book and identify how these themes are to be discussed in the chapters that follow.

Competition clearly lies at the very heart of any market approach to educational reform. The idea here is quite simple and pertains to the "supply side" of education. In the traditional system of school assignment, a system in which students are assigned to a school based on where they live, schools are monopoly providers. Given this monopoly status, schools have no reason to compete with one another, and they have no incentives to create new programs or to improve their efficiency. The underlying argument is right out of Econ 101—without the salutary force of competition, monopolists charge too much, they produce inferior products, or they do both.

Milton Friedman's classic argument in favor of vouchers placed the reform of the supply side to increase pressure on monopoly education providers in a central role. Friedman's key argument is that competition will improve the price/performance ratio of inputs to outputs (productive efficiency). Friedman did not argue that competition would automatically lead to higher performance per se—rather, he argued that we could achieve the same level of outcomes at lower unit cost.[16] One interesting outcome of this intellectual history is that voucher programs tend to set the dollar figure attached to vouchers below the cost of public education—embodying the belief that competition can produce more for less. However, perhaps because charter schools are not as closely tied intellectually to Friedman's argument for vouchers, the per-student payment in charter schools is usually higher than in voucher programs—even in the same city. For example, in Washington, D.C., per-student payments for students in charter schools total around $10,000, but in the recently approved federally supported program, vouchers are set at only $7,500.

The second dimension, *choice*, is also central to our study, for two reasons. First, as noted above, choice by itself should improve the match between what parents and students want and what they get from their schools. This in turn should improve parent and student satisfaction with their schools. Second, choice is intimately linked to competition. It is the diverse preferences and the ability of consumers to choose among a range of products that provides the foundation for competition. However, there is a "flip side" to this dimension: equity is a primary concern of most stakeholders in American education policy (see, e.g., Levin 1991).

In any market, there is always what Okun (1975) called the "big trade-off" between efficiency and equity. This trade-off may be particularly important in evaluating school reform since education plays a central role in reducing socioeconomic disparities and providing equality of opportunity in American myth and social reality (Hochschild and Scovronick 2003). In turn, successful charter school reform must not exacerbate inequalities through the "cream skimming" of students of higher socioeconomic status—even if this might improve productive efficiency or increase parental or student satisfaction. Thus, there are questions about who chooses and who loses in a system of expanded choice—and these questions are central to our analysis.

Community is not part and parcel of the market approach. However, the importance of community emerges from the distinctive nature of schooling. A system of charter-school choice should not jeopardize the social and political foundation of our communities and nation. As Levin and Belfield (2003, 20) write, "a market system that bases its appeal on differentiation and choice must adopt a mechanism to ensure common experiences across schools to prepare students for their civic rights and responsibilities." In turn, the public good or positive externality aspects of education must be considered as an important part of the final evaluation of a charter reform.

In addition, education is not a simple service. Rather, it is a production process that requires the continued input of a range of actors—that is, education is "co-produced" by students, parents, teachers, school staff, and administrators. There is clear evidence demonstrating the importance of the ties among these stakeholders in producing a high-quality education. Also, as alluded to above, schools provide a venue for citizenship or democratic education, and such education may be more effective in a well-functioning school community.

THE TWO A'S

The first "A" is *accountability,* which should increase in systems of choice. In marketlike approaches to education reform, the first line of accountability lies in consumer choice. If parents and students are not happy with the school they chose, they can exit.

Since schools of choice are directly dependent on the revenues brought in by each student, if enough students exit the school, the school either improves or disappears. Paul Hill, in one of the most comprehensive studies of charter schools to date, argues that charter schools, freed from many of the bureaucratic rules and regulations governing traditional public schools, have created new "accountability" relationships with the teachers, on whose performance the schools depend, and with families, whom the schools must attract and satisfy (Hill et al. 2001, 6). These relationships, according to Hill et al., transform the way in which teachers, administrators, parents and students deal with each other, creating strong, cooperative, working relationships leading to strong school communities and higher levels of academic success.

Second, and more specific to charter schools, is the fact that charters are granted for fixed periods of time and are subject to periodic and strict review at which time they can be revoked. Consider the following example. In January 2004, the State University of New York Board of Trustees, which has authority to charter schools, acted on the renewal of the first three charter schools established in the state. Two schools were approved without problem. However, the decision on the John A. Reisenbach Charter School in Harlem's District 5 was more difficult.

New York's Charter Schools Institute, created to administer the state's charter-school law, had recommended that the Reisenbach School be closed at the end of the school year, due to poor academic performance, governance problems, and other concerns. However, the choice was not easy. On the one hand, District 5 was one of the lowest-performing in the city, and parents in that district were desperate for better schools. On the other hand, Reisenbach's poor performance after five years and the demands of accountability argued for closing the school. As this debate unfolded, an op-ed piece by Peter Murphy, which appeared in the January 31, 2004 edition of the *New York Post*, summarized the issues at hand concisely:

> Charters differ from traditional public schools because they are held accountable for academic results. Failure has real consequences (rather than rewards of more money). This accountability system is made clear to charter-school operators up front and they commit to abide by it.
>
> To protect the integrity of all charter schools and ensure the success of this reform movement, the SUNY board needs to act on the exhaustive findings of its own institute staff and close schools, like Reisenbach, that have failed to operate in an educationally and fiscally sound manner.
>
> Accountability has to mean something in public education—at least for charter schools.

On February 24, 2004, the State University Board of Trustees voted not to renew the charter and the Reisenbach School joined the list of charter schools held accountable for failure. But how widespread are cases such as these?

While data calculating actual closure rates are hard to find, Hassel and Batdorff (2004) studied decisions to renew school charters, looking at all 506 nationwide renewal cases through 2001, and then focusing on fifty randomly selected cases. They found that 16 percent of charter schools up for renewal were terminated (conversely, 84 percent of the charter schools were renewed). The Center for Education Reform reports that 429 charter schools have closed from the inception of charter schools through 2003.[17] If we set the number of remaining charter schools in the nation at around three thousand, we can estimate a closure rate of approximately 13 percent, not much different than the Hassel and Batdorff finding of 16 percent (also see Teske, Schneider, and Cassese 2005, who look at the politics involved in authorizing and renewing charter schools).

There are two problems with these existing data (besides the fact that they are, at best, approximations). First, it is close to impossible to state precisely the reasons for nonrenewal—there is no central repository for information about these actions, and news accounts are unreliable. While Hassel and Batdorff (2003) suggest that many authorizers have been willing to close underperforming schools, many nonrenewals make the news because of financial improprieties or other newsworthy acts of malfeasance. For example, in 2004, the Washington, D.C. school board closed the Village Learning Center Public Charter School after a city audit found that the school spent hundreds of thousands of dollars on leased space it did not occupy, credit card charges for apparel and gifts, and loan repayments that lacked documentation. Similarly, in September 2004, just as the school year began, ten thousand students in the California Charter Academy's four schools (spread over sixty campuses) faced serious disruption as the state closed the schools as a result of financial audits. Whether the high incidence of media reporting on charter school closings due to financial impropriety is just another example of the media's love of scandals is an open question; we still lack convincing evidence on the extent to which authorizers are really holding charter schools accountable for low academic performance.

Second, we have no standard by which to judge whether or not this (approximate) 15 percent closure rate is high or low (public schools are rarely closed and no data on private school closings are kept as far as we can tell). Critics often argue that charter-school closures are a sign of failure in the charter movement—that the charter "movement" is creating a legion of poor schools that are failing to educate the children placed in their care (and absconding with scarce public-education money, to boot). In contrast, proponents argue that while these closures are undoubtedly a sign of failure in *individual* schools, they are a sign of success for the movement as a whole as bad schools are weeded out and good ones survive. For them, closures are clearly proof that accountability is taken seriously.

ACHIEVEMENT: THE ULTIMATE GOAL?

While many advocates of choice argue that competition, choice, community, and accountability are goals in themselves, others argue that they really serve as intermediate steps to the ultimate goal of higher school performance. Lubienski makes this point clear:

[T]hemes such as "innovation," "choice," "competition," and "diversity," although they all have some value in and of themselves, often serve as intermediate goals that structure opportunities for institutions to increase achievement. Even as intermediate goals, however, choice, competition, and innovation are cast as the necessary vehicles for advancing academic outcomes. Therefore, the extent to which school choice reforms succeed in securing these ideals indicates the likelihood of reaching the primary objective in this logic model. (2003, 397)

Thus, these structural reforms should lead the final dimension that we argue should be used to study schools: *achievement.*

Higher academic achievement is now the mantra of educational reform and the call for better test scores is heard throughout the nation. According to Amrein and Berliner (2002):

In recent decades, test scores have come to dominate the discourse about schools and their accomplishments. Families now make important decisions, such as where to live, based on the scores from these tests. This occurs because real estate agents use school test scores to rate neighborhood quality and this affects property values. Test scores have been shown to affect housing prices, resulting in a difference of about $9,000 between homes in grade "A" or grade "B" neighborhoods. At the national and state levels, test scores are now commonly used to evaluate programs and allocate educational resources. Millions of dollars now hinge on the tested performance of students in educational and social programs.[18]

Indeed, there are many ways in which charter schools should be able to take advantage of their autonomy while responding to the pressures of choice, competition, and community to achieve higher academic outcomes (Chubb and Moe 1990; Hoxby 1997; Hill, Pierce, and Guthrie 1997; and Brandl 1998). Wohlstetter and Griffin make this explicit. For them, choice, autonomy, and competition make schools more flexible and innovative "with the perceived assumption that such innovations will produce identifiable improvements in student achievement" (1998, 3).[19]

As the descriptions of the criteria suggest, it is likely that there will be tensions among the various measures in almost any real choice program—improving productive efficiency through a choice mechanism may compromise equity; increasing social cohesion through regulations requiring democratic education may reduce freedom to choose.[20] Moreover, it is difficult to measure the size of the trade-off across the different criteria, as they clearly have different metrics. We try to elucidate some of these trade-offs while assessing the success or failure of the charter schools we study in the chapters that follow.

THE PLAN OF THE BOOK

The book is organized in four clusters, and we examine *competition, choice, community, accountability*, and *achievement* throughout, although with different emphases in each cluster and in each chapter.

In the first cluster, beginning with this chapter, we describe the theoretical issues that inform our work. In the present chapter, we have identified the five broad dimensions that structure our approach to studying school choice and placed these dimensions in the larger debate over school choice and charter schools. In the next chapter, we move from general themes that underlie every school-choice plan to an exploration of the venue in which we develop and test specific hypotheses that are derived from applying the ideas we explored in this chapter to the city in which we have been studying the evolution of charter schools—Washington, D.C.

Washington, D.C., has one of the strongest charter laws in the country and has one of the largest concentrations of students attending charter schools in the nation.[21] At the time of this writing (April 2006), there are fifty-one organizations running sixty-three charter-school campuses, enrolling about 17,500 students. This represents almost a quarter of the total number of public-school students in the city and almost one-third of the schools. At least six new charter schools are scheduled to open in the school year beginning in September 2006. In chapter 2, we describe the development of the charter-school sector in D.C., touching specifically on how competition and choice have evolved since the city adopted its strong charter-school legislation in 1996.

With the themes and venue laid out, we then introduce the two research projects from which the data we use in this book are drawn. In chapter 3, we introduce the four-wave panel survey that we use to assess how parents shop for schools, how they feel about their schools, and how they participate in their school community.

A multiple-wave panel study is one of the most valuable, but least frequently created, social-science research tools. In the field of political science, studies that attempt to model the dynamics of political phenomena using such data are rare and in the sphere of charter schools—to the best of our best knowledge—are currently nonexistent.[22] However, in chapter 3 we will also introduce some of the problems that plagued us as we tried to keep the panel "alive" in an inner city where there is high mobility and where people "disappear" from the sample for many reasons.

We follow that chapter with an examination of the students in charter schools and the traditional D.C. public schools and briefly touch on the issue of student achievement. A major theme in this section is the extent to which charter-school students are any different than students in the

DCPS. One argument in the often-contentious evaluation of how well charter schools perform is that the students in them are different and "harder to educate." We explore this issue in chapter 4.

In chapter 5, we introduce our second major research tool. In 1999, we created a web site called DCSchoolSearch.com. As described in that chapter, we collected a large amount of data about each and every school in Washington, D.C. and made it available on a user-friendly web site. As visitors navigated through the information presented on DCSchoolSearch.com, we tracked their movements to see what information they were accessing and in what order. In addition, we surveyed parents who gave us their e-mail addresses to obtain more information about their search procedures.

With the sources of our data established, in chapters 6–8, we use data from both the survey and from DCSchoolSearch.com to study fundamental issues pertaining to choice. One of the main issues concerning choice has to do with what parents want from their schools, with perhaps the most important consideration being the relative weight that different parents put on academic achievement versus factors such as proximity, the racial and economic background of other students, and other, perhaps more idiosyncratic preferences. We compare the findings from our telephone survey with the search patterns parents used while "visiting" schools using DCSchoolSearch.com to present some rather different conclusions about parental preferences over school attributes.

In the two chapters that follow the introduction of our data sources, we combine theories of information search drawn from behavioral decision theory with traditional concerns of political science and theories of consumer behavior to explore how different types of parents search for information. We have two major research themes in that exploration: first, given the generally low levels of information that have been well documented, can we expect that parents will choose the right school for their child? Besides this question at the individual level, we are also concerned with a systemic one: if parents as a population of consumers have low levels of information, can the school system overall feel any competitive pressure to improve? Here we look more closely at the search patterns of the "marginal consumer" of education to see whether in the face of low information the school system may still be pressured to improve.

In chapters 9–12 of the book, we look at the consequences of choice and charters. Here we address the fundamental "so what?" question— does all the time, energy, effort, and money spent on creating these alternative charter schools matter? In chapter 9, we explore parents' satisfaction with their child's school. As noted earlier, given choice, parents should be choosing schools that do more of what they want done in education. Therefore, satisfaction should be higher among choosers—if not, this is a pretty strong indication of a failing system of choice. In this chapter, we also begin to deal with some fundamental methodological issues to which all studies of school choice must pay heed. Of greatest concern is the problem of self-selection—parents who have chosen to enroll their children in charter schools may be systematically different than parents whose children remain in traditional public schools. This self-selection into the "treatment" (i.e., charter schools) can lead to biased estimates of its effects.

We explore several statistical approaches to control for self-selection to see how robust the effects of charter schools are. We also explore the possibility that parents who choose have a psychological stake in saying that what they chose is good (often called the "rose-colored glasses" effect). To "telegraph" one of our most interesting results, we find that rather than viewing schools through rose-colored glasses, charter school parents may in fact be wearing "grey-colored" ones: they may constitute a group of parents that are particularly hard to please.

In chapter 10, we take full advantage of our panel data to explore parental satisfaction over time. We look at changes from the beginning of the school year to the end of the year and we look at how well schools did over time, comparing the 2001/2 patterns with 2003/4 ones. We also cope with some fairly difficult problems caused by attrition.

In chapter 11, we look at the extent to which charter schools and traditional public schools differ in the strength of community and the creation of social capital. Using methods established in our previous chapters, we examine the survey data for evidence of any charter-school effect on attitudes thought to be the foundation of parental civic engagement, both at the school level and in a broader context.

In chapter 12, we turn our focus from parents to students. We examine key indicators of student civic education and participation in search of empirical evidence for the contention that charter schools, like other schools of choice, build better citizens.

Finally, we conclude with an attempt to pull together the disparate empirical findings of the earlier chapters and view them through the lens of our organizing framework. We return to our central question: are charter schools, on the whole, a beneficial policy reform, or are the hope and the hype unjustified by the facts?

The Evolution of Charter-School Choice
in the District of Columbia

THE THEMES WE EXPLORE IN THIS BOOK are fundamental to the study of charter schools and school choice in general. However, empirical research is conducted in specific locales and often based on samples drawn from a defined population. The challenge is to identify trends and patterns based on the empirical data drawn from a particular milieu and balance conclusions based on such observations with the inevitable desire to make broader statements. We recognize this temptation and we try hard not to "overgeneralize" from our data.

Thus, as the reader will discover, our empirical evidence is drawn from Washington, D.C., but our reading of the literature on school choice suggests that there is very little that we document in this book that is unique or limited to D.C. We believe our analysis is a reasonable and reasoned reading of the data and we firmly believe that the lessons we draw have bearing on the ongoing debate over school choice and charter schools; nonetheless, caveat emptor is always sound advice.

We believe that political and social attitudes and behaviors develop in response to the institutional arrangements that define the opportunities, constraints, and the benefits and costs of such actions. In this chapter we begin the substantive work of the book, describing the context in which the parents, the students, and the schools we study operate. In the following pages, we present a brief history of the evolution of school choice in Washington, D.C. and present some of that school system's defining characteristics that we believe have affected the way in which charter schools have developed and the choices parents have.

SCHOOL CHOICE IN THE DISTRICT OF COLUMBIA

The District of Columbia has a long record of school reform. Much of this has been in response to a long and troubled history of poor academic performance of schools in the district coupled with more than a few management scandals. School reform in Washington also develops in response to the ever-present role of the Congress, which supervises many aspects of local government and which periodically exercises its power over the city to foster school reform (most recently in the creation of an experimental voucher program that is ongoing at the time of writing).

The central impetus for the adoption of choice-based educational reforms in the District of Columbia can be traced to the fiscal crisis of 1995, when the District's schools were faced with mounting problems stemming from fiscal mismanagement and administrative corruption. Facing a budget deficit of $722 million, the city was taken over by the Control Board, formally known as the Fiscal Responsibility and Management Assistance Authority. The Control Board in turn took over the schools, appointing an emergency board of trustees. Eventually this takeover was ruled illegal, but in the meantime the board of trustees fired several hundred teachers and staff members. This brought to the fore the chronic problem of poor academic performance, documented by the fact that test scores in the District's schools were among the lowest in the nation and its dropout rate was among the highest.

The question of how better to manage the District's schools generated considerable controversy. The Republican-controlled House of Representatives favored choice-based reforms, and included provisions for voucher, scholarship, and charter-school programs in the District of Columbia School Reform Act of 1995. That version of the reform failed to pass the Senate. A year later, stripped of the voucher and scholarship programs—by far its most controversial components—a version of the act containing only a charter-school provision was passed. Within weeks of the act's passage, the D.C. City Council enacted a separate local charter law. Despite this local legislation, charter schools in D.C. are effectively governed by the federal statute and many consider the local law (and the potential points of conflict between the two laws) more a nuisance than anything else. We discuss the two charter laws later in this chapter.

These laws provided the foundation for a rapid growth of public charter schools. Among the most important provisions supporting this growth are the following:

- a generous per-pupil funding level, equal to that for traditional D.C. public schools;
- an annual facilities allowance;
- first access to closed public school facilities and discounting of the appraised value of surplus schools for charter schools;
- direct loans and credit enhancement to reduce the cost of private debt; and
- public revenue bonds backed by the District's per-pupil facility allowance (Brookings Greater Washington Program 2004).

Research has shown that jurisdictions that have more than one authorizer tend to have a greater number of charter schools (Kucsova and Buckley 2004; Witte, Shober, and Manna 2003) and the District has two—the

Public Charter School Board, which was created specially to charter and supervise new schools, and the Board of Education, which has taken on the added responsibility of authorizing and overseeing a portion of the charter sector. In addition, while the number of charter schools that can be created in any year is capped, the limit of ten per year for each of authorizer is generous. As a result of these features, Washington currently boasts the highest density of charter schools of any "state" in the nation.

We should note that the structure of education in Washington, D.C. produces a conflict in the way in which charter schools are supervised. This conflict emerges from the role of the D.C. Public School system as both the *local* education authority (LEA) and the *state* education authority (SEA). While each charter school is an independent entity (in effect, it acts as its own LEA), charter schools are still supervised by the DCPS in its position as the SEA. Since charter schools are in competition for students and resources with the DCPS, the conflict of interest is clear. In response, a State Education Office (SEO) has recently been created to take over more of the SEA functions from the DCPS, providing oversight and playing a critical role in standard-setting and rulemaking for both the charter schools and the traditional public schools.[1] At this writing, a turf war between the SEO and DCPS is still being played out.

In the remainder of this chapter we consider several factors that are central to understanding the character of Washington's choice program: the nature of the District's charter law, the charter-school application process, a variety of operational considerations for the charter schools, the inherent tension between accountability and autonomy faced by the charter schools, and the challenges facing the schools. In reviewing these factors, we hope that the reader will gain an understanding of the context in which to judge the evidence regarding the scope and magnitude of the changes to the District's education system and its relevant stakeholders that we present later in this book.

A SNAPSHOT OF THE DISTRICT'S CHARTER SECTOR

In the 2005–6 school year, there were fifty-one organizations running sixty-three charter school campuses. These are almost equally split between those authorized by the Public Charter School Board (PCSB) and the District's Board of Education (BOE). In comparison, the DCPS is currently operating schools and programs in 156 buildings and serving about sixty thousand students.[2] Thus approximately one-quarter of the public *schools* in D.C. are charter schools, which serve close to about one-fifth of total *enrollment* in public schools (about sixteen thousand students).

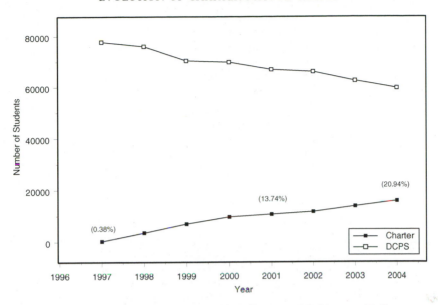

Figure 2.1. The growth of charter-school enrollment in Washington, D.C.

These numbers represent a continued and sustained growth since the first charter schools opened for business in the District (see figure 2.1). Despite this expansion, demand exceeds the supply of available spots in the charter schools—according to one Center for Education Reform estimate, over one thousand students are on waiting lists for the charter schools.

Overall, the demographic distribution of students in the charter schools is comparable to that of the DCPS schools. Both sectors serve a high number of minority students and students from low-income families. Although there is evidence that the charter schools serve an even higher percentage of African American and poor students, in chapter 4, we will show that there are not any consistent differences in the overall "educability" of students in each sector.

In what ways do charters differ from the traditional DCPS schools? Overall, charter schools are smaller and therefore may offer a more intimate educational setting than the traditional public schools. Beyond this, there is little evidence to suggest widespread innovations in curriculum or teaching methods. Concern for programmatic diversity among charter programs stems from a desire for differentiation in the supply side of this market for educational services. From a normative perspective, the schools must be sufficiently distinguishable from one other to allow parent-consumers to make choices on the basis of their educational preferences. In the idealized market for schools, parental choices provide an element of dynamism that drives the schools to improve and reflect these preferences.

Despite the importance of innovation and variety in programs, as far as we have been able to ascertain, about half of the charters offer a general liberal arts curriculum that parallels that of the traditional public schools. Many employ "innovations" that do not differ dramatically from reform efforts previously employed by the public schools (see Lubienski 2003; Teske et al. 2001). However, a number of charter schools offer extended days or longer school years.

Henig et al. (1999) found that D.C. charter schools are more likely to emphasize a particular substantive theme rather than curricular innovation. According to their study, 40 percent of the schools emphasized the arts, nonvocational math and science, or foreign languages. During the 2003–4 school year, our research team visited twenty-seven charter schools. Consistent with the findings of Henig et al., our interaction with charter school staff did not suggest that the schools were positioning themselves in terms of unique curricular or operational features. This was evident by the fact that staff in only about a third of the schools even tried to explain the curricular focus or some other distinctive aspect of the school educational program, and staff in only a handful of charter schools could provide packets of information about their school's programs or curricula. Where programmatic innovation does exist in the charter schools, it is unclear whether the schools will be able to maintain it over time. There is evidence, in practice, of a gap between the pedagogy outlined in a charter application and the "real-world" implementation of such programs.

THE DISTRICT'S CHARTER LAW

Nationwide, as of April 2006, forty states and the District of Columbia had charter laws in place, and around thirty-six hundred charter schools were in operation (Center for Education Reform 2006). Existing laws differ on a number of dimensions that affect the ease with which charter schools can be created, notably the number of schools that can be authorized in a given year, the number of entities with the authority to grant charters, whether existing traditional public schools can be converted to charter status, the duration of the charter, and requirements for faculty training and certification (Kucsova and Buckley 2004).

Gill and his colleagues illustrate the importance of such differences by comparing the situation under a very weak charter law in Kansas to that found under Arizona's very strong charter law (Gill et al. 2001). In Kansas, the number of new charters that can be established each year is capped at fifteen and the charter is granted for only three years. Local school boards are the only authorizing agency and education management organizations—for example, the Edison Corporation—are not permitted to apply for charters. Start-up funding is not available to assist new schools. Further, Kansas's charter law requires all teachers to be Board certified and allows exemptions from other district regulations only on a case-by-case basis, determined by negotiations between the charter school and the local school board that authorized it.

At the opposite end at the spectrum lies Arizona's charter law, arguably the nation's strongest. There is no limit on the number of schools that can be established in a given year and the initial charter term is fifteen years. Schools are exempt from most district regulations, and teacher certification is not required. In addition, Arizona provides start-up grants and funding for facilities maintenance. Three separate organizations (the state board of education, local school districts, and a state board of charter schools) have the authority to grant charters. Given these differences it is not surprising that in Spring 2006 Kansas had just twenty-five charter schools, enrolling fewer than two thousand students, while Arizona had close to 450 charters enrolling almost one hundred thousand students.[3]

On this continuum, Washington, D.C. falls far closer to Arizona than to Kansas. Policy analysts at the Center for Education Reform have evaluated and ranked each state's charter law on the basis of criteria that their research has linked to charter sector growth. Currently, Washington's charter law was ranked third strongest in the nation, behind only Arizona and Minnesota.[4]

Multiple Authorities in the District Can Charter Schools

What makes the District's law so strong? The provision of a dual authorizing system by D.C. charter law has often been cited as one of its many strengths. As noted above, the law grants both the District's Board of Education and an independent chartering agency, the Public Charter School Board, the authority to grant charters. Both bodies are each responsible for reviewing applications, authorizing schools, monitoring the operations of the existing schools, and renewing or revoking charters.

At the time of the law's inception, there was general recognition that the local school board was not adequately prepared to manage the charter schools, and overwhelming evidence suggested that they had failed in this role with their own schools. Beyond this, the dual structure was designed to address concerns about democratic accountability and conflicts of interest. On the one hand, involving the elected school board in charter governance is consistent with normative democratic principles. Charter schools established with the approval of a locally elected board are more likely to reflect community interests and needs. Beyond this, many thought that establishing a close connection between the traditional public schools and the charter schools might also serve to facilitate the exchange of information and innovation—recall that one of the concepts propelling the proliferation of charter schools is their potential role as "laboratories of innovation" that can leverage change throughout the school system.

Despite these potential benefits, many charter school advocates fear that local school boards do not make good authorizers, since they are likely to view charter schools as competitors for their students and funds and will, therefore, impede their creation or limit their growth.

Chester Finn, with his characteristic flair, argues that "placing school boards in charge of charter schools is akin to placing McDonald's in charge of Burger King" (Finn 2003). In less dramatic language, Finn argues that local school boards don't "want the competition, [have] scant experience in letting some schools be different from others, and [don't] know how to replace command-and-control compliance with results-based accountability." Palmer and Gau (2003) also contend that local school boards generally do not make good authorizers, while Hassel and Batdorff (2004) argue that local school boards are much more likely to be influenced by political pressure and considerations than other types of authorizers. In turn, they argue that state policy makers should grant more nonlocal authorizers power to grant charters (also see Teske, Schneider, and Cassese 2005). In any case, the D.C. charter law does support two authorizers, which is most likely to have spurred the creation of more charter schools (Kucsova and Buckley 2004).

But this spur to the creation of charter schools may incur costs: the combined expenses of the two chartering authorities in the District exceeded one million dollars for FY 2000 (DC Appleseed Center 2001)—a number that no doubt has grown as the charter sector has expanded.

Yet another issue flowing from Washington's dual accountability structure concerns the different professional capacities of the authorizing bodies. The relative competence of the two boards may manifest itself in markedly different school outcomes, and as a result is an important consideration for the success of Washington's charter schools, as applicants may choose the charter authorizer which they think has lower standards or is more charter-friendly. Such a practice among applicants might serve to systematically influence the quality of new schools (DC Appleseed Center 2001). Indeed, there is some evidence that the Public Charter School Board has performed its support and oversight role more proficiently, a point we discuss in more detail below.

Other Aspects of the District's Charter Law Matter

Aside from the dual accountability structure, several other components of the charter law warrant mention, as they clearly shape the character of the District's charter sector. First, the duration of each charter granted by either the Board of Education or Public Charter School Board is fifteen years. A long charter term was designed to improve the long-term financing options—mortgages and long-term borrowing—of the charter schools. However, the schools are subject to review at five-year intervals. These periodic reviews can (and do) result in probation or, in some cases, revocation of a school's charter. Indeed, if sufficient problems emerge before the five-year review term expires, it is possible for the chartering authority to intervene earlier.

The number of new schools that can be established in a given year is capped at twenty, with each authorizing agency having the right to approve ten applicants each year. Any person, group, or private or public organization is considered an eligible applicant. Under the law, home-based schools are not eligible to apply for charter status. Applicants may also include conversions of schools that were previously public or private, as well as new schools. When traditional public schools apply to convert to charter status, the original charter law dictated that the applicant provide evidence that two-thirds of teachers, two-thirds of the parents of minor students, and two-thirds of adult students support the conversion. Recent amendments to the law have reduced the percentage of teachers to 51 percent, which is likely to make conversion easier. At present, only one traditional public school, the Paul Junior High School, has converted to charter status. However, in the summer of 2004, one of the city's best senior high schools, Wilson, made public its exploration of the idea of converting to charter status.

Because the rationale of charter reform requires charter schools to have more autonomy than the traditional public schools, Washington's charter law dictates that each charter school must organize a board of trustees. It is this board of trustees, rather than the school district, that provides support, governance, and oversight to the charter school. In this respect, charter school administration is school-specific, that is, it is focused on the individual school and sensitive to the particular needs of its students and parents. District charter law places two requirements on the composition of each school's board of trustees. First, the law insists that a minimum of two board members be parents of children currently enrolled in the school. The second provision states that a majority of the board members must be residents of D.C. These requirements reinforce the notion of local leadership and local control.

In recent years, some of the original charter schools have begun to restructure their boards of trustees to provide an emphasis on fundraising and long-term planning. This trend is consistent with the growing importance of recruiting nonfederal funds among charter schools in the District (Henig et al. 2001). An additional way that the District's charter law facilitates local control can be found in the stipulation that petitions to establish a charter school must include a description of how local stakeholders have been involved in the design of the charter school, and the role they will play in the operation of the school should it be established.

Overall, this brief history and the "facts on the ground" suggest that existing law has established the conditions for a vibrant charter sector in the District. In the following sections, we consider the implementation of several provisions in the District's charter law.

CREATING CHARTER SCHOOLS: THE APPLICATION PROCESS

Washington's charter law enables new charter schools to be sponsored by a university, a nonprofit service provider, a museum, or a theater. Sectarian organizations can sponsor a charter school, although the school itself must be nonsectarian. Essentially any person, group, organization, or postsecondary institution—including public, private, or quasi-private entities—can apply to start a school with charter status. A notable exception to this rule is that charters may not be granted directly to for-profit organizations, although the schools may be managed by them.[5] As previously noted, existing public and private schools can apply to convert to charter status.

Potential new schools and conversions choose to file their application with one of the two District authorizers, the District Board of Education and the Public Charter School Board. The Public Charter School Board consists of seven members who are appointed by the mayor from a list of fifteen nominees provided by the U.S. Secretary of Education. Prior to 2000, the District's Board of Education was composed exclusively of elected officials until it was reconstituted by a voter referendum and changed to include four members appointed by the mayor and five elected members.

Either chartering authority may approve or reject applications. There is no administrative appeals process in place for rejected applicants, unlike in other states such as Pennsylvania or New York, although applicants can appeal to the courts. Applicants can also reapply at a later date, with a revised application.

Through 2003, the Public Charter School Board has received about twice as many applications as the Board of Education and has approved about one-third. In contrast, the Board of Education has an approval rate

TABLE 2.1
Charter School Petitions/Approvals by Year

Petition Cycle	D.C. Public Charter School Board		D.C. Board of Education	
	Number of applications	Number of approvals (approval rate)	Number of applications	Number of approvals (approval rate)
1. 1996–97 [Fall '96/'97]			5	5 (100%)
2. 1997–98 [Fall '98]	26	10 (38%)	9	9 (100%)
3. 1998–99 [Fall '99]	13	2 (15%)	12	4 (33%)
4. 1999–2000 [Fall '00]	18	6 (33%)	8	2 (25%)
5. 2000–1 [Fall '01]	12	3 (25%)	Did not accept applications	
6. 2001–2 [Fall '02]	5	0 (0%)	11	2 (18%)
7. 2002–3 [Fall '03]	5	3 (60%)	5	1 (20%)
8. 2003–4 [Fall '04]	11	6 (55%)	15	3 (20%)
9. 2004–5 [Fall '05]	16	3 (19%)	**	4
10. 2005–6 [Fall '06]	15	7 (47%)	4	3 (75%)
11. 2006–7 [Fall '07]	19	6 (32%)	Did not accept applications	

Source: Robert Cane, Executive Director, FOCUS. Data are accurate as of the end of the 2005/6 school year. *Note*: the School Reform Act passed in April 1996; BOE approved five public charter schools in August '96; D.C. Public Charter School Board began in Spring 1997 and took its first applications in September 1997.

**BOE began to require a "prospectus" to be filed in February; applicants were those who survived prospectus review

of 50 percent, but has gotten far more restrictive in recent years (see table 2.1; also see Teske, Schneider, and Cassese 2005). The different approval rates of the two charter authorities raises questions of whether the authorities have different standards or vary in their support of charter schools. Henig and his colleagues (1999) have explored the extent to which the applications approved by either authorizer differed in terms of completeness or comprehensiveness. Overall, they argue that applications to the Board of Education were less sophisticated and less complete. This is congruent with Palmer and Gau's (2003) contention that local school boards do not make good authorizers.[6]

Beyond the superficial difference in composition and an apparent difference in approval behavior, the two charter authorities are also generally considered to differ in terms of their sentiments towards the charter schools, their professional orientation, and their competence. Based on interviews with charter-school administration and staff, Henig and his colleagues (1999) suggest that the Public Charter School Board is generally considered to be more neutral, objective, and professional. The Board of Education, on the other hand, is often characterized as hostile. Hill and colleagues suggest that the charter-granting behavior of the Board of Education highlights its vulnerability to local political forces (Hill et al. 2001). A later study by Henig and MacDonald (2002) offers some corroborating evidence. The authors demonstrate that the schools chartered by the Board of Education were located in wards with higher voter turnout and a higher concentration of African Americans. In contrast, the Public Charter School Board was found to be focused on pragmatic considerations, such as operational and fiscal viability (also see Hassel and Batdorff 2004 on the greater susceptibility of school districts to political factors).

The differences between the Board of Education and Public Charter School Board may be attributable to a number of factors, including differences in staffing, resources, and organizational focus. While some D.C. stakeholders attribute the Board of Education's apparent ineptitude to willful hostility stemming from opposition to the charter movement, others maintain that it stems from bureaucratic unresponsiveness and the inability of the already heavily burdened district administration to meet its new responsibilities to the charter schools. There is some anecdotal evidence, notably evident in the reconstitution of the Board in 2000, that stakeholders in the District are pressuring the Board of Education to close this gap in competence.

To what extent do the relative competencies of the two boards show through in terms of the character of the schools they authorize? A study by Teske, Schneider, and Cassese (2005) found little evidence of systematic differences between the schools chartered by the Board of Education and those chartered by the Public Charter School Board in terms of student demographics. The most important exception concerned schools serving students at risk, where the Board of Education chartered significantly more schools designed to deal with this student population. School size was also found to differ by charter-granting authority, with the Board of Education demonstrating a tendency to authorize smaller schools.

AN OVERVIEW OF CHARTER-SCHOOL OPERATIONS

Public charter schools are considered autonomous legal entities. They are organized as nonprofit corporations and exempt from most of the regulations that govern the traditional public schools. As we discussed in the introductory chapter, the logic underlying their legal status suggests that exemption from burdensome requirements affords the schools greater flexibility in determining their operational and curricular policies, thus fostering innovation and responsiveness to school-level interests and concerns. Each school is governed by its own board of trustees, sometimes referred to as the school corporation. The board is responsible for determining the school's fiscal, administrative, personnel, and instructional policies.

There are several commonalities in charter-school operations, most of which are driven by the District's charter-law requirements. Enrollment is a prime example. All District residents are eligible to apply to the charter schools, and admission is granted on the basis of available space. Once a charter has reached capacity, applicants are placed on a waiting list. A lottery system is then used to select students as space becomes available. Preference for enrollment is given to students who have attended the school previously, siblings of these students, and district residents. Beyond this, the charter schools are prohibited from explicitly discriminating in enrollment. They cannot use entrance exams or limit who is accepted on the basis of academic ability or achievement, but they may constrain enrollment based on the curricular focus of the school. Finally, charter schools cannot require prospective students to pay any application fees.[7]

Schools in both sectors receive public funds based on the number of students they enroll. In addition, both charter schools and traditional public schools are eligible for federal categorical funds such as Title I of the Improving America's Schools Act or Part B of the Individuals with Disabilities Act (Public Charter School Board 2004). Appropriations from the D.C. General Fund are allocated according to a Uniform Per-Student Funding Formula (UPSFF). The schools are provided with a baseline or foundation level of funding. The foundation level for FY 2005, for example, was $6,900 per pupil. Additional funding is added on the basis of grade level and student needs, and determined by a weighting scheme. Generally speaking, the UPSFF provides a stable, predictable, and well-defined procedure for estimating the yearly budget. In addition, charter schools receive a capital allowance of over $2,000 per student, a revenue stream against which many charter schools borrow for capital investments.

One hundred percent of operations funding follows students to charter schools, based on the District's per-pupil expenditures (PPE) formula. That is, on average, the per-pupil expenditures received by the charter schools equal those received by the traditional public schools. The practice of offering comparable funding to the charter schools is unusual among the states with charter laws.[8] The Center for Education Reform has estimated that the average per-pupil expenditure received by the D.C. charter schools is among the highest of any school system in the nation. Charter schools were expected, by some proponents of this choice-based reform, to increase productive efficiency and provide education at a lower cost. This expectation has generally not been borne out in practice.

That the charter schools have not managed to reduce the cost of providing educational services, as many proponents had hoped, may reflect the growing pains of a newly developing educational sector or an inability to create economies of scale. Some argue that even if the funding levels are the same, many charter schools are actually doing more with the same dollars, for example, by running extended day programs or by having a longer school year. These types of activities would signify higher productivity even if overall costs are not lower (more is being produced for the same amount of dollars).

Start-up funding has proven to be a common implementation problem for charter schools throughout the nation, including in the District. In a 1999 study by Henig and his colleagues, lack of sufficient start-up funds was cited as a significant problem in almost half of the charter schools sampled. In addition, over a third of the schools complained of inadequate operating funds. Sufficient support is particularly crucial at the early stages of establishing a charter school. New charters face several substantial challenges—training new personnel, purchasing equipment and instructional supplies, securing and renovating a facility—all of which require money, experience, and expertise. Each charter has to manage its real-estate and building-improvement needs using whatever capabilities exist within their board or administrative staff and leadership.

This situation has improved over time. As of 2002, the funding stream has been smoothed out and money now arrives earlier in the year. In addition, there are several professional and grassroots public interest groups operating in the District of Columbia who help provide information, expertise, and support for charter-school applicants and newly established schools. These interest groups—notably Friends of Choice in Urban Schools (FOCUS), the DC Public Charter School Association, and the Charter School Development Corporation—constitute a significant component of the charter school infrastructure. From the inception of the charter movement in D.C., they have worked closely with Congress, the Control Board, and the City Council to ensure the viability of the charter sector.

A second and related problem faced by many charter schools concerns securing an adequate and permanent educational facility. This challenge is not limited to start-ups, but also concerns those charter schools in temporary facilities or who have outgrown their current accommodations. Across the country, a major barrier to starting a public charter school is finding and financing suitable school facilities. According to the U.S. Government Accountability Office, "obtaining an adequate facility remains a significant obstacle for charter schools, especially in those locations like the District of Columbia, where the cost of and demand for property is high" (2003, 27).

A FOCUS ON FACILITIES

In D.C., with its declining enrollments in the traditional schools, a logical source of facilities for the growing charter-school sector should be underutilized or abandoned school buildings. Because the DCPS has lost about one-fifth of its enrollment in the past seven years, many of the traditional public schools have unused space—enough, by some estimates, for twenty thousand students. Although it currently operates over 140 active schools, the District is thought to control approximately 190 buildings. Based on these figures, these properties should constitute an untapped resource for the charter sector.

However, there is a long-standing reluctance on the part of the D.C. public school system to part with its vacant facilities. Several charter schools scheduled to open in the Fall of 1998 expected to be housed in vacant DCPS buildings, only to be informed days prior to the start of the school year that the buildings would not be made available for their use. Following these events, other charters have reported bidding on vacant DCPS buildings only to have them suddenly and inexplicably pulled off the market. According to Robert Cane, the Executive Director of FOCUS, a number of public charter schools have been forced to delay opening for a year or more because of facilities problems. Others have been forced to locate in temporary or otherwise unsuitable facilities.

Despite the clear evidence that many charter schools need new space now or within the next few years as enrollments continue to grow, the DCPS has continued to turn a blind eye to these needs: approximately sixty school buildings were declared surplus by the District of Columbia Public Schools before 1998. Unfortunately, even though the School Reform Act gives the public charter schools a preference to acquire these buildings, only about a dozen of them now house public charter schools.

Financing building renovations has been another major problem. As start-up operations—essentially new businesses—the public charter schools have no credit history and have had to convince the banks that the public demand for seats in the schools and their guaranteed per-pupil capital funding is a reasonable security for long-term loans. Drawing on the available public subsidies, public charter schools have already amassed almost $200 million in debt for their schools. More than $70 million is from private loans, often leveraged by District credit enhancements. Almost $100 million has been borrowed through city revenue bonds.[9] Charter school borrowing does not just go for building improvements, as charter schools must also pay the cost of financing acquisitions and improvements.

There have been some successes in meeting these financial needs. In September 2004, Sallie Mae, the student loan company, made $28 million available to help charter schools in the District acquire or lease facilities and expand their student enrollment through loan guarantees, low-interest loans, grants for technical assistance and help in such areas as site selection and lease and purchase negotiations. This augments actions by Mayor Anthony A. Williams (D) and Sen. Mary Landrieu (D-La.), ranking member of the Senate Appropriations Subcommittee on the District, who in August 2004 launched CityBuild, a federally funded effort to create or expand charter schools in selected neighborhoods (with $5 million appropriated for FY 2004 and an additional $2 million in FY 2005). In addition, a credit-enhancement program has made over $20 million available to help finance charter schools.

Despite these gains, finding and funding facilities is still a problem, one which is exacerbated by the perennial problem of finding buildings and space in the Washington, D.C. tight real-estate market. The District of Columbia School Reform Act has been revised several times in response to persistent complaints by the District's charter schools on the matter of facilities. After the DCPS reneged on the agreement to give charters the use of their facilities in 1998, the law was revised in an attempt to affirm the rights of the charter schools in securing facilities. The changes had little impact, and additional amendments were made in 2000. Evidence to date suggests that the amendments have not resulted in a significant change, and a new set of amendments increasing the rights of charter schools is now pending in Congress.

How Do Charter-School Facilities Compare to DCPS Facilities?

One of the central arguments made in this debate over access to facilities is that current charter facilities are not educationally adequate. In an attempt to measure the quality of the District's charter schools and the appropriateness of these facilities for the mission of the charter schools, we present evidence from a survey of principals of both DCPS and charter

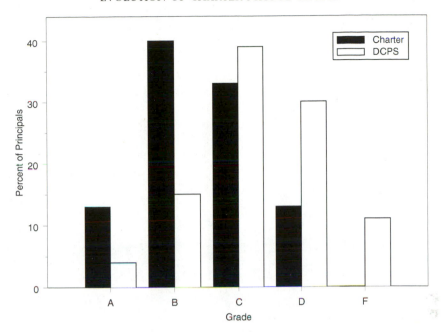

Figure 2.2. Charter-school principals grade their school facilities higher than do DCPS principals. *Note*: Results from telephone survey of *n* = 56 school principals. All differences significant at the *p* < .05 level, two-tailed.

schools, a survey that was supplemented by site visits.[10] There is one caveat to the use of the principal data: only one-third of the charter schools and a little over one-third of the traditional public schools are represented in the sample.

With this in mind, there appears to be a tendency for charter-school leaders to think their schools are in better overall condition compared to DCPS principals. When principals were asked to assign a letter grade to the condition of their school building, the grades assigned to charter facilities were, on average, higher than those assigned to the traditional public schools (see figure 2.2).[11] Interestingly, although charter-school principals are more likely to grade their schools overall higher, they are less likely to believe that their schools are adequate to meet specific aspects of the school's mission in terms of programs such as special education, science, preschool, after school, the recruitment of teachers, and attracting new students (see figure 2.3). It may be that the charter schools are adequate by the "normal" standards of public education, but once the competitive environment of the charter schools is factored in and once the ambition and desires of the charter-school principals are taken into account, charter-school facilities may, in their perception, come up short.

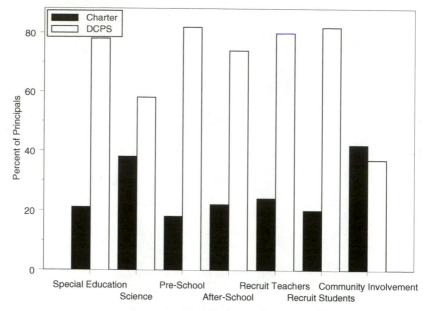

Figure 2.3. But charter-school principals find their schools less adequate in other important dimensions. *Note*: Results from telephone survey of *n* = 56 school principals. Reported percentages are based on principals reporting their schools as "somewhat" or "very" adequate. All differences significant at the *p* < .05 level, two-tailed, except for community involvement.

ACCOUNTABILITY VERSUS AUTONOMY: THE REVIEW PROCESS

As previously discussed, charter schools are exempt from most of the regulations that govern the traditional public schools. The rationale behind this autonomy is that schools will be freed from inefficient bureaucratic practices and afforded enhanced opportunities for innovation. This freedom from burdensome regulations is supposed to improve the productive efficiency of the schools. However, the desire for greater autonomy is often at odds with the perceived need for accountability.

The District of Columbia School Reform Act aims to induce both *market-based* and *performance-based* accountability. Generally speaking, performance-based accountability is founded on a performance contract between each school's board of directors and the chartering authority. If a school fails to meet its expected outcomes at the end of a five-year period, the charter-granting agency determines whether its charter will be revoked. Both charter authorizers retain the legal right to revoke a charter at any time if there is evidence that the school engaged in financial mismanagement, violation of any state or federal laws, or violation of its own charter.

What does the performance-based accountability process look like in practice? Consider the oversight procedures followed by the Public Charter School Board. Through its Program Development Review Process, every school is evaluated according to academic outcomes, compliance with special education law, and rules and regulations governing finances. After four years, schools are notified whether they will be placed on "priority review" and hence whether their charter is at risk for revocation. The schools on priority review receive a list of problems that must be rectified in order to retain their charter. The PCSB considers four criteria for continuance: (1) Is the school making progress towards achieving most of its academic and nonacademic goals? (2) Is the school well managed and fiscally responsible? (3) Can the school demonstrate that it is continuing to earn the support of parents; and (4) Is the school on an upward rather than a downward trajectory in terms of attaining its goals?

In terms of academic or quantitative standards, the PCSB requires that two of the following three be met: (1) The school must attain a majority of its performance goals over the two most recent school years; (2) The school must show improvement on a majority of academic goals of the two more recent school years; and (3) The school must come within 80 percent of the five-year Stanford 9 achievement targets in its accountability plan.[12] In terms of nonacademic standards, the PCSB holds that the school (1) should meet or exceed 80 percent of its five-year targets; (2) must maintain attendance targets (92 percent for elementary schools and 69 percent for alternative schools); (3) must maintain sufficient enrollment; and (4) experience a reenrollment rate of 75 percent or higher (Public Charter School Board 2004).

In terms of market-based accountability for the charter schools, the School Reform Act requires dissemination of information regarding school progress, usually through performance report data. On the basis of this information, parents can, in theory, decide whether to exercise their exit option and enroll their child in a different school. The extent to which this type of accountability is a viable mechanism in the market for educational services will be taken up in later chapters, where the informational and rationality assumptions underlying the role of parents as consumers will be explored in detail.

Unlike market-based accountability, in which the choices made by individual consumers either force improvement in quality or drive a school from the market in a gradual fashion, performance-based accountability involves the revocation of a school's charter by its authorizing agency. Note, however, that both forms of accountability are inextricably linked: a failure of a charter school to attract parents in the market will lead to its missing some necessary performance targets. Similarly, a school that is not performing to the level specified in its charter will likely be at a disadvantage in the market, presuming informed consumers.

Just how widespread is this accountability? Nationwide, between 1993 and 2003, 429 charter schools have been closed, with closure rates ranging from a high of 25 percent in Louisiana to zero in seven states.[13] Washington's closure rate is approximately 16 percent—virtually identical to the nationwide rate reported by Hassel and Batdorff (2004) and slightly more than the national rate calculated using Center for Education Reform numbers.[14] One issue is that the majority of charter schools that have been closed were terminated because of financial irregularities rather than lack of academic performance (Hassel and Batdorff 2004).

In the District, one PCSB-authorized school and six Board of Education—authorized schools have had their charters revoked since the School Reform Act's inception. In the case of the Board of Education closures, and consistent with national trends, four of the six schools were closed due to fiscal mismanagement and the two others due to improper reporting and poor learning conditions. The PCSB charter school, Associates for Renewal in Education, closed voluntarily prior to the completion of its fifth-year review, on the basis of the failure to make improvements required as part of its priority review status. Brown et al. (2003) attribute the higher success rate of the PCSB charters to a more rigorous application process, its participation in school development initiatives, and its greater support through the oversight process.

Some analysts propose that closures provide evidence that accountability measures are functioning properly. As a result, the low closure rate is considered evidence that the initial application process is effective in selecting viable schools, but failing schools will still not be tolerated. Jeanne Allen, director of the procharter Center for Education Reform offers a different explanation for charter closures: "To be fair, those few charters that do close—just 47, or 15 percent, of all schools in operation last year were closed—most do so not because of malfeasance but because they are underfunded or operationally undermined by regulations specifically intended to drive them out of existence" (Center for Education Reform 2004). For Allen, charter school closures suggest not the poor performance of the school per se; rather they suggest malfeasance on the part of the local school district. This attitude is not uncommon. For example, Finn, Manno, and Vanourek (2001) identify school district resistance and excessive regulations as one of the main impediments to the charter-school movement (also see Kucsova and Buckley 2004; SRI 2002).

Determining an appropriate level at which to regulate charter schools has generated considerable controversy. Several D.C. charter schools have suggested that they have been subject to more scrutiny and stricter reporting requirements than the traditional public schools (Henig et al.

1999). This perhaps reflects the so-called "principal-agent" problem of bureaucratic politics. Because the traditional public schools are subject to bureaucratic routinization, their behavior is thought to be constrained in such a way as to minimize the costs associated with monitoring or oversight. The obvious trade-off here is unresponsiveness to changing environmental conditions, in this case changing student needs or parental preferences. Charter schools, free from such constraints on behavior, can be more responsive and innovative organizations than the traditional public schools. This latitude raises questions for the bureaucratic principal—here the chartering authority—resulting in increased expenditures for monitoring and ultimately more stringent oversight.

Do the charter-granting authorities differ in their approach to or competence at charter-sector oversight? Many comparisons have been made of the two organizations' performance as wardens of the charter sector, and many accusations of mismanagement have been leveled against the District's Board of Education. In fact, the Board of Education has often been seen as less helpful and hospitable during the chartering process and has been considered to be the more intrusive party in the monitoring stage by stakeholders in D.C. Based on interviews with charter-school leaders, Henig and his colleagues (1999) conclude that the PCSB-authorized schools consider the PCSB to be exhaustively thorough, but at the same time fair and supportive. Leaders of schools authorized by the Board of Education, on the other hand, frequently described the Board as hostile, ill informed, and reluctant to provide feedback. More recently, Palmer and Gau (2003) report that the District's Board of Education charter schools consistently characterize their interaction with the Board as strained and antagonistic, suggesting not much has changed over the last five years of charter-school expansion, a conclusion verified by our own conversations with people involved with charter schools in the District.

It is unclear whether this difference can be attributed to willful hostility, simple bureaucratic indifference, or incompetence (Teske, Schneider, and Cassese 2005). Many critics of the Board of Education cite the difficulties encountered by the charter schools in securing vacant DCPS facilities and forwarding student records as a prime example of the District Board's unwillingness to form a working relationship with the charter sector. Perhaps the Board of Education fears that a thriving charter sector will serve to highlight (if not exacerbate) the many flaws of the traditional public schools. A second potential cause for concern might be that the better traditional public schools will convert to charter status, resulting in "skimming the cream" at the school level, rather than student level.

It might also be the case that differences in resources or institutional focus between the two authorizers show through in their behavior towards the charters. For the Board of Education, for example, responsibilities towards the charter schools have to fit within its large organizational structure, while the PCSB was designed for the specific purpose of regulating charter schools. In addition, the Public Charter School Board has a larger staff than does the Board of Education's chartering unit, providing them with more resources to monitor school performance and respond to school needs.

WHAT DOES THE FUTURE HOLD FOR SCHOOL CHOICE IN WASHINGTON, D.C.?

Recent developments in the District point to a reconsideration of charter governance. Within the past several years, and consistent with national trends, there have been repeated calls for mayoral control of the schools by Mayor Williams and newly elected mayor Adrian Fenty. In addition, they seem intent on increasing the scope of authority for the PSCB, all members of which are now selected by mayoral appointment. In fact, a plan released in May 2004 proposed the elimination of the District's school board as a chartering authority and suggested placing responsibility for all charter schools with the PCSB. Under this new plan, the BOE would be reconstituted with powers to set educational policy such as academic standards, attendance rules, and teacher certification/licensure requirements—a role not unlike the one proposed for the newly created State Education Office (SEO). Although supported by the *Washington Post*,[15] the Center for Education Reform, FOCUS, and other advocacy groups argued that elimination of a dual chartering system would undermine the strength of the charter law—and suggested instead the creation of another independent board similar to the PSCB. The plan for increased mayoral control failed in the Senate, but it is unlikely that Mayor Williams will drop the issue. He has often been quoted as referring to the District's public school system as "a slow-moving train wreck" and seems committed to directing educational reforms directly from the Mayor's Office.[16]

A new congressionally funded program expanded choice in the District's educational system even further. In January 2004, the D.C. School Choice Incentive Act created a scholarship program designed to offset the tuition payments for low-income students who want to attend private or parochial schools. Overall, the FY 2004 spending measure includes $13 million for charter schools (creating five new charters and supporting existing ones); $10 million for the traditional public schools for teacher training, recruitment, and supplemental academic programs; and $13 million for a D.C. school choice scholarship program, with an additional $1 million for administrative expenses. The program incorporates scholarships of up to $7,500 for as many as 1,700 disadvantaged D.C. schoolchildren, and grants preference to students enrolled in public schools that are failing to make adequate yearly progress as defined by the No Child Left Behind Act. Based on last year's figures, fifteen traditional public schools fell into that category (Hsu and Blum 2004).

This Washington Scholarship Fund is unique in that it is the first scholarship or voucher program to receive federal funding and the only such program to be administered by the U.S. Department of Education (Hsu and Blum 2004). Although marked by many implementation problems (for example, in the first year, not enough students applied at the elementary school level, while demand outstripped the supply of seats in high schools), to date the WSF has placed about one thousand disadvantaged, low-income students in fifty-three private schools across the District of Columbia for the 2004–5 school year. These vouchers may provide a challenge to charter schools: according to preliminary numbers, about 15 percent of voucher students came from charter schools, suggesting that not all charter-school students and their parents are happy with their current choices (for more on this, see chapters 9 and 10).

Given all this activity, school alternatives are more densely packed in the District than in other areas in which charter-school programs have been implemented. In addition, trends in enrollment and the length of waiting lists suggest the continued viability of the charter sector in D.C. The District's charter-school law is, for the most part, strongly supportive of the charter movement and the charter sector is situated within an infrastructure of grassroots and professional interest groups who provide both fiscal support and expertise. This is the milieu faced by the subjects of our study: the parents and the students that choose among an ever-increasing number of schools.

The Panel Study

IN THIS BOOK, we use two main sources of data to study choice behavior and charter schools. One dataset, which we describe in chapter 5, is a record of the characteristics and electronic search behavior of parents using an Internet site, DCSchoolSearch.com, that we created to help parents shop for schools. In this chapter, we describe the other major source of data, a four-wave panel survey in which we interviewed at four separate times a sample of Washington, D.C. parents with children either in the charter schools or in the traditional public schools.[1] In the last two waves, we interviewed students as well.[2]

We conducted the first wave of parent interviews in the Fall of 2001, at which time we talked with just over five hundred parents in charter schools and about the same number of parents whose children were in traditional public schools.[3] At the end of that school year (Spring 2002), we reinterviewed as many of these parents as possible. As we will see below, attrition was high even over the course of a single school year and in Wave 2 we completed interviews with just about six hundred of the parents in our original sample. Wave 3 was conducted in the Fall of 2003, when we successfully reinterviewed 395 of the original parents. In each wave of the parent survey, we asked the parent to talk about a specific child and the specific school in which that child was enrolled.[4]

In Wave 3, we asked the parent for permission to speak directly with the student if that child was enrolled in grade 7 or above. We completed interviews with 195 students. Of these, 100 were in charter schools, while the other 95 were in traditional public schools. At the end of the 2003/4 school year we launched Wave 4, during which we reinterviewed 297 parents and 149 students.

CHARACTERISTICS OF THE PANEL

There are several important characteristics of this component of our research. First, of course, our study employs a panel—a research design that is all too rare in the social sciences. As in any panel study, the structure of the data allows us to measure both stability and change in attitudes and behavior over time. This is always important when investigating the effects of institutions on individuals, but is particularly important when investigating a relatively new institutional reform, such as the charter schools we study. In addition, the structure of our panel allows us to measure conditions at the beginning of the school year and at the end of it. As we shall see later (and perhaps not surprisingly), parents and students feel differently about their schools at the end of the year than at the beginning.

There is an old adage that "hope springs eternal"—in the schools we study, hope may be less eternal than cyclical, springing up in the Fall, but drying up as the realities of inner-city education wear on everyone over the course of the school year.

Self-Selection into Charter School—and out of the Study

Given the power of panel studies, not surprisingly they are complex research instruments to design and to implement. Our panel data becomes even more complex when we consider several other issues. First, the very nature of charter-school choice creates problems caused by self-selection. Given that only some parents choose to choose, we must always keep in mind that charter-school parents as a population may be systematically different than traditional public-school parents. This is important to the extent that these differences affect outcomes independently of what the charter schools actually do and of any value charter schools add to the educational process. We discuss this potential bias due to self-selection in detail below.

Second, keeping a panel study "alive" over time is difficult under any circumstance and keeping it viable in an inner city over several years is even more so. Not surprisingly, attrition was high over the course of the study and was higher among certain types of parents (for example, the lowest-income parents) than others. As every educator knows, student mobility rates in inner-city schools are distressingly high. It is not just students who are moving about—their parents are also moving at very high rates. Furthermore in contrast to more affluent families, when many of the parents in our survey moved, they did not take their phone numbers with them nor did many contract with the phone company to give callers their new telephone number. We also suspect that some of the attrition we experienced was the result of parents' loss of phone service for a variety of financial reasons.

Modeling such nonrandom "exits" over the life of the panel is a difficult task. As will be clear in our empirical analyses later in the book, we try statistically to adjust our analyses for both self-selection and nonrandom attrition, but controlling for both simultaneously is a challenging task.

Charter Schools as a "Treatment"

Throughout much of this book, we talk about the students and parents enrolled in charter school as being exposed to a "treatment," and we refer to the public-school parents in our sample as the "control" group. We believe this is the right way to think about (and measure) the effects of the charter-school experience; however, like so much other social science and policy research, the reality of our research design and the flaws in our data may stretch the applicability of the terminology—but we believe not past the breaking point.

In a medical test of a new drug, testing the effects of a treatment is almost always done through randomized controlled trials (RCTs), often called the "gold standard" for obtaining proof of causal relationships. In RCTs, participants are randomly assigned to treatment and control groups, and this randomization "cancels out" any biases that might affect observed outcomes by ensuring that potential confounds are uncorrelated with treatment assignment. The results of RCTs provide, many argue, the strongest basis for statements regarding cause and effect.

The world of education research differs from this ideal. To be sure, there have been randomized field trials in education research—but, according to Thomas Cook, one of the nation's most astute observers of social experiments, most have been conducted by psychologists to help assess the effectiveness of different ways to prevent school violence or reduce student violence or drug use. In contrast, very few education studies with policy relevance for school system design use random assignment (Cook 2002). A major exception is the work of Paul Peterson and his colleagues, who have conducted randomized field trials to assign parents to school-voucher programs; however, to date no researchers studying the implementation of charter-school reforms have successfully completed such a study.[5] In addition, for a variety of reasons, RCTs of complex educational interventions often end up with most of the problems inherent in observational research anyway (Hanushek 1999).[6]

In Washington, D.C. (as in other cities and states introducing charters) we were faced with a highly popular reform that has grown rapidly in response to political pressure and parental demand. Given the reality of rapid growth and no central control over who can enroll in which school, we had little say over who was exposed to the treatment (since parents and students themselves choose to enroll in charter schools). Thus, in our study, the "facts on the ground" did not include random assignment to charter schools and our data are observational in nature.[7] In turn, we attempt to control statistically for potential biases caused by the self-selection of parents into the charter schools. There is argument about how effectively our methods "emulate" the power of a true randomized field trial. While this is an intense (and unsettled) debate, we do know our methods for controlling self-selection are state-of-the-art and we believe that they are sufficiently robust to counter any biases in our data that may flow from the nature of charter-school choice.

Defining the Nature of the Treatment

We recognize too that in controlled experiments, the nature of the treatment (e.g., the dose of a new drug administered, or the number of repetitions of a psychological stimulus) is under the control of the experimenter. In addition, since many causal relationships are contingent on other factors, experiments can be designed to identify the precise mix of conditions or factors that make things work. In short, a well-designed randomized controlled trial can begin to "unpack" the black box to identify the actual conditions under which treatment effects are observed.

In contrast, we have potential problems in precisely defining the treatment itself. Consider, first, the length of time a student is enrolled in a charter school. Do any hypothesized effects of charter schools on students and parents accrue to students and their parents from the moment they are accepted into the school? From the first day they enroll? From the end of the first month, the first semester, the first year? Is the effect of the treatment cumulative over time or do the effects plateau after some (unknown) period? The questions about the temporal effects of the treatment go on—and mostly have been ignored by researchers.

Given the way we constructed our sample, the length of time students were enrolled in their school varies—some students are new to a school, some have been in the school for one, two, or three years, and a few for more. In addition, as we noted above, effects may vary over the course of the school year itself. The panel nature of our study allows us to get a better reading of the temporal effects of the charter-school treatment.

There is also debate about how deeply researchers should go into defining the pedagogical or curricular changes that constitute the charter-school "treatment." One could argue that charter schools are a structural reform, not a pedagogical one, and that it is the very act of changing the institutional structure of schooling that will lead to desirable outcomes, such as increased student performance or higher satisfaction (Miron and Nelson 2002; Vergari 2002). From this perspective, there is no need to specify in detail the specific characteristics of charter schools—because creating charter schools *is* the treatment.

This position has merit and the great diversity of charter schools lends credence to the idea that the structural, rather than any specific pedagogical or curricular, challenges posed by charter schools to the existing system of public schools is at the heart of the treatment. But many proponents also think of charter schools as laboratories of innovation, as "public education's 'R&D' arm" (U.S. Department of Education 2004, v). If this is the case, then getting inside the "black box" is important—because we need to identify what it is about the curriculum and educational approaches of successful charter schools that "work" and then use this information to leverage change in the traditional system of schooling in the United States (Teske et al. 2001; Cohen, Raudenbush, and Ball 2003). From the perspective of charter schools as laboratories, research into charter schools has too often emphasized the "intention to treat" (whether or not the choice was offered) and, at best, the average effect of the "treatment on the treated" rather than working to identify the "active ingredients"—the aspects of charter schools that drive any observed effects.

Taken as a whole, neither the traditional D.C. public schools nor the D.C. charter schools are a homogeneous group—as in any large urban school district, the schools vary considerably in programs, student populations, and, ultimately, success in educating their students. Our dataset was not designed to map many characteristics of schools onto individual observations, so we cannot get very far into the black box of how the mission, curriculum, or teachers in charter schools affect outcomes. We are then faced with this question: when we observe an overall difference between the two sets of parents, does it result from something unique about the charter-school sector or from something identifiable about the structure of individual schools? As a concrete example, might parents be more satisfied with charter schools simply because they are smaller on average than traditional public schools?

Following the idea of charter schools as primarily a structural reform we could focus on the "main effect" of charter schools (that is, we could assess the extent to which outcomes in charter schools are different overall than those observed in traditional public schools). If we document superior outcomes in the charter schools, we could then argue that the combination of competition, choice, community, and accountability that define the structure of charter schools in general has produced these superior results. We would then leave it up to the market and to chartering authorities to monitor the performance of individual charter schools, expecting that these forces will weed out bad schools—but these actions would take place knowing that charter schools are overall a successful intervention.[8]

On the other hand, we could try to more closely link observed variation in outcomes to differences in the characteristics of schools. In this approach, we might find that there is nothing unique about the charter schools—they may have simply put together different combinations of programs or approaches than traditional public schools. We would then use the larger variance between all schools (charter and traditional) to identify the effects of school structure on educational outcomes. Consistent with the idea of charter schools as "laboratories of reform," this information would then be used to reform traditional public schools as well as continue to push for improvement of charter schools.

However, this is a difficult strategy to pursue. On the most basic level, the literature on the characteristics of schools that "matter" is as contentious as it is voluminous (see, for example, Burtless 1996). This makes the choice of a set of variables describing how schools differ difficult to construct and hard to measure.

Moreover, it is often difficult to decide which school conditions are exogenous and which are endogenous to the system of charter schools. Consider, for example, the difference in size between schools in the two sectors. Hypothetically, say we find that a particular measure of desired parental behavior or student outcomes is higher in charter schools. Further, let us say that some of the observed differences can be attributed to the size of the school the child attends. We could then say that it is not charter school enrollment per se that matters, rather it is small schools. But what if small schools are part of the philosophy that charter schools share? Clearly, one could legitimately argue that creating smaller schools would benefit students regardless of sector, but what if it is predominantly charter schools that choose to remain small and have the autonomy and the authority to do so? In this case, we find a contingent relationship that theoretically could be exported to schools in any sector, but for various reasons only schools in the charter and perhaps private sectors are able to create the conditions under which the desired effect can be achieved.

Our response is to empirically investigate a few characteristics of schools as they may affect outcomes—for example, we are particularly concerned with the effect of school size, where we know there are significant differences between charter schools (which are smaller) and traditional public schools. We also look in depth at how charter schools build school communities and involve parents in the process of educating their children, a process that can affect outcomes. However, in this book, we do not explore many aspects of charter school curricula, mission, or teaching that have been hypothesized to affect outcomes, leaving that to the next wave of charter-school research.

Finally, researchers and policy makers have talked a lot about how parents and students choose schools, but it should really not be surprising that, in fact, schools also choose students. As strategic players, many schools manipulate selection (and retention) processes to fashion a student body they want. Similarly, it is not only parents who choose a level at which to participate in school events; schools actively encourage or discourage parent participation (for example, see Benveniste, Carnoy, and Rothstein 2003). While the opportunities to engage in these kinds of strategic behavior may be more extensive for charter schools than traditional public schools, the extent to which such manipulation exists will affect observed outcomes. We discuss this issue in chapter 4, where we examine the charter schools and their traditional counterparts for any evidence of "cream skimming" or other selection behavior.

Describing the Schools

In addition to our parent and student data, we worked long and hard to create a reliable set of indicators on some of the characteristics of the schools that deliver public education to Washington, D.C. As noted above, we did not seek to develop extensive descriptions of school curricula or programs, looking instead for more basic descriptive information about student demographics and test scores. While it seems as though gathering such data should be easy, for many reasons, reliable objective data were extremely hard to gather for any given year. Of course, these problems intensify when we tried to reconstruct school data over several years.

Nationwide, many schools and school systems do not have the institutional capacity to produce and disseminate accurate information. In Washington, D.C., school officials often claim that their reporting systems are old and do not communicate with one another. Many officials also noted that the release of data was a highly "political" process, subject to administrative pressures from "higher up." As a result, our requests for even basic data were often refused or the data provided were either not useful or differed from data obtained from other sources (often within the same agency). In short, the difficulties of compiling such data are legion, starting with incompetence and ranging perhaps all the way up to malevolence.[9] Nonetheless, we have assembled what we believe to be a (mostly) accurate dataset over time of the objective conditions of both the traditional D.C. public schools and the ever-growing population of charter schools, and we make reference to this information often in the subsequent chapters.

WHO CHOOSES?

With these preliminaries taken care of, we can now begin to introduce more fully the sample of parents we surveyed and discuss some of the problems we encountered in conducting the panel study. We also begin our exploration of a core question of this book and indeed, a question that anyone interested in school choice must ultimately address: are the parents who choose to enroll their children in charter schools systematically different than parents whose children remain in the traditional public schools?

The answer to this question will affect how we evaluate charter schools on virtually all of the five dimensions (competition, choice, community, accountability, and achievement) described in chapter 1. If charter-school parents and students are systematically different than other parents and students, the extent to which they differ may affect our answer to every other question we pose about the effects of charter schools. Unfortunately, the likelihood that charter-school parents and students are different than those in the traditional public schools is built into the design of charter schools as a form of choice.

Charter schools, like many of today's most popular school choice plans, embody an "option-demand" form of choice (Elmore 1991; Schneider, Teske, and Marschall 2000). In contrast to a system of "universal choice" in which all parents *must* choose, option-demand choice consists of a two-stage process. In the first step, parents must "choose to choose"—that is, they must be dissatisfied enough with their existing schools or be sufficiently attracted to an alternative to their neighborhood school that they decide to exercise choice. It is only after they decide to choose that the parent then faces the second step—selecting a new and different school in which to enroll her child from among the available alternatives.

Given this two-step process, one issue that is frequently discussed is the extent to which the parents who choose are different than the parents who do not. Many critics believe that option-demand choice exacerbates inequities based on race, socioeconomic status, and special needs (see, e.g., Henig 1994; Smith and Meier 1995; Ascher, Fruchter, and Berne 1996; Fiske and Ladd 2000). These critiques are often based on a concern that parents—particularly low-income, low-education parents—will not have sufficient information, motivation, or skills to negotiate the choice process or to choose effectively.

There is also a concern that the values and preferences of different racial and ethnic subgroups might lead them to segregate into homogeneous school settings (Henig 1990; Weiher and Tedin 2002; Schneider and Buckley 2002). While much of this work has focused on the individual-level question of who chooses and why, analysts are also concerned with systemic effects: how will choice and competition affect schools? From this viewpoint, many critics worry that choice will force existing schools to lower their costs and to demonstrate the highest levels of student achievement as quickly as possible. Facing these incentives, schools may be tempted to admit only those students who will be easier and perhaps less costly to educate, to "counsel out" students who are lagging, and to engage in dubious behavior when administering increasingly common "high-stakes" tests (Zollers and Ramanathan 1998; Cobb and Glass 1999; Henig et al. 1999; Maranto et al. 1999; Fiske and Ladd 2000; McEwan 2000; Schneider, Teske, and Marschall 2000).

Despite the enduring concerns that charter schools will engage in "cream skimming," the empirical evidence is fairly convincing that, overall, at least in terms of observable demographics, charter-school populations resemble the student population in the districts in which they are located. This pattern has been documented in a number of studies both nationwide and in many different jurisdictions (see Research Policy Practice International 2001 or SRI International 2002).

However, this leaves unresolved the possibility of a different type of skimming: charter-school parents might differ from other parents in less easily observed characteristics—for example, in the level to which they are involved in the school community or the degree to which they help their child with homework. These kinds of factors can affect student and school performance and if charter schools remove the most intensely involved parents from traditional public schools, the traditional public schools may suffer. Abernathy offers a clear statement of this problem. Using Hirschman's (1970) well-known "exit, voice, and loyalty" framework, Abernathy argues that the parents most likely to choose are those that "possess the requisite skills, information and attitudes to have their needs met, and their exercise of exit could result in a concentration of politically active and effective individuals within choice schools and away from assigned public schools" (Abernathy 2004, 5).

The resulting "paralysis of voice" in traditional public schools, according to Abernathy, means that "the most troubled public schools become less constrained by and more poorly supported by a parent community that has lost its most active voices to choice options" (2004, 14–15). Thus while advocates of choice extol the virtues of the exit option, Abernathy, like many other critics of choice, highlights the potential adverse affects from "skimming" along behavioral rather than demographic dimensions. In the rest of this chapter and in the next, we explore these issues.

TURNING TO THE DATA

We begin in this chapter by describing our parent sample, which is the basis for much of our empirical analysis. In particular, we explore in depth the data collected in the first wave of our study that bear on the stratification/segregation dimensions of the debate concerning option-demand choice. We focus first on the demographic characteristics of the charter-school parents and compare them to the parents whose children remained in the D.C. public schools. We then introduce some of the nondemographic differences between these parents, reporting such things as differences in such aspects of parental behavior as involvement with the school and with their child's education. The reader should note that this is only an introduction to the parents about whom this book is about. In later chapters, we delve into the attitudinal and behavioral differences that may (or may not) distinguish parents who have chosen charter schools and those who have kept their children in traditional D.C. public schools. The reader should also note that the descriptive data presented in this chapter are only our starting place; our ultimate task is to identify how these attitudes and behaviors change over time and the extent to which charter schools may in fact be affecting those changes.

After describing the distribution of some of these variables in the Wave 1 (Fall 2001) sample, we begin describing what happened to our panel over time. As we note above, we experienced high attrition even in the short time between Wave 1 and Wave 2, and we experienced further attrition in later waves. Below we present some data on rates of attrition and how they affect the composition of our panel over time.[10]

Not surprisingly, we find that some types of parents (for example, those with less education) were more likely to drop out of the panel than were others. Similarly, people who lived in their neighborhood for less time were also more likely to leave the panel. The complexity of patterns in attrition obviously leads to many different types of statistical problems, which we deal with in many of the empirical analyses we present in later chapters.

Given these problems, the reader should again remember that the object of the preliminary explorations we present in this chapter is to introduce our sample and to highlight some of the differences between the sets of parents—those in charter and traditional public schools—and over time. As the book progresses, we will present more detailed analyses of differences in attitudes and behavior between charter- and traditional public-school parents and we will introduce more rigorous methods to explore these differences.

Are Charter-School Parents Different?

In introducing our panel, we focus on Wave 1 data—this wave of the study was the largest and was not yet affected by differential rates of attrition (hence it is the most representative of the parents who have children in the D.C. schools). We begin by reporting a set of demographic characteristics and then move on to attitudinal and behavior indicators gleaned from the survey.

Table 3.1 shows that, congruent with other studies, in terms of demographics there are few differences between the parents in our sample who chose traditional public schools and those who opted for charter schools—and any observed differences do not point to demographic "cream skimming" by the charter schools.

Turning first to self-reported racial identity, there is no evidence of a racial divide in which charter schools have become a redoubt for white students. Indeed, by an 87–73 percent margin, charter parents are significantly more likely to identify themselves as African American than are D.C. public-school parents.[11] Conversely, charter-school parents are less likely to be Hispanic or non-Hispanic white. However, this overall pattern

TABLE 3.1
Comparing Charter and DCPS Parents

	D.C. public school parents	D.C. charter school parents	Sample size
Average income	$46,560	$41,450*	833
Percent >$65,000	36%	36%	833
Years of schooling	13.3	13.5	1000
Percent non-Hispanic black	74%	87%*	1005
Percent Hispanic	10%	6%*	1005
Percent non-Hispanic white	9%	2%*	1005
Percent other race	3%	2%	1005
Years lived in D.C.	17.2	17.5	1002
Years lived in neighborhood	9.4	9.1	1001
Age	40	39	983
Percent married	45%	42%	1005
Employed	72%	74%	1001
Attended church weekly	45%	55%*	992

* $p < .05$, two-tailed. Data are from first wave (Fall 2001) of parent panel survey. Total sample size is 1,012; reported sample sizes vary due to unit nonresponse.

hides a critical fact. Given the ability of charter schools to craft distinctive programs, there are a few charter schools that are focused on the special educational needs of Hispanics. In fact, while most charter schools have very low percentages of Hispanics, a few are quite high. Most notably the Next Step Public Charter School has a student body that is around 90 percent Hispanic. This is not surprising, since the school was founded by the Latin American Youth Center (LAYC), a nonprofit youth and family center with a mission of helping Latin American students. Similarly, while the César Chávez Public Charter High School for Public Policy is not as explicitly designed to support the needs of the Hispanic community as the Next Step school, it too has a very large concentration of Hispanic students (about 40 percent).

The lack of any evidence of skimming is also repeated when we look at reported income levels. Consider first the proportion of upper-income families in the two school sectors, where we find identical proportions represented in each. Even more striking, parents who have opted for charter schools report on average a *lower* average family income than the D.C. public-school parents we interviewed: $46,560 for DCPS parents or about $5,000 higher than the $41,450 reported by charter-school parents. There is thus no skimming evident on income.

Perhaps an even more critical indicator of socioeconomic status than income when studying educational choices and outcomes of children is parental education levels. Here, once again, we find no difference between the two sets of parents in terms of the *average* years of education completed. However, the *distribution* of the level of education completed by parents does differ. Note that a higher percentage of parents in the D.C. public schools stopped their education at high school or below (49.2 percent) compared to the D.C. charter-school parents (44.9 percent). Conversely, more D.C. charter parents attended college than the public-school parents in our sample. Howell and Peterson (2002) have also found that parents who take up school vouchers when offered tend to have completed more formal education than parents who choose not to accept a voucher.

Given the importance of parental education in determining student expectations about schooling and performance in schools, this difference may be of importance to the functioning of the schools and school communities, and parental education is a covariate that we will statistically control for in the empirical explorations we conduct in later chapters.

Demographics Are Not All That Matter

While much of the debate about cream skimming and school choice focuses on observable demographics, we use our survey data to analyze the distribution of other, less easily observed parental characteristics that may affect the stability and performance of schools. As we expand our analysis from demographics to these other characteristics, we still find that, in general, the samples of charter-school and DCPS parents are closely matched. For example, high residential mobility is one of the most serious problems that affect inner-city schools and clearly contributes to poor academic performance. But we find that the parents of children in both sectors report the same average number of years that they have lived in Washington and in their particular neighborhood. Table 3.1 also shows that the parents are virtually identical in terms of average age, marital status, and employment status.

There is a difference in the characteristics of the two sets of parents that is potentially important—charter-school parents attend church more regularly than D.C. public-school parents. Note that over half of the charter-school parents (55 percent) we interviewed said they attended church on a weekly basis, about 10 percent higher than the proportion of DCPS parents who said so. The importance of religion among choosers has been found by others (see for example Moe 2001; Howell and Peterson 2002;

Howell 2004a) and may reflect the greater concern that choosers have for education that emphasizes values.[12]

Overall, our results are congruent with that of Lacireno-Paquet et al. (2002, 154), who report "that charter schools taken as a whole do not appear to be cream skimming the pool of potential students in Washington, D.C. To the contrary, in the aggregate they are serving a population that has many characteristics associated with educational disadvantages."

HOW DOES THE SAMPLE CHANGE OVER TIME?

One of the major features of our research was its panel design. Despite strenuous efforts to preserve the integrity of the sample over time we experienced significant panel attrition or dropout. Consider the following numbers: in Wave 1 (Fall 2001) we completed interviews with 1,012 parents; Wave 2 (Spring 2002), 557; Wave 3 (Fall 2003), 395; and Wave 4 (Spring 2004), 296. Thus, in the months between the first two waves, fully 45 percent of the sample was lost. Between Waves 2 and 3, 29 percent of the remaining sample left, and between waves 3 and 4, we lost another 25 percent.

Since one of our main concerns is estimating the value-added of the charter-school experience, we need to consider how attrition may affect our longitudinal findings by nonrandomly removing certain types of parents from the sample. While we deal with the methodological issues associated with attrition in more detail in the substantive chapters in which we present longitudinal findings, here we report on the demographics of the respondents in different waves. Before doing so, it is important to note that attrition was significantly higher among the charter-school parents than among the D.C. public-school parents (see table 3.2).

Table 3.3 repeats the same demographic characteristics as table 3.2 but this time for respondents according to their status in the panel. Not surprisingly, the panel data demonstrate that attrition is higher among low-income and less-educated respondents—note, for example, the increase in the average income and educational attainment in the sample over time (although higher income and better-educated parents left the sample at a relatively higher rate between Waves 3 and 4). Attrition was also lower among people who lived in their neighborhood for a longer period of time.

There are a few demographic variables in which the patterns of attrition are different among parents in charter schools versus D.C. public schools. For example, while the percentage of Hispanics in our charter-school sample remains constant regardless of panel status (around 6 percent), the

TABLE 3.2
Status of Panel over Time, by School Sector

	DCPS	Charter	Total
Wave 1 only	89 (19.87%)	167 (29.61%)	256 (25.30%)
Waves 1 and 2	51 (11.38%)	118 (20.92%)	169 (16.70%)
Waves 1, 2, and 3	113 (25.22%)	178 (31.56%)	291 (28.75%)
All four waves	195 (43.53%)	101 (17.91%)	296 (29.25%)
Total	448 (100%)	564 (100%)	1,012 (100%)

$p < .001$ based on Pearson's chi-squared.

percentage in the DCPS sample fluctuates more widely, going from 10 percent among parents in Wave 1, jumping to 14 percent among parents in Waves 1 and 2, and then falling back to 5 percent among parents who were in all four waves. Consequently we find much wider fluctuation in the proportion of African American parents represented in the DCPS population. We also find that the income level of the charter-school population rises slowly over the life of the panel, in part because attrition among low-income parents in the DCPS sample was considerably higher—the average income among DCPS parents in Waves 1 and 2 is about $37,000, jumps to around $60,000 among parents who were interviewed in the first three waves but drops to back to $42,000 among parents in all four waves. On the other dimensions, there are no patterns of differences in parents in the two sectors by panel status.

NONDEMOGRAPHIC DIFFERENCES BETWEEN CHARTER- AND TRADITIONAL PUBLIC-SCHOOL PARENTS

While most discussion of cream skimming has focused on demographics, Abernathy (2004) and others have suggested that important differences may exist between choosers and nonchoosers across a range of attitudes and behaviors that are essential for good schools. In this section, we use our survey data to look at the distribution across parents in the two sectors across some nondemographic attributes that may affect the functioning of schools.[13]

TABLE 3.3
Differences in Sample Characteristics, by Attrition

	Wave 1 Only	Waves 1 and 2	Waves 1, 2 and 3	Waves 1, 2, 3 and 4
Percent income < $35,000	41%	34%	22%	31%*
Percent income > $65,000	29%	37%	45%	34%*
Average income	$38,000	$39,000	$53,000	$42,000*
Years of schooling	12.9	13.0	13.9	13.6*
Percent non-Hispanic black	83%	78%	78%	82%
Percent Hispanic	8%	13%	5%	6%*
Percent non-Hispanic white	3%	2%	8%	5%*
Years lived in D.C.	17.4	17.5	17.5	17.4
Years lived in neighborhood	7.7	8.7	11.1	9.0*
Age	36	38	34	37*
Percent married	40%	41%	48%	45%*
Employed	74%	72%	75%	74%
Attended church weekly	48%	51%	55%	50%

* $p < .05$ based on Pearson's chi-square tests for each row.

Parental Involvement

As we will discuss in chapter 11, education researchers have come to believe that the quality of education a school delivers is improved by a higher level of parental involvement. Indeed, fueled by a desire to bring parents into cooperative, supportive relationships with teachers and administrators in order to improve the education of students, many current proposals for educational reform seek to rewrite the relationship between stakeholders. In this vision, parents are given not only the power to choose but also a central role in school governance and the creation of "effective" schools. This aspect of the school-reform movement focuses on transforming parents from passive clients of a government service to active partners entitled to a say in how schools are run and how students are taught.

In our data, which we subject to more intense multivariate analysis in later chapters, we do not find consistent evidence that charter-school parents in D.C. are more involved with their schools than are D.C. public-school parents. For example, as seen in table 3.4, there are no statistically significant differences in the percentages of parents who say that they are members of the PTA. We also find no difference in the percentage of parents in each sector who report volunteering in their schools.

TABLE 3.4
Parental Involvement with School

	D.C. public-school parents	D.C. charter-school parents	Sample size
Volunteered for school event	57%	55%	999
Member of PTA	48%	47%	999
Commuting time to school (minutes)	17%	23*	543
Talk to teachers at least once a month	72%	83%*	766
Talk to administrators at least once a month	34%	44%*	767
Got information from school staff	49%	55%*	997
Number of people talked with about education	4.65%	4.84	972
Number of educational discussants	1.64	1.77*	972

* $p < .05$, two-tailed. Data are from first wave (Fall 2001) of parent panel survey except for the commuting time questions, which was asked in Wave 2 (Spring 2002). Total sample size is 1,012; reported sample sizes vary due to unit nonresponse.

These findings differ from what Schneider, Teske, and Marschall (2000) report in their study of choice in New York City—and one possible reason for this difference highlights how the design of choice plans can affect their success. Simply put, there are geographic differences in the way in which choice in New York and Washington, D.C. is structured, and these differences may explain the different outcomes. The districts Schneider, Teske, and Marschall studied were relatively compact and all the schools in parental choice sets were easily accessible. While the District of Columbia is blessed with an excellent public-transit system (paid for with money from taxpayers across the country) and is a small city compared to New York, as a whole the city is larger than the individual school districts around which New York's school system is organized. The citywide nature of choice in D.C. affects the accessibility of schools to children and parents. As an indicator of how this factor affects choice, we found that the reported commuting time for D.C. charter students was almost 50 percent longer than that of the public-school students.

Clearly, the longer commuting time is a burden that is most heavily felt by the children who attend school every day. But this geographic dispersion may also present a barrier to involving parents in building strong schools. This simple fact of geography may pose a difficult trade-off for advocates of school choice—small neighborhoods may not have the capacity to support many alternative schools, yet eliminating neighborhood-based schools to create a larger choice set may weaken parental involvement, one of the primary supports for quality education.

We return to the issue of parental involvement in chapter 11, where we focus on the effects of choosing on the vibrancy of school communities. Here, we note that at least on this dimension, as on most demographic measures, there is no prima facie evidence that Abernathy's concern about skimming off the most involved parents is justified in D.C.

DO CHARTER SCHOOLS WELCOME PARENTAL INVOLVEMENT?

As with so many of the issues we study, the level of parental involvement depends not only on the actions of parents (the "demand side"), but also on the action of schools, the "suppliers" of educational services. Parents may want to become more involved in schools, but more intense involvement must be aided and nurtured by schools that welcome such activity.

Many analysts argue that charter schools, as schools of choice, create a more welcoming environment that brings parents into the schools and encourages their involvement with teachers, administrators, and staff. These analysts argue that choice changes the "accountability relationships" between parents and the school, creating a stronger community (see, e.g., Hill et al. 2001). Furthermore, choice may put pressure on administrators, teachers, and staff to be more "consumer-friendly" (Hassel 1999, 6). Indeed, Teske et al. (2001) found that parents visiting charter schools in Washington were treated better than parents visiting D.C. public schools. Moreover, Teske and his colleagues report that the charter schools treated parental requests for information about programs more seriously than did staff at the D.C. public schools.

Returning to table 3.4, we find evidence of these patterns. Note for example that charter parents were much more likely to talk with teachers, principals, and other school administrators on a regular basis than were D.C. public-school parents. We also find that charter-school parents were more likely to report that they received information about the schools from school staff, confirming the pattern reported by Teske et al. (2001).

Finally, we look at one other measure of parental involvement with the schooling process. There is substantial evidence that talking with other parents and word of mouth are critical tools in finding out about schools and about monitoring school performance. There is also growing evidence about the importance of networks in creating social capital and in providing a strong basis for a range of other social, economic and political activity (see especially Lin 2001).

TABLE 3.5
Parental Involvement with Homework

	D.C. public-school parents	D.C. charter-school parents	Sample size
How many nights did child have homework in previous week?	4.3	4.4	991
How much time did homework take? (minutes)	59	66	721
Homework was not enough (% agree)	17%	13%*	724
Helped with homework (% of nights homework was given)	61%	55%*	738

* $p < .05$, two-tailed. Data are from first wave (Fall 2001) of parent panel survey. Total sample size is 1,012; reported sample sizes vary due to unit nonresponse.

We report three measures that reflect how deeply engaged parents in the two sectors are in networking. First, we asked parents to tell us how many other people they talked with over the course of the previous six months about their child's school. We find that charter-school parents do not talk with more people on average than DCPS parents. However, we do find that they are more likely to have a greater number of discussants with whom they talk in detail about the schools: 25 percent of DCPS parents named no one that they talked with about education, but only 19 percent of charter-school parents had no educational discussants.[14] On the other end of our count of educational discussants, 41 percent of charter-school parents reported three educational discussants (the maximum we counted in our study), exceeding the 37 percent of DCPS parents. In short, charter-school parents are, in general, involved in bigger networks in which education and schooling are discussed—and one of the most fundamental rules of network analysis is that "bigger is better" (Schneider et al. 1997).

PARENTAL "INVOLVEMENT" WITH HOMEWORK

In table 3.5, we look at another type of parental involvement that may contribute to academic success—the extent to which children in the different sectors are assigned homework and the amount of involvement of parents with their children in doing it. We do not find significant differences in the frequency with which parents report that their child had

homework and the amount of time it took for the child to do the homework (and our results are aligned with nationwide findings—see Gill and
Schlossman 2003). However, parents in the traditional schools were
somewhat more likely to think that their children were not getting enough
homework. We also find that in terms of simple percentages, DCPS parents were more likely to have helped their child do homework than the
charter-school parents, but this is driven by the fact that the students represented in our sample in the D.C. charter schools are in higher grades
than students in our sample enrolled in the D.C. public schools (37 percent of the charter-school students in our sample were in high school, 10
percent more than students in the traditional D.C. public school sample).
Once we account for that difference in grade distribution, the charter-
school deficit disappears. In short, we again find no evidence of creaming
on this dimension—the charter-school parents and the traditional DCPS
parents have remarkably similar profiles concerning homework.

At this stage, we begin to sense the complexity of the real world of
schools and how parents' behavior and attitudes shape and are shaped
by the many aspects of schooling. Critics of choice can find some evidence
that option-demand choice can lead to adverse outcomes. For example,
parents who chose to choose are more likely to have higher education.
They are also more likely to have more frequent contact with their child's
teachers and school administrators. But they are not more likely to be
members of the PTA or to do volunteer work in the school. And at this
stage we cannot untangle the extent to which the greater contact between
parents and school personnel is a *choice* of the parents or a result of the
active encouragement of parental involvement by charter schools—and
the normative implications of these two paths to higher parent-school
contact are radically different.

Attitudes toward Schools in the Different Sectors

While we will investigate how parents evaluate their schools in considerable detail in chapters 9 and 10, here we introduce some basic data about
how parents view schools in both sectors. We asked parents to assign a
letter grade of A to F to the D.C. public schools as a whole and to the
D.C. charter schools.

Comparing the two first rows of table 3.6, we see that parents in both
sectors give higher average grades to the D.C. charter schools compared
to the DCPS. Consistent with other studies, we find that parents also
grade their own child's school higher than they do schools in general. But
at this stage we are more concerned with the sectoral differences, and they
are not surprising. Charter-school parents are significantly more negative

TABLE 3.6
Attitudes toward Charter Schools and DCPS

	DCPS parents	Charter-School parents	Sample Size
Average D.C. public school grade	2.2	1.8*	894
Average D.C. charter-school grade	3.0	2.7*	684
Hold school responsible for poor reading scores	73%	85%*	652
Charter schools are for the more affluent (% disagree)	71%	68%	864
Charter schools will pressure DCPS to improve (% agree)	53%	71%*	909
Charter schools are risky (% disagree)	74%	89%*	899

* $p < .05$, two-tailed. Data are from first wave (Fall 2001) of parent panel survey. Total sample size is 1,012; reported sample sizes vary due to unit nonresponse.

about the D.C. public schools than are other parents. In contrast, they are consistently more positive about charter schools, and they are significantly more likely to give their child's school a higher grade than parents whose children are in traditional D.C. public schools. These data are congruent with other studies that show that charter-school parents are, in general, more satisfied with their schools than other public school parents. We subject this pattern to more stringent analysis in chapters 9 and 10.[15]

Another area in which important differences emerge is the degree to which parents think their child's school should be held accountable for poor academic performance. We asked parents how much they agreed or disagreed with the following sentence: "My child's school faces so many problems that I do not expect it to do better in teaching reading." Returning to table 3.6, we find that 85 percent of charter-school parents either somewhat disagreed or strongly disagreed with that sentiment, significantly more than the 73 percent of D.C. public-school parents. We believe that this is important: charter-school parents are not easy critics and they hold their children's schools to more exacting standards. Indeed, as we will see later, in chapter 9, they view their children's schools through a very exacting lens—and that their higher levels of satisfaction emerge even as they hold schools more accountable and subject them to tougher scrutiny.

Finally, Terry Moe has investigated the extent to which parents are suspicious of choice and fear the systemic consequences of moving away from a system of public schools—he terms this a "public school ideology" (2001, 89–91). While our survey questions were not identical to his, several questions in our study reflect parental attitudes toward the balance between charter schools and the public schools. In general, we find some interesting, but not surprising, differences between parents in the two sectors in their overall evaluation of the potential effects of charter schools on education.

First, and reflecting the absence of demographic differences of students in the two sectors noted earlier, a large majority of parents in both sectors disagree with a statement that charter schools will serve only affluent families: around 70 percent of parents, regardless of the sector their child attended, disagreed with the statement that charter schools will serve only the more affluent families in the district. While this response is rooted in the reality of D.C. school demographics, the next two questions do not have such a strong grounding in fact, and thus they may be more reflective of the underlying attitude toward the role of charter schools in public education.

We asked parents if they thought that charter schools were "too risky to try out on children." Large majorities in both sectors said no—but there are still substantial differences: while almost 90 percent of charter-school parents felt this way, only about three-quarters of DCPS parents felt the same way. In analyzing this pattern further, we did not find any of the usual demographic factors affected the level of risk assessment.

We also asked parents whether they thought that charter schools will pressure the traditional D.C. public schools to improve. Here a majority of parents in both sectors said yes—but again, charter-school parents are much more likely to feel that way compared to DCPS parents (71 percent vs. 53 percent). When we investigated the effects of demographics on this evaluation, we found that higher-educated parents are less likely to think that this cross-sector effect will matter. In addition, agreement increases substantially with church attendance. But the effects of these demographic variables do not come close to the charter-school effect.

D.C. PARENTS: A SUMMARY

Overall, looking primarily at the descriptive statistics, we find that the charter schools are serving a population that is remarkably similar to the population served by the traditional public schools. This is clearly true with regard to observable parent demographic data, but the similarity between parents in the two sectors also extends to less easily observed behaviors and attitudes that may affect the operation of the school and the quality of education the students in those schools receive.

What about involvement with the school community? Here we find that as measured by volunteering and PTA membership, there is no evidence of a charter-school advantage. But charter schools in D.C., like charter schools elsewhere, have a strong commitment to parent outreach, making parents a more integral part of the school community. As a result, we do find that, compared to parents in the D.C. public schools, charter parents are more likely to talk with the school principal and with their child's teacher at least monthly. But to what extent is this a function of the characteristics of parents—and to what extent can this difference be ascribed to differences in the schools themselves? The policy and equity implications of these alternative causes are profound. In chapter 11, we look at these data in more detail to try to untangle these different causal mechanisms.

Perhaps reflecting the lack of systematic differences between the charter schools and the traditional D.C. public schools, we also found little hostility toward the charter schools among parents. Most parents, regardless of the sector in which their child is enrolled, do not think that charter schools engage in cream skimming by serving only the affluent, nor do they think that charter schools are risky, but they do believe that charter schools will pressure the traditional schools to improve. This cluster of attitudes suggests that charter schools have considerable leeway to continue to develop as alternatives to the traditional D.C. public schools.

We do find some attitudinal differences that may matter in the long run. First, charter parents have a greater propensity to hold their schools accountable for academic performance (see Hill et al. 2001 on this point). Second, there may be some "halo" effect surrounding the charter schools: parents in both sectors gave higher grades to charter schools in general than to the traditional public schools.

Together these attitudes could constitute a double-edged sword: if people have high expectations of charter schools, and parents in them hold them more accountable, then charter schools must perform. The baseline positive affect that most citizens have for public schools (Moe's public school ideology described above) gives public schools "cover" from poor performance. Our data suggest that the attitudes toward charter schools may be the mirror image: "we chose you and you had better perform."

In the chapters that follow, we subject many of these patterns to more intense analysis.

APPENDIX 3.1

Telephone Sample Design and Response Information

WAVE 1

Telephone interviews were conducted among parents with at least one child in a Washington, D.C. charter or public school. For the first wave, interviews were conducted between September 12 and December 11, 2001. All interviews were conducted by the Center for Survey Research at the State University of New York at Stony Brook. As a quality-control measure, up to fifteen callbacks were made per number and an attempt was made to convert all initial refusals. Almost 52 percent of all interviews were validated on a subsequent call after the interview had been completed.

Sample Design

Parents were drawn from two distinct samples: a random sample of parents with children in charter and public schools, created through "random digit dialing" (RDD) and a sample of parents randomly chosen from a list of charter-school parents provided by D.C. charter schools. Charter parents were thus oversampled by design due to their relatively low incidence in the population (about 50 percent of the parents in our sample have children in charter schools. But by chance we would expect to find only about 20 percent, which we thought was too small a proportion for the key variable of interest in this analysis). All analyses reported in the book adjust for this design through poststratification weighting.

RANDOM DIGIT DIALING

A list-assisted method of RDD was used to obtain phone numbers in the main state sample. Numbers were purchased from Genesys. Under the list-assisted sampling method, random samples of telephone numbers are selected from blocks of one hundred telephone numbers that are known to contain at least one *listed* residential telephone number. These blocks with at least one residential telephone number are referred to as "1-plus" working blocks. According to Survey Sampling Inc., roughly 40 percent of telephone numbers in 1-plus working blocks are residences, although percentages are as high as 54 percent when the blocks are screened for nonworking and business numbers.

CHARTER SCHOOL

A sample of charter-school parents was drawn from a list of parents in thirty D.C. charter schools. Not all numbers provided by the schools were valid, and numbers that lacked the appropriate number of digits were eliminated prior to sampling. This left a total of 7,389 valid phone numbers for charter-school parents.

RESPONSE RATES: RANDOM DIGIT DIALING SAMPLE

A total of 24,000 numbers were drawn from 1-plus blocks for the main state sample. Of those, Genesys screened out 5,214 or 21.73 percent as numbers that it detected as nonworking or listed in directories of known business numbers. This left 18,786 numbers that were actually dialed by the Center for Survey Research. Just over 46 percent of all these numbers (N = 8,734) were coded as nonhouseholds. This includes all numbers coded as disconnected, a business, government office, fax, changed number, or cell phone. It also includes 1,550 numbers estimated as nonhouseholds. These 1,550 numbers are drawn from all numbers that were called fifteen times and at which there was always only a busy signal or no answer (but no answering machine). Based on research by Westat, we estimate that 75 percent of these numbers are nonhouseholds. This number is based on national estimates. There were 2,067 numbers in this category and 1,550 were estimated to be nonworking numbers.

This left 9,956 possible households in the sample of phone numbers. Of the remaining households, 6,523 (a total of 941 parents plus 5,582 nonparents or non-D.C. parents) were successfully screened for the presence or absence of children in D.C. public or charter schools. This resulted in a screening rate of 62.81 percent for parenting status obtained by dividing the number of D.C. parent plus nonparent households by the total number of households in the sample. The total number of parenting households in D.C. is estimated at 922 or 14.13 percent of all screened households. This number omits 264 (245 nonparents and 19 not in D.C.) households that were coded in at least one contact attempt as parents in D.C. but were later recoded as nonparents. The status of these numbers is ambiguous and could reflect the actions of respondents to avoid an interview. If all of these numbers are included (probably an overestimate) the incidence of parents in the sample increases to 18.18 percent.

Of those households identified as obtaining a parent of a child in a D.C. school (N = 922), interviews were completed in 504, resulting in a cooperation rate of 54.66 percent. This results in an overall response rate in the sample of 34.33 percent. This response rate is calculated by combining the screening rate for parenting households (62.81 percent) with the cooperation rate among households identified as parents of children in D.C. schools (54.66 percent).

Charter-school parents were drawn from a list of names provided by thirty charter schools in the D.C. areas. The sample was self-weighting— unequal numbers of parents were drawn from each school. The number of parents selected from a school was directly proportional to the size of the school in relation to all charter-school parents in D.C. Thus more parents were chosen from large schools and fewer from small schools. This ensures that the final sample represents parents in charter schools across the D.C. area. The sampling fraction was 29.63 percent or just under a third; parents were drawn in successive random waves from the lists. There were 7,389 parents listed (after bad numbers were culled from the lists), and 2,189 numbers were included in the sample.

Of the total 2,189 numbers, just over 23 percent of all numbers (N = 522) were coded as nonhouseholds. This includes all numbers coded as disconnected, a business, government office, fax, changed number, or cell phone. It also includes six numbers estimated as nonhouseholds. These six numbers are drawn from all numbers that were called fifteen times, and at which there was always only a busy signal or no answer (but no answering machine). There were twenty-four numbers in the "nonhousehold" category and eighteen (75 percent) were estimated to be nonworking numbers.

This left 1,667 possible households in the sample of phone numbers. Of the remaining households, 1,321 (a total of 811 parents plus 441 nonparents and 69 non-D.C. parents) were successfully screened for the presence or absence of children in D.C. public or charter schools. Given the messy status of the sample, we assumed that numbers were not associated with parents of students in charter schools until this had been verified by an interviewer. This resulted in a screening rate of 79.24 percent for parenting status, obtained by dividing the number of D.C. parent plus nonparent households by the total number of households in the sample.

Of those households identified as containing a parent of a child in a D.C. school (N = 811), interviews were completed in 510 instances, resulting in a cooperation rate of 62.89 percent. This results in an overall response rate in the main sample of 49.83 percent. This response rate is calculated by combining the screening rate for parenting households (79.24 percent) with the cooperation rate among households identified as parents of children in D.C. schools (49.83 percent).

Since we are combining two different ways of drawing a sample, an obvious question is the extent to which the two methods might produce

TABLE 3A.1a
There Are Few Differences between the Samples Obtained
Using Different Techniques

	Random digit dialing (DCPS)	Random digit dialing (charter)	List sample (charter)
Black	73	80	88%*
Hispanic	9	9	6%*
White	9	5	1%*
Average years of education	13.3	13.5	13.5
Married/living with someone	44	41	42%
Working	72	86	73%

* $p < .05$, two-tailed.

populations that are systematically different (and thereby affect results). To assess whether or not this is a problem, we explore the extent of demographic differences between the two samples in more detail below. In addition to the data we report in the book comparing the charter sample to the RDD DCPS sample, we add here a further check on the possibility of bias. While most of our charter-school sample was drawn from a list provided by the charter schools themselves, about 10 percent of our charter-school sample were identified through random digit dialing. This type of respondent (i.e., a charter school parent identified through RDD) gives us yet a further check on the potential for bias from mixing interviewing methods.

As is evident in the data (see tables 3A.1a and 1b), there are a few indicators where the RDD and list samples differ: the RDD did produce a sample that contains fewer blacks and more Hispanics and whites than the list sample—and this is true of both the RDD charter-school parents and the RDD DCPS sample. However, when we come to other critical demographic characteristics, there are no observable education or income differences associated with the methods of obtaining the sample nor are there differences in marital status or employment condition. We believe these data indicate that relying on two different ways of constructing a sample did not materially affect our findings.

WAVE 2

A second stage of telephone interviews were conducted with parents of at least one child in a Washington, D.C. charter or public school who

TABLE 3A.1b
There Are No Income Differences between Samples Obtained
Using Different Techniques

Income category	Random digit dialing (DCPS)	Random digit dialing (charter)	List sample (charter)
<$35,000	36%	27	30%
$35–65,000	29	27	34%
>$65,000	35	46	36%

$p = 0.47$ based on chi-square for table.

were previously interviewed for the study in the Fall of 2001. Interviews were conducted between May 30 and July 8, 2002. All interviews were again conducted by the Center for Survey Research at the State University of New York at Stony Brook. As a quality control measure, up to fifteen callbacks were made per number and up to three attempts were made to convert all initial refusals.

Sample Design

The sample consisted of the list of 1,014 respondents who completed the first stage of interviews.

Response Rate

Of the 1,014 numbers attempted, just over 22 percent (N = 225) were coded as nonhouseholds. The vast majority of the nonhouseholds (N = 200) were either nonworking/disconnected numbers, or a wrong number with no forwarding number given. A small number of cases (N = 15) reported that they did not have children in the D.C. public/charter schools (these cases were validated for accuracy), and five numbers were reported to be consistently a fax or data line. This left a total of 789 available working numbers. Respondents from the first-stage study were located, and interviews were completed with 558 of these respondents, for a response rate of 70.7 percent.

WAVE 3

The third phase of interviews with parents in the Washington, D.C. school study was conducted in the Fall of 2003, between September 24 and November 9, 2003 (Time 3). Telephone reinterviews were conducted with parents who had at least one child in a Washington, D.C. charter or public school and who had previously been interviewed in the Fall of 2001 (Time 1). Parents had also been interviewed at a second time point in July 2002 (Time 2). All interviews were again conducted by the Center for Survey Research at the State University of New York at Stony Brook. In order to maximize the response of both parents and children, all eligible parents were offered a telephone calling card with seventy-five minutes of free long distance calling time to be provided after the parent had completed the survey. In order to further maximize the response rate, up to thirty-five callback attempts were made to reach each respondent, and up to three attempts were made to convert all initial refusals of parents.

Sample Design

Of the initial 1,014 parents who completed the interview at Time 1, 992 parents were contacted at Time 3. Twenty-two households were excluded from the sample at Time 3 because someone had refused the interview on at least three different occasions at Time 2.

Response Rate

Of the 992 numbers attempted, just over 39 percent (N = 391) were coded as nonhouseholds. The vast majority of the nonhouseholds (N = 369) were either nonworking/disconnected numbers, or a wrong number with no forwarding number given. Additionally, eleven numbers were consistently coded as a fax or data line, nine were businesses and two were cell phones. This left a total of 601 available working numbers.

Interviews were completed with 395 parents, comprising 66 percent (395/601) of all identified households at Time 3. This included interviews with fifty-five parents who completed a shorter questionnaire because they no longer had children in the D.C. public/charter schools. The overall response rate was 66 percent among valid households at Time 3 and the reinterview rate among all parents interviewed at Time 1 was 39 percent (395/1,014). The remaining valid households at Time 3 were either refusals (16 percent, including straight refusals, hang-ups, and incomplete callbacks) or parents who were difficult to reach (15 percent, including answering machine, busy, or no answer). In addition, five cases were coded as physically/mentally unable/deceased (one was critically ill, four were deceased), 2 percent no longer lived in the D.C. area, and three respondents were temporarily unavailable because they were in the military.

Parents were asked to discuss the same child who had been identified during the Time 1 interview. If that child was no longer in a D.C. public or charter school, or no longer lived in the household, the parent was asked to identify another child in the household who did attend a D.C. public or charter school. If more than one child was eligible, the parent was asked to select the child who had celebrated the most recent birthday.

An attempt was made to interview a child in each household in which a parent completed an interview at Time 3. Children in grades 7 or higher were eligible for this interview. Of the 395 interviewed parents, 192 (49 percent) had a child who completed the survey, 145 (37 percent) did not have an eligible child, and 58 (15 percent) refused or their child refused the survey (or only partially completed the survey). Interviewers requested permission to speak with the child discussed in the Time 3 parent interview if the child was in grade 7 or higher ("original child" if the child is the same child interviewed at Time 1, "new child" if the original child was no longer eligible and a new child was selected for the Time 3 interview). If that child was not eligible because he or she was not yet in grade 7, an "older child" was selected. In households in which there was only one other child attending a D.C. public or charter school, that child was chosen. In households with more than one eligible older child, the child with the most recent birthday was selected. This resulted in an overall cooperation rate among children of 77 percent in households in which a parent had been interviewed and there was an eligible child.

The sample of parents who completed interviews at Time 3 was originally drawn from two different sources: parents obtained though an RDD telephone sample (N = 490 were contacted out of the original 504 respondents at Time 1), and those selected through the charter list sample (N = 502 contacted out of the original 510 at Time 1). Response rates were almost identical in the two groups. Among eligible households at Time 3, the response rate for the RDD sample was 69 percent (198 completes / 288 eligible households) and the reinterview rate was 39 percent (198 completes / 504 respondents at Time 1). In the charter list sample, the response rate among parents was 62 percent (197 completes / 313 eligible households) and the reinterview rate was 39 percent (197 completes / 510 respondents at Time 1).

The two samples also yielded comparable cooperation rates among children of interviewed parents. There were 108 or 55 percent (108/198) of households in which an RDD parent who had been interviewed at Time 3 had a child who was eligible to be interviewed. Of this group, 84 children participated to produce a cooperation rate of 78 percent (84/108). Thus, in the RDD sample a child completed the survey in 45 percent of households in which parents had completed the survey (84/198). In the charter sample, there was an eligible child in 142 of the 197 households in which a parent completed the interview (72 percent), a higher percentage than in the RDD sample. Of this group, interviews were completed with 108 children to produce a cooperation rate of 76 percent. In this sample a child completed the survey in 55 percent of households in which a parent completed the survey (108/197), a slightly higher rate than for the RDD sample because of the larger number of households containing an eligible child.

The RDD and charter list subsamples can be further divided into parents who had participated in both previous interviews (Times 1 and 2) or only Time 1. Not surprisingly, there was a higher percentage of invalid numbers in the group that had only been interviewed at Time 1. Response and reinterview rates were higher among those who had been interviewed twice before.

WAVE 4

The fourth phase of interviews with parents in the Washington, D.C. school study was conducted in the Spring of 2004, between April 28 and July 12, 2004 (Time 4). Telephone reinterviews were conducted with parents who had at least one child in a Washington, D.C. charter or public school and who had previously been interviewed in the Fall of 2001 (Time 1). Parents had also been interviewed at a second time point in July 2002 (Time 2), and/or at a third time point in November 2003 (Time 3). All interviews were conducted in English or Spanish, by the Center for Survey Research at the State University of New York at Stony Brook. In order to maximize the response, all eligible parents were offered a telephone calling card with 120 minutes of free long distance calling time to be provided after the parent had completed the survey. In order to maximize the response rate, up to thirty-five callback attempts were made to reach respondents, and up to three attempts were made to convert all initial refusals of parents. In addition, during the last two weeks of the interviews, a bonus incentive of $25 was offered to engage respondents who had been previously contacted but had either refused or were difficult to reach.

Sample Design

Of the initial 1,014 parents who completed the interview at Time 1, a total of 878 parents were contacted at Time 4. Of these, 395 completed the interview at Time 3. The sample also included 483 records that completed the interview at Time 1, and/or Time 2, did not complete the interview at Time 3 because they were not reached, but had not refused to participate. Finally, 114 households were excluded from the sample at Time 4 because the eligible parent refused to participate in the interview on at least three different occasions at Time 3.

Response Rate

Of the 878 numbers attempted, just over 49 percent (N = 431) were coded as nonhouseholds. The vast majority of the nonhouseholds were either nonworking/disconnected numbers, or a wrong number with no forwarding number given (N = 406). Additionally, eight numbers were consistently coded as a fax or data line, fifteen were businesses and two were cell phones. This left a total of 447 available working numbers.

Interviews were completed with 288 parents, comprising 64 percent (288/447) of all identified households at Time 4. This included interviews with eighteen parents who completed a shorter questionnaire because they no longer had children in the D.C. public/charter schools. The overall response rate was 64 percent among valid households at Time 4 and the reinterview rate among all parents interviewed at Time 1 was 28 percent (288/1,014). Of the remaining 159 valid households at Time 4, 15 percent refused to participate (71 cases of refusals, hang-ups, and incomplete callbacks) and 17 percent were parents who were difficult to reach (75 cases of answering machines, busy, or no answer). In addition, one case was coded as physically/mentally unable/deceased, and in three cases the eligible parent was unavailable for the duration of the study. Finally, in nine cases the eligible parent completed only part of the questionnaire.

During the interview, parents were asked to discuss the same child who had been identified during the Time 1 interview. If that child was no longer in a D.C. public or charter school, or no longer lived in the household, the parent was asked to identify another child in the household who did attend a D.C. public or charter school. If more than one child was eligible, the parent was asked to select the child who had celebrated the most recent birthday.

Interviews were also conducted with eligible children. In households where a child was interviewed at Time 3, an attempt was made to reinterview the same child. Children in grades 7 or higher were eligible for this interview. We refer to the child interviewed as "original child" if the child is the same child interviewed at Time 3, "new child" if the original child was no longer eligible and a new child was selected for the Time 4 interview. If the child interviewed at Time 3 was not eligible because he or she was not yet in grade 7, an "older child" was selected. In households in which there was only one other child attending a D.C. public or charter school, that child was chosen. In households with more than one eligible older child, the child with the most recent birthday was selected.

Of the 288 interviewed parents, 270 (94 percent) had a child who was able to participate. For the remaining 18 cases, there were no longer any children going to a D.C. public or charter school. Of the 270 eligible parents, 146 (54 percent) had a child who completed the survey at Time 4. In addition, 77 (29 percent) did not have an eligible child, and 47 (17 percent) refused or their child refused the survey (or only partially completed the survey).

At Time 3, there were 187 children who completed the survey. Of these 136 also completed the survey at Time 4. This resulted in a reinterview rate among children of 73 percent. The additional 10 who completed surveys at Time 4 were interviews with a new child.

The sample of parents who completed interviews at Time 4 was originally drawn from two different sources: parents obtained though an RDD telephone sample (N = 440 were contacted out of the original 504 respondents at Time 1), and those selected through the charter list sample (N = 438 contacted out of the original 510 at Time 1). Response rates were almost identical in the two groups. Among eligible households at Time 4, the response rate for the RDD sample was 63 percent (137 completes / 218 eligible households) and the reinterview rate was 27 percent (137 completes / 504 respondents at Time 1). In the charter list sample, the response rate among parents was 66 percent (151 completes / 229 eligible households) and the reinterview rate was 30 percent (151 completes / 510 respondents at Time 1). The RDD and charter samples also yielded comparable cooperation rates among interviewed children.

In the RDD sample, there were 130 or 95 percent (130/137) of households in which an parent interviewed at Time 4 had a child who was eligible to be interviewed. Of this group, 63 children participated, giving a cooperation rate of 48 percent (63/130). Thus, in the RDD sample a child completed the survey in 46 percent of households in which parents had completed the survey (63/137). At Time 3, there were 84 children who completed the survey. Of these 57 also completed the survey at Time 4. This resulted in a reinterview rate among children of 68 percent. The additional six completed surveys at Time 4 were interviews with a new child.

In the charter sample, there was an eligible child in 140 of the 149 households in which a parent completed the interview (94 percent). Of this group, interviews were completed with 83 children to produce a cooperation rate of 59 percent (83/140). In this sample a child completed the survey in 55 percent of households in which a parent completed the survey (83/151), a higher rate than for the RDD sample because of the larger number of households containing an eligible child. At Time 3, there were 108 children who completed the survey. Of these, 79 also completed the survey at Time 4. This resulted in a reinterview rate among children of 73 percent. The additional four completed surveys at Time 4 were interviews with a new child.

The RDD and charter list subsamples can be further divided into parents who had participated in previous interviews (Times 1, 2, 3, and 4) or only Times 1, 2, and 4, but not 3. Not surprisingly, there was a higher percentage of invalid numbers in the group that had only been interviewed at Time 1 and 2, but not 3. Response and reinterview rates were higher among those who had been interviewed three times before.

Are Charter-School Students Harder to Educate than Those in the Traditional Public Schools?

IN THIS CHAPTER we begin our in-depth empirical investigations of the issues we have presented in the first three chapters. Here, we investigate further the extent to which the families and students in charter schools are different than those in traditional public schools—the point upon which we ended chapter 2. In this chapter, we investigate the extent to which charter-school students may be easier or harder to educate than students who have remained in traditional public schools.

STUDENT POPULATION AND ACHIEVEMENT

For many involved in the school-choice debate, the ultimate test of a reform is whether or not the academic achievement of students improves. Answering this question is much more complex than it may first appear, as many decisions must first be made about how achievement can be measured and how research should be designed to properly attribute causality to the reform. A consensus is growing in the educational research field that the gold standard for such research involves a design that examines longitudinal data on student test scores subsequent to random assignment to the reform. Even this design, however, has proven fraught with difficulties for the statistical analyst.[1] We do not have such data and, thus, we do not enter directly the fray surrounding this issue. However, another point of debate in the recent controversy in the media and among policy analysts over the academic achievement of charter-school students is whether charter students are harder to educate than their counterparts enrolled in traditional public schools.

In this chapter we examine this question using data from the 2002–3 school year in Washington, D.C. We begin by examining a simple binomial model of the proportion of students in key demographic and programmatic categories linked to educability. As explained below, we then turn to the estimation of a more theoretically appropriate mixture model that assumes two latent categories of charter schools. We then present an analysis that moves beyond simple demographic/programmatic factors to consider measures of educability using our individual-level survey data from charter- and traditional public-school students described in chapter 3. With the question of differential educability addressed, we end the chapter by presenting some data on test scores for schools in the two sectors.

A Heated Debate on Achievement in Charter Schools

A report published by the American Federation of Teachers (AFT) in August 2004 added fuel to the already spirited debate over the value of charter schools as a tool to improve education in the United States (Nelson, Rosenberg, and Van Meter 2004). The report compares the performance of charter-school students and their counterparts in traditional public schools using math and reading test-score data from fourth and eighth grade students collected as part of the 2003 National Assessment of Educational Progress (NAEP), often referred to as "the Nation's Report Card." The authors reported that, on average, charter achievement was lower, based on both average scaled scores and differences in proficiency levels, for fourth and eighth grade math and reading (although the difference in eighth grade math scaled scores was not statistically significant).[2]

The report, which was described favorably in a front-page *New York Times* article (Schemo 2004), drew a swift and often heated response. Pro-school-choice policy analysts, academics, think-tankers, and other partisans in the debate quickly wrote op-ed pieces, response papers, and even took out a full-page advertisement in the *Wall Street Journal*, at a cost of $125,000, denouncing the methods and conclusions of the AFT report.[3]

One of the most repeated arguments used to counter the finding of lagging charter school performance presented in the AFT report was that the students in charter schools are harder to educate. For example, in an op-ed piece in the *Wall Street Journal*, a group of Harvard education researchers responded to the AFT study by proclaiming: "Big deal. These results could easily indicate nothing other than the simple fact that charter schools are typically asked to serve problematic students in low-performing districts with many poor, minority children" (Howell, Peterson, and West 2004). Similarly Jeanne Allen, a noted charter advocate and president of the Center for Education Reform, penned a response which included a quotation from then Secretary of Education Ron Paige: "It is wrong to think of charter schools as a monolith. There are schools for dropouts, schools for students who've been expelled, schools serving the most economically disadvantaged families" (Center for Education Reform 2004).

While other aspects of the methodology of the AFT study were criticized, including its cross-sectional nature, its failure to employ multivariate analyses, and the small sample size of charter students participating in the NAEP, the claim that the population of charter students is somehow harder to educate was the most prevalent and, perhaps, most persuasive rejoinder to the AFT's report.

It is also, in many ways, the most important. The crux of the argument is that, since the charter schools really serve a different population, it is unreasonable to hold them to the same standard as the traditional public schools—even those located in the same urban school districts from which many charter schools draw their students.[4]

There is an irony in the argument that may illustrate the tendency of education partisans to talk past each other: while charter-school proponents were now claiming that charter schools are serving a *less* privileged population, opponents of charter schools have long claimed that charters served children from relatively *more* advantaged families, with more involved parents, who are easier, on average, to educate. Indeed, school-choice skeptics and other researchers have long contended that any research purporting to show beneficial effects of choice reforms must be questioned on precisely this point of "cream skimming" on the part of the charters or self-selection into choice schools by parents, and that to identify the "real" effects of charter schools after eliminating the benefits of creaming, either randomized field trials must be conducted (Hoxby 2004), natural experiments should be sought (Schneider, Teske, and Marschall 2000), or more advanced statistical methods must be applied (Goldhaber and Eide 2003; Schneider and Buckley 2003).

In the rest of this chapter, we seek to provide evidence to help resolve empirically this fundamental issue. Are charter-school students harder to educate, or do they attract the most motivated or highest socioeconomic status families of their areas? Or, as we should add in the interest of completeness, do they do both? That is, are charter schools not, in Secretary Paige's words, a "monolith," but instead sufficiently heterogeneous that many charter schools choose the hardest to educate while others attract (and perhaps use strategies to retain) only the best students?

Creaming, Cropping, or What?

Although concerns about equity have long been a staple of the research on school-choice reforms (e.g., Henig 1994; Smith and Meier 1995; Ascher, Fruchter, and Berne 1996), there has been relatively little research on the question of the educability of charter students. In a report released in 2000, the U.S. Department of Education, using data from 927 charter schools in the twenty-seven states with charter laws at the time, found that the charter schools had, on average, higher proportions of black and Hispanic students (who are almost always assumed in this literature to be harder to educate), although a smaller proportion of students with disabilities or requiring special educational services relative to the traditional public schools in their state (Research Policy Practice International 2000). Proponents of charter schools have taken these data to imply that the population of students in charter schools is not "creamed" from the general student population.

Others, such as Wells et al. (1998), Lopez et al. (2002), and Yancey (2000), have provided evidence that at least *some* charter schools do enroll proportionately more minority students, as some charter operators deliberately create schools designed to serve the particular needs of African American or Hispanic students—lending some support to the quotation from Paige cited above. This provides an arguably more positive interpretation to the oft-observed predilection of American parents to self-segregate their schools through residential mobility or other choice programs (e.g., Henig 1990; Schneider and Buckley 2002), although others worry that racial or ethnic segregation for any reason could have deleterious effects (Fuller 2000b).

It is thus possible that any study of the educability of charter-school students in the aggregate (i.e., at the national, state, or even district level), such as the 2000 Department of Education study described above, which finds differences between the charters and their traditional counterparts in racial composition or other educability proxies like the proportion of free/reduced price lunches or special education, may be subject to a form of aggregation bias or Simpson's paradox due to extreme heterogeneity across the population of charter schools.[5]

Recognizing this, Lacireno-Paquet et al. conducted a careful study of cream-skimming behavior, using data on the charter schools of Washington, D.C. in the 1999–2000 school year. They conclude that, in the aggregate, the D.C. charters in this period "are serving a population that has many characteristics associated with educational disadvantages" (2002, 155).[6] Furthermore, when they disaggregate their data into what they term "market-oriented" and "nonmarket-oriented" schools, they find some evidence that the latter are more likely to have a disproportionate share of theoretically harder-to-educate students. They further argue that this is not due to the market-oriented schools creaming the best students, but instead "cropping" the hardest (and most expensive) to educate. Nevertheless, they conclude that "no charter schools in the District of Columbia are serving an elite population" (155).

While the Lacireno-Paquet et al. study is probably the best examination of this question to date, it leaves several questions unanswered. First, the authors measure educability only using demographic proxy measures, ignoring possible differences in educability at the level of parent and student attitudes and behavior. Second, we do not know if the Lacireno-Paquet

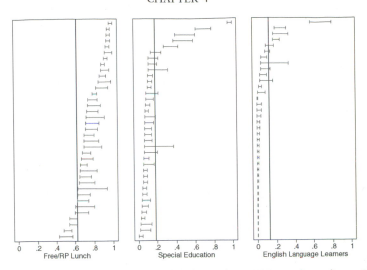

Figure 4.1. Comparing the charter schools to the DCPS on three dimensions. *Note*: 95 percent highest posterior density intervals of the estimated proportion of students in each demographic category, using independent Jeffreys priors. Each interval represents a charter school in Washington, D.C. and is estimated using data from the 2002–3 school year. The vertical lines indicate the proportion of students in each category in the D.C. public schools overall. For visual presentation the schools are sorted independently for each measure; the same school is thus not in the same horizontal position across all three plots. Number of charter schools = 37.

(.620 for free/reduced price lunch, .183 for special education, and .125 for English language learners).[11] Our decision rule is simple: we compare the 95 percent HPD of each school on each measure to the point value of the DCPS proportion on this measure. If the DCPS proportion is less than the lower bound of the charter estimate, we conclude that the charter school has more students, proportionally, in this category than the DCPS. Similarly, if the DCPS value is larger than the upper bound, we conclude that the charter has proportionally fewer students in this category. Finally, if the 95 percent HPD contains the DPCS point estimate, we conclude that we cannot distinguish between the proportions. We summarize our results in table 4.2.

Figure 4.1 and table 4.2 suggest that, considering each charter school individually, many charter schools in D.C. enroll a disproportionately high number of free/reduced-price lunch–eligible students. On the other hand, the vast majority of charters have proportionally fewer special education and English language learning students. Our estimates provide some support for the idea that a small set of charter schools are specifically targeted at these latter two groups, but most are not. Note that, in com-

Table 4.1
D.C. Charter Schools Have More Free/RP Lunch Students, but Fewer Special Education and English Language Learners. Naïve Comparison.

Measure of educability	Charter > DCPS	Charter < DCPS
Free/RP lunch	33	4
Special education	7	30
English language learners	6	30

Results are computed from comparisons of reported proportions for 37 D.C. charter schools to the reported overall DCPS proportions. See chap. 4, n. 6 for sources of data.

et al. findings have persisted into more recent years, when the number of charter schools has dramatically increased. We now turn to an empirical investigation of precisely these questions.

EXAMINING EDUCABILITY: DEMOGRAPHIC FACTORS

We first examine the charter schools in our study, using the proportion of students eligible for free or reduced price lunch, the proportion of students classified as special education students, and the proportion of students classified as English language learners—demographic and programmatic measures often cited in the educability literature.[7] Our data come from the 2002–3 academic year.[8] Our general strategy is, for each key variable, to compare the proportion in each charter school to the average proportion in the traditional D.C. public schools (DCPS).

In table 4.1 we present the results from a "naïve" version of this comparison, in which we simply compare the reported proportions of each measure from each charter school to the aggregate proportions reported by the DCPS schools. In 2003, the DCPS reported that 62 percent of students were eligible for free/reduced price lunches, 18.3 percent were special education students, and 12.5 percent were English language learners. Thus, for example, looking at table 4.1, we see that thirty of the thirty-seven charter schools reported that they had more than 62 percent of their students who qualified for free/reduced-price lunches in 2003.

An important issue in an analysis of this type is how to properly model uncertainty. In one sense, we have data on the entire universe or population of D.C. charter schools and any proportions we compute are thus (in the language of classical or "frequentist" statistics) "true" parameters and not estimated quantities. However, for a number of reasons, it is desirable to model the uncertainty surrounding these values. First, although we have population data, we have them only for a fixed period of time, the

2002–3 academic year. If we wish to generalize our results beyond this period, we may need to account for the likely fact that our estimated values will fluctuate over time.

Similarly, but a bit more esoterically, it is possible to imagine that our population of schools and the students within them are but one realization or sample drawn from a hypothetical infinite population. This "superpopulation" argument, which is often found in the sampling literature in statistics (e.g., Cochran 1946; Brewer 1963; Hartley and Sielken 1975), uses the concept of a stochastic population to reintroduce variability to the quantities of interest. For example, in the literature on state politics and public policy, hypotheses are frequently tested using the population of all fifty states but standard errors are almost always reported and statistical tests of quantities of interest are reported (Gill 2001).

Applied research in education policy (among many other areas) often implicitly adopts this approach, perhaps unwittingly. For example, in her response to the charter school performance debate outlined in the introduction to this chapter, Hoxby presents data analysis that she argues is superior to the AFT's research. One reason for this superiority, according to Hoxby, is that her data source "is not a sample: it is all charter students for whom results are reported" (2004, 3). Nevertheless, she goes on to compute standard errors of her differences in achievement (which are based on a theoretical model of a sampling distribution), even going as far as to not report differences which she decides are statistically insignificant, presumably based on some level of significance selected a priori. Nowhere, however, is there reference to the source of the stochastic component of these data.

An alternative method to modeling uncertainty in population data can be found in the Bayesian approach to statistics. While a full description is beyond the scope of this chapter, the general idea is that Bayesian statistics are founded on a different philosophy of probability than is the more familiar, frequentist approach. To a Bayesian, probability is not necessarily defined by appeals to hypothetical infinitely repeated trials of an experiment. Rather, Bayesian statistical analysis attempts to draw inference by taking into account both the observed data at hand and the researcher's a priori information or beliefs about the parameters of interest. In addition, under the usual Bayesian approach, the researcher need not assume that population parameters are fixed or "true" values, but instead that they can be characterized by an a posteriori probability distribution. These posterior distributions can be thought of as a weighted combination of information from the observed data and the priors; when the prior information is weak or noninformative, the results of a Bayesian analysis will typically be similar to those of a frequentist one, albeit with a different interpretation.[9]

Our approach here to estimating the proportion of students in each charter school who are members of the various demographic groups that have been assumed to be harder to educate, and our related uncertainty about our estimate, is fundamentally Bayesian. Our general strategy is to treat the observed proportion of charter school students in a given category (e.g., English language learners) in a given school as a discrete random variable modeled as the result of a binomial experiment. We assume that we have no prior information about the various quantities of interest, and we model this assumption of a priori ignorance using the Jeffreys (1946) prior.[10]

Specifically, let x be the number of students out of a total enrollment of n in a given school who possess a particular demographic characteristic of interest. We assume that x has a binomial distribution with parameters n and π, where π is the unknown proportion of x in n. Thus:

$$p(x \mid \pi) = \binom{n}{x} \pi^x (1 - \pi)^{n-x} \qquad (4.1)$$

It can be shown that the Jeffreys prior for this likelihood model (assuming that the prior is distributed beta, the conjugate prior to the binomial likelihood; see Lee 1997, 77–90) is:

$$\pi \sim \text{Be}\left(\frac{1}{2}, \frac{1}{2}\right) \qquad (4.2)$$

thus yielding a posterior probability distribution of π that is also beta:

$$\pi \sim \text{Be}\left(\frac{1}{2} + x, \frac{1}{2} + n - x\right) \qquad (4.3)$$

We use equation (4.3) to estimate the posterior probability distribution of the proportion of students in each charter school who are eligible for free or reduced price lunch, classified as special education, or English language learners, independently. We present our results graphically in figure 4.1. Instead of presenting the entire posterior distribution for each school on each measure, we instead present the 95 percent highest posterior density (HPD) for each. For the current model, this region is analogous to the conventional two-sided 95 percent confidence interval, except that the HPD may actually be interpreted such that that the proportion of interest is in the estimated region with .95 probability.

In figure 4.1, we present the estimated 95 percent HPDs for the proportion of students in each of thirty-seven charter schools who are members of each of three of the demographic measures that have been linked to educability. For comparison to the DCPS, we include a vertical line at the overall proportion of traditional public school students in each category

TABLE 4.2
D.C. Charter Schools Have More Free/RP Lunch Students, but
Fewer Special Education and English Language Learners

Measure of educability	Number of charter schools with proportions > DCPS	Tie	Number of charter schools with proportions < DCPS
Free/reduced-price lunch	30	5	2
Special education	5	8	24
English language learners	4	5	28

Results are computed from comparisons of estimated proportions for 37 D.C. charter schools presented in figure 4.1 to DCPS point estimates of overall proportions.

parison to the "naïve" results of table 4.1, there is quite a bit of uncertainty is these results, as reflected in the "ties" column of table 4.2 and in many of the HPDs plotted in figure 4.1.

We are also interested in a test of the hypothesis that charter students are differently educable than their traditional public school counterparts on each of these measures overall, or in the aggregate. One method for conducting such a test is to return to the Bayesian conjugate beta-binomial model described above and extend it to a fully hierarchical specification (Gelman et al. 1995, 129–32). In such a model, for each of the three demographic measures, we would treat each charter school as a binomial experiment for which the probability of "success" varies for each school (here of a student being a member of the category) but is drawn from a common distribution shared by all of these experiments.

The problem with this approach is that we have reason to believe that the proportion in each schools is *not* drawn from a common, "monolithic" distribution. As we note above, one way of interpreting the results for special education and English language learning presented in figure 4.1 is that a number of charter schools in D.C. are targeting these groups (this interpretation is also supported by the literature available from several charter schools in the district and from interviews with experts on the D.C. charter schools). To account for this data-generating process, we propose instead a mixture model that allows for the mixture of two binomial distributions and assumes that the distribution to which any particular school belongs is a latent (unobserved) but estimable categorization.[12]

We assume that the observed number of students x_s in a given category in each school s is a random variable with an unknown distribution $\varphi(x_s)$ that can be approximated as a sum of $K = 2$ binomial distributions:

$$\varphi(x_s) \cong \sum_{k=1}^{K} \theta_k \binom{n_s}{x_s} \pi_{ks}^{x_s} (1 - \pi_{ks})^{n_s - x_s} \qquad (4.4)$$

That is, we assume that the charter schools are drawn from a heterogeneous population containing two subgroups each of which is modeled with a binomial distribution with probability of success parameter π_{ks}. The two latent subgroups or subpopulations are mixed together with proportions θ_k (we constrain $\Sigma_k \theta_k = 1$).

Although we recognize that the true population of charter schools may, in fact, be composed for more than two subpopulations, our small sample size of thirty-seven schools suggests that limiting our model a priori to two groups will allow us to relax the "monolithic" property of our simple model without sacrificing model fit or reliable estimation. Moreover, the choice of two subpopulations reflects a coarse but substantively sufficient dichotomy in which a given set of charter schools are "better" or "worse" than the DCPS on a particular measure.

Since our model is fully Bayesian, we also need to specify a prior distribution on the θ_k's; we assume that they are jointly distributed Dirichlet (the multivariate analogue of the beta distribution):

$$p(\pi) \sim \frac{\Gamma\left(\Sigma_{k=1}^{K} u_k\right)}{\Pi_{k=1}^{K} \Gamma(u_k)} \Pi_{k=1}^{K} \pi_k^{u_k - 1} \qquad (4.5)$$

where, again, $K = 2$ and u_k are the prior counts of the number of schools in the two groups. As a minimally informative prior, we assume that all schools are in the same subpopulation on each measure except for the one reporting the largest proportion.[13]

We estimate the model using Markov Chain Monte Carlo and obtain simulations of the posterior distributions of each π_{ks} and θ_k, as well as the posterior predictive distribution of $\varphi(x_s)$, a posterior distribution which takes into account all sources of uncertainty in the model (see Gelman et al. 1995, 140–47).[14]

We present the results of the mixture model estimation in table 4.3. The table provides the estimated posterior means and standard deviations of π_k (the proportion of students in each educability measure) and θ_k (the proportion of schools in each of the two subpopulations) for each of the three outcome measures. Thus, for each measure, we compute two estimated proportions, one for each of the "high" and "low" groups, as well as an estimate of the proportion of schools in each group.

Interpretation using the means of these posterior distributions as point estimates is fairly straightforward. For free/reduced price lunch, for example, we estimate that the number of students eligible in about 65 percent (θ_1) of the charter schools is drawn from a binomial distribution with $\pi_1 = .690$, while the remaining 35 percent (θ_2) of the schools have a common

TABLE 4.3
Estimated Parameters from Binomial-Mixture Models of
Educability Demographic/Programmatic Factors

Measure of educability	Posterior mean (standard deviation) of π_1	Posterior mean (standard deviation) of π_2	Posterior mean (standard deviation) of θ_1	Posterior mean (standard deviation) of θ_2	95% HPD from posterior predictive distribution of $\varphi(x_s)$
Free/reduced-price lunch	.690 (.005)	.934 (.004)	.651 (.077)	.349 (.077)	[.740, .814]
Special education	.095 (.003)	.547 (.022)	.846 (.056)	.154 (.056)	[.122, .223]
English language learners	.003 (.001)	.152 (.007)	.692 (.073)	.308 (.073)	[.029, .072]

Results are computed from Markov Chain Monte Carlo estimation of Bayesian hierarchical models for proportion data from the 37 D.C. charter schools. Quantities of interest are computed from 20,000 iterations after discarding 180,000 as burn-in. The π_k's denote the estimated probability (or proportion) parameters of the two binomial components of the mixture. The θ_k's denote the estimates of the mixing constants (the proportion of schools in each distribution). The DCPS point estimate is contained within the 95% HPD for special education, but is below the free/reduced-price lunch HPD and beyond the English language learner HPD, suggesting that the charters, on average, have fewer ELL students, more F/RPL students, and statistically the same proportion of SPED students.

$\pi_2 = .934$. In the case of special education, it appears that the vast majority of charter schools (85 percent) have a fairly low proportion of special education students, as reflected in their estimated $\pi = .095$; the remaining 15 percent of schools have an estimated $\pi = .547$. Finally, for English language learners we estimate that 69 percent of the charter schools have virtually no students in this category ($\pi = .003$) while the other 31 percent suggest $\pi = .152$. The standard deviations of the posteriors suggest that, on all three outcome measures, the charter schools can be separated into two quite distinct subpopulations.

In the final column of table 4.3, we present the 95 percent HPDs from the posterior predictive distributions for each $\varphi(x_s)$, the overall mixture distribution. We also present the entire posterior predictive distribution for each of the outcomes graphically in figure 4.2. If we compare the DCPS point estimates again to these 95 percent HPDs, we find varying results. The mixed model suggests that the D.C. charter schools have, on average, proportionally more free/reduced price lunch–eligible students (the lower bound on the 95 percent HPD is .740, which is greater than the DCPS proportion of .620). The 95 percent HPD for special education, however, includes the DCPS value of .183, suggesting little evidence of a difference. Finally, the DCPS proportion of English language learners of

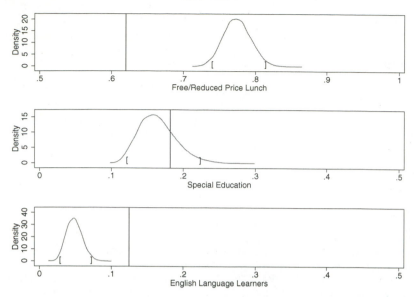

Figure 4.2. Posterior densities of mixture models. *Note*: Estimated posterior pre-dictive densities, assuming independent binomial mixture models for each demo-graphic/programmatic measure. Results are computed from 20,000 Markov Chain Monte Carlo iterations after discarding 180,000 as burn-in. Data are num-ber of students in each category and total enrollment for thirty-seven D.C. charter schools in 2003. Brackets denote 95 percent HPD as reported in table 4.3. Vertical lines indicate DCPS proportion for reference.

.125 is larger than the upper bound of the charter schools' 95 percent HPD of .073, from which we infer that the charter schools on average enroll proportionally fewer of these students.

In sum, we find mixed evidence for a difference in educability using the demographic/programmatic data. Our findings in the case of the free/reduced price lunch measure support the argument advanced by Howell et al. (2004). However, while charter schools in D.C. may enroll, on average, more students with a lower SES background, they appear to have propor-tionally fewer English language learners and about the same fraction of special education students.

ARE THERE DIFFERENCES BEYOND DEMOGRAPHICS?

Measures such as free/reduced price lunch and special education do not necessarily indicate *real* differences in educability; rather they are proxies for family context, peer effects, school practices, and student-level attitudes, ability, and behaviors that theoretically combine to predict a student's educability. Accordingly, we now shift our focus away from the broad demographic measures to examine a set of more precise indicators.

To compare charter and traditional DCPS students on these measures, we use our Wave 3 data from the telephone survey of both charter and traditional public school seventh to twelfth grade students conducted September–October 2003.[15]

We examine eight key measures of educability at the individual student level, which we now describe in some detail. First, we look at the number of different schools attended by the student. Student mobility has long been linked to negative consequences for academic achievement and progress. A variety of empirical studies conclude that changing schools disrupts the social and academic life of students (see, for example, Ingersoll, Scamman, and Eckerling 1989; Brent and DiObilda 1993; Fitchen 1994; Wood et al. 1993; U.S. General Accounting Office 1994). However, other research has shown that this negative effect may be offset if the move is out of an educationally disadvantaged school to a healthier environment (Brawner 1973; Lee 1951). Thus, the move from an underperforming traditional public school to a charter school or other option might not be as potentially harmful as remaining in place—and the federal government certainly seems to be taking this position as evidenced by the choice provisions in the No Child Left Behind Act. However, it is reasonable to expect that, on average, excessive mobility predicts a decline in educability.

Next we look at indicators of student attitudes and the home environment. Since the publication of the Coleman Report, research has documented the importance of family background in predicting academic achievement. While this has often been operationally defined as socioeconomic status, here we use two sets of indicators of the nonschool environment that we believe affect student performance. First, we consider the student's own expected level of educational attainment, asking the student to report on the highest level of education that they expect to complete.

Next we consider measures of parental involvement with the child's education. The "effective schools" movement and a large body of subsequent work have shown the importance of such involvement. For example, Bryk and his colleagues have repeatedly demonstrated that parents must be involved in schooling to ensure the quality of schools as institutions serving the community. They also show that children from low-income and minority families gain the most from parent involvement (see, for example, Bryk and Schneider 2002; Bryk, Lee, and Holland 1993; Bryk, Sebring, and Rollow 1998). Reflecting the importance of such involvement, we asked students:

- How often their parents talk to them about school;
- How much they think their parents know about their school.

These outcome variables are measured as categorical survey responses, which we treat in the subsequent model as continuous dependent variables.

Finally, we consider the peer groups of the students in both the charters and the DCPS. A growing body of research has documented the importance of peer effects on learning (Coleman 1961; Bishop 1999; Nechyba 1996; Epple and Romano 1998; Hoxby 2000a). One of the most disturbing findings of this body of research is how peers in many inner-city schools pressure each other away into antisocial activities at the expense of learning and studying (Steinberg, Brown, and Dornbusch 1996; Betts and Morell 1999; Brooks-Gunn, Duncan, and Aber 1997). To tap peer group effects, we consider four measures (all are self-reported by the student):

- What proportion of a student's close friends like school;
- What proportion get good grades;
- What proportion frequently get in trouble with teachers; and
- What proportion use bad language.

We construct each proportion by dividing the number of close friends in each category by the total number of close friends reported by each student.

In general, we are interested in comparing the charter- and traditional public-school students on the set of measures outlined above. However, because of the extent of panel attrition and thus the possibility of selection bias in any simple comparison, we adopt a slightly more complex modeling approach. We assume that the attrition process is a function of observable covariates—that data are "missing at random" or MAR in the terminology of Rubin (1987)—and we use the method of propensity weighting (Cassel, Sarndal, and Wretman 1983). That is, we estimate a model predicting the probability of each family unit remaining in the student sample, based on the observed data for the parents in the first wave. These predicted probabilities are obtained using a Bayesian analogue of the familiar probit model for dichotomous dependent variables and subsequent analyses are weighted by the inverse of these predicted probabilities.

More precisely, we assume,

$$\text{Pr (student } i \text{ in sample} = 1 \mid \mathbf{x}_i) \sim \text{Bernoulli } (\pi_i), \pi_i = \Phi (\mathbf{x}_i\beta) \quad (4.6)$$

where $\mathbf{x}_i$ is a vector of predictors of the student's family remaining in the sample, including a constant, β denotes the coefficients on these covariates, and Φ denotes the standard Normal cumulative distribution function. As predictors of sample retention, we include covariates measuring the parent's socioeconomic status (MaCurdy, Mroz, and Gritz 1998): the responding parent's employment status; the parent's marital status; the respondent's years of formal education; and a set of three dichotomous variables for parent self-reported race (white, Hispanic, and other, with black as the excluded and modal category).

We also consider the respondents' strength of community ties by measuring their frequency of church attendance (a seven-category measure, treated as continuous) and their history of residential mobility, as measured by the number of years the respondent's have lived in D.C. and in their particular neighborhood.

Finally, we consider two aspects of their children's education as possible predictors of sample retention. First, we measure their satisfaction with the DCPS overall using an A–F letter grade the respondents reported in the first interview, which we treat as a continuous predictor. Our logic here is to allow for the possibility that highly dissatisfied parents exit the schools—and the sample—altogether, and for the possibility that satisfaction may influence whether or not the parent allows the child to be interviewed. We also include a dichotomous indicator for whether their children were enrolled in a charter school during the first interview, to account for the possibility of differential rates of attrition or interviewing between the charter and DCPS sectors.

We model each of our k outcome variables as independent normal variates:

$$y_{ik} \sim \mathrm{N}(\mu_{ik}, \pi_i \tau_{ik}) \tag{4.7}$$

where, for each outcome, the precision (inverse variance), τ_{ik}, is weighted by the probability of sample retention π_i (Hahn 2000). In each case, μ_{ik}, the mean, is modeled as:

$$\mu_{ik} = \gamma_{0k} + \gamma_{1k} \text{ Charter Student}_{ik} + \gamma_{2k} \text{ Grade Level}_{ik} \tag{4.8}$$

where each γ_{1k} are the key quantities of interest to allow inference about the differences between charter and DCPS students, controlling for the student's grade level and adjusting for attrition probability.

We estimate each of the eight outcome models and the propensity weighting model simultaneously to allow for the proper propagation of estimation uncertainty from the weighting model to the outcome models. Our approach to estimation is fully Bayesian and we again employ the Markov Chain Monte Carlo estimator, after specifying independent, diffuse normal priors on the parameter vectors, β and γ, and independent and diffuse gamma priors on the precisions, τ.

Finally, since our sample size is small, we are especially concerned with avoiding the loss of any further cases due to listwise deletion of missing

TABLE 4.4
Predicting Which Families Remain in the Sample

	Posterior mean (standard deviation)	95% highest posterior density
Parent employed	−.023 (.104)	[−.241, .181]
Parent married	.049 (.141)	[−.221, .340]
Parent's church attendance	.065 (.034)	[−.002, .135]
Parent's time in D.C.	−.019 (.014)	[−.050, .009]
Parent's time in neighborhood	.028 (.012)	[.006, .055]
Parent white	.367 (.380)	[−.328, 1.177]
Parent Hispanic	−.184 (.313)	[−.804, .440]
Parent other race (nonblack)	−.331 (.313)	[−.968, .273]
Parent's DCPS grade	.019 (.030)	[−.045, .066]
Parent's years of education	.040 (.027)	[−.012, .095]
Student in charter school	.082 (.143)	[−.201, .368]
Constant	−1.088 (.501)	[−2.139, −.161]

Results are computed from Markov Chain Monte Carlo estimation of the sample-retention propensity portion of the Bayesian model using data from 479 parents of students in grades 7–12 at the time of student interviews. Quantities of interest are computed from 200,000 iterations after discarding 600,000 as burn-in.

data.[16] Accordingly, we take advantage of the flexibility of the Markov Chain Monte Carlo approach and treat missing values as parameters to be estimated conditional on the observed data (MAR), thus imputing missing values "on the fly" (Jackman 2000), after specifying their prior distributions again as independent, diffuse normals.[17]

In table 4.4, we first report the results of the propensity-weighting portion of the model. As in the case of our earlier results, we provide the mean and standard deviation of the simulated posterior distributions as point estimates, as well as the 95 percent highest posterior density.

Although most of the covariates do not appear to be strong predictors of sample attrition, the posteriors for parent's frequency of church atten-

TABLE 4.5
There Are Few Differences between Charter Students and Their DCPS Peers

Measure of educability		Posterior mean (standard deviation)	95% highest posterior density
Number of schools	Student in charter	.492 (.160)	[.178, .806]
	Grade level	.258 (.050)	[.159, .356]
	Constant	.582 (.482)	[−.361, 1.534]
Highest grade expected	Student in charter	.037 (.176)	[−.310, .382]
	Grade level	−.006 (.056)	[−.116, .104]
	Constant	5.348 (.536)	[4.294, 6.406]
Parents talk about school	Student in charter	−.025 (.227)	[−.471, .420]
	Grade level	.031 (.072)	[−.109, .172]
	Constant	4.871 (.682)	[3.527, 6.201]
Parents know about school	Student in charter	.036 (.092)	[−.144, .217]
	Grade level	−.011 (.029)	[−.069, .045]
	Constant	1.783 (.273)	[1.245, 2.318]
Proportion friends like school	Student in charter	.038 (.038)	[−.035, .112]
	Grade level	.011 (.012)	[−.011, .034]
	Constant	.746 (.112)	[.525, .966]
Proportion friends good grades	Student in charter	.013 (.029)	[−.044, .070]
	Grade level	.010 (.009)	[−.007, .028]
	Constant	.799 (.087)	[.629, .969]
Proportion friends in trouble	Student in charter	.014 (.044)	[−.073, .101]
	Grade level	.004 (.014)	[−.022, .031]
	Constant	.491 (.132)	[.232, .750]
Proportion friends bad language	Student in charter	−.079 (.049)	[−.176, .018]
	Grade level	.049 (.016)	[.019, .079]
	Constant	.325 (.147)	[.039, .616]

Results are computed from Markov Chain Monte Carlo estimation of the sample retention propensity portion of the Bayesian model using data from 201 students in grades 7–12, with attrition of families controlled for by weighting by the estimated inverse probability of remaining in the sample. Quantities of interest are computed from 200,000 iterations after discarding 600,000 as burn-in.

dance and number of years lived in the neighborhood suggest that stronger community ties, not surprisingly, decrease the probability of attrition. Furthermore, the results for the parent's years of education are somewhat suggestive that higher SES parents are more likely to remain (or to permit their child to be interviewed).

Table 4.5 presents the results of the outcome models. The only charter coefficient with a 95 percent HPD that does not include 0 is found in the model for the number of schools attended. On average, we find that charter students have attended .49 (standard deviation = .16) more schools than their traditional DCPS counterparts. This, however, is not surprising: we expect that many charter students, unless their parents moved them to a charter at the natural break point between elementary and middle or middle and secondary schools, have attended one more school than their traditional public peers. Stronger evidence of a difference in educability would be a difference in the number of schools greater than 1; our 95 percent HPD for this coefficient is [.178, .806], which we do not believe provides support for a difference between charter- and traditional public-school students.

The only other result that appears suggestive of a difference is the charter coefficient for the proportion of friends who use bad language. The estimated posterior mean of this coefficient is –.079 (.049) with a 95 percent HPD of [–.176, .018], providing some support for the conclusion that charter school students have better-behaved peer groups in school. We suspect that this difference, which is not found in the other peer group outcomes, may be a result of the focus by some charter schools on policies of stricter discipline.

Are There Differences in Test Scores?

In general, we find scant evidence that charter-school students in D.C. are harder to educate than students in the traditional schools. Given this, what do the data show about the relative test performance of students in the two sectors? Again, we note that our test-score data are not value-added or gain measures.[18] Nonetheless, we present the following analysis because in the charter-school debate ignited by the AFT report, educability and test scores both were central issues—and much of that debate focused on the type of data we analyze next.

For example, in her response to the AFT report, Hoxby (2004) criticizes the AFT researchers for their methodology and choice of data. But more importantly, she presents empirical evidence that she claims shows that charter schools are actually outperforming their traditional counterparts on standardized achievement measures. This research, not surprisingly, was praised by critics of the AFT report and was widely used to refute the claims that charter schools were lagging.

Hoxby's ingenious method involved matching each charter school to its nearest neighboring public school, both geographically and in terms of racial composition, and then computing the difference in percent proficient in math and reading at the fourth grade level on the appropriate state test. In Washington, D.C., for example, Hoxby reports that the charters outperformed their competition by 35.3 percent or 36.6 percent in reading (the first number is her geographic match result, the second is

TABLE 4.6
Students in Charter Schools Do Not Appear to
Have Increased Academic Achievement

Percent proficient or advanced	Difference in means charter — DCPS (standard error)	95% confidence interval
Mathematics, source 1	−10.21 (4.73)	[−19.49, −1.10]
Mathematics, source 2	−13.96 (4.95)	[−23.66, −4.25]
Reading, source 1	−3.64 (4.95)	[−15.02, 5.67]
Reading, source 2	−4.60 (5.84)	[−14.67, 7.67]

Results are estimates of difference of mean percent proficient or advanced between 20 charter elementary schools and their nearest neighbors selected (with replacement) via Mahalanobis metric matching from a space defined by the number of students enrolled, the percentage of students eligible for free and reduced-price lunch, and the percentage of English language learners. Standard errors and confidence intervals are computed using a non-parametric bootstrap procedure (1,000 replications). Achievement data were obtained from two sources; source 1 is DCSchoolSearch.com; source 2 is the DCPS Office of Educational Accountability and Assessment. Both sets of results are included for comparison.

the racial composition match) and 40.0 percent or 41.5 percent in math. Nelson, however, reports a variety of problems with these results in D.C., including the omission of more than half of the charter schools from Hoxby's sample, the use of different proficiency standards for the charters and comparison schools, and errors in the identification of closest neighbors (as cited in Matthews 2004).

As a first step, we have attempted to replicate Hoxby's findings using 2002–3 test-score and demographic data. Using both multiple and multivariate regression models controlling for demographic/programmatic factors, and various matching models on percentage of students eligible for free or reduced price lunch (similar to Hoxby's racial composition match but more relevant to D.C., given its demographics), we do not find any statistically significant evidence for a charter effect in achievement at any level of school (elementary, middle, or secondary) once *all* charter schools are considered. In fact, given several choices of model (including several matching approaches), we find some evidence that the traditional schools are outperforming their charter counterparts.

For example, in table 4.6 we present the results of one such comparison of the average academic achievement of the charters and the traditional public schools. To conduct this analysis, we use test-score data from the

2002–3 school year obtained from two sources (the first is a web site, www.dcschoolsearch.com (described later in chapter 5) created by us but now operated by the DCPS; the second is performance data provided by the DCPS Office of Educational Accountability and Assessment). Following Hoxby, we restrict our analysis to just elementary schools. We match the twenty elementary-level charter schools to their nearest neighbors—not geographically, but in terms of a hypothetical space consisting of their size (number of students), the percent of students eligible for free/reduced price lunch, and the percent of English language learners. We find the nearest neighbor in this multidimensional space, drawing from the set of DCPS schools with replacement.[19] We then compute the difference in mean percent of students scoring at or above the proficient level and obtain standard errors of this difference and 95 percent confidence intervals via the nonparametric bootstrap (Efron and Tibshirani 1995; Mooney and Duval 1996).

As table 4.6 illustrates, we find that in the case of mathematics achievement, charter schools, on average, have about 10 percent (from the first source of data) or 14 percent (from the second) fewer of their students performing at or above the level of proficiency in math compared to the set of matched traditional public schools. In the case of reading achievement, we find no statistically significant difference using either data source. These differences are robust to alternative matching methods and matching metric specifications. While we again caution the reader that these are not gain scores, using a technique similar to that used by Hoxby, we find no evidence of charter schools outperforming matched traditional public schools on academic achievement measured by test scores.

Are Charter School Students Different?

Both proponents and opponents of charter schools have recently argued that charter schools attract and retain different student populations than the traditional public schools—but they disagree on what those different populations are.

Opponents have argued that charters, through selective recruitment and retention or through differences in parent knowledge and motivation, will be composed of easier-to-educate students from more intact, higher-socioeconomic-status families. More recently, charter-school advocates have pointed to a presumed difference in educability in the opposite direction as an explanation for some recent empirical evidence that the charter schools may not be living up to their promise of higher academic achievement.

In this chapter, we tested these competing claims. We find little evidence supporting either position. At the school level, looking at demographic measures of educability—proportion of free/reduced price lunch, special education, and English language learning students—our data show that there are indeed several D.C. charter schools with a higher percentage of students in each of these categories, particularly in the case of the free/reduced price lunch students.[20] However, when considering a heterogeneous data-generation process, we find mixed results: D.C. charter students, on average, appear to be more likely to be eligible for free/reduced price lunch, but less likely to be English language learners, and about equally likely to be special education students.

At the student level, the data from our survey of charter- and traditional public-school students again suggest little difference on measures of attitude, parental involvement, and peer group quality. We find evidence of a difference, on average, in the number of schools attended, but this is likely explained by the simple fact that many charter students are expected to have switched schools one additional time.

We concluded the chapter with a brief investigation of student achievement. Given that, overall, students in the two sectors are roughly comparable in terms of educability, we find that charter schools are not outperforming a matched sample of traditional public schools. However, using only the measures we have employed in this chapter, we may not have fully captured differences in the charter schools versus the traditional public schools. In the next chapters, we continue to study how schools, parents, and students differ across these two sectors.

Shopping for Schools on the
Internet Using DCSchoolSearch.com

SOCIAL SCIENTISTS HAVE CONSIDERABLE experience with telephone surveys—and as noted earlier, we use survey data in this book. However, the revolution in information technology that blossomed in the mid- to late-1990s created many new tools for research, and here we use such technology as another window into how parents make decisions about schools. Specifically, we use data gathered from a school-choice web site we constructed to help further our understanding of how parents go about choosing schools. In this chapter, we describe that website. In the next section of the book, we explore some of the data generated by the site to further illuminate parental information search patterns.

CREATING DCSCHOOLSEARCH.COM

With the support of the National Science Foundation and the Smith Richardson Foundation, we worked with two D.C.-based not-for-profit organizations focused on school policy, the 21st Century Schools Fund and Friends of Choice in Urban School (FOCUS), to create DCSchoolSearch .com, an Internet-based site that contained information about every traditional and public charter school in Washington, D.C.

The creation and design of DCSchoolSearch.com was driven by two simple beliefs. First, we believed that as school choice proliferates, parents need more and better information about schools. Second, we believed that modern information technologies have the potential to make information about schools cheap and accessible. The marriage of these two ideas—that the need for information was increasing at the same time that technology was reducing the cost of providing it—drove us to create DCSchoolSearch.com.

However, while the cost of *disseminating* information has been reduced by modern information technologies, we discovered that the cost of *gathering* that information was still high. In particular, we incurred high costs because we were dependent on the cooperation of people, both DCPS officials and charter-school officials, who needed to give us the information we wanted to provide to parents. Despite the fact that data we were seeking were (or should have been) readily accessible public information, many D.C. school officials felt they had little reason to cooperate in our effort.[1]

We begin this chapter with an in-depth discussion of the motivation behind the creation of DCSchoolSearch.com, noting some of the problems we experienced. While most of the analysis in this book is based on the surveys described in the previous chapter, we also use data collected from visitors to DCSchoolSearch.com to explore aspects of school-choice behavior that could not be studied using only telephone surveys. It is therefore incumbent upon us to explain in more detail the way in which these data were generated. We should note that while it is relatively easy to write a technical appendix for a survey (such as the appendix to chapter 3) and for the reader to judge the quality of the survey data using the information contained in such an appendix, writing such a standardized appendix for DCSchoolSearch.com is virtually impossible—hence the long narrative.

THE VISION: INFORMED CHOOSERS MAKING THE RIGHT CHOICE

The vision of parents gathering information to make informed choices about an expanded set of schools among which their children can enroll is central to the theory of choice. However, while we focus on how the search for information affects school choice, the implications of the distribution and use of information transcend any single policy domain. Indeed, the extent to which individuals engage in a rational search for information and the way they use the information they have, most notably the level of information citizens have about candidates and policy issues, is central to many debates in political science.

The importance given to information levels is not surprising—as Delli Carpini and Keeter argue, "an informed citizenry is an implicit requisite for any theory of democracy" (1996, 583). Yet despite the importance of an informed citizenry, especially in an environment giving them choice over an increasing range of public goods, political scientists have repeatedly shown that most citizens know very little about politics and public policies (see, for example, Bartels 1996; Lupia and McCubbins 1998). Kuklinski and Quirk (1998) demonstrate that the level of information about specific public policies, even in highly salient domains, tends to be quite low (also see Gilens 2001). In the field of education policy and school choice, Schneider, Teske, and Marschall (2000) show that many parents cannot even name the principal of their child's school, let alone accurately report on basic aspects of school performance and composition, such as the average class size and test scores.

While there are many avenues being explored as to why such low information levels are endemic to American politics and how these affect decision making, a recurring theme links low information levels to benefit/cost calculations. The argument is simple: information is costly and individuals must make a decision about how much to invest to get it (Downs 1957; Aldrich 1993). Since the costs of gathering information about public goods are high relative to the benefits of such information, citizens (rationally) remain uninformed. Using this "instrumental-quantitative" perspective, researchers focus on the amount of information available, the costs of obtaining it, and the degree to which it reduces uncertainty and clarifies options (Bimber 2001, 56). To the extent that information costs are high, it follows that options are neglected and decisions may be faulty. Indeed, a wide range of research focuses on the costs of information as an impediment to decision making and political participation more broadly. In turn, many researchers have explored the ways that people can reduce the costs of gathering and processing information.

This research perspective is evident across a wide range of work studying how consumers shop for goods, both public and private. It is not surprising that this perspective has also affected the discussion of school choice—indeed, the cost of information gathering and processing has been one of the main avenues of criticism employed by critics of choice. In fact, early in the school-choice debate, Bridge (1978) called the quality of information available to parents and their ability to use it the "Achilles' heel" of choice.

While some critics have questioned the extent to which parents *overall* have the capacity to make good schooling decisions (see, for example, Ascher et al. 1996), most criticism has been based on the belief that less-educated parents will be particularly disadvantaged in the search for and use of information (see Carnegie 1992; Bridge 1978; Wells 1993). The argument is not surprising: good information processing and decision-making skills are linked to cognitive ability, which is often linked to and signaled by higher education.

However, good decision-making skills are also linked to the degree to which a person is "involved" in the decision and the stakes at hand. Here proponents of choice argue that increasing the benefits of gathering information that follow from expanding school choice would in fact provide a strong incentive to improve parental decision skills. This is a cornerstone of Chubb and Moe's argument for school choice; they assert that in a market-based system of choice, parent choices "would have consequences for their children's education, and their incentives to become informed and involved would be dramatically different" (1990, 564).

From Chubb and Moe's perspective, the benefits of acquiring information about schools are reduced by the centralized control of school enrollment found in most school districts—it makes little sense to gather extensive information about the quality of the school your child attends if the "choice" of the school has been dictated bureaucratically. But Chubb and Moe argue that given choice, people will have incentives to become informed (see Schneider, Teske, and Marschall 2000 for empirical evidence on this point).

While linking choice to the greater benefits of becoming informed is taken as a "given" by proponents of school choice, less studied are the *costs* of being an informed parent. The idea of using new technologies to reduce the cost of disseminating information about schools motivated us to create DCSchoolSearch.com.

Gathering Information about Schools Is Difficult

Historically, the costs of acquiring information about schools have been very high. Basic information about local schools is generally not widely circulated and local school officials have few incentives and often no legal requirement to report information. This is a long-standing problem. For example, one explanation for the low information levels found in the oft-cited Alum Rock voucher studies is simple: principals and the school board simply did not provide information about school performance (Henig 1994, 120). Similarly, Wilson (1992) found that even the most basic information about schools in the districts he studied was not generally available. Carver and Salganik (1991, 75) report that they were unable to gather information about test scores, grade retention, graduation, and college attendance rates from many schools of choice. In their study of choice, Schneider, Teske, and Marschall (2000) report that it took months to track down data on school performance over time in New York, and even after they located a school official who had the data, arranging access entailed time-consuming negotiations. They were even more stymied in efforts to gather data on New Jersey districts over time—at the time they were doing their research, New Jersey's commitment to reporting school data seemed to be a direct function of its budget situation. And their efforts to get data about private schools yielded little information.

It is perhaps not surprising that essential data are hard to find: historically, schools have had few reasons to disseminate information widely, and may in fact have incentives to misreport data. Given the widespread reports of school failures and poor test scores, many school officials feel besieged. Subjected to constant criticisms, the ability of school officials to isolate themselves behind a veil of professionalism and expertise has been eroding for decades. In addition, teaching is a difficult job, and the rewards are often few and far between. Organizations under attack, and not just schools, often "circle the wagons" rather than seek positive ways of dealing with the problems at hand.

Moreover, as Hess (1999) has argued, while there are very strong incentives built into the governance of school systems for ambitious administrators to announce and launch new programs (and thereby create a "name" and win promotion to a more prestigious, higher paying position), there are few incentives to put in place a monitoring system to assess the effects of these reforms. And there are no incentives at all to broadcast failures. In addition, even given the right incentives and good intentions, many school systems lack the capacity (or the willingness to redeploy their existing resources) to support a serious effort to disseminate high-quality educational information.

NCLB and the Requirement to Report Information

While this problem has been chronic, the Federal 2001 No Child Left Behind Act (NCLB) may be changing the situation. NCLB expands the federal government's role in kindergarten through grade 12 public education and may ultimately result in higher levels of information dissemination and transparency in all schools in the nation. Among its many provisions, NCLB mandates that states must furnish annual report cards showing a range of information on school performance. Districts must provide similar report cards showing school-by-school data. Among the data NCLB requires are aggregate student achievement on state academic assessments and performance data disaggregated by race, ethnicity, gender, disability status, migrant status, English proficiency, and status as economically disadvantaged. Other provisions require schools to make available detailed information about over-time change in test scores and data about teacher credentials. In addition, schools have the option of reporting the extent and type of parental involvement in the schools and data about advanced placement tests and accountability systems.

Clearly, to the extent that these provisions of the law are enforced, schools face a new world in terms of reporting requirements. But the law does not mandate the exact form in which these report cards are to be reported—and therein lies a problem.

Gormley and Weimer (1999) identify six criteria for evaluating organizational report cards, which is what essentially the NCLB law requires of schools. These criteria are the following:

- *Validity.* To what degree are the measures reported linked to outcomes?
- *Comprehensiveness.* Does the good/service have multiple dimensions? Is information about all of them presented?

- *Comprehensibility.* Can consumers understand the data?
- *Relevance.* To what extent do the report cards produce news of use to the consumer?
- *Reasonableness.* To what extent do the report cards put reasonable demands on the user?
- *Functionality.* Do the report cards facilitate appropriate behavior or do they encourage poor judgments and decision making?

There are many approaches to releasing school report cards—and most of them do not meet these criteria. Some states and districts rely on printed documents, others on posting PDF files on the Internet, while others display static information on often hard to locate web pages.[2] In most of these approaches, parents can be overwhelmed with lots of data but little usable information. Data are almost never designed to help a parent identify the set of schools that she would consider appropriate for her child and data designed to facilitate comparisons between schools are almost never reported. While posting such information may allow states and districts to claim to have met the requirements of NCLB, they fail to meet most, if not all of the criteria for a good organizational report card.

There is another problem with the ongoing push for more information—the data do not necessarily reflect what parents really want to know. There is consensus among parents about what type of school conditions they say are most important and about which they want to know. Below (table 5.1) we report the results from Wave 1 of our telephone survey in which we asked parents to tell us what they thought were the most important aspects that define a good school. In general, this list, which is virtually identical to the results from every other survey of this topic, shows that parents say they want information about fundamental characteristics of schools that we are all likely to agree are important. However, the devil is in the details.

Consider the first item on the list. In our research, the majority of parents identify good teachers as the characteristic of schools about which they care the most. But what specific data should a state or district report to allow parents to judge the quality of teachers? The number of teachers with advanced degrees? The average salary or experience level of teachers? Some more complex "value-added" measure constructed from a statistical model of student test-score data?

To get a more intense look at what parents want in report cards, one of our DC partners, the 21st Century Schools Fund, assembled two focus groups to help design a user-friendly report card and to gauge parental reaction to the provisions of the NCLB law. The parents in these groups all agreed that information on teacher quality was essential and they were all upset that they did not currently get this information. Furthermore,

TABLE 5.1
What Do Parents Say Is Important in Defining a Good School?

	Most Important	Next Most Important
Teacher quality	34%	22%
Academic environment/curriculum	16%	14%
Parental involvement cooperation	13%	12%
Discipline/safety	12%	16%
Class or school size	9%	5%
Administrators/principal/staff	7%	13%
Morals and values	3%	3%
Facilities	3%	8%
After school programs/extracurricular	1%	3%
Test scores	1%	1%
Location	1%	1%
Diversity of students	0%	1%

Data are from two open-ended survey questions asked in Wave 1 of the telephone survey. The number of observations was 1,012 parents.

when given a list of indicators of teacher quality, parents found it most important to get two specific pieces of information: Does the teacher meet state qualification and licensing criteria for the grade levels and the subject areas in which the teacher provides instruction? And is the teacher teaching under emergency certification or other provisional status?

These results clearly confirm that parents want their children taught by a "good" teacher, and the measures they want may actually reflect the quality of the teacher; however, the correlation between these indicators and the outcome parents want is subject to significant noise. Indeed, there are intense debates about the relationship of experience, certification, and other standards to teaching effectiveness—and therefore little guidance to parents seeking information or professionals seeking to make reliable teacher-quality indicators available (see, for example, Goldhaber and Anthony 2003).

Does the Capacity to Produce Reliable Data Exist?

There is another problem: put simply, many schools and school systems may not have the institutional capacity to produce and disseminate accurate information. We noted earlier the problems that many researchers have encountered trying to gather information. In Washington, D.C., while trying to create and maintain DCSchoolSearch.com, we found that school officials often claimed that their reporting systems were out-of-date and did not communicate with one another. In turn, our requests for even very basic data were refused.

Of course, this refusal, while couched in terms of the inability of the school system to provide the program information requested, was no doubt also driven by their suspicion that the project was going to hurt their schools and benefit the charter schools. Nonetheless, their lack of capacity is evident: DCPS has almost always run into a variety of technical problems that has repeatedly led to the late release of school report cards. Moreover, after DCSchoolSearch.com became operational, one of the heaviest classes of users was D.C. school officials, who were accessing the centralized database we created as a management information system! How the mandates of NCLB interact with the capacity of school districts to gather and report data is an ongoing story.

There is also one further problem in terms of data reporting (and perhaps an area where schools are *too* good at data handling): as high-stakes testing has taken root, schools are under intense pressure to produce good results—and they now often cheat on assessment tests.

According to Figlio and Getzler (2002), schools facing the high-stakes Florida Comprehensive Assessment Test (FCAT) reclassified students as disabled, putting them into special education programs exempt from the state tests, and therefore exempt from the school's aggregate test scores. Moreover, these reclassifications were concentrated among the low-income schools most likely to be on the margin of failing the state's accountability system. Similarly, Jacob and Levitt (2003) use Iowa Test scores from third through seventh grade students in the Chicago public schools to identify likely cases of teachers or administrators who cheat by systematically altering student test forms. They suggest that cheating occurred in 3–5 percent of the elementary classrooms in their sample (also see Haney 2000 for a similar story in Texas).

In short, we must always remember that schools are strategic players in the world of school choice and their incentives will affect the amount and accuracy of information they gather and report. With this in mind, we turn toward a description of DCSchoolSearch.com.

LINKING IT AND INFORMATION

Our work in creating DCSchoolSearch.com fit into a larger movement. We, like many others, recognized that individuals are using the Internet to gather information about a wide range of goods and services. We also recognized that the Internet could be a means to include citizens in govern-ment policy making and administrative processes. In fact, a number of studies assess the extent to which this potential has been turned into a reality (inter alia, Bimber 1998, 1999, 2000, 2001; Hale et al. 1999; Dahl-berg 2001; Stanley and Weare 2004). While shopping for private goods clearly dominates Internet activity, information about local public goods and services is widely available on line.

Not surprisingly, given the importance of education to parents, local governments, and extragovernmental supporters of school choice, infor-mation about local schools is also now available online. Such efforts are often linked directly to the growing number and range of options being presented to parents via intradistrict choice, interdistrict choice, charter schools, and vouchers. The provision of more and better information is critical for choice since, as we have seen, information about schools has been difficult to obtain. Providing information via the Internet has be-come one way to address this shortage.

The Internet and School Report Cards

The Internet is becoming one of the main routes for meeting the reporting requirements of the NCLB. We see several problems with current re-sponses. First, there is still considerable inequality in computer access—the so-called digital divide (which we will return to below). Second, as more information appears on the Internet, many critics believe that the information is displayed in a static format that ignores one of the web's most important features—interactivity.

It was in response to these two specific problems that we designed DCSchoolSearch.com. Our goal was to tap the Internet to reduce the cost of gathering information about the schools. We engaged in extensive out-reach activities to tell the population of D.C. parents about the site, and then assessed the extent to which changing the benefit/cost ratio regarding information and choice affected behavior. We also wanted to create a site that was interactive and user-friendly, and in particular allowed parents to create their own choice sets of schools by facilitating the comparison of schools on multiple dimensions.

However, an important question is whether the Internet will reach indi-viduals more equally than it does at present, bridging existing inequalities in resources and access to information (Tolbert, Mossberger, and McNeal 2002). Thus even as information becomes more widely available, some fear that a "digital divide," a gap between information "haves" and "have-nots," will exacerbate existing levels of inequality in American so-ciety. In this view, only more affluent parents will be able to overcome the entry barriers to using the Internet. In terms of school choice, the digital divide will undercut the spread of Internet-based information sites, since the divide will allow only more affluent parents to gather better information about their options and make better choices, while lower-income parents will continue to be relatively uninformed.

In our work, we tried to deal with these issues. In the following pages, we briefly identify the nature of the digital divide and we assess DCSchoolSearch.com's success at bridging it.

DEFINING THE DIGITAL DIVIDE

The digital divide is built on at least two different components.[3] First, and by far better known, is that part of the divide built on inequalities between income groups in the distribution of electronic consumer goods and access to modern information technologies. As clearly documented by the U.S. Department of Commerce, the use of computers and the Internet increases with income and education (Commerce 1998, 2000; also see Wilhelm, Carmen, and Reynolds 2002). There are also race/ethnicity effects—at every income level blacks and Hispanics are much less likely to be accessing the Internet than non-Hispanic whites and Asian Americans. The issue of access will likely remain serious despite the continuing drop in the price of computers themselves—as broad bandwidth connections proliferate, the costs of high-speed connections can create different entry barriers for low-income individuals.

Even as evidence has emerged showing that differences in access to hardware are narrowing and usage patterns converging, some analysts have identified a second component to the digital divide—the lack of content appropriate for low-income Americans. Among the dimensions of this content-based digital divide are the lack of local information about critical services, such as low-cost housing, local employment opportunities, and the schools; literacy barriers, since the vast majority of information on the Internet is written for an audience that has average or above-average literacy skills; and language barriers, since most of the information on the Internet is written in English. These barriers can be even more formidable than those based on hardware. Indeed, the argument about the digital divide has moved away from a simple question of access to hardware to a new set of questions relating to who is actually benefiting from modern IT and how different people are using the information that is on the Internet.[4]

We thought that school-based information sites presented perhaps the single best domain for crossing this "new frontier" of the digital divide. If the argument of Chubb and Moe is correct, the importance of schools to the well-being of their children provides parents with incentives to find out about schools. And, to extend this logic, as choice proliferates, the incentive for making an informed decision about the schools should increase.

WHAT IS DCSCHOOLSEARCH.COM?

DCSchoolSearch.com presented detailed information on about two hundred traditional public and charter schools,[5] all in the District of Columbia.[6] The site was "rolled out" in November 1999 and cost about $200,000 to design, implement, and keep online through the 1999–2000 school year. Maintenance costs were much lower, although they soon became a perennial issue. In part to ensure the long-term survival of the site, in 2003 we turned DCSchoolSearch.com over to the city government.

Between its rollout in November 1999 and February 2003 (when the city took over the site and the research component ended), DCSchoolSearch.com had over forty-eight hundred unique identifiable parent visitors and about nine hundred student visitors (an additional twenty-eight hundred visitors signed on as "other," which included researchers, school officials, and a variety of other people just curious about the site). These are of course small numbers relative to the number of parents with children in any of the school systems covered, and leads to a question about the effect that these sites can have on school choice and school systems (but see Schneider, Teske, and Marschall 2000 on the role that a small number of "marginal consumers" can have on school systems).

As noted, there was a research component to the D.C. site and all visitors to the site were asked to fill out a short, five-question profile in order to use it. Patterns of movement through the site were tracked. A set of site visitors who gave their e-mail addresses and permission to be contacted were surveyed via e-mail to get more detailed information about their attitudes toward the schools and their school-choice behavior (more about this later in this chapter and again in the next one). Thus, DCSchoolSearch.com combined an action component and a research component—that is, the site was designed to do something good for parents (providing them information to make better choices) while applying social-scientific and behavioral-decision theoretic concepts and models to better understand how parents search for and use information in the school-choice process.

Figure 5.1 shows an example of a typical page of information on the site when it was first made public.[7] Each school in the district had a similar set of pages constituting a profile describing the school's programs, student body, and academic performance. Note that detailed information about each of these attributes was accessed by pointing and clicking on a tab that takes the parent to a page with more detailed information about a school in the choice set. So, similar to the way a traditional information board is used by behavioral-decision scientists, parents could gather information by pointing and clicking through sets of alternatives and attributes.[8]

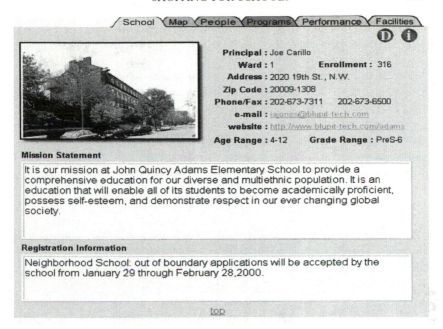

Figure 5.1. A sample page from DCSchoolSearch.com.

One central theme in research into education and school choice is the distribution of attitudes and behaviors of parents of different educational, class, and ethnic backgrounds. And indeed in any telephone-based survey, there is a fairly extensive (and fairly standard) set of demographic questions about education level, income, marital status, racial identification, and the like that is routinely gathered and used in subsequent analysis. We of course wanted similar types of information from parents using DCSchoolSearch.com. We had three mechanisms to get this information.

First, as noted earlier, anyone wishing to use the site had to supply us with five pieces of information in order to access to the site. Using "pop-up" boxes, each user had to tell us their (a) status as a student, a parent, or "other" type of user; (b) education level; (c) frequency of Internet use; and (d) extent of voluntary activity in schools in the last year. We also asked from where they were signed on (home, work, library, and so on). As researchers, we wanted to make the supply of more information mandatory, but the more information one asks for, the more likely a visitor is to exit the site without providing any information.

Second, visitors were asked to fill out voluntarily a more detailed online survey. In this survey, parents were asked to provide information about each of their children in the D.C. public schools, to evaluate the overall quality of the school, and to report on how well the school was performing on a variety of indicators. Parents were also asked to report on how many different kinds of choice activity they engaged in during the past year (for example, did they apply for an out-of-boundary transfer permit from the DCPS? Did they apply to a D.C. charter school or a private school? Did they move into a more desirable school's catchment area?).

Third, we asked visitors to give us their e-mail addresses. Social scientists (and commercial polling firms) have begun moving away from telephone-based interviews to e-surveys. Given the rapidly increasing use of e-mail coupled with the cost advantage of e-mail surveys, and given plummeting response rates from telephone polls, this migration is not surprising, although results are still somewhat mixed.[9]

Like some other work using e-mail surveys, our experience was salutary. Since a visitor could not access the site without answering the first five questions, "response rates" to these were 100 percent (of course, people did leave the page without providing any information—and as is always the case with web sites, we had many more "hits" than we had actual users). The object of using only five questions as the cost of entry was to "lure" users into the site, assuming that once they had made the initial investment of time and energy, they would be more likely to provide additional information. We discovered that this assumption was optimistic. Of all the registered users, only a handful bothered to take the online survey. We are not alone in finding low response rates to site-based surveys and that research tool proved unusable.

Since our plan to have parents supply much of the information we needed via online surveys linked to the site was frustrated, we had to rely more on the e-mail survey to gather detailed data. We conducted the e-mail survey when the site was active for a little more than one year. At the time of the e-mail survey, the site had slightly more than two thousand registered unique users, about eighteen hundred of whom were parents. Approximately five hundred of these parents provided their e-mail addresses, and of those 169 responded to the e-survey, for a response rate of about 10 percent of all parents (or 34 percent of those parents surveyed by e-mail). We use these data later in the book.

Spanning the Digital Divide

In contrast to Chubb and Moe, we believed that simply providing valuable content was not enough—underserved low-income parents had to be made aware of the information and how to access it. The staff of DCSchoolSearch.com tried extensive outreach activities to inform parents about these sites and about the importance of becoming an informed consumer of education. But we quickly discovered how hard it is to reach the target communities.

We partnered with the D.C. metro system and put posters in over three hundred D.C. buses. We had a slide shown in the Union Station multiplex cinema, mixing in information about our service with slides for the local laser eye surgery and the local carpet store. We hired a PR company and had press coverage, with stories in the *Washington Post* and several local television and radio stations, as well as on some local TV stations. These had some "one-time" effects boosting usage—in fact our biggest surge in hits was after a local TV show focused an entire half-hour show on DCSchoolSearch.com.

However, the media campaign was only a "sideshow" to an endless cycle of community meetings, parent groups, church groups, and school fairs. This was a labor-intensive activity, consuming significant amounts of staff time at DCSchoolSearch.com. Unfortunately, we were never able to identify "wholesale" methods of making the contacts, conducting training, and keeping interest alive in these sites. The key lesson here is that Internet-based school sites do not live in a "build it and they will come" field of dreams, but rather require hard work to achieve even limited penetration into an underserved, low-income, and minority population.

As we argued earlier, demographic differences in Internet access are probably the most widely discussed aspect of the digital divide. In addition, there is also a stratification component to the divide—those who already use the Internet will use it more, while those who do not use it will fall further behind. We now turn to our data to examine the evidence for these claims.

THE CHARACTERISTICS OF PARENT VISITORS

Our data show that despite the content, the site design, and the extensive outreach activity, DCSchoolSearch.com was less than successful in crossing the digital divide. Consider figure 5.2, which plots the frequency of Internet use of site visitors. Note that just about 80 percent of parents said that they used the Internet on a daily basis, and almost all the rest said that they used the Internet one or two times a week: There was not a noticeable expansion of the population into less frequent users (note that all the figures in this chapter are based on the 100 percent response to the required registration questions).[10]

Figure 5.3 indicates another factor contributing to the digital divide— almost two-thirds of parents who visited the site signed on from home, and almost all the other parents signed on from their workplace. In contrast, very few users signed on from a public place such as a library, school, or community organization. Clearly entry barriers limit the use of the Internet. On the one hand, there are the costs of purchasing and maintaining a home computer; of paying for an Internet service provider and having either a separate phone line or an existing phone line tied up for long periods of time; or paying for a high speed DSL or cable connec-

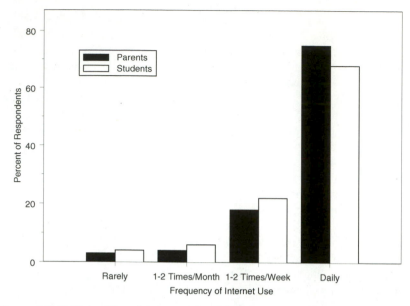

Figure 5.2. DCSchoolSearch.com attracted frequent Internet users. *Note*: Source of data is the required registration survey for www.DCSchoolSearch.com web site. $N = 2{,}168$ parent and 235 student users.

tion. On the other hand, people who are unemployed or work in places with no computer access are also denied a major route to the Internet and DCSchoolSearch.com.

But even more telling is the breakdown of users by education level (see figure 5.4). Note that the modal education category of parents who visited DCSchoolSearch.com was a college education.[11] About half of the site visitors either graduated from college or had some college education. Comparing this distribution to the one we obtained from our telephone survey shows clearly that the user population was far more educated than the general population of parents whose children are in the D.C. schools.

THE CHARACTERISTICS OF STUDENT VISITORS

While the site was designed with parents in mind, students are another population that could benefit from more information about their schools. While they may also be subject to the digital divide, they may in fact be better positioned to cross it. Yet returning to figures 5.2 and 5.3, the pattern of student access to the site shows a digital divide among current students as well.

First, students who signed on were, like parents, already heavy users of the Internet. While the percentage of students who were daily users of

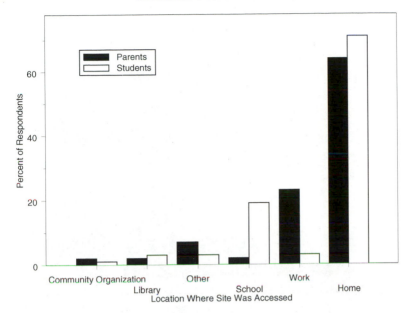

Figure 5.3. From where did parents and students access DCSchoolSearch.com? *Note:* Source of data is the required registration survey for www.DCSchoolSearch .com web site. N = 2,168 parent and 235 student users.

the Internet was about 10 percentage points lower than parents, this still represented over 70 percent of students. The percentage of infrequent users among students was somewhat higher than among parents, but nonetheless, there is little evidence that infrequent users were lured onto the Internet by the availability of school information.

As with parents, we again find that the modal location for using the Internet for students was home. Not surprisingly, compared to parents, students were more likely to access the site from their schools and less likely to access the site from work. Students were also more likely than parents to access the site from libraries (but still fewer than 3 percent of students signed on from libraries), and there was no reported access from community organizations.

THERE IS NO "FIELD OF DREAMS" IN DISSEMINATING INFORMATION ABOUT SCHOOL CHOICE

For many advocates of school choice, the expansion of choice, such as that seen in D.C., should provide strong incentives for parents to seek out information about their options. Thus, one possibility is that parental

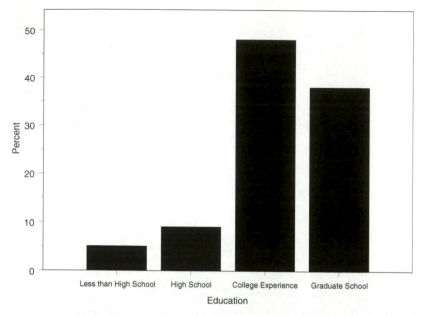

Figure 5.4. DCSchoolSearch.com attracted highly educated parents. *Note*: Source of data is the required registration survey for www.DCSchoolSearch.com web site. N = 2,168 parent users.

interest in taking advantage of choice to change their children's schools would yield heavy use of DCSchoolSearch.com, and perhaps even help span the digital divide. As noted earlier, this argument is congruent with the position staked out by Chubb and Moe (1990). But while Chubb and Moe argue that choice alone may create sufficient incentives for all parents to search for information, our data show that choice is not yet a sufficient bridge across the digital divide. We built it, and still they did not come.

6

What Do Parents Want from Schools?
It Depends on How You Ask

RANGING FROM THE EXPANSION of inter- and intradistrict choice to the rapid diffusion of charter schools and including the hotly contested spread of vouchers, the opportunities for parents to choose their children's schools continue to grow. As choice has proliferated, researchers have increasingly focused on the role of parents as "citizen/consumers" and studied how parent-choice behavior will affect schools under more marketlike schooling arrangements (see, e.g., Chubb and Moe 1990; Smith and Meier 1995; Henig 1996; Schneider, Teske, and Marschall 2000; Moe 2001; Howell and Peterson 2002).

While many dimensions of parent-choice behavior have been analyzed, one of the most important, and one of the most contentious, is the question of what aspects of schools parents prefer and how these preferences will affect the socioeconomic and racial composition of schools, as well as their academic performance. At the core of these studies of parental preferences is the debate about whether or not, given choice, parents will select schools on educationally sound dimensions or make choices based on noneducational ones. In this chapter, we use both our survey and our Internet data to gain insight into parental preferences.

Our survey data confirm what virtually all other surveys find: parents *say* that the academic aspects of schools are most important to them in choosing and evaluating schools. These patterns, remarkably consistent across a growing number of studies, are reassuring to proponents of choice—because they seem to settle one of the most fundamental issues surrounding choice reforms. Indeed, given the consistency of results, it is even possible to believe that the issue is resolved: if we trust what they say, parents of all races and all socioeconomic strata will choose schools on educationally appropriate grounds.

But we believe that the issue is far from settled. After analyzing how parents search for information on DCSchoolSearch.com and how they responded to our e-mail survey, we will argue that the standard findings in the literature, based largely on telephone interviews, may not be as solid as they appear. We will show that in the privacy of their own homes or offices and "talking" only with their computers, parents reveal a different set of preferences than those that they routinely state in surveys. Spe-

cifically, given the cloak of privacy, parents are consistently more interested in race than they ever will admit to when talking to someone who
is interviewing them. We will also show that these less reactive, noninter-
view data are more congruent with a smaller body of research findings
based on the actual choice behavior of parents.

WHO CHOOSES WHAT?

Despite the rapid expansion of school choice, many analysts have long
doubted the ability of parents to make good choices. The Carnegie Foundation (1992) concluded that "many parents base their school choice decision on factors that have nothing to do with the quality of education,"
including the availability of day care, convenience, social factors, and the
range and quality of interscholastic sports. A Twentieth Century Fund
report argued that parents are not "natural 'consumers' of education"
and that "few parents of any social class appear willing to acquire the
information necessary to make active and informed educational choices"
(Ascher, Fruchter, and Berne 1996, 40–41). But perhaps even more important, many researchers have argued that the tendency to make ill-in-
formed choices is stronger among low-income parents. Again, according
to the Carnegie Foundation, "School choice works better for some parents than for others. Those with education . . . may be able to participate
in such programs" (Carnegie Foundation 1992, 20; also see Smith and
Meier 1995; Ascher, Fruchter, and Berne 1996; Henig 1994, 1996; Henig
et al. 1999).
    A supporting line of research has been based on the examination of the
choice of courses exercised by high school students. In public high schools
where students have the freedom to choose from among a wide range of
courses, Ravitch (1996) has shown that white and Asian American students take more traditional academic courses than African American and
Hispanic students (also see Bryk, Lee, and Holland 1993), suggesting that
choice (in this case, within schools) can lead to increased stratification,
as minority students disproportionately choose to enroll in nonacademic
courses. Linking these results to school choice, some argue that stratification will be replicated across entire school systems as less-advantaged parents choose less rigorous schools.
    Moe summarizes the terms of this debate. He argues that a common
criticism of parental choice is the idea that "parents cannot be counted
on to make choices by reference to sound educational criteria or values."
He continues by noting that critics often argue that "parents—especially
low-income parents—supposedly care about practical concerns, such as
how close the school is or whether it has a good sports team, and put little

emphasis on academic quality and other properties of effective schooling" (Moe 1995, 26–27).

Moe's comments highlight the two dimensions underlying the commonly expressed concern for parental-choice behavior. The first is the broad indictment that *many* parents will fail to choose schools for their children based on educational quality. If, indeed, large numbers of parents do not value appropriate educational values and base their choice on ancillary or irrelevant school characteristics, schools, facing pressures to keep their consumers happy, will have incentives to emphasize the "wrong" performance criteria—for example, the number of football games won rather than the number of students reading at grade level or going on to college. To the extent this occurs, school choice could prove disastrous for the quality of learning across the country. With apologies to Gresham's law, we could see bad schools driving out good ones as a large number of parents choose schools for the wrong reasons.

While this broad-based criticism is often found in the literature, there is a corollary that *only certain types* of parents will be prone to choosing their children's schools for the wrong reasons. As is evident in Moe's statement, this concern is almost always phrased in terms of the particular susceptibility of low-income and less-educated parents to fall for the attraction of nonacademic (and thus "wrong") school attributes. Here, the issue of the values held by different parents and the concern that, given choice, some schools will skim off of the best students are joined. If low-income parents are unduly influenced by nonacademic factors while high-income parents focus their choice of schools on academic dimensions, then the schools will become more stratified as higher socioeconomic-status individuals with a concern for academics choose better performing schools, leaving the children of lower SES parents behind in low-performing schools. This bias in the selection process could fuel cumulative intergenerational inequality (Levin 1989; Wells 1993; Cookson 1992).

While this aspect of the debate has usually been focused on the presumed predilection of parents with lower incomes and educational attainment to choose schools on nonacademic grounds, there is another possibility worth considering that could also have adverse effects on schools. If parents are concerned with student body characteristics, will choice exacerbate stratification by class and segregation by race, countering one of the enduring policy and social commitments of educational policy of the last fifty years? If white and wealthier parents select schools on the basis of racial makeup regardless of a school's instructional quality or curriculum, the end result could be highly segregated schools chosen on the basis of race and not academic achievement. To the extent that demographics displace academic performance in the choices of higher-status parents, this could *reduce* pressure on schools to enhance performance—negating one of the main promises of choice.

Similarly, if parents select on the basis of the economic characteristics of the student body, stratification may increase, again with adverse learning outcomes. A body of research has documented the importance of peer effects on learning (Coleman 1961; Bishop 1999; Nechyba 1996; Epple and Romano 1998; Hoxby 2000a, inter alia). One of the most disturbing findings of this body of research is how in many inner-city schools students pressure each other away from learning and studying and into anti-social activities (Steinberg, Brown, and Dornbusch 1996; Betts and Morell 1999; Brooks-Gunn, Duncan, and Aber 1997). To the extent that parental preferences are focused on student-body characteristics and their resulting choices increase stratification and the isolation of students from more motivated peers and students with more mainstream career and academic aspirations, then schools and our society will suffer.

In short, the stakes are high in this debate.

SURVEY DATA SUPPORT THE IMPORTANCE OF ACADEMIC VALUES

There are numerous examples of surveys showing that parents endorse the "right" academic values. Armor and Peiser (1998) found that in the Massachusetts interdistrict choice program, high academic standards, curriculum, and facilities were the three most often cited reasons that parents give for exercising their right to choose. Similarly, Vanourek, Manno, and Finn (1998) found that in evaluating charter schools, most students stressed academics—in their list of what they thought important about the charter schools, "good teachers" was number one, followed by "they teach it until I learn it," and "they don't let me fall behind." Greene, Howell, and Peterson (1998) found that the decision to apply for vouchers in Cleveland was motivated by academic concerns, paralleling the results Kleitz et al. (2000) found in Texas. The Public Policy Forum (1998) reported that when asked about what kind of information they most want about schools, 85 percent of parents surveyed say that they want information on teacher quality. This result comports with the survey data reported by Schneider et al. (1998) in which teacher quality was the modal response to a question about what parents valued most in education, and with the results we reported in table 5.1.

Survey data also show that the preference for academic aspects is as strong, if not stronger, among parents with lower socioeconomic status and those from racial minority groups as it is among other parents. Kleitz et al. (2000), studying why parents chose charter schools in Texas, report that parents across all income and ethnic groups say they chose charter schools in the hope of achieving a better education for their children and for smaller classes in particular—if anything the percentage of black and Hispanic parents saying that educational quality motivates their choice of charter schools is higher than that among Anglo parents. Kleitz et al. also report that support for educational quality is stronger among low-income parents than among higher-income ones, a finding similar to that reported by Schneider et al. (1998—but see Weiher and Tedin 2002).

A study by Public Agenda demonstrates that parents and students from racial minority groups are *not* more likely than whites to undervalue academics. Their nationwide study of the attitudes of high school students found that "contrary to some conventional wisdom, minority youngsters are not less dismissive of traditional academic course work than their white counterparts." Moreover, Public Agenda reported that "minority teens—both African-American and Hispanic—are more likely than white students to consider a strong academic background as the chief component of future career success" (1999, 31). These patterns among high school students are similar to those of African American parents also surveyed by Public Agenda.

These patterns are replicated in the responses of parents we interviewed. In our survey instrument, we asked parents an open ended question: "When you think about what makes a school good, what is the most important quality of the school you think about?" We recoded these answers into twelve substantive categories.[1]

We begin with the response patterns broken down by the two major dimensions of concern in this debate: race and education level (as a proxy for SES more generally). And we ask a very simple question: is there any evidence that parents from racial minority groups or parents with less education express interest in dimensions of education that are substantively different than other parents?

Across the Board, Parents Express Interest in Academic Quality

Consider figure 6.1. Note that almost *every* category that parents mention with any frequency is fundamentally important to the quality of education—and parents virtually never mention sports teams or other of the extraneous nonacademic items that some fear would drive choice. The modal category that parents of every race say is important to making a good school is teacher quality, with over 40 percent of Hispanic parents and about one-third of black and white parents giving this response. Close behind, parents also endorse the importance of the school's academic environment and curriculum. It is interesting to note the importance of parental involvement—there is a body of research that has identified the importance of parental support for high-quality education and this is

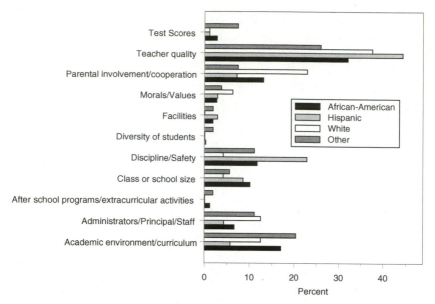

Figure 6.1. The most important aspect of schools, according to parents (by racial identification).

clearly supported by stated parental preferences. Note that discipline and safety are particularly important for Hispanic parents, but these too can be considered an essential foundation to academic performance.

At this stage it is important to note that almost no parents refer to the racial composition of the student body, and location also does not rank high on the list of things that parents *say* is important in defining a good school. Note, too, that while there are some differences between parents according to racial identification, virtually everything parents of all racial groups say contribute to good schools is in fact reasonable and believed by many to be related to effective education.

Similarly, as evident in figure 6.2, differences among parents by education level are relatively minor. The most highly educated parents assign somewhat less importance to teacher quality, and tend to view the quality of education more holistically, mentioning more frequently the importance of the academic environment and the quality of the principal than less-educated parents, but again, despite these differences, the pattern of responses indicate a strong endorsement of academic qualities in making a good school across the board.

While most previous work has focused on race and class differences and how these differences in stated preferences might affect choice behavior, in figure 6.3, we look at that question from a slightly different angle. Here we compare the differences between parents who have already chosen

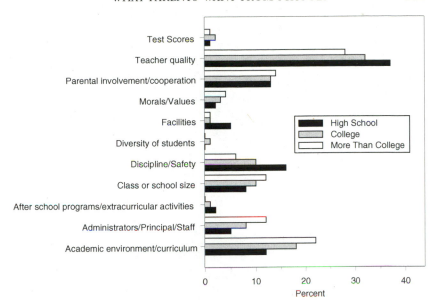

Figure 6.2. The most important aspect of schools, according to parents (by educational attainment).

charter schools and other parents. Again, there are few differences—and all of them make sense given the nature of charter schools. For example, charter-school parents are more likely to rank location among their most salient attributes of schooling. Given that most DCPS schools are neighborhood-based and charter schools are not, this is clearly reasonable. Charter schools also tend on average to be smaller than DCPS schools, so again, charter parents are not surprisingly somewhat more attuned to school and class size than are DCPS parents. Note too that charter-school parents are more likely to say that morals and "values" are important to the making of a good school than are DCPS parents. Indeed, there is evidence about the importance of values to strong schools that derives heavily from studies of Catholic schools (e.g., Bryk, Lee, and Holland 1993). Some charter-school parents obviously endorse the importance of values as a way of improving schools.

In short, results drawn from our survey data, as in the case of other parent surveys, support the idea that parents are interested in academic performance and academically sound criteria in defining a good school. While many analysts might take these results as proof that choice will be driven by academic values and that it will not exacerbate segregation or stratification, there is a potential skunk at the garden party—these optimistic findings are based on telephone survey data. In contrast, the observed search and choice behavior of parents yields more complicated (and potentially less benign) results.

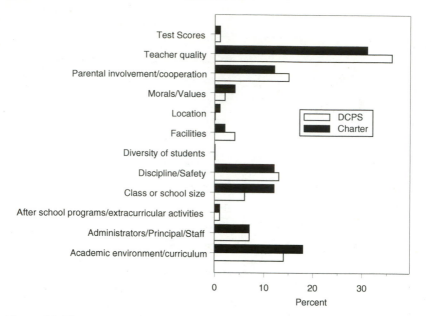

Figure 6.3. The most important aspect of schools, according to parents (by charter enrollment).

The Evidence on What Parents Want from Schools Is Mixed Using Different Data

There are fewer studies based on actual behavior than studies based on survey data. One of the most widely cited is Henig's (1990) study of enrollment patterns in Montgomery County magnet schools, in which race and class concerns were found to be central to parental choices. Henig found that both whites and minorities tended to choose schools in which their children would be less likely to be racially or socioeconomically isolated. But clearly this choice strategy points students in different directions: white families were most likely to request transfer into schools with low proportions of minorities (these schools were also located in higher-income neighborhoods), while minority families were more likely to opt for schools with higher proportions of minority students (which tended to be in low-income neighborhoods).

Similar to Henig's results, in a study of school choice in Minneapolis, Glazerman (1997) found evidence for an "own-group preference" among minorities and a strong peer group SES effect. While there was also a tendency of parents to select schools with higher test scores, the racial effect was especially strong when choosers faced the prospect of their child being in a small minority. Weiher and Tedin (2002) show that in their choice of charter schools, Texas parents were likely to "sort themselves along racial/ethnic lines . . . *in spite* of their expressed preferences, rather than in conformity with those expressed preferences."

In their study of the extensive interdistrict choice behavior in Massachusetts, Armor and Peiser (1998) found evidence of "skimming" in that families exercising choice were more affluent and more highly educated than the average in the districts they were leaving. The students who changed districts were also less likely to be minorities and their test scores were higher. Choosers were also more likely to transfer to wealthier districts, a result reported by Fossey (1994) as well.

It should be noted that given the correlation between socioeconomic status and academic performance, parents choosing to enroll their children in more affluent districts were usually also enrolling their children in higher-performing school districts and sorting out the two effects is therefore difficult. Nonetheless, the bulk of this evidence points to a much stronger effect of race and class on school-choice behavior than identified in survey data.

We should also note that the evidence of preferences based on actual behavior is constrained by rules governing choice. Henig argues that the existing composition of magnet schools is only partially a reflection of parent preferences, because regulations regarding racial balance rule out transfer requests that would lead to racial imbalance.

In sum, research based on surveys tends to find that parents of all races and social classes say they prefer schools that have good teachers and high test scores. And very few admit to being concerned by the racial or class composition of the student body. However, these stated preferences are not congruent with observed parental behavior, where researchers have found significant effects of race and class.

Using our Internet-based research, we have two other sources of data that can be used to examine the extent of the mismatch between parental stated preferences and their behavior. We will look first at results from our e-mail survey and then we turn to the data from DCSchoolSearch.com documenting parental search behavior.

WHAT DO PARENTS LIKE ABOUT SCHOOLS?
RESULTS FROM OUR E-MAIL SURVEY

As noted one of the datasets that we use in this chapter is based on an e-mail survey that we sent to users of DCSchoolSearch.com. In the e-mail survey we reminded parents of the schools that they had viewed on their recent visits to DCSchoolSearch.com. We then asked them to tell us which of the schools they viewed was their favorite. Once they noted their favor-

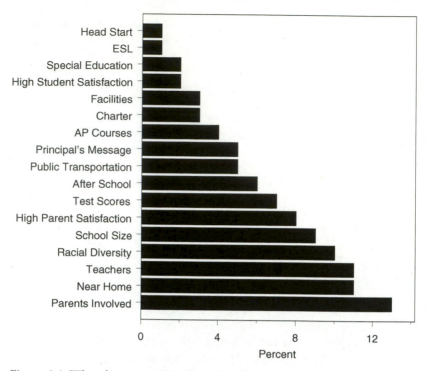

Figure 6.4. What do parents like about their favorite school? (E-mail survey.)

ite school, we presented them with a list of school attributes and asked them to assign numbers to the things they liked about the school. We treated as the most important school attribute the condition assigned the number 1, the second most important attribute was the one marked 2, and so on. We assumed that if a respondent did not assign a number, the item was not a significant contributor to the status of the school as their favorite.

Our goal was quite simple—we wanted to know the extent to which the list of school attributes that parents tell interviewers is important matches the things they "tell" their computer. We believe that this method and the one we use in the next section of this chapter may sidestep the social-desirability bias inherent in interview situations. We recommend that the reader view this evidence cautiously: there were only a small number of respondents, and how representative they are of the whole D.C. parent population is unknown (although we do a rough check later; also see our description of the survey instrument in chapter 5).

Keeping these caveats in mind, consider figure 6.4. In this analysis, we summed up the total number of attributes mentioned (we study the rank assigned to the attributes next) and then measured the relative frequency

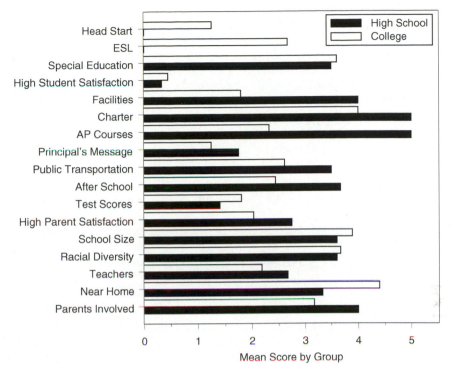

Figure 6.5. What do parents of different educational attainment like about schools? (E-mail survey.) *Note*: Bars show mean scores assigned by educational group. Higher scores indicate a more positive attitude toward the attribute.

with which each attribute was mentioned. Using this simple metric, teacher quality remains among the most important characteristics. Parental involvement is high on the list, indeed even edging out the quality of teachers. The "importance" of these characteristics differs from telephone-survey data, but together they seem to confirm the importance of sound educational attributes in making a school a parental favorite. But note that, in contrast to the telephone-survey results, the demographic makeup of the student population and the location of the school are far more often cited as contributing to the favorite status of a school than would be predicted from the survey data. Thus, while in surveys parents hardly ever *say* that these factors matter, when we use this more anonymous e-mail research tool, we find that these factors do matter.

Another way of viewing this data is presented in figure 6.5. Here we take the average score given to each attribute,[2] and following earlier analyses, we stratify the sample by education level and report their mean "liked" score for each attribute. As with survey data, there are hardly any differences by education level. But note that while there is clearly great attention given to academic considerations such as teachers, race and proximity again appear more important than in the telephone results.

We admit that these results must be qualified—the number of parents involved is small and our ability to subject these results to rigorous statistical analysis limited, but our results using the electronically collected survey results suggest that person-to-person interviews may lead to biased reports endorsing the "correct" aspects of schools and discounting factors such as race that behavioral studies have found to be important. In the next section, we turn to another way of looking at what parents consider important in defining preferred schools, which supports the findings of this exploratory e-mail survey and again calls into question the results of traditional surveys.

PREFERENCES REVEALED BY SEARCH BEHAVIOR

As explained in our description of DCSchoolSearch.com in chapter 5, we monitored the search behavior of parents as they accessed information from that site. Using these data, we hope to transcend the bias in survey research toward socially acceptable response patterns, a bias that may account for the strong verbal endorsement of academic criteria not evident in actual choice behavior. Because the search behavior we study is not as "costly" as actually moving a child to another school or school district nor is it constrained by the balancing rules inherent in many choice programs, we may get an even better idea of the place of demographics versus academics in parental preferences than by observing (expensive and constrained) actual choice.

First, we again need to note that these parents were not reflective of the general population of D.C. parents—in fact, as we have noted earlier, they were much more highly educated than D.C. parents in general. Given the discussion in chapter 5, such a skewed distribution is not surprising. In some research, this skewed distribution could cause serious problems. However, we argue that the more educated and motivated parents who are overrepresented in our sample are the most relevant group to study because it is their preferences and behavior that matters most in school-choice programs such as found in Washington.

Why? Recall that the charter schools create what Elmore (1991) calls an "option-demand" system of choice. Unlike universal-choice programs, under an option-demand system new schooling alternatives (such as charter schools) exist alongside neighborhood schools. Option-demand choice does not eliminate traditional schooling arrangements but instead seeks to implement change by offering a set of alternatives to those parents and students who actively choose to opt out of their neighborhood schools. In fact, the vast majority of choice programs currently in place in school districts across the United States are of this option-demand type.

The characteristic feature of option-demand choice is a two-stage choice process. The first stage involves the decision to leave one's own zoned neighborhood school (a parent or student "chooses to choose"). At the second stage of option-demand choice, parents/students choose their preferred school from the set of possible alternatives.

In their study of the option-demand system in New York City's District 4, Schneider, Teske and Marschall (2000) extensively studied the parents who took advantage of choice. They call these choosers "marginal consumers," and they show how the preferences and behavior of this highly motivated subset of parents mattered the most in an option-demand system. They also show that the marginal consumers are more highly educated and of higher social status than the average parent in the district (also see Meier, Wrinkle, and Polinard 2000).

Building on this work, we believe that the parents using DCSchool Search.com reflect the population of "marginal consumers" in the D.C. system. Thus, if we want to know one of the key factors affecting how option-demand school choice works and what dimensions are important in the choice process, these are the very parents we should study.

What Do Parents Search For?

What do the search data show about the preferences of these consumers? In figure 6.6, we report the percentage distribution of school attributes actually looked at by all parents overall and within the first five "steps" or "moves" they made during their visits to DCSchoolSearch.com.

The key assumption of our analysis is that search patterns reveal preferences, and, more specifically, that the attributes examined early in a search are more important to the decision maker than dimensions looked at later. We draw this assumption from several prominent psychological theories of judgment and decision making. For example, the importance of the order of search is the foundation of Tversky's (1972) elimination-by-aspects model and is supported empirically by Payne (1976; Payne, Bettman, and Johnson 1993) in his study of complex decision tasks (which certainly would include school choice). This assumption is also the foundation for the lexicographic decision rule (Hogarth 1987) and, more broadly, underlies the notion of "satisficing" (Simon 1955, 1957, 1978).

In figure 6.6, we can clearly see a strong bias toward accessing the demographic characteristics of the student population, which is in marked contrast to verbal reports about the importance (or lack thereof) of race. In our survey-data study, for example, less than 5 percent of the

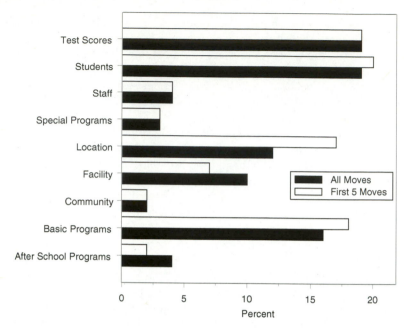

Figure 6.6. What school attributes do parents care about? Evidence from DCSchoolSearch.com.

parents who were surveyed said that the race and economic background of the students in a school were among the most important characteristics of schools. Yet almost 30 percent of parents looked at student demographic information early in their visit to DCSchoolSearch.com, making it the modal "response" category.

Aside from demographic information, parents were most likely to look at a map showing the location of the school. While the location of a school is important for a variety of obvious reasons (distance from home, access to public transportation, and so on), in a highly segregated and stratified city such as D.C., school location also conveys information about the student body.

Furthermore, while many parents *say* that they are concerned about high-quality teachers, in their search behavior, very few parents actually visited the part of the school profiles that reported that information. On a more positive note, parents did access test-score data and program data in fairly high numbers—but nowhere near a level congruent with verbal reports of preferences.[3]

In figure 6.7 we look at the effect of education on these patterns. Here, as earlier in the chapter, we simply divide the population into those with any level of college education and those without college. The concern for

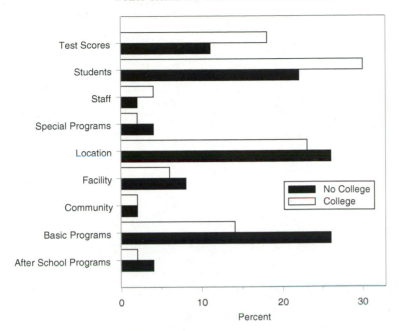

Figure 6.7. What do parents search for using DCSchoolSearch.com? (By educational attainment.)

student demographics remains the modal category of action for higher-educated parents and, indeed, is *more* evident among them than among less-educated respondents.[4]

In short, the data presented in figures 6.6 and 6.7 suggest that parents value demographic information much more highly than they admit when responding to surveys.

Another way of assessing the relative importance of race and academic performance is to look at the search paths of parents over time. While most parents are unlikely to have detailed information a priori about many schools on any given dimension, some parents are moderately or even well informed (Schneider, Teske, and Marschall 2000). If we study the aggregate search behavior of all parents, the "signal" from these more knowledgeable parents, which reflects their underlying preferences, can be detected amid the random "noise" of the others. In the literature on mass public opinion, this statistical process, in which most people have little information and yet aggregate evaluations are accurate, rational, and reflective of preferences, is sometimes referred to as the "miracle of aggregation" (Kinder 1998; see also Stimson 1991; Converse 1990).

In the next stage of analysis, we examine the aggregate search paths of all parents and we focus on the characteristics of the schools they are

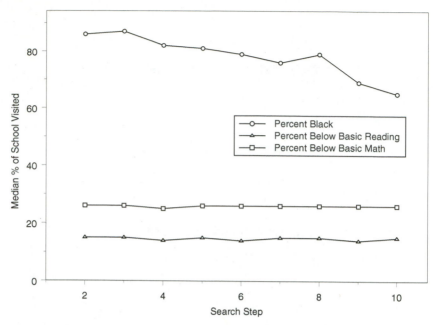

Figure 6.8. As the search progresses, the percent of black students in the school "visited" decreases. *Note*: Paths begin at step 2 because specific school information is unavailable on the first menu screen. The number of observations also varies (between 860 and 1,662) over steps as some parents travel between search menus and lists of schools repeatedly.

visiting. We record the academic performance of these schools, reflected in the percentages of math and reading scores below the basic level on the SAT-9 standardized test. And we record the demographic makeup of these schools, reflected in the percentage of black students. We gathered these data for each school visited during the first ten moves of each parent user, aggregate the results over the entire sample by computing median school characteristics, and present the results in figure 6.8.[5]

We compare the academic performance and demographic characteristics of the schools parents are visiting to the overall characteristics of all D.C. schools, and we chart the characteristics of the schools visited over time. If the racial composition of the student body does not matter to parents, then, at any given step in the search process, we should see the median percent black of the schools visited approximate the median in the District's schools as a whole and we should expect no systematic change in the pattern over the course of search (i.e., there will be no "signal" in the "noise"). But if race matters, we should see a pattern of re-

TABLE 6.1
Percent Black and Academic-Performance Indicators in the D.C. Public Schools
at Time DCSchoolSearch.com Data Were Collected

	Median	Minimum	Maximum	Mean	Standard deviation	Number of schools
Percent black	97%	9%	100%	84%	26%	166
Percent below basic, reading	27%	1%	82%	29%	17%	161
Percent below basic, math	36%	1%	100%	42%	24%	162

sponses and, by looking at the aggregate search paths over time, we should be able to determine the direction of preferences. The same argument holds for search as an indicator of the importance parents attach to academic performance.

Turning first to academic performance, figure 6.8 compares the academic performance of the schools visited by users of DCSchoolSearch.com with the overall levels of performance for all D.C. schools reported in table 6.1. On average, parents are looking at academically better-performing schools: at every point in the search, the median percentages of students scoring below basic for reading and math for the schools "visited" are lower than the actual medians for the entire population of D.C. schools. In short, a set of parents are using their existing knowledge to cull schools with poor academic performance from their choice set without even looking at the detailed school profiles. Following Tversky's (1972) elimination-by-aspects model of search, we take this as indicative of a "first elimination"—poorly performing schools have been dropped from consideration, confirming that parents are concerned about academics.

Turning to racial composition, we again compare figure 6.8 with table 6.1, and we see that the median percent black of the visited schools is lower at all times than the median for all schools. We argue that this reflects the fact that site visitors care about student-body demographics and are coupling this concern with information they already have to choose schools with fewer minority students than found in D.C. schools overall. But note that, in contrast to the pattern for academic scores, the median percent black has a downward trend as search proceeds. This, we believe, is a function of how parents learn about schools using the search features of the site.

The number of parents looking at specific school attributes at any given step charted in figure 6.8 fluctuates as some of them return to one of the

TABLE 6.2
The Decrease in Percent Black of Schools Searched Is Significant
While There Is No Significant Change in Test Scores

	Step coefficient (robust std. error)	Constant (robust std. error)	R^2	Estimated ρ
Percent black	−2.5 *	93.1	.89	−.17
	(.35)	(1.7)		
Percent below basic reading	−.02	14.7	.99	−.64
	(.04)	(.22)		
Percent below basic math	.04	25.7	.99	−.27
	(.04)	(.26)		

* $p < .01$.

Each row of table 6.2 reports the estimates of a simple regression of the school characteristic of interest on the step in the search process. Since these data are, loosely, time series, we tested for autocorrelation. Since standard diagnostic methods suggest an AR(1) process (ρ measures the amount of first-order autocorrelation in the residuals), the models are estimated using Prais-Winsten (1954) regression with robust (heteroscedasticity-consistent) standard errors to account for the variation in sample size over time. As an additional test, differences between the endpoints (step 2 and step 10) and between each step in the path are tested using a conservative nonparametric test for differences in matched pairs of observations that requires no assumptions about the distributions of the random variables (Arbuthnott 1710; Snedecor and Cochran 1989).

site's several search engines to generate a new list of alternative schools that meet criteria they specify—such as geographic location, test scores, and student-body demographics. Indeed, at any given step, 20–25 percent of parents are assembling new lists of schools using one of the site's search mechanisms and then, at subsequent steps, delving deeper into the specific characteristics of the schools that met their search criteria.

We believe that a number of these parents are combining the information they already have about the demographic composition of schools and the demographic makeup of D.C. neighborhoods with new information learned from their search to select a new school to view in depth. As they do this, they focus on specific schools and schools in neighborhoods that they believe have a lower percentage of black students—a selection that is often correct. Thus, as search proceeds, parents increasingly "visit" schools that have lower percentages of black students. As reported in table 6.2 in the case of the percent of black students, the median viewed at step 10 is significantly lower than that at step 2 ($p < .01$). For reading and math below basic level these differences are not significant ($p = .44$ and .17 respectively). Furthermore, only the coefficient for percent black is statistically significant ($p < .01$). Substantively our analysis predicts that the median percent black of schools viewed declines from 88 percent to 68 percent in nine steps, while the percent below basic reading and math stays the same over the number of search steps.

Searching for Schools Is a Complex Task

Education is a complex good with many dimensions, and as parents evaluate schools they have to strike a balance between the different attributes of education schools represent. The complexity of that task is compounded by the fact that the level of existing information they have about schools is often limited. In turn, parents using DCSchoolSearch.com are engaged in a complicated search over a large number of schools representing very different combinations of attributes, and they are being presented with information that is more comprehensive and more detailed than most parents have. As any complicated search progresses, searchers have to meld existing information with new information, a process that is structured by existing preferences.

While we would need other techniques developed by behavioral-decision researchers to confirm this proposition more fully, one possible explanation for our findings is not that parents care more about racial composition than academics, but that they are concerned about the level and quality of the information they do have about demographics. In other words, they are engaged in a more intense search for information about student demographics for one of several related reasons: because they have less a priori information, because they have less confidence in that information, and/or because they want more accurate information than they already have. Any of a combination of these conditions would yield behavior consistent with the elimination-by-aspects theory discussed above.

Despite our limited ability at present to specify which decision- and information-processing rules actually drive the search strategies of different parents, it is clear from our existing data that parents care about the racial composition of schools as reflected in their search processes.

In short, consistent with verbal reports, parents in our study are "visiting" schools with better academic performance—but, despite an unwillingness to admit this in telephone or face-to-face surveys, they are also seeking out schools with a lower percentage of black students. Thus, when we move our research technique away from surveys, in which social desirability clearly affects response patterns, to more anonymous search behavior, the results are not as optimistic as those based on survey data. Moreover, this search behavior is congruent with preferences revealed by the studies of actual-choice behavior—parents do care about academics but they also care very much about school demographics—something they will not admit to verbally.

We return to this issue in the conclusion of the book, when we integrate this finding along with the others we are about to present to offer our overall assessment of the hype and the hope surrounding charter schools.

School Choice and the Importance
of Parental Information

ONE OF THE CENTRAL BATTLEGROUNDS in the fight over school choice is information: Who has it? Who uses it? To what effect? In this chapter we review some of the relevant theories regarding how individuals gather and use information about politics, public goods, and schools. This sets the background for the analysis we present in the next chapter, where we explore how parents gather and use information about schools using data from our web site, DCSchoolSearch.com (described in chapter 5).

The arguments over choice have taken on many dimensions but, at their core, many rest on the link between choice and the (presumed) superiority of markets. Proponents of choice, whose contributions range from those of seminal economist Milton Friedman (1962) to the work of traditional education researchers such as Goldring and Shapira (1993), to the neoinstitutional work of political scientists Chubb and Moe (1990), have advanced strong normative arguments in favor of parent/consumer sovereignty. While coming from diverse perspectives, these works share the belief that by expanding the right to choose, parents and students will be more satisfied with the education they receive. Furthermore, the argument continues, under the pressure of consumer demand, schools will improve, boosting student performance and the overall quality of American education.

In response, others have argued that choice programs may not provide the efficiency gains assumed by supporters, and that choice may further erode an already inequitable education system (see, for example, Henig 1994; Smith and Meier 1995a). At the theoretical center of this debate is the reasoning of neoclassical microeconomics, market theory, and the efficacy of consumer choice. As we noted in chapter 1, asymmetries of information play a central role in this aspect of the debate over school choice. Here the debate centers on who has information about schools and how choice will affect the acquisition and use of information.

Even proponents of school choice recognize that the information requirements of fully formed competitive markets will likely not be met in the market for schools. Education is a difficult product to describe and people will continue to disagree about the outcomes by which to judge its quality: Is it test scores? Self-esteem? Graduation rates? Earnings? Socialization into democratic norms? The list goes on.

Moreover, the level and quality of information about schools is often poorer than information about consumer goods, and there are few intermediaries or third parties (such as the Consumer Union) that independently "test" products and disseminate information about the quality and reliability of schools. In turn, most parents have very low levels of reliable information about the schools their children attend.

In response, debate has often focused on the incentives for "rational" parents to learn more about the schooling options available to them due to the introduction of choice. As we argued earlier in the book, from this perspective, a prime reason for such low information levels is a simple benefit/cost calculation: in a system without school choice, the costs of gathering information about schools are high relative to the benefits of such information—why invest time and resources in gathering information about schools when your "choice" of schools is determined by geographic attendance zones? Faced with this adverse calculation, most parents remain "rationally" ignorant. The next step in the argument is clear: if, through choice, parents are given a reason to know more about schools, they will become more informed. As Chubb and Moe put it: "In a system where virtually all the important choices are the responsibility of others, parents have little incentive to be informed or involved. In a market-based system, much of the responsibility would be shifted to parents (their choices would have consequences for their children's education), and their incentives to become informed and involved would be dramatically different" (1990, 564).

Other scholars exploring levels of information about public policies and politics have developed similar ideas. Lupia and McCubbins argue that the search for information is driven by a "calculus of decision" that is anchored by three fundamental points: "First, learning requires effort. Second, effort is a scarce resource for everyone. Third, and as a consequence of the first two facts, *people choose* what and when to learn" (2000, 51, emphasis in the original). Clearly, Lupia and McCubbins's calculus points in the same direction as Chubb and Moe's: paying the cost of gathering and processing additional information makes sense only if the decision maker knows that the new information will help her avoid a mistake or help her make a better choice.

This calculus is evident in an ongoing conceptual shift among cognitive scientists in which humans are no longer viewed as "cognitive misers" (who invariably seek to reduce the effort needed to make good decisions) but who are now viewed as "cognitive managers," individuals "who deploy mental resources strategically as a function of the perceived importance and tractability of the problem" (Tetlock 2000, 240). From this viewpoint, people "decide how to decide," choosing decision tools that reflect the benefits (decision accuracy) and costs (cognitive effort) of the particular decision task.

The ongoing shift in theoretical perspectives to situational decision making and humans as cognitive managers has not yet been incorporated into the debate over school choice. Rather, there is a long-standing argument made by critics of choice that education is a complex good, difficult to describe in a way that people understand, and that less-educated parents (who probably stand to benefit most from any system of expanded choice) are the least able to access and analyze information. Recall the Twentieth Century Fund report we cited earlier that argued that parents are not "natural 'consumers' of education" and that "few parents of any social class appear willing to acquire the information necessary to make active and informed educational choices" (Ascher, Fruchter, and Berne 1996, 40–41). Also recall that Bridge (1978) called the lack of information the "Achilles' heel" of choice.

In short, critics of choice argue that, given the lack of good information among "parent/consumers," the success of choice reforms is unlikely, especially for less-educated parents. But they don't address the argument that under certain circumstances enough parents may find shortcuts to decisions or otherwise be sufficiently motivated to gather information to make reasonable choices.

PARENTS (AND CITIZENS) HAVE LOW INFORMATION LEVELS

While many issues surrounding school choice have been a battleground for conflicting ideologies and the results of studies are often dismissed as ideologically motivated, even for analysts sympathetic to choice the fact that parents know so little about their children's schools should come as no surprise—social scientists have long documented that citizens have little information about politics and a wide range of public policies besides education.

Dating back to at least as early as the classic studies of elections by Lazarsfeld et al. (1944), political scientists have shown that most citizens have poor information about their political choices. The data are so consistent that Bartels asserts that: "The political ignorance of the American voter is one of the best documented data of modern political science" (1996, 194).

Since electoral politics are removed from the daily world of most citizens, some analysts have argued that their knowledge about candidates might be lower than their knowledge about the *policies* of government that may directly affect them. However, in several studies, Kuklinski and his colleagues find a citizenry woefully misinformed about basic aspects of public policies (see, for example, Kuklinski et al. 1996). More generally, Zaller and Feldman dismiss the suggestion that citizens are likely to learn more about matters important to them, arguing that the "tendency appears not to be very great or very widespread" (1992, 18; also see Price and Zaller 1993; Delli Carpini and Keeter 1996).

Empirical evidence about what parents know about schools, even in districts with choice, reflects this lack of information—a pattern that is more pronounced among parents with lower socioeconomic status. For example, data from the Alum Rock demonstration program showed that awareness of the voucher program was lower among parents with less formal education and those who had lower expectations for their children's educational attainment. In a survey of parents in Montgomery County, Maryland, Henig (1996) found that, even among parents whose children attended magnet schools, many, especially minority parents, said that they had never heard the terms "magnet school" or "magnet program." Schneider, Teske, and Marschall (2000) found that parents from lower socioeconomic status had poor information-search strategies and were isolated from social networks, one of the most efficient ways in which parents with higher socioeconomic status learn about schools. Howell (2004b) reports that less than 30 percent of parents in underperforming schools in Massachusetts knew that their schools had failed to meet the NCLB standards of "annual yearly progress." Reflecting Schneider, Teske, and Marschall's finding regarding the effects of socioeconomic status on knowledge, Howell found that minority and disadvantaged parents had less information about their child's school than white and more advantaged parents, and parents with limited English proficiency had even less.

Parents in Our Study Also Know Little about Their School's Performance

Given this research, it is not surprising that we too find low levels of information among parents in our study. As an example consider parental accuracy regarding test scores—one of the prime indicators governments throughout the nation advocate as a way to judge schools and to enforce accountability. Our measure of information accuracy was constructed by computing the difference between the response to the Wave 1 survey question: "What do you think is the percentage of children in your child's school reading at or above the basic level?" and the actual percent at or above basic on the SAT-9 standardized test reported by the school. We treat this difference in the perceived and the actual level of test performance as an indicator of the quality of information parents have.[1]

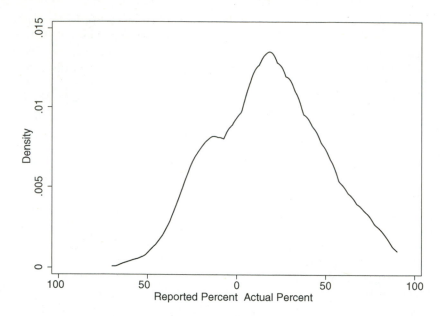

Figure 7.1. Parents tend to overestimate the academic success of their child's school. *Note*: Kernel-smoothed density plot of parent's error in response when asked about the percent of pupils in their child's school reading at or above the basic level. Number of observations = 518.

One indicator of the poor quality of information parents have about academic performance is immediately evident: about one-third of the parents we interviewed simply said that they were unable to answer the question. But even when parents did estimate the test scores of their children's schools, we find considerable error. In figure 7.1, we present a kernel-smoothed density plot of the parent's observed error, computed using the difference in percentages described above.[2] As the figure shows, the range of observed error is large (the standard deviation is approximately 30 percent) and the mean error is about +18 percent, indicating that, on average, not only are parents likely to be wrong, but they are likely to err by *overestimating* the academic quality of their child's school. We believe that the propensity to overestimate academic performance is congruent with findings we will present in chapters 9 and 10, where we show that parents are quite satisfied with their own child's school, often despite a dismal reality.

Presaging another theme we explore in later chapters, we turn now to a brief examination of the degree to which charter-school parents are more or less likely to have erroneous information about their school's test scores. To do so, we estimate the following simple regression of the absolute error on charter enrollment and a set of control variables:

$$
\begin{aligned}
|\text{Error}_i| = {} & \beta_0 + \beta_1 \text{Charter}_i + \beta_2 \text{White}_i + \beta_3 \text{Hispanic}_i + \beta_4 \text{Other Race}_i \\
& + \beta_5 \text{Time in DC}_i + \beta_6 \text{Time in neighborhood}_i + \beta_7 \text{Employed}_i \\
& + \beta_8 \text{Frequency of volunteering at school}_i + \beta_9 \text{PTA member}_i \\
& + \beta_{10} \text{Married}_i + \beta_{11} \text{Frequency of church attendance}_i \\
& + \beta_{12} \text{Number of organizational memberships}_i \\
& + \beta_{13} \text{Number of educational discussants}_i + \beta_{14} \text{School Grade}_i \\
& + \beta_{15} \text{Years of education}_i + \beta_{16} \text{Years of education}^2_i \\
& + \beta_{17} \text{Time in school}_i + \beta_{18} \text{Student's grade level}_i + \varepsilon_i
\end{aligned} \tag{7.1}
$$

where $\varepsilon_i \sim N(0, \sigma^2)$.

Most of the variables in equation 7.1 are self-explanatory and are ones that are frequently used by education analysts (and will be used throughout this book). Charter is an indicator variable coded 1 if the student is enrolled in a charter school—and is the key variable of interest in this analysis.

Other variables in the equation are used as controls. White, Hispanic, and other race are a series of binary indicators for self-reported race, with black the modal and omitted category. Time in D.C. and in the neighborhood, and time in school are measured in years, as are the amount of formal education and its square (to allow for likely nonlinearity in the effect of socioeconomic status on error/information levels). Employed, married, and PTA membership are all measured with binary variables. The frequency of church attendance, included as a measure of social connectedness and involvement, is a seven-category response, treated here as continuous. The number of social organizations and educational discussants are included as additional measures of social involvement and the potential strength of information networks (see Schneider et al. 1997 on the importance of networks). School grade is a measure of the parent's satisfaction with the school (see chapter 9) and here is simply the numerical conversion to the 0.0 to 4.0 scale of the letter grade (F, D, . . . , A) that the parent assigns to her child's school. Finally, grade level is simply the child's reported grade, K–12, with K coded as 0.

We estimate the vector of coefficients, β using the least squares estimator and present the results in table 7.1. As the table shows, controlling for the other covariates we find that charter parents are an average of 4.1 percentage points *less* correct in their report of the percent of students reading at grade level in their child's school. In short, parents as consumers do not have accurate information about the test scores of their child's schools—and, equally important, they are likely to think that their schools are doing better than they really are.[3] Moreover, this occurs even in a system with extensive choice and is even more pronounced among parents who have

TABLE 7.1
Charter Parents Make Larger Errors in Reporting the
Academic Achievement of Their Schools

	Coefficient (Standard Error)
Charter	4.11* (2.14)
White	−3.78 (5.13)
Hispanic	.412 (4.96)
Other	.027 (4.78)
Years in D.C.	−.150 (.254)
Years in neighborhood	−.151 (.184)
Employed	4.84* (2.59)
Frequent volunteer	−.650 (2.75)
PTA member	2.84 (2.29)
Married	−6.35* (2.21)
Frequency of church attendance	−2.81 (2.54)
Number of organizations	−1.47* (.535)
Number of discussants	−.337 (.245)
School grade	−4.14* (1.22)
Years of education	−3.48 (3.26)
Years of education^2	.158 (.122)
Time in school	−.688 (.707)
Student's grade level	−.214 (.356)
Constant	65.79* (22.28)
Omnibus F	3.69*

* $p < .10$ two-tailed. $R^2 = .11$, RMSE = 19.14.

Source of data is Wave 1 of panel survey; final number of observations is 489 after listwise deletion of missing values. Dependent variable is the absolute difference between the reported percent of students in the respondent's child's school reading at or above the basic level and the actual percent.

taken advantage of the opportunity to choose. We will return to the importance of this pattern at several points throughout the book.

Consumers of Private Goods Also Have Low Information Levels

While a pattern of low information about politics and public policies is well known to social scientists, research on how much information consumers have about private goods points to a surprisingly similar pattern. According to Kardes, the "typical consumer is exposed to a relatively small subset of available information about products and services, and the consumer attends to an even smaller subset of information to which he or she has been exposed. Not all information is encountered, and not all encountered information is attended to and processed" (1994, 400). Similarly Bloch, Sherrel, and Ridgway argue that "consumers have surprisingly little enthusiasm for the pursuit [of information], even when buying expensive or socially risky goods" (1986, 119). In short, even in markets for private goods, consumers typically spend little time gathering and analyzing information about the products and services they purchase (see, e.g., Fiske and Taylor 1991; Bettman 1986; Cohen and Chakrovarti 1990; Tybout and Artz 1994).

Economists, especially those in business schools, have been struggling for some time to explain how markets can be efficient given poorly informed consumers—and advocates of school choice are coming to realize that they are faced with the same challenge. It is simply not enough to say that given choice parents will become informed—there is too much evidence to the contrary. But there is also too much evidence to simply say that since information levels are low, parents should not be given choice. Indeed, America's markets for consumer goods are remarkably efficient even given low information levels. By extension, there may be no reason to expect that markets for schools cannot operate given low parent-information levels.

Given the puzzling disjuncture between low information and reasonably well-functioning markets and given a similar disjuncture between low political information and a reasonably well-performing democracy, many social scientists have begun to study ways in which citizens can make good decisions about politics and public policies in the face of low information levels.

There are at least two research traditions that have sought to "square" the empirical evidence demonstrating low information with the functioning of markets. Not surprisingly, these lines of argument have also appeared in the study of school choice. One line of argument emphasizes cognitive shortcuts; the other emphasizes the importance of a small cadre of "market makers." We review these in turn.

HEURISTICS AND SHORTCUTS TO DECISIONS

Given that the calculus of decision making involves balancing benefits and costs, many researchers have looked at how individuals can reduce the costs of decision making by employing heuristics, often described as "cognitive rules of thumb." The literature on heuristics is large, and much of it is rooted in the work of Daniel Kahneman (see, for example, the classic collection of studies in Kahneman, Slovic, and Tversky 1982). Current research employs economic, psychological, and often ecological theories to move away from traditional models of rationality in which decision makers have limitless knowledge and lots of time in which to make choices to develop models that show how humans employ simple rules for making decisions with limited mental resources (see, for example, Todd and Gigerenzer 1999). According to these studies, heuristics allow decision makers to make smart choices, judgments, and predictions in a way congruent with Simon's concept of bounded rationality.

Researchers have identified three main categories of heuristics that affect the way people make decisions: the availability heuristic, the representativeness heuristic, and the anchoring and adjustment heuristic. When the availability heuristic is used, events that evoke emotions, and are vivid and easy to imagine, are likely to be available in the memory of an individual and hence influence the decision maker. The representativeness heuristic makes the decision maker assess the likelihood of an event occurring based on experiences with similar events before. The anchoring and adjustment heuristic is invoked when decision makers make assessments by starting at an initial value and continuously adjusting it to reach a final decision. While many argue that heuristics can lead to quick and often effective decisions, as we will see later, the psychological processes imbedded in heuristics may lead to inferences that are systematically biased and error prone.

While work on heuristics has proceeded the furthest in psychology and is having profound effects on economics, the idea of heuristics as shortcuts is increasingly known in policy studies. For example, central to Popkin's concept of the "Reasoning Voter" is the concept of "low information rationality," which refers to a method of economically combining learning and information from past experiences, daily life, the media, and political campaigns (1994, 7). The use of heuristics and information generated as a by-product of other aspects of life makes citizen choices easier and more rational than are typically portrayed.

Along these lines, Kuklinski and Hurley argue that there is evidence that the use of heuristics, specifically taking cues from political elites, serves citizens well: "[O]rdinary citizens can make good political judgments even when they lack general political acumen or information about the specific issue at hand by taking cues from political actors" (1994, 730). In a similar vein, Lupia argues that, as

an alternative to the costly acquisition of encyclopedic information, voters may choose to employ information shortcuts. For example, voters can acquire information about the preferences or opinions of friends, coworkers, political parties or other groups, which they may then use to infer how a proposition will affect them. The appeal of these information shortcuts is that they generally require relatively little effort to acquire. (1994, 63)

Lupia and McCubbins extend this position, arguing that in contrast to "encyclopedic knowledge," citizens can use shortcuts to acquire sufficient knowledge to make the same decisions they otherwise would if they were expert. For Lupia and McCubbins, people "who lack information solve enormously complex problems every day" (1998, 5). In their approach, people who lack encyclopedic information not only use simple cues, but they are systematic, selective, and strategic about the cues they do use.

Regarding school choice, Stein and Bickers rely on heuristics to explain how people gather and use information about school quality as they choose places to live. For these authors, "direct factual information is only one means for making a link between preferences and the locational choices. We find that, controlling for direct factual information, movers are able to sort themselves into jurisdictions in which their children can attend objectively better schools. What we infer from this is that movers have access to information that enables them to make rational choices, but this information is generated through the use of heuristics" (1998, 90).

There are many types of shortcuts to information. Some rely on identifying expert decision makers and taking cues from them. Others rely on networks in which members tap the flow of information among friends and colleagues.[4] While most of these works rely on verbal information passed along through personal contacts or by relying on experts, another shortcut uses visible cues.

The most popular example comes from the work of George Kelling, who has argued that people can use simple visual cues to judge the safety of urban neighborhoods. In developing this idea, Kelling and his colleagues (Kelling and Coles 1996; Kelling and Wilson 1982) present the compelling image of *broken windows* as an indicator of neighborhood quality. The process they describe is deceptively simple: If windows in a factory or a shop are broken and remain that way, a passerby walks away with the idea that no one cares about the neighborhood. In turn, more windows will be broken and the sense of disorder intensifies. In a self-propelling process, law-abiding individuals avoid the area, thinking that the area is dangerous. This leaves the area open to criminals—in turn, the area becomes increasingly unsafe. Thus, in Kelling's view, even small disorders can lead to larger and larger disorders and high crime rates.[5]

While this body of work is mostly concerned with the relationship between observable conditions and crime, there are in fact visual cues that parents can use to tell how well a school is "working." Schneider et al.

(1999) have shown that the observable physical condition of schools is correlated with performance and that simply walking by a school and noting the presence of graffiti or the condition of the school building provides cues to school performance.

In short, visual cues can aid parents in their selection of a school by allowing parents to relatively easily find out about the conditions about which they care. If a school building is in good working order and free of graffiti (especially the inside of the building), parents who care about academic performance can infer that these conditions mean better test scores. And parents who care about safety can infer that a school that is relatively free of graffiti is also a safer school (Schneider et al. 1999). From this perspective, the fact that parents have a hard time estimating the actual test scores in a school may not be that important—they can develop a set of heuristics that can guide them to knowing if a school is a good school or not without incurring the costs of pinpoint accuracy.

While much of this work on heuristics initially led to a "new optimism" about rational decision making, questions are now accumulating about how well heuristics actually work. Backing off from his earlier endorsement of the benefits of heuristics, Kuklinski more recently has argued that at the same time that political scientists are stressing the importance of heuristics as aids to rational decision making, cognitive psychologists are refocusing on how the automatic and unconscious use of heuristics can produce dysfunctional effects. Basically, behavioral-decision theorists have now identified many biases and problems in human decision-making processes that affect the quality of decisions that flow from relying on heuristics. For Kuklinski and Quirk, among the most important impediments to good decision making are the facts that "people use arbitrary starting points to anchor estimates, use accessibility in memory to estimate frequency; use a source's attractiveness to judge her credibility; and draw inferences from predetermined scripts and stereotypes" (2000, 166). It is bad enough that these practices can lead to flawed judgments, but, according to Kuklinski, these practices are "hardwired" so that people use unreliable rules of thumb without even realizing they are doing so, and the resulting errors may not be easily corrected (see also Piattelli-Palmarini 2000). From this perspective, heuristics can produce biased and inaccurate decisions that are hard to avoid and hard to correct.

Jones also shows fundamental biases in decision making derive from "hardwired" limits in the information-processing capacity of humans. In Jones's view, as humans are presented with information, they process it and in so doing transform it: "To react to information, people must attend to it, interpret it, and devise an appropriate strategy to act on it" (2001, 8). And, as they do so, Jones argues humans become "disproportionate decision makers."

At the core of this idea of proportionate and disproportionate decision making is the importance of the context in which information is presented. Also central to Jones's argument is the idea of attention shifts. In some contexts, information will be ignored, but if the context changes, the same piece of information may become central. For Jones, this shifting attention is built into the structure of the human brain (we are presented with many parallel streams of information, but we can only process information serially; cf. Holyoak and Spellman 1993) and leads to lurching changes in the attention that humans (and their institutions) pay to problems.

Also building on the link between the "hardwiring" of human information-processing systems and choice, Lodge and his colleagues question the "rational" foundation of political and policy decision making. In Lodge's model, beliefs and attitudes are strongly driven by affect. For Lodge, as people form or revise their overall impressions of persons, places, events, or issues, they extract the affective value of the message and virtually instantaneously update their summary evaluation "online" and in real time (Lodge and Steenbergen 1995; Lodge and Taber 2000). This "running tally" represents an integration of all prior evaluations of the object and is available for subsequent evaluations of persons, groups, events, or issues. The key to Lodge's model is that affect is linked *immediately* to objects in long-term memory and decays slowly; but the cognitive considerations that went into the evaluation associations appear to be forgotten far more quickly. In short, *affect,* not rational cognition, is the key to understanding evaluations and decision making.

Lodge and his colleagues also show that all political leaders, groups, issues, symbols, and ideas are "affectively tagged"—they are valued as positive or negative—and this evaluation is linked directly to the concept in long-term memory. This affective component comes automatically and inescapably to mind upon exposure to the associated object. The result has been termed "hot cognition"—political beliefs are affectively charged and rather than dispassionate, rational, "cold" cognition, people's judgments are driven by affect.[6]

Sniderman also raises question about the role of heuristics. While not as pessimistic about heuristics as Kuklinski or as questioning of the basis for cognitive decision making as Lodge, Sniderman is concerned with the context of decision making and that those studying heuristics often do not pay sufficient attention to the task environment in which heuristics are invoked. According to Sniderman, "[v]ariations in the organization of alternatives across issues, era, and regimes have much to do with the conditional dynamics of public choice" (2000, 83). In Sniderman's view, while heuristics may be hardwired into humans, which heuristic is invoked and how much effort is used by the individual to counter the biases of heuristics is conditional on the benefits and costs (that is, the calculus) of the decision task, which in turn is at least partly driven by the institutional milieu in which the decision is embedded. It should be noted that the importance of how people's options are structured and presented has been long recognized by individuals who study policy agendas and the dynamics of public choice (see, for example, Riker 1982, 1984; Austen-Smith and Riker 1987, on the importance of the alternatives in structuring the outcome of decisions; or Baumgartner and Jones's 1993 work on agendas and policy outcomes).

THEORIES OF DECISION MAKING AND SCHOOL CHOICE

These types of issues are central to theories of decision making, but they have not substantially affected how people go about studying school choice. But clearly, for example, affect may bias judgment about schools: for example, if a person has a positive affect toward charter schools, then judgments about schools will be driven by that affect, resulting in biased choice. In this light, the fact that charter schools are supported by a "movement" generating positive news stories and great expectations may have a profound effect on how people judge them. In fact, we have already noted that charter-school parents are likely to overestimate the test scores of the schools their children attend. And, as we shall see in chapters 9 and 10, charter schools do benefit from very positive, perhaps inflated, affect, reflected in highly positive evaluations across a whole range of school conditions at the time when parents first enroll their children in them. However, we also see that the harsh realities of urban education erode that positive affect over time.

We deal with this pattern and other issues of affect and choice in later chapters, but next we focus on an alternative explanation to how education can be improved by choice in the face of low information, focusing on what Schneider, Teske, and Marschall (2000) call the "marginal" consumer.

THE "AVERAGE" CONSUMER VERSUS THE "MARGINAL" CONSUMER

While (overly) simple models of markets employ assumptions of full information and rational consumers, empirical studies of competitive private markets show that only a subset of consumers gathers information about their purchases (Katona and Mueller 1955; Newman 1999; Slama and Williams 1990; Thorelli and Engledow 1980). These consumers are more "involved" with the product and can leverage change in markets, even when the average consumer is not well informed. For many, it is the behavior of this subset of consumers that creates competitive markets.

These consumers have attracted a variety of labels. Thorelli and Engledow (1980) call them "information seekers" and estimate that they comprise 10–20 percent of the population. Feick and Price (1987) have an even smaller population in mind: they label the upper third of this already small population of information seekers "market mavens" and credit this subpopulation with driving competitive markets.

The popular press has weighed in on this issue as well. In his popular book, *The Anatomy of Buzz,* Emanuel Rosen (2000) focuses on a population about the same size as Feick and Price identify and links the actions of this small group of individuals to social and purchasing trends. In his even more widely read book *The Tipping Point,* Gladwell (2000) emphasizes the importance of a relatively small population in driving market and societal change. Gladwell develops "the law of the few" and shows how "connectors, mavens, and salesmen" can drive social and economic "epidemics." Similarly, Berry and Kellery (2003) stress the importance of "influentials" in spreading information and informing purchase decisions by their ability to control word-of-mouth discussions.

In a more scholarly study, Goldsmith, Flynn, and Goldsmith write that market mavens:

> are very involved in the marketplace. They are exposed to a variety of media where they seek out and acquire information about products, services, stores, and shopping and buying in general. Thus, they are quite knowledgeable about shopping and buying and are eager to share their expertise/opinions with other consumers, who often request information from them. . . . The characteristics of the market maven suggest that they tend to be opinion leaders. (2003, 54)

To use Kellery and Berry's term, market mavens are important because of the "social capital of conversations" and how they affect the flow of information through networks, which in turn influences decisions and product evaluation.[7]

Teske et al. (1993) extended the idea of market mavens from work in the market for consumer goods to the local market for public goods, identifying a set of "marginal consumers" who are informed about schools and who exert pressure on local schools to be more efficient (see also Dowding, John, and Biggs 1994; John, Dowding, and Biggs 1995). Teske et al. applied this concept in their examination of households that gather extensive information about municipal services (especially education) prior to moving. They conclude that:

> High-income movers have more accurate information about their schools and those who report they care about local schools are also more accurate

about local public services and taxes. These important households gather accurate comparative information and they act upon this information when shopping around before entering a community. But even more important for understanding the local market for public goods, these citizens are the very people that communities have the strongest incentives to attract. As communities seek to attract these higher-income individuals, the resulting competition may benefit all citizens, including non-movers. (1993, 709)

From our perspective, one of the most important roles marginal consumers play is the systemic effect their choices have: by becoming informed and shopping around, the marginal consumer can help the entire market become more competitive and efficient. As Rhoads argues, in many markets these marginal consumers generate "competitive pressures that help keep prices reasonable for less-informed, non-searching consumers as well" (1985, 144).

Indeed, there is evidence that even a small number of parents exercising choice can affect entire school systems. Such leverage was clearly evident in the reaction of poorly performing schools in Florida facing sanctions under the Opportunity Scholarships Program, created under the Bush/Brogan A+ Plan that went into effect in 1999 (Chatterji 2004). This was evident in Mesa, Arizona, where the loss of 1,600 students to charter schools was enough to pressure the 70,000-student school district into making reforms (Toch 1998). Armor and Peiser (1998) show a similar change in Massachusetts, after the adoption of interdistrict choice. The United States is essentially embarked on a nationwide experiment incorporating this idea, as evident in the transfer provisions built into the No Child Left Behind Act.

How can this happen? Teske et al. (2001) identify two mechanisms by which a small number of parents choosing charter schools can leverage systemic change in the public schools. The first is built on the diffusion of innovation. As we have seen at several points earlier in this book, many proponents of charter schools argue that, because of their greater freedom and fewer bureaucratic rules, charter schools can be "laboratories" for change and experimentation that will provide examples for the reform of the traditional public schools. Advocates believe that, given their greater freedom, charter schools will design new and original curricula and programs, that they will experiment with new models of school organization, and that they will develop new methods to encourage parental involvement. Those innovations that prove successful, the argument goes, will be conveyed to the education community at large and eventually adopted by traditional public schools (see especially Miron and Nelson 2000, 2002; Wohlstetter and Griffin 1998; but see Lubienski 2003).

The second mechanism is built directly on the idea of market competition. Specifically, to the extent that the traditional public schools lose students to charter schools and to the extent that penalties accrue for this loss, then schools losing "market share" should respond by improving their product. In this view, the elements necessary to propel change are competition and the prospect of financial reward or penalty based on performance and "customer" response. This financial incentive could aid in the flow of information concerning successful education programs and techniques between charter and traditional schools: if traditional schools face budget losses from declining market share, the incentive to adopt programs that have been successful elsewhere should increase. Indeed, charter school laws around the country have in effect "codified" this argument by mandating that some percentage of per-pupil educational expenses follows the child to the charter school, leaving less money in the traditional public school district (although also leaving fewer children to educate).

In these approaches, change is leveraged by the behavior of a small number of parents who opt out of the traditional public schools. The recent explosion of school-choice options within single school districts expands dramatically the ability of parents to shop around for schools without incurring the high cost of relocating to a different community or incurring the tuition costs of private education. Schneider, Teske, and Marschall (2000) examine the effects of intradistrict choice in their study of two New York City school districts. They found a large enough subset of active and informed parents to drive the demand side of the marketlike setting and pressure schools to compete. In other words, choice has created the conditions for a corps of "marginal consumers" to emerge who pressure the schools to perform better.

The implications of the concept of the "marginal consumer" for schools is fundamental. While proponents such as Chubb and Moe (1990) and Coons and Sugarman (1978) imply that the full competitive benefits of choice at the systemic level require high levels of information across *all* parents, the idea of the marginal consumer suggests that the behavior of a smaller group of parents may be sufficient to produce significant benefits. If competitive markets require that some but not all consumers be sufficiently informed so as to pressure producers to deliver services efficiently, then the critiques of school choice based on the argument that *on average* parents have too little information to drive education reform are wrong.

There is clear appeal to this idea of markets driven by a small number of mavens—empirically we know that most parents remain uninformed of much that goes on in their children's schools. But it is also true that we can find a set of parents highly involved in and knowledgeable about schools. Thus shifting the analytic focus from the average to the marginal consumer avoids one of the most seemingly telling critiques of choice. But there are also major problems with the shift of focus to the marginal consumer—most fundamentally, the concept is underspecified.

For example, the number of marginal consumers necessary to drive the market is vague. While there seems to be a consensus that around 10 percent of the consumer population is enough to drive change, there is little or no scientific evidence underlying this estimate. The definition of who is a marginal consumer is also less than precise. In Teske et al. (1993), it is high-income movers; in Meier, Wrinkle, and Polinard's (2000) study of choice in Texas, it is Anglo parents; in Schneider, Teske, and Marschall (2000) it is all individuals who have chosen to exercise their right to choose in an option-demand system. In each case, there are two shared ideas—that the individuals who have been characterized as marginal consumers are seeking more information about schooling and education policy, and that marginal consumers are more valuable "consumers" in the market (either because they are more affluent, more involved with the schools, or, in the case of charter schools, carry with them substantial funding). Clearly, while the body of work on private markets and schools strongly suggests a mechanism by which choice by a small number of people can create pressure for more efficient outcomes, just as clearly, the concept is still in the early stages of development.

MARGINAL CONSUMERS AND CHOOSING SCHOOLS

While we recognize that the exact definition of the marginal consumer will need to be explored further, we turn next to a set of questions that straddle the theory of the marginal consumer and the literature on heuristics and decision theory. While research has identified the importance of the marginal consumer in the market, little attention has been paid to the actual mechanics of their choice behavior—do they engage in full search? If not, how do they search? Are these efficient means of finding information?

In the next chapter, we examine the information-gathering and decision-making processes of a set of consumers of education who are actively seeking out information about the schools and attempt to identify the implications that these may have for school-choice programs and education policy in general. We begin by specifying in more detail alternate theories of judgment and decision making, and then we develop specific hypotheses about how these consumers may search for information about the schools.

How Do Parents Access and
Process Information about Schools?

IN THIS CHAPTER we use data from our Internet site, DCSchoolSearch .com, to learn more about how parents search for information about schools. To explore this issue, we merge insights from the marginal-consumer perspective developed in the last chapter with insights from decision theory, which we outline in the following pages.

HOW PEOPLE CHOOSE: A BEHAVIORAL-DECISION-THEORY PERSPECTIVE

In the past fifty years there has been a great deal of interdisciplinary scholarship concerned with the processes of judgment and decision making, producing well over a dozen distinct theoretical approaches.[1] Beach and Mitchell (1998) divide these competing theories of decision analysis into three major categories: *normative models*, *behavioral-decision theory*, and *naturalistic-decision theory*.

Normative models—such as expected-utility decision theory (Keeney and Raiffa 1976; Von Neumann and Morgenstern 1943), subjective expected-utility decision theory (Edwards 1954), and the analytic hierarchy process (Saaty 1986)—are prescriptive, focusing primarily on how decisions *should* be made. Grounded in mathematical theories of probability and economic theories of utility, the normative models are often described as "elegant" and are frequently used by formal theorists.

Despite the attraction of these normative models and their widespread application in fields as diverse as sociology, anthropology, political science, and, of course, economics, many researchers have taken issue with their cognitive demands and their Herculean assumptions. Perhaps the most cogent criticisms are built on the seminal work of Herbert Simon (1955, 1957, 1978, 1985). In particular, Simon's concept of "bounded rationality" is widely recognized as providing the foundation for what is now termed behavioral-decision theory.[2]

In general terms, behavioral-decision theory seeks to apply empirical psychological findings concerning cognitive limits, shortcuts and suboptimal judgment to the normative models discussed above. Prominent approaches include judgment analysis (Cooksey 1996; Hammond et al.

1975); heuristics (Tversky and Kahneman 1974); prospect theory (Kahneman and Tversky 1979; Kahneman, Slovic, and Tversky 1982); search for dominance structure (SDS) theory (Montgomery 1983); fuzzy decision theory (Zadeh et al. 1975; Smithson 1987) and differentiation and consolidation theory (Svenson 1999). In political science, Bryan Jones (2001) has been among the most active scholars applying the insights of bounded rationality to studies of both individual and collective decision making in his efforts to delineate what he calls the "architecture of choice."[3] While these theories modify, sometimes extensively, the assumptions of the normative models, they often retain a normative focus on prescriptions for "good" decision making.

Beach and Mitchell's third category, naturalistic-decision theory, consists of theories of judgment and decision making derived from observed decision behavior, not normative ideas about what such behavior ought to be. These naturalistic theories are rooted in cognitive science; they are relatively "messy" and intractable by simple formal analysis. The category includes image theory (Beach and Mitchell 1987, 1998); recognition-primed decision theory (Klein 1993); and conflict/constraint theory (Janis 1989; Janis and Mann 1977).

In the area of policy analysis, researchers have long been attracted to normative models; after all, much of their argument is about how to make the "best," or at least a "good," decision (see, for example, Munger 2000; Weimer and Vining 2004). Accordingly, policy choices are often evaluated by comparison to the normative ideal, and when policy success is dependent upon the aggregation of many human decisions, as in the case of school choice, decision makers are generally presumed to be "rational actors."

We believe that adopting this model is a mistake, since, as with any model that uses a full information standard, the "rational-decision-maker" model sets the standard too high for most parents (and indeed for most actors) to meet. In our approach, we follow March's observation that:

> Time and capabilities for attention are limited. Not everything can be attended to at once. Too many signals are received. Too many things are relevant to a decision. Because of those limitations, theories of decision making are often better described as theories of attention or search than as theories of choice. They are concerned with the way in which scarce attention is allocated. (1994, 10)

March's position is congruent with the new emphasis on individuals as "information managers," discussed in the last chapter, and with Jones's architecture of choice based on the idea of bounded rationality. In this chapter we are concerned with the naturalistic question, "How are decisions made?" and the evaluative one, "Are the decisions good relative to some objective standard?" And we focus on "How do parents gather information?" more than on "How do parents use that information?"

School Choice and Decision Making

Many behavioral and naturalistic theories are broad in scope, and attempt to describe the entire decision process, from predecision editing to the psychology of postdecision reinforcement. This broad purview makes it challenging for researchers to derive hypotheses that enable tests of the theories in their entirety. Accordingly, we have not adopted a specific theory as the foundation for this component of our study; instead we identify a set of core ideas about decision making common to several theories that are both relevant to the school-choice decision and amenable to empirical verification. We then test to see the extent to which a set of parents who fit the profile of marginal consumers of education follow these precepts.

WHAT MAKES A "GOOD" DECISION MAKER?

Working in the tradition of others we discussed in the previous chapter who describe the contingent nature of the search and use of information, Payne convincingly demonstrates that individuals should be adaptive in their decision making (1976; Payne, Bettman, and Johnson 1993). According to Payne, people have a repertoire of strategies available for solving problems of varying complexity and they make use of different decision strategies in response to different tasks. As "information managers," this choice of strategy may be informed by a "metarational" cost/benefit analysis weighing accuracy against cognitive effort, but, ultimately, the repertoire of strategies from which the individual chooses has been acquired through some combination of training and experience with decision making.[4]

Frisch and Clemen (1994) advance an alternative normative framework for evaluating decision making that relies not on matching outcomes to the predictions of the expected utility model but rather on the observed quality of the decision process. Specifically, they identify three features of a "good" decision process: the decision maker must use a strategy that allows trade-offs between dimensions (a "compensatory rule"), she must identify the consequences of the decision ("thorough structuring"), and she must be concerned with the consequences of the choice ("consequentialism"). A reasonable application of Payne's strategy-selection model to the Frisch and Clemen criteria results in the prediction that good decision makers will use compensatory rules (comparing many dimensions among choices) when resources permit and when the consequences of the decision are sufficiently important.

A TWO-STAGE DECISION STRATEGY

In their discussion of thorough structuring, Frisch and Clemen (1994) point out that the detailed analysis of options and outcomes is not only a function of resources, but also of the size and complexity of the option set. In the face of extreme complexity or myriad options, many researchers have argued that efficient decision makers will follow a two-stage strategy. Kahneman and Tversky (1979) distinguish between an "editing phase," during which decision makers structure the problem and attempt to eliminate options that seem to be dominated by other options, and an evaluation stage, during which the decision maker more systematically compares the remaining options. In the naturalistic literature, Beach (1990) has described a "screening" process, during which decision makers eliminate some subset of alternatives prior to making a choice among them. Montgomery's analysis of how decision makers search for dominance structure and Svenson's differentiation and consolidation theory also include a prechoice or editing phase (Montgomery 1983; Svenson 1999). Perhaps the best known of this class of two-stage decision process is Tversky's idea of "elimination by aspects." This is a noncompensatory strategy in which options are winnowed from the choice set. After employing this relatively quick noncompensatory elimination process, decision makers then shift to a more compensatory strategy to evaluate the remaining alternatives (Tversky 1972).

CONSTRUCTING A CHOICE SET

Schools are a complex multidimensional "good," and for parents actively seeking to choose among a set of alternatives, the task can be quite demanding.[5] Accordingly, the balance of behavioral and naturalistic theories of decision making predict that some form of prechoice editing will be used to reduce the selection set to a more manageable level. We argue that marginal consumers of education, the set of informed and active education "market mavens" discussed in chapter 7, are more involved in the product (schools) and are more likely to employ a two-stage strategy of decision making, wherein an initial editing phase is followed by a more compensatory comparison of remaining options.

Measuring Parental Information Processing

To test our hypotheses, we need a way of capturing information about the decision process of real parents in a complex, real-world environment. The decision-theory literature provides several examples of methodology that might be used to address this problem. Early research, such as the work of Kahneman and Tversky (1979; Kahneman, Slovic, and Tversky

1982; Tversky and Kahneman 1974), generally gave written question-naires to experimental subjects in a controlled setting.[6]

Later research by cognitive scientists centered on two distinct approaches to the study of decision making: process tracing and "representative design."[7] The first attempts at process tracing used verbal protocols in which subjects discussed their decision-making process "out loud" while decisions were made (Ericsson and Simon 1984). The disadvantages in time and validity of this approach led to the development of the "information board," first used in the study of consumer behavior in private-goods markets and later used by a broader array of social scientists.

An information board is essentially a matrix of information presented to laboratory subjects either physically or, more recently, in a computerized format. The subjects use the board to search for information relevant to a choice (made at the conclusion of the experiment), while researchers record the information selected and, often, the time spent reviewing the information in each "box."

The information board allows for subtle experimental manipulation and the gathering of data directly related to cognitive-decision processes. For these reasons, it has long been a dominant process-tracing methodology (Ford et al. 1989). Critics, however, point out that the artificial nature of the choice under examination presents problems for external validity (cf. Adamowicz, Louviere, and Williams 1994), a problem that, not surprisingly, has also plagued the study of school-choice decisions by parents.

Figure 8.1 shows an information board designed by Schneider for a laboratory experiment on school choice. The board embodies the classic "alternatives-by-attributes" structure and the use of buttons that the subject clicks to reveal "hidden" information about the choice set of schools. In this classic laboratory approach, the structure of the data is manipulated by the experimenter and the number of alternatives as well as the number of attributes altered to change the difficulty of the decision task. Also, using basic computer technology, the time parents spend looking at any piece of information can be timed to the microsecond. These experimental manipulations and the precise timing of parent information processing can together yield data to test sophisticated models of decision making.

However, parents outside the laboratory do not gather information about schools from an information board—and they must make choices from a real and not a hypothetical set of schools.[8] Thus, while we recognize the power of the information board for testing specific hypotheses, we wanted a way to take the information board out of the laboratory and increase the complexity of the information provided to make our experiment more in accordance with the principles of representative design.

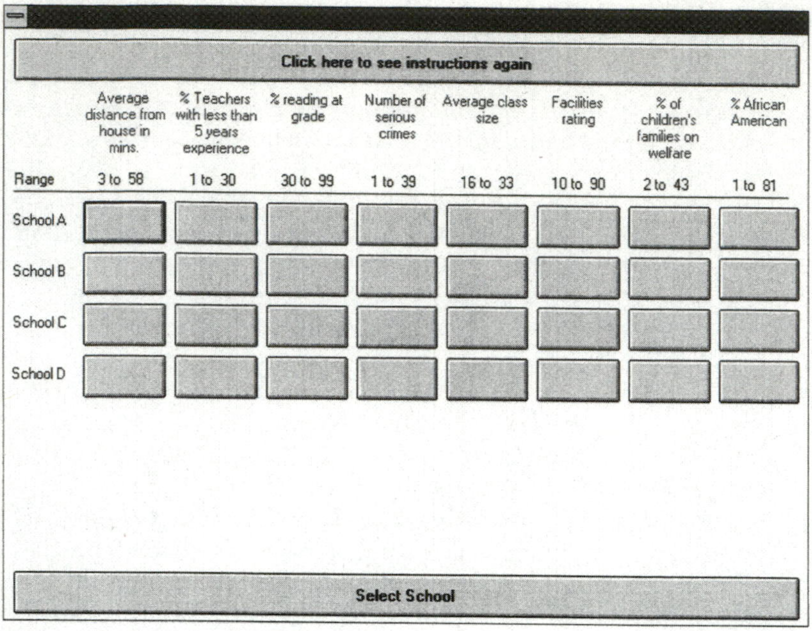

	Average distance from house in mins.	% Teachers with less than 5 years experience	% reading at grade	Number of serious crimes	Average class size	Facilities rating	% of children's families on welfare	% African American
Click here to see instructions again								
Range	3 to 58	1 to 30	30 to 99	1 to 39	16 to 33	10 to 90	2 to 43	1 to 81
School A								
School B								
School C								
School D								
Select School								

Figure 8.1. Example of an information board.

As described earlier, our solution was to create an Internet site that allows real parents to search for information about real schools in their district at their own pace, while allowing us to record data describing their search.

DCSCHOOLSEARCH.COM AS AN INFORMATION BOARD

In figure 5.1 in chapter 5 we presented a "screen shot" of a typical DCSchoolSearch.com page introducing a school. Compare this to the classic information board presented in figure 8.1, and the structural similarities are immediately apparent. As in the information board, DCSchoolSearch.com presents "subjects" with a number of alternatives each described by a number of attributes. These "tabs," which resemble the tabs on a file folder, are the functional equivalent of the "buttons" characteristic of information boards. And just as a researcher using an information board would capture the pattern of search (which then becomes the data by which to test models of decision making), it is a fairly routine task to capture the way in which Internet users negotiate through a site (although given the vagaries of Internet connections and variation in the computers that people used for accessing our site, it was virtually impossible to monitor how long parents looked at any specific piece of information).

When accessing DCSchoolSearch.com, parents can use a variety of search mechanisms to narrow down their choice set (for example, they can use a preprogrammed search function to find all charter schools in the district or to find all elementary schools where more than 50 percent of the students are reading and doing math scores at or above the basic level) or they can elect simply to browse the list of schools. This selection of a search strategy creates the list of alternatives essential to tests of choice behavior.[9]

Each school in the resulting choice set has a school profile describing the school's programs, student body, and performance (that is, each alternative school in a parent's choice set is now described by a set of attributes). Note that detailed information about each of these attributes is accessed by pointing and clicking on one of six major or nine minor "tabs" that take the parent to a page with more detailed information about a school in the choice set. So, in a manner similar to the traditional information board, parents point and click through sets of alternatives and attributes to access information.

As with any study using a traditional information board, the search pattern of every user of DCSchoolSearch.com was recorded. As the reader will recall, users of the site were also required to fill out a brief registration survey, and users who identified themselves as parents were asked to answer a brief survey after their initial log-on to the site. As noted below, we also surveyed parents via e-mail.[10] The specifics of these combined data and how we measured our quantities of interest are described below.

First, however, we describe how we operationalize the measures of decision making we test in this chapter.

Measuring Compensatory Rule Usage

Recall that one of the ways in which the quality of decision making is evaluated is by how compensatory it is. We distinguish empirically between compensatory and noncompensatory rule usage by tracking the information subjects seek when faced with a choice task. Using a classic information board in a laboratory, researchers usually gather data on the total amount of information processed, as well as the amount of time spent viewing information and the proportion of time spent exploring each attribute and alternative. Unfortunately, as noted earlier, given the "real-world" (or at least the real world of the Internet) basis of our experiment, we do not have reliable data for the time spent at any page on the DCSchoolSearch.com site. Thus our test of compensatory rule usage is limited to a "searches-per-school" measure, defined as a count of the total number of search actions taken by each user divided by the number schools examined.

Since a defining feature of a compensatory rule is that low values of one attribute of an alternative can be compensated by a high value on another attribute, a decision maker using such a rule must view much of the available information for all alternatives under consideration. This predicts that a compensatory decision maker would seek out, on average, more information per alternative than an individual using a noncompensatory decision strategy. Despite measurement limitations, we believe that our operational definition of compensatory rule usage captures its core characteristic.

Measuring Two-Stage Search Processes

Recall that in addition to employing compensatory strategies, many argue that efficient decision makers will employ a two-stage search process. We measure the extent to which such a search process is employed, and by whom.

After registering on the site, users were presented with a choice of browsing the entire alphabetical list of schools or creating a more structured choice set (essentially "editing" or "screening" the information) by either performing a predefined search of the database or via an open-ended Boolean search that allows for "editing" by user-defined parameters. We operationally define the two-stage strategy as a parent who begins a visit by the selection of either the quick or advanced search option, followed by a compensatory search of at least 7.5 attribute "tabs" (half the fifteen available) of information per school examined after the choice set is returned. We argue that parents who begin their search by browsing through the list of schools, or who use a quick search but then fail to undertake a detailed, compensatory comparison of the unscreened results, are not employing a two-stage search strategy.[11]

In this case, the Internet as a research tool grants us an advantage over traditional information-board methodology. Rather than choosing from among relatively few information options under laboratory conditions, our subjects face a bewildering array of facts and figures (all drawn from and reflecting the real world of schooling alternatives they face in Washington, D.C.). The ready availability of the data, as well as the predefined search options, allow for a relatively "frictionless" search, with none of the painstaking school visits and telephone calls required to shop for schools without such a database. Thus we are able to observe our subjects navigate complex, real-world data at their own pace. And more importantly, their pattern of navigation reveals their search strategies and their preferences over attributes.

HOW DO PARENTS SEARCH FOR INFORMATION?

As noted in chapter 5, DCSchoolSearch.com was launched in the middle of November 1999. Between November and June 2000, the site had close to eight thousand "hits," which translated into a much smaller usable dataset. First, the eight thousand hits were generated by about sixteen hundred unique users, about half (55 percent) of whom where parents—the population of interest to us in this research. Since very few parents answered our online survey (a common problem with school-oriented web sites),[12] we decided to gather more information about our users via an e-mail survey. Of the 944 parents who signed on to our site during the time period we study here, less than five hundred supplied their e-mail addresses, and of these, 169 responded to our e-mail survey. Data were collected on educational background, Internet use, time spent waiting for the site to respond (lag), and whether the parent had engaged in a variety of school-choice activities.

Merging these ideas of behavioral-decision theory and the importance of the marginal consumer is critical. As noted above, the precise nature of the marginal consumer is not well defined; however, existing research suggests that marginal consumers are engaged in an active search for information across alternatives, and that they are more likely to use that information to inform their choice of the product. In other words, we believe that marginal consumers or active shoppers for schools are more likely to employ a two-stage search process and a compensatory search for information about schooling options. While all parents who are searching for information *may* employ these strategies, in accordance with Payne's theory of adaptive decision making, active choosers will expend the additional effort and energy on a "higher quality" search.

As table 8.1 illustrates, it is clear that many of the individuals who responded to our survey were in fact active shoppers for schools. For example, over three-quarters of the parents said they had thought of moving their child to a school they thought was better and almost half actually did move a child to a different school.

Building on this table, on our discussion in the previous chapter and on Schneider, Teske, and Marschall (2000), our definition of marginal consumers is based on choice behavior rather than on search behavior. In this chapter, we operationally define marginal consumers of education as parents who report that they have actively shopped for a different school for their child over the default neighborhood school that their child would "normally" attend, either by actually transferring their child, or by applying to one or more schooling alternatives.[13] With this behavioral definition in mind, we argue that marginal consumers of education are

TABLE 8.1
Site Users Were Likely to Be Active Shoppers for Schools

	% Agreeing
In the past few years have you thought about moving your child to a different school you thought was better?	77%
In the past few years have you actually moved any of your children to a different school because you thought it was better?	44%
Has the information about the schools you saw using DCSchoolSearch.com made you think more about moving your child to a different school?	53%
Because of the information you got through DCSchoolSearch .com, have you actually tried to change your child's school?	33%

Source: E-mail survey of DCSchoolSearch.com site users; number of observations = 169.

more likely to use compensatory decision strategies and employ a two-stage search than are other parents.

Do Marginal Consumers Engage in Better Decision-Making Practices?

As a preliminary finding, our data show that some parents do appear to engage in the selection of search strategies. About 24 percent of parents studied used a two-stage decision strategy (as operationally defined above), while the remainder used one of several different decision approaches. While this is not by any means a comprehensive test of adaptiveness, it is an important existence result upon which our other findings are based.

Our next concern is the extent to which marginal consumers of education compare their options in a more thorough, compensatory way. To assess this, we treat the number of searches per school as count data and estimate the following model:

$$\text{Search/School}_i \sim Poisson(\mu_i)$$
$$\mu_i = \exp\left(\beta_0 + \beta_1 \text{Marginal Consumer}_i + \beta_2 \text{Moved}_i + \beta_3 \text{Degree}_i + \beta_4 \text{Lag}_i\right) \quad (8.1)$$

where:

- "Marginal Consumer," a measurement of active "shopping," is a continuous variable created by factor analysis of six dichotomous school-choice behavior covariates: whether the parent actually changed her child's school in the past year and whether she applied for a public charter school, a private school, an out-of-boundary transfer, or a special citywide high school, or whether she home schooled her child in the previous six months.[14]

TABLE 8.2
Search Procedures of Marginal Consumers Are More Compensatory

	Coefficient (standard error)
Marginal consumer	.10*
	(.04)
Moved	.01
	(.11)
Degree	−.06
	(.06)
Lag	.03
	(.02)
Constant	2.22*
	(.07)

* $p < .05$.
Results are from maximum-likelihood estimation of Poisson regression of searches per school on the covariates. Number of observations = 136, log-likelihood = −49.38.

- "Moved" refers to parents who changed their residence to secure a better education for their child. We treat this as separate from the marginal-consumer effect because of the limitation of the web site information to a single school district.
- "Degree" is a dichotomous variable coded 1 if the subject has a college degree and 0 if not. We use this variable as a control variable since education is clearly a fundamental individual-level factor that is correlated with cognitive abilities, information search processes, and various behaviors relating to school choice.
- "Lag" is a scaled (1–5) subjective estimate of the amount of time the user waited for information to download to her computer. We use this as a variable to try to control for various technological factors that may affect the extent to which a person is willing to engage in extensive search on the Internet.

Table 8.2 shows that clearly that, on average and holding the other factors constant, marginal consumers do indeed have a higher propensity to engage in more thorough searches of information than the average consumer. System lag, moving residence, and college (or higher) education are not statistically significant predictors.

What do the coefficients reported in table 8.2 mean substantively? Using the method of stochastic simulation (King, Tomz, and Wittenberg 2000; Tomz, Wittenberg, and King 2000), we can estimate the effect of changes of the values of the covariates on quantities of interest. Table 8.3

TABLE 8.3
Stochastic Simulation Results for Compensatory-Rule Model

	Mean search/school (standard deviation)
Sample	9.5
	(6.90)
Average consumer	8.0
	(0.57)
Marginal consumer	10.5
	(0.88)

shows the results of this simulation, compared to the actual sample mean. The "average-consumer" condition is a parent with a college degree who experienced minimal system lag, did not move, and had the lowest in-sample value for the marginal-consumer variable. In contrast, the "marginal-consumer" condition is a parent with a college degree, experiencing minimal computer lag, with the highest in-sample value for the marginal-consumer variable. The result of the simulation is that the expected value of searches per school increased by more than two, from below the actual sample mean to above it. In other words, when compared to the least active shoppers, the most active shoppers look at, on average, about 2.5 more attributes of their choice alternatives.

Our second question focuses on whether or not marginal consumers are more likely to employ a two-stage search model. To address this, we estimated the following probit model using the same covariates as above (the data used here again from the e-mail survey):

$Pr(\text{Two Stage Search}_i = 1) =$
$$\Phi(\beta_0 + \beta_1\text{Marginal Consumer}_i + \beta_2\text{Moved}_i + \beta_3\text{Degree}_i + \beta_4\text{Lag}_i) \qquad 8.2$$

where $\Phi(.)$ denotes the standard cumulative normal distribution.

We estimate the model using the usual maximum likelihood approach. As shown in table 8.4, we find that the marginal consumer is more likely to engage in a two-stage decision process, while college degree, lag, and moving are found to have no discernable effect on the probability of using a two-stage search.

As above, we use simulation techniques to better illustrate the impact of changing schools on the predicted probability of using a two-stage model. Our results, presented in table 8.5, show that the predicted probability of using a two-stage model increases by .44 for marginal consumers, holding the other covariates constant with a college degree, minimal lag, and not moving.

TABLE 8.4
Marginal Consumers Are More Likely to Use a Two-Stage Search

Variable	Coefficient (standard error)
Constant	−.43
	(.28)
Degree	−.20
	(.25)
Lag	−.11
	(.11)
Marginal consumer	.52*
	(.18)
Moved	.12
	(.24)

*$p < .01$.

Results are from maximum-likelihood estimation of probit regression of search method (coded 1 for two-stage and 0 for other) on the covariates. Figures in column 2 are unstandardized probit coefficients. Number of observations = 136; log-likelihood = −67.44.

Does Information Affect Choice?

Our data suggest that the marginal consumer engages in better search practices than other consumers of education. In the next section, we address an even more critical question: does more information affect the likelihood that parents will find a school in which they would rather enroll their child?

The short answer is yes. Recall from table 8.1 that over half of the parents who shopped for schools on DCSchoolSearch.com said that the information they gathered increased the likelihood that they would change their child's school, and large proportions also engaged in other choice behavior.

Of particular interest to us, however, is a more precise measure of the extent to which information affects choice. In its purest form, a market model of education requires "rational" parent/consumers to make choices consistent with their ordered preferences. Even if one recognizes bounds to parent rationality, such as incomplete and imperfect information regarding available options, the market model still predicts that more information will lead, on average, to an ordering of the available alternatives that is more consistent with underlying preferences over school attributes that matter to the parent. Except for the case in which the new information obtained confirms the consumer's original ranking of options (or the case in which the difference between alternatives is vanishingly small or not salient to the chooser), an increase in the amount of information

TABLE 8.5
Simulation Results for Two-Stage Search Model

	Probability of using two-stage search (standard deviation)
Sample	.24
	(.03)
Average consumer	.10
	(.06)
Marginal consumer	.54
	(.13)

should, ceteris paribus, increase the likelihood that the consumer will choose a new supplier of education.[15] We test this assumption next.

Information Affects the Propensity to Exercise Choice

Our goal is to estimate the effect of quantity of information, measured two ways—the total number of search actions and the number of searches per school—on the probability of a parent moving her child to a new school.[16] To do so, we estimate the following probit model:

$$
\begin{aligned}
\Pr(\text{Changed School}_i = 1) = \Phi(&\beta_0\text{Constant} + \beta_1 \ln(\text{Search Actions}_i \\
&+ \beta_2\ln(\text{Search/School}_i) + \beta_3\text{Tried to Change School}_i \\
&+ \beta_4\text{Already in Favorite}_i + \beta_5\text{Some College}_i \\
&+ \beta_6\text{College}_i + \beta_7\text{Post-College}_i + \beta_8\text{Lag}_i \\
&+ \beta_9\text{Did DCSS Help}_i + \beta_{10}\text{Frequent Volunteer}_i \\
&+ \beta_{11}\text{Daily Internet User}_i + \beta_{12}\text{Charter School}_i \\
&+ \beta_{13}\text{Private Religious School}_i + \beta_{14}\text{Teaching Rating}_i \\
&+ \beta_{15}\text{Principal Rating}_i + \beta_{16}\text{School Quality}_i + \beta_{17}\text{School Safety}_i)
\end{aligned}
\tag{8.3}
$$

In addition to our dependent variable and the two search variables,[17] we included a number of controls. To account for whether the parent is a habitual "shopper," we used the responses from a dichotomous question concerning past attempts to move their child to another school. We also controlled by whether or not the parents already had their child in their favorite school, an obvious confound. The next three covariates in the model are dichotomous measures of educational attainment, included as a measure of socioeconomic status and information-processing capacity. We also included as controls: system lag (defined above), general affect toward the site ("Did DCSchoolSearch.com help you learn things about the schools that you really wanted to know?"), whether the respondent volunteered three or more times in the last year at her local school, and whether he or she uses the Internet daily. Additionally, we include dichotomous responses to whether the child was in either a D.C. public charter school or a private religious school (there were no nonsectarian private students in the sample) and responses to a battery of four questions in which the parents rated their current schools on teacher quality, principal quality, overall school quality, and school safety as controlling covariates.

Missing values were imputed using the method of multiple imputation (Rubin 1987; Little and Rubin 2002; Allison, 2002; Honaker et al. 1999; King et al. 1998; King et al. 2001). A total of five datasets were imputed and estimated coefficient values and standard errors were averaged in accordance with Rubin's method (1987; Little and Rubin 2002, 210–12).

Table 8.6 presents the estimates from the probit model. We find support for the idea that information affects the likelihood of changing schools in that the coefficient for the natural log of the total number of search actions is significant and in the expected direction. Interestingly, however, we do not find the coefficient of the natural logarithm of searches per school to be significantly different from zero.[18]

Due to the nonlinear nature of the model, however, the values of coefficients tell us little about their substantive importance. Accordingly, predicted probabilities varying each covariate over its entire range while holding all others at their means (or modal values for dichotomous variables) are given in table 8.7. We have opted to present predicted probabilities for *all* covariates, not just those that we find to be statistically significant. Again, as in the analyses presented earlier in the chapter, predictions were made using stochastic simulation.

As the table shows, varying over the complete sample range of the natural logarithm of search actions yields a change in probability of reporting that the respondent actually tried to change her child's school of 0.44. To further explore this information, we transform the independent variable to the total number of search actions, and then calculate predicted probabilities (ceteris paribus) and a 95 percent confidence interval at a variety of points. These results are plotted in figure 8.2.

The transformation allows us to see a classic "diminishing-returns" pattern to the effect of further search on the probability of changing schools. This probability doubles in slightly more than one hundred pieces of information viewed, but the next *one thousand* "clicks" only yield a 38 percent increase.

CONCLUSIONS: MARGINAL CONSUMERS DO IT BETTER

Our goal in this chapter is ambitious: we use information technology to combine and advance two disparate areas of research—behavioral-decision theory and school choice.

TABLE 8.6
More Information Increases the Chance of Choice

Variable	Coefficient (standard error)
Some college	1.10* (0.50)
College	1.02* (0.52)
Post-college	0.43 (0.55)
Did DCSS help?	0.67 (0.46)
Frequent volunteer	−0.30 (0.40)
Already in favorite school	−0.45 (0.34)
Daily internet user	0.76* (0.38)
D.C. public charter-school parent	0.35 (0.45)
Private religious-school parent	0.64 (0.86)
Teacher rating	0.35 (0.45)
Principal rating	0.16 (0.20)
School quality	−0.11 (0.21)
School safety	−0.24 (0.29)
Lag	−0.52 (0.46)
Tried to change school in past	0.83* (0.28)
Natural log of search actions	0.20* (0.09)
Natural log of searches/school	−0.30 (0.23)
Constant	−3.71* (1.53)
Number of observations	169
Log likelihood	−77.8
Percent correctly predicted	78%
Estimated PCP	70%
Percent reduction in error	33%
Estimated PRE	9%
Chi square of the model	57.6* (17 d.f.)

$p < .05$, two-tailed.
Results are from maximum-likelihood estimation of probit regression of the probability of changing schools. All results are averaged over five multiply-imputed datasets.

TABLE 8.7
Predicted Probabilities for Probit Model

Variable	Range in sample	Mean (mode for dichotomous variables)	Predicted probability over range		
			Low	High	Δ
Some college	0–1	1	.11	.40	.29
College	0–1	0	.11	.38	.27
Post-college	0–1	0	.11	.20	.09
Did DCSS help?	0–1	1	.20	.40	.20
Frequent volunteer	0–1	0	.40	.30	−.10
Already in favorite school	0–1	0	.40	.25	−.15
Daily internet user	0–1	1	.17	.40	.23
D.C. public charter-school parent	0–1	0	.40	.53	.13
Private religious-school parent	0–1	0	.40	.62	.22
Teacher rating	2.0–4.6	3.5	.26	.54	.28
Principal rating	1.0–5.8	3.4	.28	.55	.27
School quality	1.0–5.3	3.1	.48	.32	−.16
School safety	1.0–4.9	3.4	.61	.29	−.32
Lag	0–1	0	.40	.24	−.16
Tried to change school in past	0–1	0	.40	.71	.31
Natural log of search actions	0.7–7.2	3.7	.22	.66	.44
Natural log of searches/ school	0.0–3.7	1.5	.57	.21	−.36

Despite the conceptual and measurement challenges involved in merging these research themes, we find evidence that not all parents search for information (and, by extension, make decisions) the same way and that the search strategy of the active chooser, or marginal consumer of education, can be characterized as being, on average, "better"—that is, more compensatory and more likely to consist of a predecision editing phase followed by in-depth comparison of options. Moreover, in general we find that an increase in the amount of information searched for is linked to an increase in the probability of choosing a new school for one's child.

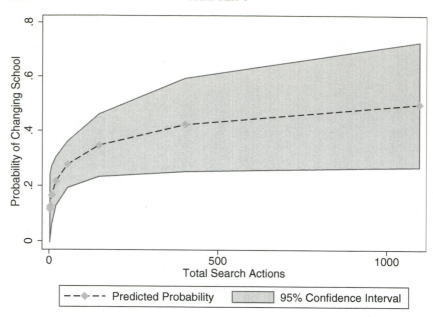

Figure 8.2. Probability of changing school as a result of DCSchoolSearch.com information.

Our findings are an important contribution to our understanding of the functioning of a market for education. Proponents of the theory of marginal consumers (in any market) inevitably rely upon these individuals to carry the burden of information seeking and processing. The marginal consumer must be a "better" shopper in order to create an efficient market. Our findings show that active choosers of education use "smart" shortcuts to reduce their decision problem to a more manageable size and search more thoroughly; they also appear to do a better job of weighing the pros and cons of the education options available.

We must caution that our results are not an unqualified support for the normative superiority of marginal consumers in market decision making. There may still be significant flaws in the reasoning and choice processes of even these parents who are using better techniques while searching for information. We do not address, for example, the issue of bias or motivated reasoning—which ironically these marginal consumers may be most prone to. As Lodge and Taber argue:

> biased processing is most likely among those whose general political knowledge and domain-specific political knowledge is rich, for it is sophisticates who typically hold the strongest attitudes, with the most confidence, and have the most facts at hand, thereby making them more able to assimilate

supporting evidence and better equipped to discredit arguments that challenge their established beliefs or attitudes. (2000, 211)

Thus a marginal consumer might process more information in a more thorough and efficient manner, but still perceive that information in an inaccurate (from a hypothetically objective perspective) fashion due to entrenched opinions or biases. Indeed it does not require a stretch of the imagination to construct numerous examples of such motivated reasoning in a policy area as ideologically charged as education and in a world where charter schools are so regularly promoted as a great policy innovation.

One key lesson from the work of Lodge and his colleagues is that "hot cognition" may drive judgments and evaluations—that is, that what people feel about charter schools may reflect their choices and their behavior regardless of the reality of school performance. In later chapters, we explore further the evaluations given to their schools by choosers and try better to measure the foundation upon which these evaluations rest.

9

Satisfaction with Schools

FROM THE MARKET STANDPOINT, the foundation upon which so much of the argument for school choice rests, people who can choose should choose things they think best meet their needs. In turn, they should be more satisfied with them. By extension, parents who choose their children's schools should be more satisfied than parents who do not.

In this chapter, we begin our empirical investigation of the effects of charter schools using the survey data described in chapter 3. Here we look at the extent to which parents and students are satisfied with their schools. While we have panel data—repeated measures on the same survey respondents over time—we begin our investigation with cross-sectional analyses.[1] We devote a great deal of space to the question of satisfaction for two reasons.

First, the structure of our data is complicated and we use several methods to account for potential problems for inference common to most observational studies, such as self-selection to the policy "treatment" and missing data due to nonresponses by parents. These problems and the methods we use to deal with them are discussed at length in this chapter, but we will refer to this discussion in later chapters.

Our other reason for devoting so much time to the issue of how parents view their child's school has to do with the importance of parental satisfaction to theories of choice. While much of the current debate about school choice focuses on achievement gains, as noted above, greater parental satisfaction with schools of choice has been a long-standing outcome that advocates have used to buttress their argument for expanding choice. If parents in charter schools do not prefer them to the traditional public alternative, this may signify that differences between the two sectors are illusory or perhaps that there is a serious shortfall in the range and type of charter schools available.

Satisfaction is also critical to the politics of school reform. Charter-school advocates have no qualms in talking about a charter-school *movement*, linking charter schools to a larger political effort to reform the system of education in the United States. If this movement is to have traction and gain adherents, parents who are satisfied with their children's schools represent a potential pool of supporters (and, not incidentally, voters) who will favor further expansion of charter schools and choice in general. In contrast, if charter-school parents are not satisfied with their schools, then an important foundation for the "movement" is missing.[2]

MEASURING HOW PARENTS EVALUATE THEIR CHILD'S SCHOOL

In the first of this pair of chapters exploring satisfaction, we present some basic information on the relationship between the sector in which a child is enrolled and how parents evaluate that child's school. As noted earlier, in this chapter we confine ourselves to cross-sectional analysis. We use a broad set of measures of parental evaluation of their children's schools and we show a consistent pattern: when we control for many factors that may affect the relationship between choice and satisfaction, we find that charter-school parents in our study consistently evaluate their children's schools more highly than do parents with children in the traditional public schools.

Many of the factors that we control in our empirical analysis are the "usual suspects"—socioeconomic status, education levels, church attendance, and so on. However, one of the factors that must be controlled may be less evident but is embedded in the very nature of charter schools as schools of choice.

As noted earlier in this book, charter schools are an "option-demand" form of choice, in which parents are free, but not required, to choose. In this two-step process, parents first choose to choose, and only then do they choose a school. Given the nature of this process, the parents who choose to choose are "self-selecting" into the charter-school system and may not be representative of the entire population of parents. In turn, the characteristics that are motivating them to choose may affect their subsequent behavior and attitudes toward the schools. To the extent this is true, a self-selection bias may enter into the data and simple comparisons of choosers and nonchoosers will be affected by these parental characteristics independent of the quality of the charter schools themselves. That is, higher evaluations of charter schools may be a function of the factors that led charter-school parents to choose in the first place. This problem is increasingly well known to social science researchers and a variety of techniques have been introduced to deal with this potential self-selection bias.

While our substantive task in this chapter is to explore differences in satisfaction with charter schools, an equally important task is methodological: to see how well any observed differences stand up to controls for self-selection into charter schools and to tests of sensitivity for hidden bias due to unmeasured covariates that may be predictors of both opting to choose and satisfaction. In this chapter, we also examine the possibility that any observed positive evaluations given to charter schools may be the result of a form of motivated reasoning (a topic that we briefly discussed in chapter 8 in a different context). As we discuss in more detail below, the potential problem is simple to state: if a parent chooses her child's school, she may need to believe that the choice was the right one. In turn, she may view the chosen school through what Erikson (1982) calls "rose-colored glasses." Later in this chapter, we investigate the likelihood that the very act of choosing charter schools creates such a positivity bias.

While social scientists have developed a wide range of tools to fix the self-selection problem, the potential bias from donning rose-colored glasses is less well studied.

Choice and Charter Schools Have Been Linked to Higher Satisfaction

In our introductory chapters, we documented the rapid increase in the number of charter schools and the number of students enrolled in them. One likely reason for this growth is that parents and students think charter schools are better than the traditional public schools in which they were previously enrolled. For example, Finn et al. (1997) find that a large majority of parents feel that charter schools in which their children are enrolled are better than the traditional public schools they left, with respect to class size, school size, teacher attentiveness, and the quality of instruction and curriculum. In contrast, less than 5 percent think charter schools inferior. Finn et al. also find high levels of student satisfaction across a gamut of school attributes, including teachers, technology, class size, and curriculum. Teachers also seem to like charter schools, with high levels of satisfaction found among charter-school teachers (Koppich, Holmes, and Piecki 1998).

There are several possible foundations for this greater satisfaction with charter schools. Perhaps the strongest is that of "allocative efficiency"—education is a complex, multifaceted "good," and choice allows parents to select schools that emphasize the kind of education they want for their children (Schneider, Teske, and Marschall 2000).[3] This foundation for higher parent satisfaction in schools of choice dates at least as far back as Milton Friedman's original argument in favor of vouchers in the 1950s and has been used to support choice ever since.

In his pioneering work, Friedman (1955) made a strong case for consumer sovereignty, arguing that higher levels of satisfaction with schools will flow from maximizing the freedom of parents to choose schools. From this perspective, choice leads to higher parental evaluation of choice schools because it increases the ability of parents to match their preferences for specific values, needs, or pedagogical approaches with the school. As Goldring and Shapira put it, the "sovereignty position suggests choice leads to greater satisfaction in that it accommodates individual family preferences, mainly in the areas of curricula, teaching philosophy, and religion. Parents will be satisfied in exercising their fundamental right of individual choice and freedom of belief about the best education for their children" (1993, 397; also see Coons and Sugarman 1978; Raywid 1989).

In addition to increasing this match between consumer and provider, choice may change the schools themselves—making better "products" available for parents to choose among. Indeed, fundamental to the push for choice is the idea that choice unleashes competitive pressure on the schools that makes them improve—and charter schools are often seen as a central tool to leverage such change (see, e.g., Hill, Pierce, and Guthrie 1997; Teske et al. 2001; Hoxby 2000c).

While the debate still rages about the effect of choice on academic outcomes, there are other outcomes from choice that are less contested—any of which can increase parental satisfaction. For example, many charter schools are designed to change the relationship among administrators, teachers, parents, and students, which may foster what Coleman (1988) refers to as "functioning communities." In these communities, the tighter links from the school to parents, families, and students are associated with better educational experiences and all parties, including teachers, will be more satisfied (Driscoll 1993). This link underlies the basic findings developed in the research on "effective schools," showing that good interpersonal relations among members of the school community and shared beliefs and values combine to promote good teaching and a positive learning environment (see especially Bryk and Schneider 2002).[4]

Indeed, many charter schools have a culture (and sometimes even a written contract) that provides parents opportunities to influence school management and to become more involved with the processes of school governance and functioning (see, for example, Peterson and Campbell 2001; Finn et al. 1997). To the extent that this occurs, parental evaluations of their children's' schools should improve (Chubb and Moe 1990; Raywid 1989; Goldring and Shapira 1993; but see Benveniste, Carnoy, and Rothstein 2003, chap. 3, on the possibility that such contracts may function as ceilings on participation).

It is also important to remember that choice seeks not only to empower parents but also to change the role of students, making them more central in the design of education programs and in the functioning of the schools. In short, one goal of choice is to increase the attention paid by schools to student needs (Hill, Pierce, and Guthrie 1997). In turn, choice seems to improve student-teacher relations. For example, in her study of the effects of choice, Driscoll found that choice students were more likely to report "they got along well with teachers, that the quality of teaching was high, and that teachers praised them and listened to them" (1993, 158). In a similar vein, Finn et al. (1997) found that large numbers of charter-school students liked the "good teachers" in their schools, who, according to these students, teach until the students learn the material and don't let them fall behind. To the extent that this behavioral change strengthens the ties between students and teachers, and increases the level of student satisfaction with the schools, parental satisfaction with the schools should in turn increase.

Finally, choice may put pressure on administrators, teachers, and staff to be more "consumer-friendly." As Hassel observes, "charter schools cannot take their 'customers' for granted. Their very survival depends on the degree to which families believe the schools are responding to family preferences and working hard to provide the education they demand" (1999, 6; also see Teske et al. 2001; Buckley and Schneider 2004). Thus, the competitive pressures on charter schools should increase their responsiveness to parent demands—and such responsiveness should lead to higher evaluations.[5]

In short, there is reason to believe that parents with children in charter schools should evaluate their schools more highly. In the first part of this chapter we explore this relationship among the parents in our study. We begin by looking at a way of evaluating schools that should be familiar to readers: we asked parents to assign letter grades ranging from A to F to their child's school overall and for three specific aspects of the school: their child's teacher, principal, and school facilities.

A Caveat about Using Grades

Before proceeding with the analysis, note that there is a well-known pattern when using grades as measures of parent evaluations of schools—parents almost always give high grades to their children's schools. For example, Phi Delta Kappa regularly asks a sample of parents to grade their children's schools. In their 2005 survey, the society's magazine found that 48 percent of respondents assigned an A or a B to schools in their community with an additional 29 percent assigning the grade of C. This pattern of high grades has remained remarkably durable over time. Further, the grades parents give to their own children's school are consistently higher than the grades they assign to the nation's schools as a whole: The number of A's and B's rises to 57 percent for public school parents and to 69 percent for parents asked to grade the public school their oldest child attends (Rose and Gallup 2005). However, we believe that pattern is not important for our analysis, since we are interested in comparing parents in the charter schools and the traditional public schools in the

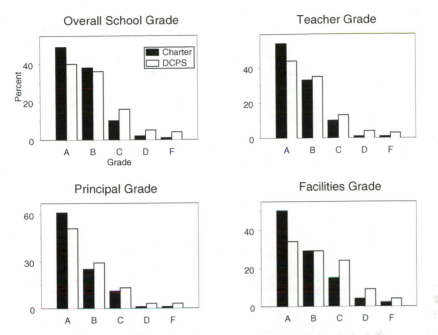

Figure 9.1. In Wave 1, charter-school parents grade their schools higher on every dimension. *Note*: Percentages are unadjusted responses from the wave 1 (Fall 2001) data, missing values deleted. Number of observations = 995.

same city; in addition, we ultimately control for conditions that could affect parents in the two sectors differently.

CHARTER SCHOOLS RECEIVE HIGHER GRADES

We start with a simple exploration of the distribution of these parent-assigned grades in our first wave of interviews. We then explore the extent to which the observational nature of our study may be confounding these results.

In figure 9.1, we present the marginal distributions of grades using the data from the first wave of the survey. In the upper left corner, we graph the overall grades parents give to their child's school by enrollment in charter school or traditional D.C. public schools. We see that 49 percent of charter parents gave their child's teachers a grade of A, fully 10 percent more than parents whose children were in DCPS. At the opposite end of the spectrum, 3 percent of DCPS parents gave their child's school an F, while only 1 percent of charter-school parents gave this failing grade. The differences displayed in figure 9.1 are all significant at $p < .01$ level, two-tailed.[6]

We find virtually the same pattern for parental evaluations of teachers and principals (the upper right and lower left corners of figure 9.1), where charter parents were again 10 percentage points more likely to give an A than DCPS parents and even more so for facilities, where 17 percent more charter parents gave a grade of A compared to DCPS parents. Thus, on each of these three specific dimensions of schooling, there is a clear shift in the distribution of grades in favor of charter schools.

We can convert these letter grades into numerical ones (using the familiar A = 4, B = 3, . . . , F = 0 scale) and create an overall grade point average (GPA). Using this summary score, charter schools overall earn a GPA of 3.3, about 10 percent (or a third of a "letter grade") higher than the 3.0 of DCPS schools.

Are These Differences a Function of Self-Selection Biases?

The results shown in figure 9.1 do not control for any characteristics of the parents in our sample. As we have noted earlier, the option-demand nature of charter schools may lead to a selection bias in who chooses: charter-school parents are not likely to be a random sample of the wider population of parents. A simple way to test the robustness of the charter-school effect on satisfaction is to estimate a linear regression model of the grades on likely confounding covariates. Our first models are independent linear regressions of the four grades on the following characteristics:

- a charter-school indicator, coded 1 if the respondent's child is in a D.C. charter school;
- a set of three dichotomous variables for self-reported race (Hispanic, white, other, with African American the excluded—and modal—category);
- residential mobility measured by the number of years the person has lived in her current neighborhood and by the years the person has lived in D.C.;
- whether or not the respondent was employed;
- whether or not the respondent reports that she is a frequent volunteer at her child's school;
- whether or not the respondent was a member if the PTA;
- the respondent's marital status;
- the respondent's frequency of church attendance (a seven-category variable, treated here as continuous);
- the number of people with whom the respondent reports frequently discussing her child's education;
- the number of nonschool organizations in which the respondent reports membership;

- the grade the respondent assigned to the D.C. public schools in general;
- the respondent's years of schooling and years of schooling squared;
- how long the respondent's child has attended the school, and;
- the child's grade level.

While most of these covariates are included for obvious reasons, several require further explanation. A particular issue in evaluating a policy program such as charter schools with observational data is that participants in the program may differ in important and difficult-to-measure psychological dimensions such as motivation or dissatisfaction with previous choices. In this first approach, we attempt to control for this possibility with their school participation (volunteerism, PTA membership) and the overall grade they assign the D.C. schools (general dissatisfaction). We return to this issue of controlling for motivation below, but first we present our initial model.

Let Y_{ig} denote respondent i's grade assigned to each dimension of schools we measured (g). We thus estimate four independent models of the form:

$$Y_{ig} = \beta_0 + \beta_1 \text{Charter}_i + \beta_2 \text{White}_i + \beta_3 \text{Hispanic}_i + \beta_4 \text{Other Race}_i$$
$$+ \beta_5 \text{ Years Lived in D.C.}_i + \beta_6 \text{Years Lived in Neighborhood}_i$$
$$+ \beta_7 \text{ Employed}_i + \beta_8 \text{Frequent Volunteer}_i + \beta_9 \text{ PTA}_i + \beta_{10} \text{Married}_i$$
$$+ \beta_{11} \text{Church Attendance}_i + \beta_{12} \text{Number of Organizations}_i \qquad (9.1)$$
$$+ \beta_{13} \text{ Number of Dicussants}_i + \beta_{14} \text{DCPS Grade}_i + \beta_{15} \text{ Years of Education}_i$$
$$+ \beta_{16} \text{ Years of Education}^2_i + \beta_{17} \text{Years Child in School}_i + \beta_{18} \text{ Grade Level}_i$$
$$+ \varepsilon_{ig}$$

where $\varepsilon_{ig} \sim N(0, \sigma^2)$.

In this first cut, the assigned grades are treated as continuous (0–4) variables. To handle missing data due to item nonresponse, we impute five complete datasets of 995 observations each using a predictive mean-matching model (Little 1988; Little and Rubin 2002; Allison 2002, 59–63; King et al. 2001; Van Buuren, Boshuizen, and Knook 1999) and average the results of the analyses using Rubin's method (Rubin 1987; Little and Rubin 2002, 210–12). One particular advantage of Rubin's partially parametric predictive mean-matching approach over other techniques used in the applied literature is the restriction of imputed values to those observed in the sample. The results of the models using this imputed data set are presented in table 9.1.

As table 9.1 shows, the observed effect of charter-school enrollment on parent satisfaction remains strong in this simple linear regression. We find the coefficients on charter enrollment (which range in magnitude from .28 for principals to .54 for facilities) to be positive and statistically significant (all $p < .01$, two-tailed) on all four parental evaluation measures.

TABLE 9.1
A Simple Linear Model of Charter Effect

	School	Teacher	Principal	Facility
Charter	.41* (.07)	.35* (.07)	.28* (.07)	.54* (.08)
White	.06 (.14)	.14 (.14)	.27* (.16)	−.46* (.18)
Hispanic	.20 (.17)	−.05 (.17)	.18 (.13)	.13 (.19)
Other	−.18 (.17)	−.09 (.16)	.13 (.15)	.03 (.18)
Years in D.C.	.01 (.01)	−.02 (.01)	.01 (.01)	.0004 (.01)
Years in neighborhood	.01 (.01)	.01 (.01)	.002 (.006)	−.005 (.007)
Employed	.03 (.10)	.05 (.10)	−.06 (.11)	−.11 (.11)
Frequent volunteer	.08 (.09)	.21* (.08)	.27* (.10)	.05 (.10)
PTA member	.13 (.09)	−.04 (.08)	−.12 (.09)	.01 (.10)
Married	.07 (.08)	−.06 (.08)	.03 (.09)	−.10 (.10)
Church attendance	−.01 (.02)	−.001 (.02)	.03 (.02)	.01 (.02)
Number of organizations	.01 (.04)	.01 (.03)	−.001 (.04)	.03 (.04)
Number of discussants	−.01 (.01)	−.02* (.01)	−.01 (.02)	−.01 (.01)
DCPS grade	.30* (.04)	.27* (.04)	.21* (.04)	.27* (.05)
Years of education	−.10* (.05)	−.03 (.05)	−.03 (.05)	−.08 (.07)
Years of education^2	.005* (.002)	.001 (.002)	.001 (.002)	.004* (.003)
Time in school	−.04* (.02)	−.03 (.03)	−.04 (.03)	.02 (.03)
Student's grade level	−.03* (.01)	−.03* (.01)	.01 (.01)	−.05* (.01)
Constant	2.87* (.37)	2.92* (.41)	2.54* (.35)	2.74* (.47)
Omnibus F	6.30*	6.81*	3.39*	6.74*

* $p < .10$, two-tailed.

Number of observations = 995 (555 charter, 440 DCPS). Results are coefficient estimates from independent linear regressions of outcome measures, weighted to correct for oversample of charter parents and averaged over five multiple-imputation datasets constructed via predictive mean matching. Standard errors in parentheses. The omnibus F-test reported in the last row is the test of the null hypothesis that all coefficients are jointly equal to zero.

Controlling for Self-Selection Using Propensity-Score Matching

There are several limitations of this simple linear approach that we must consider before concluding that our data support the hypothesis that charter schools *cause* an increase in satisfaction. First, we are assuming that our model is correctly specified—that the covariates predict the outcome in a linear, additive function and that our assumption of normality of the dependent variables is appropriate. Second, we are assuming that there is no endogeneity among the outcomes and their predictors. Finally, we are assuming that there are no omitted variables that are correlated with both charter enrollment and our satisfaction outcomes; it is well known that results from quasi-experimental studies of the effects of public policy (or other "treatments") are potentially biased when the factors predicting self-selection into the program (here, charter schools) are correlated with the outcome measures.

A variety of techniques have been developed to deal with this last cause of bias. One solution is the estimation of some form of "Heckman-type" parametric treatment-effects model, usually by means of a consistent two-step or full-information maximum-likelihood model that relies on assumptions about the error structure for identification (Maddala 1983). Instead, in our analysis we use a semiparametric estimator, propensity-score matching, originally introduced by Rosenbaum and Rubin (1983, 1985) in a biometric context and increasingly used in econometric studies, ranging from evaluating the effects of training programs on subsequent earnings (e.g., Bryson, Dorsett, and Purdon 2002; Dehejia and Wahba 1999, 2002; Heckman, Ichimura, and Todd 1997), to evaluating successful techniques of heart catheterization (Hirano and Imbens 2001), to evaluating education policy (Schneider and Buckley 2003).

The logic underlying this method is to construct, from quasi-experimental data, a new variable, the propensity score, that summarizes pretreatment (and other potentially confounding) characteristics for each respondent. This score is essentially the conditional probability of the subject selecting the treatment. Based on these propensity scores, a new sample consisting of the treatment group and their matched controls is created and the size and significance of the treatment effect can be estimated using this sample.

Propensity-score matching has several advantages over the Heckman-type treatment-effects models, such as the relaxation of restrictive parametric assumptions and of the need to find instrumental variables for practical model identification (see LaLonde 1986 and Puhani 2000 for a discussion of the sensitivity of Heckman-type of models to misspecification and to violations of their parametric assumptions). Moreover, as Dehejia and Wahba (1999) argue, matching provides estimates of the treatment effects more similar to randomized field trials than can be obtained using other corrections for self-selection.

However, the propensity-score model produces correct causal inference only if selection to treatment is independent of outcomes, conditional on the covariates used in the matching procedure. Thus there is a trade-off: The Heckman-type modeling strategy relaxes the assumption of observability of all covariates correlated with both the treatment decision and the outcome, but imposes a strong assumption about the error structure. Conversely, the more intuitive propensity-score matching approach assumes selection on the observables, but does not require strict parametric assumptions for estimation. Our strategy is use the propensity-score approach combined with a test of sensitivity to hidden bias introduced by Rosenbaum (2002, 105–38) and discussed by DiPrete and Gangl (2004) in the context of unemployment insurance.

Our approach is thus superior to the classical linear-regression model both in adjusting on the observable covariates without strong assumptions and in testing for hidden bias. However, we have not considered yet the issue of endogeneity. Our strategy is to take advantage of the longitudinal nature of the "treatment" (that is, enrollment in charter schools) to better disentangle cause from effect.

To do that, in the next analysis we select the 226 (137 charter, 89 DCPS) parents whose children were new to their schools in Fall 2001, the time of the first panel interview. We match these new charter parents to the new DCPS parents (sampling with replacement) on their estimated propensity scores, and then consider the differences between these matched pairs using the grades assigned by parents in the Spring of 2001, the second panel wave. This method of analysis allows us to draw more valid causal inference about the effects of charter-school enrollment by correcting for self-selection factors *prior* to the treatment but considering outcomes one school year later. The trade-off is a potential reduction in power to detect effects due to the decrease in sample size caused by our restriction of the sample to students new to their school.

We assume that all missing data, including panel attrition, is missing at random (MAR) conditioned on the observed covariates, so we impute these missing values using the same predictive mean-matching method discussed above.

To implement this propensity-score matching procedure, we first estimate a probit model (other generalized linear models or semiparametric models for dichotomous data would also be appropriate) to generate each individual's predicted probability of choosing a charter school (that is, the propensity score). The covariates we use to estimate the propensity score are a subset of the covariates discussed in the regression model above. If C_i is the indicator of treatment (charter enrollment) for parent i and $\hat{p}$ is the estimated propensity score for a vector, $\mathbf{w}_i$, of predictors, the full model is thus:

TABLE 9.2
Predicting Who Chooses Charter Schools

	Coefficient (standard error)
White	−1.22* (.47)
Hispanic	−.68* (.34)
Other	.04 (.32)
Years in D.C.	−.02 (.02)
Years in neighborhood	.02* (.01)
Employed	.06 (.20)
Frequent school volunteer	−.18 (.20)
PTA member	.27 (.21)
Married	−.10 (.18)
Church attendance	.11* (.04)
Number of organizations	−.01 (.11)
Number of discussants	−.01 (.02)
DCPS Grade	−.24* (.09)
Years of education	.13 (.13)
Years of education squared	−.01 (.01)
Constant	−1.27 (.88)

* $p < .10$, two-tailed.

Number of observations = 226 (137 charter, 89 DCPS, sample limited to parents with children in new school). Results are estimates from maximum-likelihood probit model of charter-school enrollment, weighted to correct for oversample of charter parents and averaged over five multiple-imputation datasets constructed via predictive mean matching.

$$\hat{p}\,(C_i = 1 \mid \mathbf{w}_i) = \Phi\,(\beta_0 + \beta_1 \text{White}_i + \beta_2 \text{Hispanic}_i + \beta_3 \text{Other Race}_i$$
$$+ \beta_4 \text{Years Lived in D.C.}_i + \beta_5 \text{Years Lived in Neighborhood}_i$$
$$+ \beta_6 \text{Employed}_i + \beta_7 \text{Frequent Volunteer}_i + \beta_8 \text{PTA}_i$$
$$+ \beta_9 \text{Married}_i + \beta_{10} \text{Church Attendance}_i \qquad (9.2)$$
$$+ \beta_{11} \text{Number of Organizations}_i + \beta_{12} \text{Number of Dicussants}_i$$
$$+ \beta_{13} \text{DCPS Grade}_i + \beta_{14} \text{Years of Education}_i$$
$$+ \beta_{15} \text{Years of Education}^2_i)$$

where $\Phi(.)$ is the normal cumulative distribution function. The results of the propensity-score estimation model are presented in table 9.2.

Once the predicted probabilities from this model are estimated, we match each charter parent to a single DCPS parent who is their "nearest neighbor" on the propensity-score metric.[7] We then verify that the balancing property is satisfied by examining the first and second moments of the distribution of propensity scores for treated and nontreated units. This property ensures that the pretreatment characteristics of the respondents within equally spaced intervals of the propensity score, independent of their treatment status, have the same mean and variance (Rosenbaum 2002, 295–328; Becker and Ichino 2002).

To test the hypotheses that the charter parents have higher levels of satisfaction reflected in the grades they assign, we use the nonparametric Wilcoxon signed-rank test for the matched pairs, a nonparametric test which has the added advantage of allowing us to relax the assumption that the outcome measures are continuous and normal. Since the Wilcoxon procedure tests the null of equality of samples but does not produce a point estimate, we also compute the Hodges-Lehmann point estimates of the difference between charter and DPCS parents on each measure (Rosenbaum 2002, 47–50).

As before, we average the results of the point estimates over the five imputed datasets to account for missing values. We also produce averaged p-values for the Wilcoxon tests by averaging their approximate z scores (under the large sample assumption of the signed-rank test) following Li, Ragunathan, and Rubin (1991). Finally, we also compute a multivariate satisfaction variable using the technique suggested by Rosenbaum (2002, 50–53) for partially ordered outcomes that enables us to consider the satisfaction results on all four dimensions simultaneously.[8] The results of these analyses are presented in table 9.3.

The first column of table 9.3 provides the averaged Hodges-Lehmann point estimates and the second column gives the averaged p-values of the signed-rank test. All four of the outcome measures, as well as the multivariate combination of them, are significantly larger in the charter group than in the matched control group, and the point estimates of the difference are similar in size to the estimates from the regression models in table 9.1.

The final column of table 9.3 presents the results of our sensitivity test for hidden bias discussed above. Rosenbaum's Γ (2002, 110–19) is the ratio of the odds that the two cases (treatment and control), matched on the propensity score computed from observable data, will select the treatment. Here, we present the estimated value for Γ at which the signed-rank test is no longer significant at the .05 level. Thus, for the case of the overall school-grade outcome, for example, if we hypothesize that there is an unmeasured covariate correlated with both selection to charter schools and the outcome, this covariate would have to be of sufficient size to increase the odds ratio of selecting treatment by 1.64. That is, the charter parent would have to be 1.64 times more likely to choose the charter school due to this hidden bias in order for the Wilcoxon test to fail to

TABLE 9.3
Charter Parents Grade Their Schools Higher

	Hodges-Lehmann point estimate	Wilcoxon signed-rank test p	Critical level of Γ
School grade	.5	<.001	1.64
Teacher grade	.4	.004	1.41
Principal grade	.7	<.001	1.29
Facilities grade	.4	.007	1.91
Multivariate satisfaction	1.1	<.001	1.72

Hodges-Lehmann point estimates and Wilcoxon p-values (two-tailed) are averaged over five datasets imputed via predictive mean matching. The Rosenbaum's Γ column provides the values of Γ for which the upper limit of the confidence interval on the p of the signed-rank test is exactly .05. Sample size varies between 135 and 136 matched pairs depending on different imputed datasets due to discarding of observations not on the common support of the estimated propensity score.

reject the null of equivalent samples at the .05 level. As the table shows, we find values of Γ ranging from 1.29 (principal grade) to 1.91 (facilities). These values may appear fairly small, suggesting that hidden bias, if it exists, may be able to explain at least some of the results. However, to place them in a social-science research context, they are all larger than the reported critical Γ's in DiPrete and Gangl's (2004) study of the behavioral effects of unemployment insurance. Also it should be emphasized that this test does not allow one to reach conclusions about the *existence* of such bias—only to assess the sensitivity of the results in the case where such an unmeasured covariate exists.

We believe that these statistical techniques confirm that charter-school parents evaluate their schools more highly than DCPS parents and that the observed higher grades are not the result of self-selection. We now turn to one further method for confirming this conclusion.

JUDGING THE VALUE ADDED OF CHARTER SCHOOLS: THE RESULTS OF A NATURAL EXPERIMENT

Randomized field trials are often held up as the "gold standard" for policy evaluation. In a well-known series of studies of the effects of school-voucher programs on academic achievement, Peterson and his colleagues (see, e.g., Howell and Peterson 2000; Peterson et al. 2002b) randomly assigned parents who have applied for vouchers to a "treatment condition" in which parents are given vouchers and to a "control condition" in which parents who sought vouchers are denied them. Since all the parents in these experiments sought vouchers and their assignment to the treatment and experimental group was randomized, the factors that contaminate so much social-science evaluation work, including differences in motivation to seek the "treatment," are ideally uncorrelated to the outcomes by design.[9]

Peterson's ability to even attempt random assignment was the result of a unique set of conditions, including the fact that the voucher programs he studied were privately financed. Most education reforms do not present researchers this type of opportunity, and given that charter schools are publicly financed and popular among parents and policy makers alike, a carefully constructed randomized field trial has up to now been difficult to implement.[10]

However, since the demand for charter schools in Washington, D.C. exceeds supply and charter schools facing excess demand conduct lotteries, there is a population whose motivation to choose charter schools is at the same level as that of charter-school parents (that is, both sets of parents have chosen to choose), but who, through the luck of the draw, were denied access to charter schools. In our random sample of parents whose child was in the traditional public schools, approximately 13 percent of the parents (sixty in all) said that they had tried to enroll their child in a charter school but failed. While not as elegant as a fully controlled experiment, we believe that the comparison of charter-school parents (who received the "treatment") and these other parents who sought the treatment but were denied access presents yet another way of assessing the sensitivity of our results to hidden bias.

As in the propensity-score models, our outcome measures are the grades assigned in Spring 2002 by charter parents whose children have completed their first year in the school. Here, however, we compare them to the Spring 2002 evaluation measures of all sixty "denied-access parents" (DAPs), regardless if their child has completed their first year or if they have been in the school longer. Partly we choose this comparison group due to the small sample size, but we also believe it to be a theoretically appropriate group, since both groups shared the motivation to try to get into charter schools, but one group was denied enrollment in the charter schools at random via a lottery.

We analyze the data using the Wilcoxon rank-sum test for the univariate outcomes and Leach's (1991) multivariate nonparametric test for two samples for multivariate satisfaction. Once again, we average these statistics over all five multiple imputation datasets. We present the results of these analyses in table 9.4.

TABLE 9.4
Comparing Charter Parents to Parents Denied Access to Charter Schools

	Wilcoxon rank-sum test p	*Leach two-sample test p*
School grade	.007	
Teacher grade	.317	
Principal grade	.624	
Facilities grade	.001	
Multivariate satisfaction		.025
Multivariate satisfaction (school grade removed)		.028

Wilcoxon and Leach *p*-values are averaged using the method of Li, Ragunathan, and Rubin (1991) over five multiply imputed datasets. Sample size is 197 (137 charter parents and 60 parents who sought but were denied access to charter schools "DAPs").

Here our results are somewhat different than in the regression or propensity-score models presented above. The charter sample's mean outcomes are higher for all four univariate measures, but we find a statistically significant difference between the charter and DAP parents only for the facilities and overall school grades. Note that the two measures for which the Wilcoxon rank-sum test fails to reject the null hypothesis—the evaluation of teachers and principals—are also the measures which had the smallest critical values of Γ in the propensity-score sensitivity analysis (i.e., the results potentially most sensitive to bias due to an omitted variable). The multivariate comparison suggests that there is still a significant difference between charter and DAP parents overall ($p = .025$). Since it is possible that the facilities effect is strongly affecting the overall school grade, we also conduct a multivariate comparison of the two samples omitting the school-grade measure, with similar results.

While it is clear from our data that charter parents on average evaluate their child's school more highly than their counterparts in the traditional public schools in D.C., the results of the DAP comparison raise questions about the charter effect in the areas of teacher and principal satisfaction. It is possible that the small sample size of the DAPs, combined with additional uncertainty caused by the missing data imputation, has left us with insufficient power to detect the difference at conventional levels of significance. It is also possible that the DAPs are not perfect counterfactual controls to the charter parents—either because the lotteries did not perfectly randomize the groups or because of dissatisfaction or "randomization bias" (Heckman and Smith 1995) induced by their failure to win the school lottery.[11]

We suspect that the truth is somewhere in between. Parents in charter schools are, in general, more satisfied after a single school year. However, this difference in satisfaction is sensitive to other factors, perhaps especially in their evaluation of teachers and principals. We return to this question in the next chapter, where we examine the persistence of this difference in satisfaction over time. Before doing so, however, we look at parental responses to four other important indicators of satisfaction.

SATISFACTION WITH OTHER DIMENSIONS OF SCHOOLS

In the last section, we used grades to reflect parent evaluation of their child's school; however, most existing work has focused explicitly on reported levels of satisfaction with various characteristics of schools. Therefore, we queried parents specifically on their level of satisfaction with several other dimensions of the schools their children attended—each of which has important implications for the quality of schooling. Our empirical model here is identical to the second model for grades discussed above—we use estimated propensity scores of parents with children new to their schools to match charter parents to their DCPS controls and then measure the outcome variables at the conclusion of the school year.

Satisfaction with Values

One of the more interesting findings in this chapter has to do with parental satisfaction with the attention paid to values in their child's school.[12] A consistent theme in the research on effective schools is the importance of values in creating a strong community around which effective schools can be built. This theme is particularly evident in the analysis of the success of Catholic schools, where many scholars believe that the communal nature of these schools, built on a shared sense of values, helps produce academic success (Bryk, Lee, and Holland 1993; Coleman, Hoffer, and Kilgore 1982; Hoffer, Greeley, and Coleman 1985). While there is not much research on the extent to which *public* schools of choice, including charter schools, create a commitment to values, we believe that charter schools also have the potential for using shared values to create stronger communities and through such stronger communities, greater academic success. While we explore the issue of the strength of school communities in greater detail later in this book (chapters 11 and 12), in table 9.5 we see that charter-school parents are significantly more satisfied with the attention to values in their schools compared to DCPS parents.

TABLE 9.5
Charter Parents Are More Satisfied on Some Other Dimensions

	Hodges-Lehmann point estimate	Wilcoxon signed-rank test p	Critical level of Γ
Discipline	0.0	.194	1.00
Values	.5	<.001	1.70
School size	.6	<.001	2.10
Class size	.6	<.001	1.69

Hodges-Lehmann point estimates and Wilcoxon p-values (two-tailed) are averaged over five datasets imputed via predictive mean matching. The Rosenbaum's Γ column provides the values of Γ for which the upper limit of the confidence interval on the p of the signed-rank test is exactly .05. Sample size varies between 135 and 136 matched pairs depending on different imputed datasets due to discarding of observations not on the common support of the estimated propensity score.

Satisfaction with Discipline

We turn next to satisfaction with the discipline in the school. Unfortunately, urban public schools are all too often not safe and secure learning environments and inner-city parents often seek out safe schools for their children. To measure satisfaction with discipline, often one of the selling points of charter schools to parents in D.C., we asked parents how satisfied they were with the discipline in their child's school using a five-point scale. The results in table 9.5 below suggest that parents in charter schools in our cross section are *not* more satisfied with the level of discipline than are parents in the traditional D.C. public schools.

We also asked parents how satisfied were they with two other aspects of schools that have been associated with higher academic performance: school size and class size.

Satisfaction with Size of School

There is an increasing body of evidence that suggests that small schools are generally better than large ones and that the benefits of small schools are particularly pronounced in enhancing student achievement in lower-income communities (Fowler and Walberg 1991; Duke and Trautvetter; Cotton 1996; Lee and Smith 1997; Howley, Strange, and Bickel 1999).

While there are many reasons small schools may work better, from our perspective Wasley et al. (2000) make the most important link. They argue that small schools improve education by creating intimate learning communities in which students are well known to each other and to their teachers and are encouraged by adults who care for them and about them. These smaller, more intense communities, in turn, reduce the isolation that adversely affects many students, reduce discrepancies in the achievement gap that plagues poor children, and encourage teachers to be more creative in their ways of thinking and teaching styles.

Small schools have also been linked to higher levels of cooperation between teachers, better relations between teachers and school administrators, and more positive attitudes toward teaching (see, for example, Stockard and Mayberry 1992; Lee and Loeb 2000). In addition, small schools often foster parental involvement, which benefits students and the entire community (see Nathan and Febey 2001; Schneider, Teske, and Marschall 2000).[13]

In short, there is a wide range of benefits that accrue to smaller schools—and many of these benefits flow from fundamentally shifting the nature of the school community. As the reader will recall from chapter 3, at the time these data were collected, charter schools in D.C. were, on average, smaller than traditional public schools. Charter elementary schools averaged 271 students, compared to almost 450 students for D.C. public schools and charter middle schools averaged 354 students compared to 543 students for D.C. public schools. The difference at the high school level was even greater: around 150 for charter high schools compared to around 600 students for D.C. public high schools.[14] Given these large objective differences, it is probably not surprising that charter-school parents are more satisfied with the size of their children's schools than are other DCPS parents.

Satisfaction with the Class Size

While the research linking school size and desired outcomes has accumulated in a relatively straightforward manner, the research linking class size to learning outcomes has been much more contentious—but there is a growing consensus that students in smaller classes do better.

Some researchers have argued that educational inputs, including class size, are not associated with higher performance. While economist Rick Hanushek has been a leader staking out this position (see, e.g., Hanushek 1997), other researchers using a range of data also have also found that reducing class size has no effect on educational outcomes (see, for example, Hoxby 2000b or Johnson 2000) or can have unintended consequences in the distribution of teachers across schools of varying socioeconomic status (Bohrnstedt and Stecher 2000). But this work, and Hanushek's in particular, has been subject to criticism (see, for example, Greenwald, Hedges, and Laine 1996 and Krueger 2000), and there is a growing body of empirical work documenting the importance of smaller classes (for example, Ferguson 1991; Folger and Breda 1989; Ferguson and Ladd 1996; Wenglinsky 1997).

While the econometric evidence has been intensively fought over, there have been a series of experiments in which class sizes have been reduced, and the results of these experiments clearly support the benefits of smaller class size. Studies in a number of states have found positive results of smaller class size (see, for example, Egelson, Harmon, and Achilles 1996; Molnar et al. 1999), but the STAR program, authorized by the Tennessee legislature in 1985, has received the most attention. The results from the STAR experiment have shown significant positive effects, especially for lower SES students and for African American students (see, for example, Mosteller 1995 or Krueger 2000 and Krueger and Whitmore 2000). While the debate about small class size continues among researchers, parents, educators, and policy makers have already made their preferences clear: throughout the nation, small class size is one of the most popular school reforms.[15]

While we have no objective data available about average class size in the D.C. schools, we do see from table 9.5 that parents in charter schools are significantly more satisfied with their child's class size than are parents with children in the traditional public schools.

ARE CHARTER-SCHOOL PARENTS WEARING ROSE-COLORED GLASSES?

Parents in charter schools evaluate their child's school more highly and are more satisfied with many dimensions of those schools than parents with children in traditional D.C. public schools. These differences survive a wide range of tests to control for possible biases introduced by self-selection built into the option-demand nature of charter schools. In the next section of this chapter, we turn to another source of potential bias that might be inflating the evaluations of charter-school parents.

In our earlier discussion of behavioral-decision theory, we briefly mentioned the theory of motivated reasoning: when people choose a program or a service, they have a psychological bias toward evaluating it positively. In the literature on school choice, this is sometimes referred to as "rose-colored glasses" or a "rose-colored glasses effect" (Erikson 1982, 1986; Goldring and Shapira 1993).

If true, this phenomenon complicates the task of the analyst who uses self-reported levels of satisfaction from attitude surveys to evaluate the perceived quality of schools. While virtually every study of schools of choice finds higher levels of satisfaction among participating parents and students versus their counterparts in the traditional public schools (e.g., Bridge and Blackman 1978; Peterson 1998; Schneider, Teske, and

Marschall 2000; Moe 2001; Schneider and Buckley 2003), the possibility of the rose-colored glasses effect raises questions about the origin of these positive results.

To try to untangle this problem, we treat the rose-colored glasses effect as a measurement issue. We compare traditional public-school and charter-school parents on three measures of school satisfaction employing a relatively new model, the CHOPIT (Compound Hierarchical Ordered ProbIT) model designed explicitly to aid applied empirical research comparing across groups using ordinal survey responses (King et al. 2003).

We will show that choice alone does *not* appear to systematically bias perception. In fact, we show that the demographic characteristics of choosers tend to predict bias in the opposite direction: the type of parents who are dissatisfied enough to change their child's school tend to be *tougher* critics of the new school as well.

Rose-Colored Glasses as a Case of Differential Item Functioning

The central assumption of our approach is that the rose-colored glasses effect is closely related to what is known in the educational-testing literature as differential item functioning or DIF (Holland and Wainer 1993). From this perspective, the rose-colored glasses effect implies that parents in charter schools (or other schools of choice) who have the same true levels of satisfaction with their child's school respond to evaluation questions with a different set of response probabilities than those in traditional public schools—the very act of choosing creates a "positivity" bias.

For ordinal responses, the act of choosing can be viewed as acting to shift the "cutpoints" that partition a hypothetical continuous latent variable into the measured discrete ordinal categories, rather than acting as an influence solely on the latent continuous random measure of satisfaction or evaluation. The CHOPIT model is designed to account for precisely this problem and to produce estimates not only of the outcome model of interest, but also the effect of a set of covariates that are hypothesized to affect these cutpoints (King et al. 2003).[16]

Central to CHOPIT is the use of "anchoring vignettes"—hypothetical cases designed by the researcher with a known relative ranking on a dependent variable of interest. In our study, this meant presenting parents with descriptions of hypothetical schools that are fixed a priori to have a known and transitive ranking (for example, a best, middle, and worst school on a particular dimension such as parent-principal communication). The respondents are asked to evaluate the anchoring vignettes and these evaluations are then used to properly scale the true question of interest (referred to as the "self-assessment question").

More precisely, in the context of the familiar ordered-probit model with a latent continuous variable (Zavoina and McElvey 1975), CHOPIT allows the researcher to estimate the cutpoints that transform the underlying latent variable to the observed categorical response (and the contribution of a vector of covariates to those cutpoints) simultaneously with the mean model that is usually estimated. It is thus possible to model the potential differential-item functioning and properly compare (with cutpoints estimated at the individual level, if data allow) categorical responses.

The rose-colored glasses effect, in our CHOPIT model, is estimated by the contribution of an indicator variable for having a child in a D.C. charter school as opposed to a traditional public school to the estimation of the cutpoints of the mean evaluation model, holding the effects of demographics and other attitudes constant.

Anchoring Vignettes

To implement the CHOPIT model, we asked parents to evaluate their child's school on three different dimensions (parent-parent relations, parent-teacher relations, and parent-principal relations), and then to evaluate three hypothetical schools on each dimension.[17] We present parent-principal relations as an example.

We begin with the self-assessment question, in this example asking the parent to grade the relationship between the parent and the principal in their child's school on the familiar A, B, . . . , F scale.[18] We then presented the following anchoring vignettes:

Anchoring Vignettes: Parent-Principal Relations

Let's consider this situation: there is a child who routinely disrupts class and gets sent to the principal's office on a regular basis.

1. At this school, the principal calls the parents, follows up with a letter, and actively tries to find out the source of the child's behavior problem. How would you grade the relationship between the principal and the parents at this school?
2. At this school, the principal sends a letter home notifying the parents of the problem but doesn't do anything else. How would you grade the relationship between the parents and the principal at this school?
3. At this school, the principal just has the child sit in the main office for a few hours and never notifies the parent. How would you grade the relationship between the principal and the parents at this school?[19]

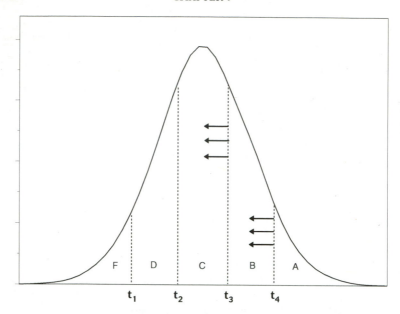

Figure 9.2. How rose-colored glasses may affect evaluations. A possible hypothetical shift of cutpoints due to the rose-colored glasses effect. The combined results
of the shifts are to make it more likely for a respondent with a given latent score
to report an A or B grade, and less likely to report a C. Here the probabilities of
reporting a D or F remain unchanged.

If charter parents are viewing their child's school through rose-colored
glasses, then the coefficient on the charter variable in the equations for
the higher-valued (more positive evaluation responses) cutpoints will be
negative, while those of the lower-valued cutpoints may be positive, negative, or indistinguishable from zero. For example, figure 9.2 illustrates one
possible scenario that is consistent with the rose-colored glasses effect. In
the figure, which shows a hypothetical distribution of the latent variable
for charter parents, the cutpoints between the grades of A and B and B
and C are shifted to the left as a result of the effect of a negative coefficient
on charter enrollment, while the other cutpoints remain unchanged. Thus
the probability of a parent reporting an A or B for a given latent score
is increased, while the probability of reporting a C is decreased.

Does Choice Create Rose-Colored Glasses?

The first model we estimate for each of the dependent variables is a simple
model in which parents' responses are modeled using the same vectors of
covariates for each of the three school-community dimensions, and the

cutpoint models contain only a constant and an indicator variable for charter-school enrollment. For the mean model in each dimension,

$$E(Y^*_i) = \beta_1 \text{Charter}_i + \beta_2 \text{White}_i + \beta_3 \text{Hispanic}_i + \beta_4 \text{Other Race}_i +$$
$$\beta_5 \text{Education}_i + \beta_6 \text{Education}^2_i + \beta_7 \text{Married}_i + \beta_8 \text{Employed}_i +$$
$$\beta_9 \text{Church Attendance}_i + \beta_{10} \text{DC Public Schools Attitude}_i + \quad (9.3)$$
$$\beta_{11} \text{Time Lived in DC}_i + \beta_{12} \text{Timed Lived in Neighborhood}_i +$$
$$\beta_{13} \text{Female}_i$$

and for the cutpoint model:

$$\tau^1_i = \gamma^1_0 + \gamma^1_1 \text{Charter}_i \quad (9.4)$$

for the first cutpoint and,

$$\tau^k_i = \tau^{k-1}_i + \exp(\gamma^k_0 + \gamma^k_1 \text{Charter}_i) \quad (9.5)$$

for the subsequent ones, where Charter is a dichotomous variable indicating that the parent's child is in a charter school and the remaining covariates are as defined earlier in the chapter. The constant is omitted in the mean equation to allow for the estimation of all cutpoints.

Table 9.6 compares the results of the CHOPIT mean model to results from a typical ordered probit. The results are comparable, although note that the coefficients on charter enrollment are generally larger in the CHOPIT models (but are not readily interpretable given the nonlinearity of the model). Table 9.7 presents the results of the cutpoint models—the information we need to evaluate the presence of rose-colored glasses.

The model provides only slight support for the rose-colored glasses effect: the only statistically significant coefficient on the charter indicator is the negative coefficient on the third cutpoint of the teacher-community model. Note, however, that because of the parameterization of the model, a change in one cutpoint has the effect of also shifting subsequent cutpoints—in this case the remaining cutpoint between A and B. In other words, choosing a charter school appears only to make parents more likely to give the teacher-parent relations in their school a grade of A or B (at the expense of C, as in the hypothetical example in figure 9.2), holding all the effects of the mean model constant.

Before drawing conclusions about the rose-colored glasses effect on the basis of this evidence, we turn to a model of the cutpoints that includes additional covariates whose omission may be biasing the results presented in table 9.7.

Table 9.8 presents the results of the cutpoint models. The first cutpoint is now modeled by:

$$\tau^1_i = \gamma^1_0 + \gamma^1_1 \text{Charter}_i + \gamma^1_2 \text{White}_i + \gamma^1_3 \text{Hispanic}_i + \gamma^1_4 \text{Other Race}_i +$$
$$\gamma^1_5 \text{Education}_i + \gamma^1_6 \text{Education}^2_i + \gamma^1_7 \text{DC Public Schools Attitude}_i + \quad (9.6)$$
$$\gamma^1_8 \text{Female}_i$$

TABLE 9.6

Comparing Standard Ordered-Probit to CHOPIT Estimates for Three School-Community Measures, Mean Model (1), Cutpoint Models (2) and (3)

Variable	Parent-teacher		Parent-parent		Parent-principal	
	Ordered-probit coefficient	CHOPIT coefficient	Ordered-probit coefficient	CHOPIT coefficient	Ordered-probit coefficient	CHOPIT coefficient
Charter	.19 (.11)	.23 (.15)	.23* (.11)	.28* (.14)	.19 (.11)	.18 (.14)
White	-.04 (.24)	-.10 (.26)	.37 (.24)	.37 (.25)	.09 (.24)	.16 (.25)
Hispanic	-.34 (.22)	-.46 (.24)	.10 (.22)	.18 (.24)	-.11 (.21)	-.18 (.24)
Other	.07 (.23)	-.13 (.27)	-.15 (.23)	-.08 (.25)	-.08 (.22)	-.24 (.26)
Education	-.35* (.14)	-.38* (.17)	-.29* (.11)	-.24* (.12)	-.31* (.13)	-.21 (.14)
Education^2	.01 (.01)	.01 (.006)	.01* (.004)	.01* (.004)	.01* (.004)	.01 (.01)
Married	.06 (.11)	.05 (.13)	-.03 (.11)	-.04 (.12)	.01 (.11)	-.02 (.12)
Working	-.24 (.13)	-.25 (.14)	-.31* (.12)	-.26* (.13)	-.19 (.12)	-.21 (.13)
Church	-.02 (.03)	-.01 (.03)	.02 (.03)	.02 (.03)	.01 (.03)	.02 (.03)
DCPS grade	.02 (.05)	-.01 (.06)	.18* (.05)	.15* (.05)	.11* (.05)	.10* (.05)
Time in DC	-.01 (.01)	-.01 (.01)	.01 (.01)	.02 (.01)	.01 (.01)	.01 (.01)
Time in neighborhood	<.01 (.01)	.01 (.01)	<.01 (.01)	<.01 (.01)	<.01 (.01)	-.01 (.01)
Female	-.02 (.14)	-.03 (.16)	.05 (.14)	.06 (.15)	-.05 (.14)	-.10 (.15)
Cutpoint 1	-4.60* (.98)		-2.90* (.79)		-3.46* (.92)	
Cutpoint 2	-4.07* (.98)		-2.48* (.78)		-3.04* (.92)	
Cutpoint 3	-3.39* (.97)		-1.58* (.78)		-2.41* (.92)	
Cutpoint 4	-2.46* (.97)		-.53 (.78)		-1.50* (.92)	
Vignette 1		-1.95 (1.19)		.17 (.85)		-.33 (.97)
Vignette 2		-3.24 (1.19)		-.92 (.85)		-2.45* (.97)
Vignette 3		-4.52* (1.20)		-2.55* (.85)		-3.28* (.98)
ln σ		.02 (.07)		.09 (.06)		

* $p < .05$, two-tailed.
Number of observations = 374; standard errors in parentheses.

TABLE 9.7
A Simple Model of the Cutpoints Provides Only Modest Support
for the Rose-Colored-Glasses Effect

	Cutpoint 1			Cutpoint 2		
	Teacher	Parent	Principal	Teacher	Parent	Principal
Charter	.14	.05	.11	.19	−.06	−.08
	(.11)	(.10)	(.08)	(.15)	(.14)	(.11)
Constant	−5.17*	−2.59*	−3.08*	−.52*	−.43*	−.40*
	(1.21)	(.85)	(.97)	(.13)	(.11)	(.10)

	Cutpoint 3			Cutpoint 3		
	Teacher	Parent	Principal	Teacher	Parent	Principal
Charter	−.21*	.01	−.13	−.10	.04	−.03
	(.10)	(.09)	(.11)	(.09)	(.08)	(.10)
Constant	−.11	−.09	−.27*	−.10	−.06	−.20*
	(.09)	(.08)	(.09)	(.08)	(.07)	(.08)

* $p < .05$, two-tailed.
N = 374. Standard errors in parentheses.

and each subsequent cutpoint by:

$$\tau_i^k = \tau_i^{k-1} + \exp(\gamma_0^k + \gamma_1^k \text{Charter}_i + \gamma_2^k \text{White}_i + \gamma_3^k \text{Hispanic}_i + \gamma_4^k \text{Other Race}_i + \gamma_5^k \text{Education}_i + \gamma_6^k \text{Education}^2_i + \gamma_7^k \text{DC Public Schools Attitude}_i + \gamma_8^k \text{Female}_i \tag{9.7}$$

where the covariates are the same as described above.

Table 9.8 compares the results of this second set of CHOPIT mean models to results from their ordered-probit counterparts. Again, the results of the two models are comparable, although note that here the coefficient on charter enrollment is generally smaller in size (and in some cases no longer statistically significant at conventional levels) in the CHOPIT models. Table 9.9 presents the results of the revised cutpoint models (4) and (5). Here the result is clear: although a variety of demographic covariates have a statistically significant effect on the cutpoints or thresholds in the CHOPIT model, the coefficients on charter enrollment are statistically indistinguishable from zero. This suggests that the thresholds with which respondents partition their underlying attitude into categories is not influenced, ceteris paribus, by choice alone.

Is there any difference, then, in the evaluations of charter and traditional parents? The answer is found not from the marginal effect of charter enrollment, but instead in considering the differences between charter and traditional public school parents on the variables used in the cutpoint model presented in table 9.9.

TABLE 9.8

Comparing Standard Ordered-Probit to CHOPIT Estimates for Three School-Community Measures, Cutpoint Models (4) and (5), with Additional Covariates

Variable	Parent-teacher		Parent-parent		Parent-principal	
	Ordered-probit coefficient	CHOPIT coefficient	Ordered-probit coefficient	CHOPIT coefficient	Ordered-probit coefficient	CHOPIT Coefficient
Charter	.19 (.11)	.15 (.13)	.23* (.11)	.23 (.13)	.19 (.11)	.07 (.13)
White	−.04 (.24)	−.29 (.29)	.37 (.24)	.08 (.28)	.09 (.24)	−.07 (.28)
Hispanic	−.34 (.22)	−.47 (.26)	.10 (.22)	−.02 (.26)	−.11 (.21)	−.05 (.25)
Other	.07 (.23)	.01 (.27)	−.15 (.23)	−.37 (.26)	−.08 (.22)	−.21 (.25)
Education)	−.35* (.14)	−.13 (.15)	−.29* (.11)	−.17 (.14)	−.31* (.13)	−.04 (.14)
Education^2	.01 (.01)	.01 (.01)	.01* (.004)	.01 (.01)	.01* (.004)	<.01 (.01)
Married	.06 (.11)	.07 (.12)	−.03 (.11)	−.01 (.11)	.01 (.11)	.02 (.11)
Working	−.24 (.13)	−.24 (.13)	−.31* (.12)	−.26* (.12)	−.19 (.12)	−.18 (.12)
Church	−.02 (.03)	−.02 (.03)	.02 (.03)	.02 (.03)	.01 (.03)	.01 (.03)
DCPS grade	.02 (.05)	−.01 (.06)	.18* (.05)	.11 (.06)	.11* (.05)	.04 (.06)
Time in D.C.	−.01 (.01)	−.01 (.01)	.01 (.01)	.01 (.01)	.01 (.01)	.01 (.01)
Time in neighborhood	<.01 (.01)	−.01 (.01)	<.01 (.01)	<.01 (.01)	<.01 (.01)	<.01 (.01)
Female	−.02 (.14)	−.01 (.17)	.05 (.14)	.08 (.16)	−.05 (.14)	.12 (.16)
Cutpoint 1	−4.60* (.98)		−2.90* (.79)		−3.46* (.92)	
Cutpoint 2	−4.07* (.98)		−2.48* (.78)		−3.04* (.92)	
Cutpoint 3	−3.39* (.97)		−1.58* (.78)		−2.41* (.92)	
Cutpoint 4	−2.46* (.97)		−.53 (.78)		−1.50 (.92)	
Vignette 1		−.17 (1.10)		.44 (1.01)		.85 (1.03)
Vignette 2		−1.47 (1.10)		−.60 (1.01)		−1.15 (1.02)
Vignette 3		−2.79* (1.10)		−2.23* (1.02)		−1.99* (1.02)
ln σ		.03 (.06)		.05 (.05)		−.09 (.06)

* $p < .05$, two-tailed.

Number of observations = 374; standard errors in parentheses.

As table 9.10 shows, charter and DCPS respondents in the sample are alike in many ways, but differ in their attitude toward the D.C. public school system and in their likelihood of reporting their race as white. In order to see what effect these differences have on the cutpoints in the CHOPIT model, we compute predicted values for each τ_i, using one vector of sample mean values on the demographic and DCPS grade covariates for charter respondents, and a second vector of sample mean responses for DCPS parents. The results for all three outcome measures, presented in figure 9.3, are interesting.

TABLE 9.9
Choice Alone Does Not Lead to Biased Evaluations

	Cutpoint 1				Cutpoint 2		
	Teacher	Parent	Principal		Teacher	Parent	Principal
Charter	.01 (.11)	.003 (.10)	−.06 (.08)	Charter	.07 (.14)	−.06 (.13)	−.02 (.12)
White	−.61* (.30)	−.19 (.21)	−.51* (.17)	White	.26 (.34)	−.18 (.30)	.45* (.21)
Hispanic	.33* (.20)	.30 (.19)	.20 (.15)	Hispanic	−.08 (.26)	−.37 (.30)	.06 (.22)
Other	.26 (.21)	−.23 (.21)	−.02 (.15)	Other	−.39 (.34)	−.11 (.26)	−.23 (.25)
DCPS Grade	−.06 (.05)	−.10* (.04)	−.03 (.03)	DCPS Grade	.01 (.06)	−.04 (.05)	−.02 (.05)
Female	.02 (.13)	−.03 (.12)	.18* (.09)	Female	.04 (.18)	.09 (.17)	.11 (.14)
Education	.15 (.13)	−.06 (.08)	.10 (.08)	Education	.79* (.30)	.90* (.28)	.69* (.22)
Education^2	−.01 (.01)	.01 (.01)	−.01 (.01)	Education^2	−.03* (.01)	−.03* (.01)	−.02* (.01)
Constant	−4.02* (1.32)	−1.50 (1.04)	−2.60* (1.05)	Constant	−6.22* (2.11)	−6.98* (2.02)	−5.62* (1.61)

	Cutpoint 3				Cutpoint 4		
	Teacher	Parent	Principal		Teacher	Parent	Principal
Charter	−.09 (.10)	−.003 (.09)	−.07 (.11)	Charter	−.06 (.09)	.08 (.08)	−.02 (.10)
White	.13 (.20)	.09 (.20)	.29 (.21)	White	.10 (.17)	−.01 (.16)	−.39 (.24)
Hispanic	−.40* (.24)	−.50* (.25)	.03 (.22)	Hispanic	−.44* (.22)	.07 (.16)	−.57* (.25)
Other	−.22 (.24)	.03 (.18)	.12 (.20)	Other	.01 (.18)	−.18 (.18)	−.10 (.20)
DCPS Grade	.03 (.04)	.02 (.04)	−.04 (.05)	DCPS Grade	.01 (.04)	−.01 (.03)	−.02 (.04)
Female	−.11 (.12)	.04 (.12)	−.11 (.13)	Female	.02 (.11)	−.12 (.10)	−.06 (.12)
Education	.04 (.22)	.14 (.15)	.11 (.15)	Education	−.17* (.09)	−.11 (.08)	−.16* (.09)
Education^2	−.01 (.01)	−.01 (.01)	−.01 (.01)	Education^2	.01* (.003)	.01* (.003)	.01* (.003)
Constant	−.52 (1.52)	−1.14 (1.07)	−.79 (1.06)	Constant	.83 (.62)	.71 (.62)	1.01 (.65)

* $p < .10$ level, two-tailed.
N= 374. Standard errors in parentheses.

The relative heights in the figure are like different-sized "hurdles" that must be overcome by the latent evaluation variable in order for the next highest grade to be reported. In all three measures, the predicted values for the charter τ_i's are larger than those of the DCPS parents (although the differences are not significant for the parent-parent measure). Because higher thresholds means a more positive latent attitude is required to report a given categorical grade level, according to these results charter parents are *tougher* graders.

The findings of the CHOPIT model, using community measures of hypothetical schools to anchor parental evaluation of actual schools, thus have an interesting interpretation: charter parents do not appear to wear

Table 9.10
Charter and DCPS Demographics in Sample

	Mean for charter parents	Mean for DCPS parents
White	.01	.15
Hispanic	.06	.07
Other	.04	.06
DCPS grade	1.77	2.18
Female	.84	.74
Education	13.77	14.00
Education squared	194.66	205.09

Sample size = 374 complete cases, 200 charter and 174 DCPS.

rose-colored glasses as a function of choice; in fact, quite the opposite appears true considering the demographic and prior attitudinal differences between the groups of parents. Choosers may be more demanding consumers, even after they have invested the time and energy to change their child's school. Rather than viewing their schools through rose-colored glasses, the type of people who choose may actually be wearing "grey-colored" ones.[20]

Clearly, parental satisfaction is a serious consideration in evaluating the success of charter schools, but students are ultimately the prime "consumers" of schooling. We look next at how students evaluate their schools to assess the extent to which greater parental satisfaction with charter schools is mirrored by higher student satisfaction.

HOW DO STUDENTS EVALUATE THEIR SCHOOLS?

Paralleling the method we used to gauge parental satisfaction, we began by asking students in our study to grade their teachers, their school's principal, the school facility, and the school overall. We treated responses as ordered-dependent variables and used ordered probit to explore differences between students in the two sectors. In the ordered-probit equation, we controlled for the students' racial identification, their grade level, and the length of time they were in the school. Because church attendance had a significant effect in some of our analyses of parental attitudes and behavior and because others have found religiosity to affect attitudes toward choice and the functioning of schools (see, for example, Moe 2001), we control for the student's frequency of church attendance. We also con-

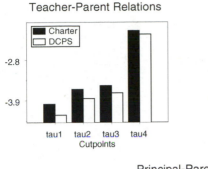

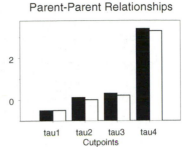

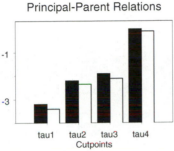

Figure 9.3. Charter parents have *higher* mean thresholds due to demographic differences.

trolled for the number of students in the school, since school size may have a significant effect on a large number of student behaviors and attitudes. In this section analyzing grading patterns, we also included the overall grade that students assigned to the D.C. public schools. To deal with the missing-values problem, as earlier in this chapter, we employed multiple imputation and the results reported in the next section are based on that procedure.

As is evident in table 9.11, we find no charter school enrollment effect on the assignment of any of the four grades—while charter parents clearly grade their child's school higher than their DCPS counterparts, student evaluations are not any different.

As with our analysis of the parent-satisfaction data, we next move beyond the analysis of grades, and we asked students what they thought about other characteristics of their school. First, we asked them how much they agreed with the following statements that pertain to the level of orderliness in the school:

- Rules for behavior are strict in my school.
- There is a lot of cheating in my school.
- I don't feel safe in my school.

TABLE 9.11
Charter-School Students Do Not Grade Their Schools Differently

	School	Teacher	Principal	Facility
Charter	−.05 (.20)	.25 (.21)	.02 (.22)	.26 (.19)
Hispanic	.30 (.33)	.17 (.37)	−.01 (.42)	−.89 (.33)*
Other race	−.44 (.48)	−1.40 (.45)*	2.60 (2.51)	−.52 (.40)
Time in school	−.21 (.06)*	−.07 (.06)	−.14 (.06)*	.04 (.06)
Student's grade level	−.02 (.06)	−.06 (.07)	−.02 (.07)	−.16 (.06)*
School size (hundreds)	.01 (.02)	−.04 (.02)	.07 (.02)*	.003 (.02)
Church attendance	−.03 (.06)	−.15 (.06)*	−.12 (.07)*	−.05 (.06)
DCPS grade	.25 (.10)*	.32 (.10)*	.33 (.10)*	.34 (.09)*
Cutpoint 1	−2.50 (.77)*	−1.9 (.79)*	−1.94 (.80)*	−2.96 (.75)*
Cutpoint 2	−1.83 (.74)*	−.44 (.78)	−1.37 (.78)*	−2.27 (.73)*
Cutpoint 3	−.95 (.74)	N/A	−.42 (.77)	−.88 (.72)
Cutpoint 4	.61 (.73)	N/A	.40 (.77)	.28 (.72)

* $p < .10$, two-tailed.

Number of observations = 165. Results are coefficient estimates from independent ordinal probit regressions of outcome measures, weighted to correct for oversample of charter parents and averaged over five multiple-imputation datasets constructed via predictive mean matching. Standard errors in parentheses.

We also asked students how satisfied they were with the level of discipline in their school and with their school's attention to values.[21]

As evident in table 9.12, and paralleling the data we report for school grades, there are no significant differences in the responses of DCPS students and charter-school students. So while charter *parents*, for example, are far more satisfied with the attention to values paid by the school, the students do not differ on this nor any other characteristics we measure.

We turn next to two measures that reflect Hirschman's well-known exit, voice, and loyalty options. First, there is no statistical difference in student interest in the exit option: for example, while 74 percent of traditional public school students disagreed with the sentence "I wish I could go to a different school," this was not significantly higher than the 68 percent of charter-school students who felt the same way.

We do find a charter school effect (at $p = .08$, two tailed) for how proud students are of their school. More specifically, 38 percent of DCPS students agreed strongly with the statement that "Students are proud to go to my school," significantly higher than the 26 percent of the charter students who agreed.[22]

TABLE 9.12

Charter-School Students Are Less Proud of Their Schools, but Otherwise Not Different

	Rules are strict	A lot of cheating	Don't feel safe	Satisfied with discipline	Satisfied with values	Would go to different school	Students proud of school
Charter	.08 (.21)	.23 (.22)	-.004 (.21)	.21 (.21)	-.30 (.21)	.02 (.20)	-.34 (.20)*
Hispanic	.78 (.40)*	.85 (.34)*	.51 (.41)	-.70 (.36)*	.25 (.34)	-.08 (.35)	.54 (.35)
Other race	-.33 (.54)	.17 (.50)	-.20 (.47)	-1.60 (.50)*	-.38 (.44)	-1.13 (.46)*	1.10 (.50)*
Time in school	.003 (.06)	-.05 (.06)	.01 (.06)	-.05 (.06)	-.01 (.06)	.10 (.06)	-.01 (.06)
Student's grade level	-.07 (.07)	.002 (.06)	.01 (.07)	-.04 (.07)	-.09 (.06)	.02 (.07)	-.08 (.06)
School size (hundreds)	.01 (.02)	.03 (.03)	.06 (.03)*	.02 (.03)	-.07 (.03)*	.08 (.03)*	.04 (.03)
Church attendance	-.05 (.06)	.11 (.07)*	.07 (.07)	-.11 (.06)*	.09 (.06)	.07 (.06)	-.06 (.06)
DCPS grade	.15 (.10)	.09 (.10)	.03 (.10)	.11 (.10)	-.11 (.11)	.01 (.10)	.06 (.10)
Cutpoint 1	-2.36 (.78)*	-.33 (.75)	-.79 (.81)	-3.34 (.91)*	-3.72 (.82)*	-.12 (.79)	-2.13 (.76)*
Cutpoint 2	-1.47 (.77)*	.18 (.75)	-.12 (.80)	-1.96 (.82)*	-3.06 (.81)*	.62 (.79)	-1.36 (.75)*
Cutpoint 3	-.49 (.77)	1.06 (.76)	.44 (.80)	-1.92 (.82)*	-1.30 (.79)*	1.24 (.79)	-.39 (.75)
Cutpoint 4	N/A	N/A	N/A	.01 (.80)	1.17 (.82)	N/A	N/A

* $p < .10$, two-tailed.
Number of observations = 165. Results are coefficient estimates from independent ordinal probit regressions of outcome measures, weighted to correct for oversample of charter parents and averaged over five multiple-imputation datasets constructed via predictive mean matching. Standard errors in parentheses.

CONCLUSIONS

We began this chapter by confirming the findings that many other analysts studying schools of choice have previously found—parents who choose their children's schools are more satisfied. However, we establish a much stronger footing for these findings than is the norm, by explicitly addressing the possibility of bias emerging from self-selection and from rose-colored glasses. This is clearly good news for proponents of charter schools and, more generally, school choice—one of the most fundamental tests of the benefits of markets, greater consumer satisfaction, has been met. In addition, given the higher levels of satisfaction, charter parents may represent a political force for the further expansion of choice.

However, when we turned to the students who are the ultimate consumers of the product schools offer, we find far weaker results—students in both sectors are remarkably similar in their evaluations of their schools. The disjuncture between parent and student evaluations is an interesting phenomenon. In several other chapters we present later in this book, we will again see that charter-school parents are more enthusiastic about the charter schools than are the children who actually attend them. We explore some potential reasons for this in our concluding chapter. But next, we turn to an analysis of the durability of these patterns over time.

APPENDIX 9.1

The CHOPIT Model

MATHEMATICALLY, THE CHOPIT MODEL is straightforward (although in practice estimation can be time-consuming). To begin with, let Y_i^* denote the latent self-assessment measure (the parent's true grade for their child's school's parent-teacher relationship, for example). As in the case of a standard ordinal probit model, $Y_i^* \sim N(\mu_i, 1)$, where $\mu_i = X_i\beta$. The actual reported self-assessment, y_i is a choice of K ordered categories. The latent variable is assumed to be converted to the observed measure via a vector of thresholds, τ_i such that $y_i = k$ if $\tau_i^{k-1} \leq Y_i \leq \tau_i^k$, $k = 1, \ldots, K$, where $\tau_i^0 = -\infty$ and $\tau_i^K = \infty$. Note that the cutpoints are indexed over the individual observations—the crucial difference from the standard model. These individual-level cutpoints are themselves defined as a function of another vector of covariates V_i and parameters γ. The first cutpoint is defined: $\tau_i^1 = \gamma^1 V_i$, and the subsequent cutpoints are constrained to increase monotonically by assuming the functional form: $\tau_i^k = \tau_i^{k-1} + \exp(\gamma^k V_i)$.

As discussed above, the vignettes are used to identify (anchor) the cutpoints. Let θ_j denote the mean response or evaluation by subjects (parents in the data discussed here) to vignette j. We assume normal variability in i's perception of θ_j, Z_{ij}^*, where $Z_{ij}^* \sim N(\theta_j, \sigma^2)$. Z_{ij}^* is measured using a survey instrument with the same K response options again partitioned by cutpoints so that the categorical response $z_{ij} + k$ if $\tau_{i1}^{k-1} \leq Z_{ij}^* \leq \tau_{i1}^k$, $k = 1, \ldots, K$. These cutpoints are determined using the same coefficient vector γ as in the mean model and the same vector V of covariates. It is this assumption of identical γ's that identifies the model and allows the vignettes to be used to correct DIF at the individual level. The CHOPIT model, once specified, is then estimated via standard maximum-likelihood methods, where the likelihood function maximized is

$$L(\beta, \sigma^2, \theta, \gamma \mid y, z, V, X)$$

In the King et al. (2003) article, a more general model is presented that includes an individual-level random effect in the mean equation. This is strongly identified only in the context of a latent variable analysis of several simultaneous self-assessment questions. Although it is possible to estimate this variant of the model in which the three dependent variables discussed here are treated as multiple measures of a latent school-community strength factor, we choose not to here because we believe that the disaggregated models are of greater substantive interest to education-policy analysts. We should also note that we estimate the CHOPIT models here using the *gllamm* user-written add-on for Stata 7.0 or above (Rabe-Hesketh and Skrondal 2002). The model may also be estimated using code for the R statistical environment that can be downloaded from http://anchors.stanford.edu/

Will You Still Love Me Tomorrow?
Parental Satisfaction over Time

IN THE PREVIOUS CHAPTER, we used our survey data to identify differences in parental satisfaction with charter schools compared to the satisfaction experienced by parents' counterparts in traditional public schools. Using a variety of methods, we found that charter parents are more satisfied with their schools on many important dimensions, even after controlling for bias caused by self-selection and "rose-colored glasses." A centerpiece of our approach was a study that used matched pairs of charter and DCPS parents to examine the treatment effect of charter enrollment and test for the sensitivity of the results to confounding unobserved covariates. This method suggests that there is a reasonably strong effect of enrollment in charter schools, but in our desire to minimize the risk of bias and to minimize the assumptions of the functional form placed on the model, we used only a fraction of our data, studying only parents with children newly enrolled in schools over the course of a single school year. In this chapter, we switch to a different modeling approach in an attempt to better understand what happens to levels of parental satisfaction in both charters and traditional public schools as the parents and their children experience the schools over several years. But first, we highlight the importance of this temporal analysis.

People form judgments about the quality and usefulness of most goods and services as they use them over time. Everyone loves a new car. But what happens as time passes? Does the car hold up, or do the wheels fall off after thirty thousand miles? Often it is only over time that we discover whether love at first sight endures or whether we bought the proverbial pig in a poke.

In some cases, this dimension is so important to our judgment of the quality of a good that economists define some items as "experience goods."[1] Experience goods present problems to consumers because their quality, and hence their value, cannot be precisely determined by buyers at the time of purchase. In addition, when it comes to experience goods, there is a pronounced information asymmetry between producers and consumers—producers have more knowledge of the real value of the good and have no incentive to reveal that quality to the consumer. This asymmetry can create what Akerlof (1970) famously called a "market for lemons," in which only low-quality goods are produced and sold for low prices and high-quality goods disappear from the market.

Clearly, we do not want to imply that the market for charter schools unravels like the used-car market described by Akerlof (nor do we wish to imply that charter schools are lemons); however, we do want to note that schools are very complex institutions for parents to judge *before* they have had extensive experience with them. While we can avoid some of the unpleasant experiences of buying cars that turn into lemons by reading consumer reviews, or paying for a prepurchase inspection, information about schools is often hard to find and harder to digest (despite the reporting requirements of No Child Left Behind and other state and local efforts to disseminate information). As we have noted earlier in this book, for a variety of reasons, most parents simply do not have enough information before their child enrolls in a school to make a good judgment about its quality (also see Schneider, Teske, and Marschall 2000).

Our own experience in gathering data in big cities further suggests that a lot of the data that *are* reported would not pass an independent audit, assuming that such a thing existed (to put it politely, we suspect that the data are often "cooked"). In addition, in many cities, including Washington, D.C., the "movement" pushing school choice (including charter schools) may create a heightened sense of quality surrounding schools of choice and, as we saw in Chapter 7, such positive affect can bias how people process information.

Put all these factors together and a single snapshot of parents' satisfaction may not be sufficient to reflect their true evaluation of schools. As with any experience goods, the quality of the school (and the corresponding level of parental satisfaction with it) may only be revealed over time, when the educational equivalent of the new-car smell has worn off and the frustration of the daily struggle to get the car started in the morning replaces the warm and fuzzy feeling we felt when the car was new.

OUR APPROACH TO STUDYING CHANGE OVER TIME

Perhaps the ideal research design for addressing this question would be a long panel study or longitudinal analysis of the same parents over their children's entire school career. A less powerful, but more feasible alternative would be the inclusion of a covariate for the number of years that a child has been in his school in the analysis of data from a cross-sectional study.

Unfortunately, all too often studies of parental satisfaction in charter schools and other educational reforms take neither approach. Even when the dynamics of satisfaction *are* considered, they are often modeled with restrictive assumptions that limit the value of the model. For example, in a one-year cross-sectional study of parental satisfaction in the Arizona charter schools prepared for the Arizona State Board for Charter Schools, Solomon (2003) regressed the grades assigned by parents on the number of years that the child has been enrolled and reports a positive and statistically significant coefficient—implying that, other things being equal, the longer the charter-school parents are involved with a school the higher they will evaluate it. This approach assumes, however, that time has a simple linear additive effect on satisfaction. But what if the effect of time is curvilinear? For example, what if there is a diminishing marginal return to time—that is, the time does lead to higher valuations, but at a decreasing rate? Such possible complexities are not captured in Solomon's model, but are often found in the real-world dynamics of attitude change and opinion formation.

Because of the nature of our survey data, our approach to measuring the dynamics of parental satisfaction falls somewhere between the full panel approach and the cross-sectional covariate approach. Since we have four panel waves, we are able to estimate "true" panel data models, such as unit fixed-effects regressions or simple difference-in-differences models. However, since our parents enter the study with their children at different lengths of time in their schools, we can also use a model-based approach to take advantage of this additional source of variation.

In much of the literature on applied longitudinal data analysis in the social sciences, there is a presumed trade-off between fixed- and random-effects models. The simpler, fixed-effects models are often cited as having the advantage of eliminating potential unmeasured confounds through differencing, but at the cost of also differencing out interesting covariates that do not vary with time or vary slowly, such as respondent demographics (Baltagi 2001, 11–20). Others, however, have recently pointed out that under a variety of plausible violations of modeling assumptions, such as endogeneity of treatment (Belsley and Case 2000) and serial correlation in the residuals (Bertrand, Duflo, and Mullainathan 2004), difference-in-differences or fixed-effects models may lead to errors in inference. Furthermore, time-varying unit effects, such as the celebrated "Ashenfelter's Dip" in which participants self-select to a job-training program as a result of an unusual shock to their earnings (Ashenfelter 1978), may also negate the ability of the fixed-effect model to account for omitted variable bias.

Random-effects models, on the other hand, allow the inclusion of time-invariant regressors but with the additional and often highly tenuous assumption that these covariates are uncorrelated with the unit effects. Although researchers have proposed instrumental-variable models to account for this problem by modeling the unit random effects as correlated with other explanatory variables (Hausman and Taylor 1981; Amemiya and MaCurdy 1986), these models can be difficult to specify and are sensitive to the decision about which covariates are exogenous to the random effects.

Plumper and Troeger (2004) have proposed an alternative approach which is not overly difficult to implement, has desirable small sample properties, and appears to be more efficient under many conditions than the alternatives sketched briefly above. Their procedure, the *fixed-effects vector-decomposition* model, involves a first stage in which the outcome measure is regressed on the time-varying covariates using a standard fixed-effects model. In the second stage, the unit effects from this model are regressed on the time-invariant variables using the least-squares estimator. Finally, in the third stage, a pooled least-squares model is estimated, regressing the dependent variable on all covariates and the residual from the second stage—which is the part of each unit effect that is not explained by the stage two regressors. A particular advantage of the model is that it allows for the joint estimation of the effects of time-varying and time-invariant covariates without making overly restrictive assumptions about the correlations between the unit effects and covariates.[2]

More precisely, the Plumper and Troeger model assumes that we have a vector of outcomes y_{it} measured for each individual i at time t. Let x_{it} and z_i denote vectors of time-varying and invariant covariates. The first stage of the fixed-effects variance-decomposition model is the familiar "within" fixed effects estimator:

$$y_{it} - \bar{y}_i = (x_{it} - \bar{x}_i)\,'\beta_{FE} + \varepsilon_{it} - \bar{\varepsilon}_i \tag{10.1}$$

or, if we denote the differencing with a tilde,

$$\tilde{y}_{it} = \tilde{x}_{it}\,'\beta_{FE} + \tilde{\varepsilon}_{it} \tag{10.2}$$

where β_{FE} is the vector of population coefficients and ε_{it} is the residual vector. Once β_{FE} is estimated, the estimated unit fixed effects, $\hat{u}_i$ are obtained via:

$$\hat{u}_i = \bar{y}_i - \bar{x}_i\,'\hat{\beta}_{FE} \tag{10.3}$$

In the second stage, the fixed effects are themselves regressed on z_i, "purging" them of the part that can be explained by the time-invariant regressors (including a constant term in z_i):

$$\hat{u}_i = z_i\,'\gamma + \eta_i \tag{10.4}$$

where γ is the vector of second stage coefficients and η_i is the second stage residual vector. We then estimate η_i by rearranging and solving per equation (10.3).

In the third stage, we again regress the outcome variable on the time-varying covariates, the nonvarying covariates, and the purged residual, using pooled ordinary least squares, adjusting the degrees of freedom of the variance-covariance matrix (Plumper and Troeger 2004, 9–10):

$$y_{it} = \alpha + x_{it}'\beta_{Pooled} + z_i'\gamma_{Pooled} + \eta_i + \varepsilon_{it} \tag{10.5}$$

Following Plumper and Troeger, we estimate (10.5) with Huber-White robust standard errors (White 1980; Huber 1967).

Our set of time-invariant covariates is similar to that used in the previous chapters:

- A set of three dichotomous variables for self-reported race (Hispanic, white, other, with African American the excluded—and modal—category);
- residential mobility measured by the number of years the person has lived in her current neighborhood and by the years the person has lived in D.C.;
- the respondent's frequency of church attendance (a seven-category variable, treated here as continuous);
- the respondent's marital status;
- whether or not the respondent was employed;
- the respondent's years of schooling and years of schooling squared; and
- the grade the respondent assigned to the D.C. public schools in general.

In addition, we include the following variables that are more time sensitive:

- the panel wave for each observation, coded 1, 2, 3, or 4, to allow for a rough linear approximation of any common attitudinal trends over time across the whole population (such as an increase in positive media attention to charter schools);
- an indicator for waves 2 and 4 to account for their timing at the end of the school year (here we assume that due to fatigue or other factors, attitudes will be qualitatively different at the end of the school year than at the beginning—a point we discuss in more detail below);
- the child's grade level; and
- an indicator variable for children who have remained in a particular school for six or more years to account for the likely deterioration in satisfaction engendered by such a long tenure.

Our major variables of interest are time and sectoral effects, and we specify these by the following:

- how many years the respondent's child has attended the school, and the square and cube of this amount of time to allow for nonlinearity in this relationship;
- a charter-school indicator, coded 1 if the respondent's child is in a D.C. charter school (this is time-varying in that students may change schools during the panel);

- the interaction of the charter indicator with the time, time-squared, and time-cubed covariates to further capture differences in temporal dynamics between charter and DCPS parents.

To examine the dynamics of parent satisfaction with the charter schools versus traditional public schools, we estimate independent fixed-effects vector-decomposition regressions of the eight main outcome measures we used in the previous chapter: overall-school, teacher, facility, and principal grade (with A–F letter grades coded as 4, 3, 2, 1, 0); and satisfaction with discipline, values, school size, and class size (coded 1–5, with higher numbers describing greater satisfaction). In the models reported in this chapter, we treat the outcome measures as continuous.

DOES SATISFACTION VARY OVER TIME?

We present the results of our eight fixed-effects vector-decomposition models in table 10.1. Note that at this stage of our analysis, the number of observations varies across the models because of listwise deletion of varying amounts of missing data on the dependent variables. Recall too that, in the case of satisfaction with class size and school size, these questions were not asked in wave 1. Also, as we discussed earlier in the book, there is substantial panel attrition (more on this point below).

The results of this first estimation are presented in table 10.1.[3] These results can be regarded as yet another sensitivity check on the findings reported in the previous chapter. We find that the charter indicator is positive and statistically significant for the overall-school, teacher, and facility grades, and for satisfaction with discipline and values. In contrast to the estimates reported in chapter 9, here we do not find a significant charter-school effect on principal grade, school size, or class size. The initial treatment effect of charter enrollment, however, is not the object of inference for this set of models, and we believe that the results of the previous chapter are a more appropriate estimate of these relationships.[4]

More relevant to the present investigation of dynamics is the pattern of coefficients on the various polynomial and interacted time covariates. At first glance, it appears that satisfaction decreases over time on almost all outcome measures, but at a decreasing rate. However, it is difficult to divine the trajectories over time due to the many terms for time in the model.

We remedy this by computing predicted values of the dependent variables, based on the model, and plotting them versus time in school in figure 10.1. The various plots in the figure allow for the rapid interpretation of our model—the dark lines are loess-local regressions (Cleveland 1979) of the predicted values on time and the dashed lines are loess-

TABLE 10.1
The Dynamics of Satisfaction

	Overall school grade	Teacher grade	Facility grade	Principal grade	Satisfaction with discipline	Satisfaction with values	Satisfaction with school size	Satisfaction with class size
Charter	.51* (.03)	.20* (.03)	.40* (.04)	.01 (.05)	.31* (.05)	.46* (.04)	-.07 (.08)	-.15 (.10)
Time in school	-.08* (.03)	-.15* (.03)	-.26* (.03)	-.31* (.04)	-.26* (.04)	-.13* (.03)	-.28* (.066)	-.52* (.08)
Time²	.02* (.01)	.06* (.01)	.04* (.01)	.09* (.01)	.10* (.01)	.04* (.01)	.11* (.01)	.20* (.02)
Time³	-.002* (.001)	-.005* (.001)	-.002* (.001)	-.007* (.001)	-.008* (.001)	-.004* (.001)	-.008* (.001)	-.01* (.002)
Time × charter	.02 (.04)	.15* (.04)	.24* (.06)	.20* (.07)	.24* (.08)	.20* (.05)	.73* (.10)	1.08* (.12)
Time² × charter	-.06* (.02)	-.08* (.01)	-.01* (.02)	-.05* (.02)	-.10* (.03)	-.07* (.02)	-.38* (.03)	-.48* (.04)
Time³ × charter	.01* (.00)	.008* (.002)	-.002* (.003)	.001* (.003)	.009* (.004)	.007* (.003)	.04* (.004)	.05* (.00)
Panel wave	.02* (.01)	.03* (.001)	-.06* (.01)	.01* (.01)	.03* (.01)	.02* (.01)	.10* (.01)	.13* (.02)
End of year	-.13* (.01)	-.13* (.01)	-.12* (.02)	-.22* (.02)	-.27* (.03)	-.21* (.02)	-.009* (.03)	-.08* (.03)
Grade level	-.02* (.002)	-.01* (.002)	-.02* (.00)	.01* (.003)	-.02* (.003)	-.03* (.003)	-.002* (.004)	-.04* (.005)
6 years	.22* (.10)	-.35* (.111)	-.08* (.13)	-.10 (.17)	-.18 (.15)	.23* (.11)	.04 (.13)	-.42* (.25)
White	.19* (.03)	.15* (.02)	-.26* (.05)	.13* (.04)	.27* (.05)	.17* (.04)	.002 (.06)	-.10* (.07)
Hispanic	.22* (.03)	-.05* (.030)	-.14* (.04)	.13* (.04)	-.09* (.05)	-.05 (.04)	-.12* (.05)	-.19* (.06)
Other race	-.14* (.03)	-.04* (.03)	-.03 (.045)	.08* (.04)	-.17* (.06)	-.09* (.04)	-.08 (.05)	-.10 (.08)
Years in D.C.	.01* (.002)	.006* (.002)	.01* (.002)	.007* (.002)	.002 (.002)	.007* (.002)	.01* (.002)	-.01* (.003)
In neighborhood	.0004 (.001)	-.001 (.001)	-.005* (.001)	-.002 (.002)	.001 (.002)	.002* (.001)	-.003* (.002)	.005* (.003)
Church	.0001 (.004)	.001 (.003)	.002 (.005)	.007 (.005)	-.003 (.006)	.012* (.004)	.023* (.006)	.008 (.008)
Marital status	.07* (.01)	.02* (.01)	-.07* (.01)	.004 (.02)	.05* (.02)	.04* (.01)	.05* (.02)	.05* (.03)
Employed	-.02 (.01)	.009 (.01)	-.13* (.02)	-.01 (.02)	-.03 (.02)	-.02 (.02)	.06* (.02)	.16* (.04)
Education	-.13* (.01)	-.08* (.01)	-.24* (.02)	-.08* (.01)	-.09* (.02)	-.11* (.02)	-.02 (.02)	-.10* (.02)
Education²	.005* (.001)	.003* (.001)	.009* (.001)	.003* (.001)	.003* (.001)	.005* (.001)	.0001 (.001)	.003* (.001)
DCPS grade	.14* (.007)	.09* (.007)	.16* (.009)	.09* (.01)	.13* (.01)	.13* (.009)	.04* (.01)	.09* (.01)
η	1* (.01)	1* (.01)	1* (.01)	1* (.01)	1* (.01)	1* (.01)	1* (.01)	1* (.01)
Constant	3.49* (.09)	3.55* (.09)	4.13* (.15)	3.58* (.13)	4.60* (.15)	4.41* (.14)	3.73* (.22)	4.59* (.17)
Number of obs.	1847	1803	1848	1701	1852	1837	969	971

* p < .10, two-tailed.

Results are coefficients from fixed-effects variance decomposition panel regressions for four waves of panel data, robust standard errors in parentheses, listwise deletion of missing values due to panel attrition. School and class size models are estimated using only three waves of data.

smoothed regressions of +/– 2 standard errors of these predictions. The results are informative.

First, several of the trajectories for the charter parents appear to follow an approximate "U" over time. That is, on average, parental satisfaction with the charters seems to decline from an initial point, and then increase again later. In contrast, in the traditional public schools, the general pattern is one of a similar decline and then a leveling off (or perhaps a slight decline, although the standard errors of the predictions become increasingly large as the number of parents observed in their schools for long periods is quite small).

Based on the predictions and standard errors, this "U" trajectory for the charter parents' satisfaction is mitigated or does not appear to be present for the teacher-grade, principal-grade, or satisfaction-with-values outcomes. Also, the DCPS parents' satisfaction with school size does not follow the same decline-and-level path of the other outcomes. Nevertheless, overall, the data appear to suggest that charter parents begin their school experience with higher levels of satisfaction than their noncharter peers, and that they end their experience also on a positive note, but that their satisfaction reaches a nadir somewhere in the middle.

Before accepting this as an empirical regularity in need of explanation, however, we must consider whether or not this unusual difference in trajectory is an artifact. As we note in chapter 3, panel attrition is a particular problem in our survey data, leading to a large amount of missing data. Accordingly, as in earlier chapters, we again employ a method of multiple imputation, here predictive mean matching to impute the missing values (jointly for both panel attrition and item nonresponse within panel waves), assuming again that the absence is conditional on the observed data (MAR or missing-at-random). We then estimate the same models as above on the imputed datasets and average the results appropriately (Little and Rubin 2002, 210–12).

We present the results from the models using the imputations in table 10.2. As the table shows, there are several important differences between these results and those presented in table 10.1, in which missing values were simply listwise-deleted. First, we now find that the coefficient on charter enrollment is statistically significant for all eight outcome measures, although its magnitude is smaller for most cases. Regarding dynamics, with the exception of teacher grade and facility grade, we no longer find any of the coefficients for the various polynomial and interaction terms for time statistically significant. Once again, to aid in interpretation of this large table, we present locally smoothed linear predictions and +/– two standard error bands graphically in figure 10.2.

The most striking difference between the plots in figure 10.2 and those in figure 10.1 is that we no longer observe the "U" trajectory for the

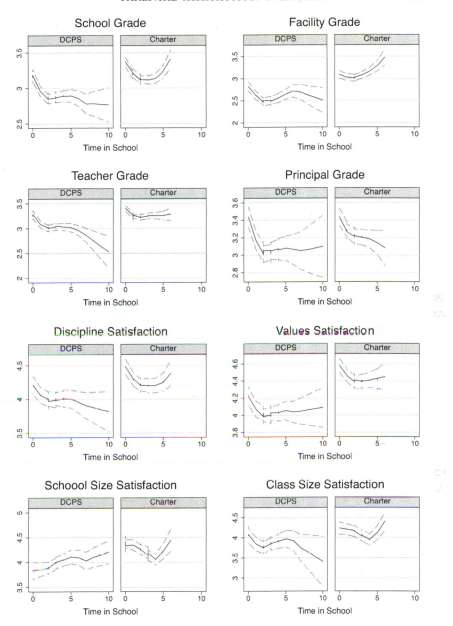

Figure 10.1. The dynamics of satisfaction, predictions based on listwise deletion of cases. *Note*: The dark lines are loess-local regressions of predicted values of the dependent variables from the fixed-effects vector decomposition models versus time. The dashed lines are +/− 2 standard errors of the prediction.

TABLE 10.2
Dynamic Models with Multiple Imputation

	Overall school grade	Teacher grade	Facility grade	Principal grade	Satisfaction with discipline	Satisfaction with values	Satisfaction with school size	Satisfaction with class size
Charter	.29* (.10)	.14* (.05)	.33* (.10)	.13* (.07)	.37* (.09)	.39* (.11)	.48* (.08)	.33* (.18)
Time in school	-.07 (.07)	-.07* (.04)	-.19* (.06)	-.09 (.08)	-.006 (.05)	-.005 (.08)	.11 (.15)	.04 (.11)
Time²	.01 (.01)	.02* (.01)	.05* (.01)	.02 (.02)	.008 (.02)	-.001 (.02)	-.01 (.03)	.01 (.02)
Time³	-.001 (.001)	-.003* (.001)	-.004* (.002)	-.002 (.002)	-.002 (.003)	.0001 (.002)	.001 (.003)	-.002 (.002)
Time × charter	-.09 (.09)	.0001 (.08)	.19* (.11)	-.11 (.12)	-.23 (.15)	-.16 (.14)	-.26 (.17)	.005 (.28)
Time² × charter	.02 (.06)	.007 (.03)	-.05 (.05)	.06 (.12)	.05 (.047)	.05 (.03)	.03 (.08)	-.06 (.09)
Time³ × charter	-.002 (.009)	-.003 (.006)	-.001 (.020)	-.01 (.007)	-.004 (.006)	-.005 (.005)	-.002 (.01)	.008 (.01)
Panel wave	.003 (.025)	.04* (.02)	-.04 (.04)	-.002 (.01)	.01 (.03)	.02 (.03)	.03 (.03)	.05 (.05)
End of year	-.08* (.03)	-.13* (.03)	-.10 (.06)	-.17* (.05)	-.17* (.07)	-.12* (.06)	-.08 (.07)	-.09 (.07)
Grade level	-.02* (.005)	-.01 (.02)	-.03* (.006)	-.01* (.006)	-.01* (.007)	-.02* (.005)	-.003 (.01)	-.01 (.009)
> 6 years	.02 (.23)	-.07 (.19)	-.16 (.13)	-.04 (.18)	-.08 (.24)	.04 (.16)	.02 (.25)	.02 (.20)
White	.16* (.05)	.06 (.09)	-.39* (.08)	.07 (.09)	.10 (.13)	-.05 (.114)	-.004 (.09)	-.04 (.15)
Hispanic	.02 (.09)	-.02 (.07)	-.03 (.13)	.10 (.08)	-.03 (.08)	-.08 (.08)	-.11 (.10)	-.14 (.10)
Other race	-.17* (.07)	-.01 (.04)	-.08 (.08)	.04 (.05)	-.11 (.07)	-.07 (.07)	-.19* (.10)	-.19 (.14)
Years in D.C	.01* (.003)	.006* (.004)	.01* (.005)	.008* (.003)	.005 (.005)	.009* (.003)	.008 (.005)	-.006 (.006)
In neighborhood	-.001 (.002)	-.001 (.003)	-.008* (.004)	-.001 (.003)	.0001 (.01)	.001 (.003)	-.003 (.004)	.004 (.004)
Church	.002 (.007)	-.006 (.009)	.003 (.01)	.005 (.009)	-.005 (.01)	.008 (.008)	.005 (.01)	-.005 (.01)
Marital status	.08* (.02)	.03* (.02)	-.07* (.03)	.06 (.04)	.058 (.03)	.08* (.02)	.008 (.03)	.03 (.04)
Employed	-.01 (.09)	.03 (.03)	-.11* (.05)	.01 (.03)	-.004 (.04)	.007 (.03)	.03 (.03)	.08 (.07)
Education	-.06 (.07)	-.05* (.03)	-.12* (.03)	-.04 (.04)	-.01 (.03)	-.04 (.05)	.03 (.04)	-.05 (.03)
Education²	.002* (.001)	.002* (.001)	.005* (.001)	.002 (.002)	.001 (.001)	.03 (.002)	-.001 (.001)	.002 (.001)
DCPS grade	.11* (.01)	.08* (.02)	.12* (.02)	.08* (.01)	.11* (.02)	.11* (.01)	.06* (.03)	.09* (.03)
η	1* (.01)	1* (.02)	1* (.02)	1* (.02)	1* (.02)	1* (.02)	1* (.03)	1* (.03)
Constant	3.18* (.16)	3.41* (.17)	3.61* (.27)	3.36* (.28)	3.94* (.24)	3.97* (.34)	3.44* (.35)	4.07* (.35)

* $p < .10$, two-tailed.

Note: Results are coefficients from fixed-effects variance decomposition panel regressions for four waves of panel data, standard errors in parentheses. All results are averaged over five multiply imputed datasets. School- and class-size models are estimated using only three waves of data. Total number of observations is 4,008, 3,006 for school and class size.

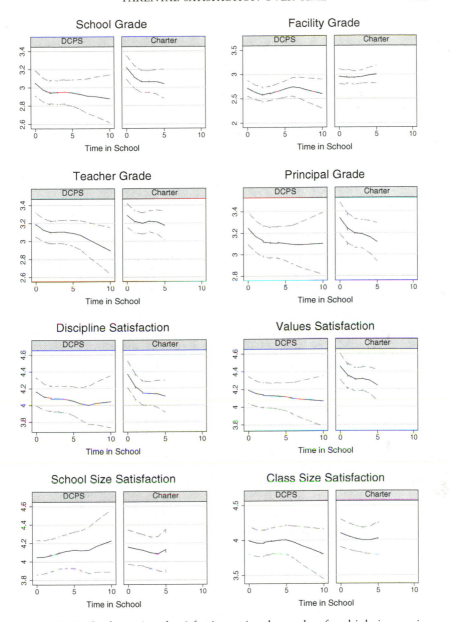

Figure 10.2. The dynamics of satisfaction, using the results of multiple-imputation datasets. *Note*: The dark lines are loess-local regressions of predicted values of the dependent variables from the fixed effects vector decomposition models versus time. The dashed lines are +/– 2 standard errors of the prediction.

charter parents' predictions. Charter parents' satisfaction with the various dimensions of the schools now generally declines over time, with the exception of satisfaction with facilities, which is essentially constant. The figure illustrates that any positive charter-school effect diminishes over time; if we treat the +/– 2 standard-error lines as an approximate test of statistical significance at the .05 level, we find that by the end of five years in the schools, there appears be only a small difference between charter and traditional public school parental satisfaction on *any* of the outcome measures, and probably no statistically significant difference on most. In particular, there appears to be a slight charter-school advantage for satisfaction with facilities, values, and perhaps teachers—although the differences in average grades at the end of five years are quite slight.

The difference between the listwise deletion results reported in the table 10.1 and figure 10.1 and the multiple imputation results in table 10.2 and figure 10.2 raises the obvious question: which ones do we accept?

It is natural when faced with two alternatives to appeal to dialectical reasoning and conclude that "the truth is somewhere in the middle." Often, however, this is an example of the logical fallacy of "false compromise," especially when the middle is not really defined or, in our case, statistically estimated. In an influential paper on missing data in applied statistical analysis, King et al. conclude that "almost any disciplined statistical model of multiple imputation would serve better than current practices. The threats to the validity of inferences from listwise deletion are of roughly the same magnitude as those from the much better known problems of omitted variable bias" (2001, 65). In our data there are many missing values. Naïvely assuming that these missing values can be ignored and respondents simply deleted from the analysis seems likely to lead to inferential error. In turn, we believe that the results based on the imputed dataset are the ones more likely to reflect the true pattern of parental beliefs over time.

Hope Springs Eternal—but Only in the Fall

The reader will remember that one of the variables we included in our estimates was the timing of the interview at the beginning or the end of the school year. We noted in an earlier chapter that parent attitudes and behaviors at the end of the school year often differ markedly from the beginning of the year, as the difficult realities of urban education all too often erode the optimism and excitement that marks the opening of school in September.

In figure 10.3, using the same imputed datasets as above, we present the effects of the beginning versus the end-of-school-year measurement. The erosion of parent satisfaction with schools (measured by the grades

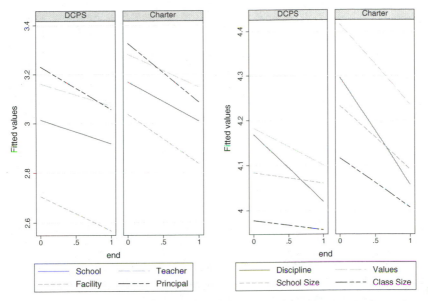

Figure 10.3. Satisfaction at the end of the year is lower than at the beginning. *Note*: Average predicted declines in satisfaction due to surveys at the end of the school year (end = 1) versus the beginning (end = 0) for the eight outcome measures. Predicted values used are from the multiple-imputation models presented in table 10.2. Total number of observations is 4,006, 3,008 for school size and class size. Lines are simple linear-regression fits.

they assign or by their explicit reports of satisfaction) is pronounced across dimensions and across schools in both sectors. Controlling for many factors, the same as we do in our other empirical models in this chapter, the grades assigned by parents drop by as much as 10 percent over the course of the school year. The rate of decline in the explicit satisfaction measures is even steeper. Perhaps one of the most disturbing findings is the fall-off in parental satisfaction with discipline. We know that one of the main concerns that parents have about urban schools is the level of safety and discipline. We infer from these data that neither Washington's traditional public schools nor the charter schools are delivering schools safe enough and orderly enough to meet parental expectations.

HYPE OR HOPE? THE CASE OF SATISFACTION

The effects of charter schools on parental satisfaction are complex and not easy to measure. In turn, the answer to the seemingly simple question, "Are charter-school parents more satisfied with their child's school?"

yields a resounding "maybe." The conditions contributing to this "maybe" are based on the time frame one uses and, unfortunately, the assumptions one makes about the data that we collected—or failed to collect because of attrition.

In the previous chapter, we showed that using cross-sectional data, charter parents are more satisfied with their children's schools—and we showed those differences are remarkably robust to many different types of model specifications and corrections for endogeneity, self-selection, and perceptual bias. Given the strength of these findings and the rigor of the tests to which we subjected them, our findings add weight to a growing body of research that shows charter-school parents are likely to be more satisfied than parents with children in traditional public schools. This, of course, is congruent with theories of choice and with the claims of charter-school proponents.

However, the results of our longitudinal analyses are more complex and less supportive of the idea that charter schools produce positive outcomes. Unfortunately, the results we report are more than a little sensitive to how one handles missing data. On the one hand, if we use listwise deletion of data, we find that over time charter-school parents tend to maintain slightly more positive evaluations of their children's schools than do other parents. However, rather than increasing over time, which we would expect if charter schools were a truly better educational experience, even in this most optimistic measurement, the charter-school advantage tends to narrow as experience with the schools increases.

Making other reasonable assumptions about how to handle missing data through imputation, we find that any charter-school advantage found in cross-sectional analysis is wiped out across all measures of satisfaction.

Of course one could argue (as some no doubt will) that these results are themselves remarkable. Given that charter schools are new, given the birth pains of launching these schools in the fractious and highly charged world of educational policy, and given the possibility that parents with hard-to-educate children often choose charter schools (although see chapter 4 above on this point), the fact that charter-school parents are on par with traditional-school parents may be viewed by some as a success. As we saw in chapter 4, this argument has been used in debates about the academic performance of charter-school students versus students in traditional schools.

This is a plausible and perhaps even a justifiable position. However, it is a far cry from the claims that were behind the original (and no doubt exaggerated) promises of the charter-school movement that choice would be a panacea, a "silver bullet" to solve the problems of urban education.

If charter schools are such a magical cure, the parents who constitute one of the prime stakeholders in schooling don't seem to know it.

In the next chapter, we explore another domain, the relationship of choice to social capital and parent involvement in the child's school and beyond. One again, we will examine our data both in cross section and over time to probe for evidence of charter-school effects.

Building Social Capital in the Nation's Capital: Can School Choice Build a Foundation for Cooperative Behavior?

A RECURRENT THEME IN POLICY STUDIES links the structure and performance of public institutions to citizens' attitudes toward government and their willingness to participate in politics and the policy process. Ostrom (1998) argues that identifying the ways that government institutions can be designed to encourage cooperative behavior is one of the central issues in contemporary political science (also see Lubell et al. 2002). However, the literature on social capital portrays a decline in cooperative attitudes and behavior (Putnam 1995, 2000) and questions the extent to which government can nurture them (see especially Fukuyama 1995).

In this chapter, we focus on schools as arenas in which parents can develop the norms and expectations essential for cooperative behavior. We pay particular attention to the extent to which reorganizing schools through the introduction of school choice affects such attitudes. We believe that by analyzing how a change in the way an important government service, in this case, schooling, is organized and then linking this institutional change to the attitudes parents hold toward each other and toward teachers allows us to address three fundamental questions:

- Can government institutions build the foundation for interpersonal trust, cooperation, and participation in the policy process?
- If the answer to the first question is yes, is this effect domain-specific or are the effects more general, spilling over into attitudes in other, broader, domains?
- And, do these effects endure over time?

Specifically, we examine the effect of a particular institutional reform—charter schools—on parental civic participation. After reviewing the literature linking the design of government institutions to civic participation and attitudes, we turn to an empirical analysis using our longitudinal survey data. We begin by assessing the effect of enrollment in charter schools on a variety of familiar measures of school and broader civic attitudes.

We find some evidence that the foundations for cooperation and trust in the domain of schooling—but not in other domains—are higher among parents with children in charter schools. Using a propensity-score matching technique similar to that employed earlier in the book, we show that this finding is robust when controlling for self-selection into charter schools. We then turn to a dynamic analysis of this difference over time as we did in the previous chapter. We find little persistence of any charter-school advantage.

As we proceed, we must keep in mind that, while schools are an important government institution in the lives of parents, they nonetheless represent only one venue in which parents interact with each other and with public employees. In turn, there are "real-world" constraints on the extent to which we should expect changes in the way schools are organized to effect broader changes in political attitudes. While we should therefore expect modest effects at best, existing research suggests that these links do exist.

INSTITUTIONS CAN AFFECT POLITICAL ATTITUDES AND BEHAVIOR

A wide range of work shows that institutions, such as religious congregations, neighborhood associations, and schools can serve as training grounds for the development of civic and political skills. Rosenstone and Hansen (1993) show that political participation is firmly rooted in the institutions and organizations that mobilize individuals and structure their involvement. Verba, Schlozman, and Brady (1995) find that networks of recruitment, which in turn are embedded in institutions and organizations, are critically important for explaining civic volunteerism. Similarly, Skocpol, Ganz, and Munson (2000) argue that civic associations and citizen participation in the United States developed less from the purely local decisions of individuals and more as a consequence of the institutional patterns of federalism, electoral politics, and political parties (also see Berry, Portney, and Thomson 1993; Vallely 1996; Minkoff 1997; Cortes 1996). Complementing this line of research is work by Mutz and Mondak that shows how the everyday environment affects political attitudes and participation. While they focus on the workplace, rather than schools, Mutz and Mondak (2006) suggest that an environment in which diverse people interact increases the level of exposure people have to a wide range of policy and political information. This is important because such "crosscutting exposure" contributes to an awareness of rationales for oppositional political views, a necessary condition for political legitimacy, and crosscutting exposure contributes to political tolerance.

Another body of work investigating "policy feedback" shows how the treatment clients of government programs receive affects their broader orientations toward government and political action. The key questions in this line of research, according to Mettler and Soss, include such issues as "whether policies render citizens more or less engaged in politics and how public programs shape citizens' beliefs, preferences, demands, and power" (2004, 60).

The idea of a feedback loop was raised at least as long ago as the study by Lowi (1964), who argued that public policies are not only the product of politics but have an independent effect on the range and level of political activity associated with them. Contemporary work in this tradition moves from the systemic level that Lowi had in mind to study the links between different institutional arrangements and the behavior of individuals.[1] Research investigating this feedback loop links the way that policies are structured to the sense of responsibility, duty, and obligation possessed by policy recipients. Completing the loop, these attitudes in turn shape political behavior of policy recipients pertaining to the policy and even spill over to broader policy and political domains. As Schneider and Ingram argue, the way in which government policies are implemented "affect people's experiences with the policy and the lessons and messages they take from it. These, in turn, influence people's values and attitudes . . . their orientations toward government, and their political participation patterns" (Ingram and Schneider 1995, 442; also see Schneider and Ingram 1997; Soss 1999; A. Campbell 2000; Mettler 2002).

This idea has been explicitly tested in the domain of social-welfare programs. For example, Verba, Schlozman, and Brady (1995, chaps. 7, 14) show that beneficiaries of non-means-tested programs are more likely to be involved in welfare-related political activity than are recipients of means-tested programs, such as AFDC. Andrea Campbell (2000) has also demonstrated the existence of this feedback loop, which may be particularly strong among lower-income recipients of social security (also see Mettler 2002 for a discussion of the greater effects of the GI Bill on less-advantaged recipients). Similarly, Soss (1999) shows that recipients of SSDI believe more strongly in their political efficacy compared to recipients of AFDC, who are more likely to be poorly treated by bureaucrats and who, in turn, develop feelings of powerlessness.

Closer to the education-policy domain we study in this book, Soss also shows that Head Start, a program that encourages parental participation and involvement, consistently mitigates the demobilizing effects of AFDC, from which he concludes that "a more participatory program design encourages more positive orientations toward political involvement. Head Start provides clients with evidence that participation can be effective and fulfilling. From the perspective of participatory theory, it is not surprising that these experiences have spill-over effects" (Soss 1999, 374).

Yet another line of research, developed in the field of public administration, has explored the importance of "coproduction"—how citizens and government officials interact in the delivery of specific services and how these interactions are related to broader patterns of civic engagement. Scholars in this tradition have noted that for many public goods, such as community policing (for example, Neighborhood Watch or Crime Stoppers), or sanitation-removal programs that depend on residents' cooperation in curbside recycling or transporting waste to specific areas for collection, cooperative behavior among citizens and between citizen/consumers and providers is essential.

Unfortunately, the term coproduction has all too often been confined to a limited set of citizen activities focused on particular acts involved in narrowly defined public services. Yet the benefits of coproduction may extend beyond the specific service and can, like other institutional arrangements that encourage citizen involvement, positively affect political behavior and attitudes. According to Levine:

> Coproduction lays the foundation for a positive relationship between government and citizens by making citizens an integral part of the service delivery process. Through these experiences citizens may build both competence and a broader perspective, a vision of the community and what it can and should become. (1984, 181; also see Marschall 2004)

POLICY FEEDBACK AND SOCIAL CAPITAL

The connection between government and citizen behavior also plays a central role in recent explorations of social capital. Many analysts argue that social capital is essential to the smooth functioning of markets and democratic politics (e.g., North 1990; Putnam 1993; Fukuyama 1995; Schneider et al. 1997; Adler and Kwon 2002)—but the role of government institutions and practices in fostering social capital has been debated.

For example, Fukuyama (1995) stresses the importance of social capital to politics and markets, but does not think much of the ability of government to create or nourish it. Similarly, for Putnam, social capital is generated mostly through the quality of secondary associations and not through government action. Putnam suggests that "civic virtue" comes from experience in associational life, which teaches "skills of cooperation as well as a sense of shared responsibility for collective endeavors" (Putnam 1993, 90). In this regard, Putnam's reference to the "amateur soccer clubs, choral societies, hiking clubs, bird-watching groups, literary circles, hunters' associations, Lions Clubs, and the like in each community" (91) is often cited. But it is his image of "bowling alone" (Putnam 1995) that captures his notion of the decline of associational life in the United States as indicative of declining social capital. In more recent work, Putnam (2000) has argued for a broader view of the foundations of social capital, including a much more expansive role for government, but the essence of his social-capital framework is built on the claim that civil societies that are characterized by a richly variegated associational life will also tend to exhibit norms of political equality, trust, and tolerance, and active participation in public affairs.

Clearly even the most "resolutely society-centered" views of social capital (to use Levi's [1996] characterization of Putnam's early statement of his theory) must recognize that institutional and bureaucratic context helps define the boundaries of civic engagement and the way in which citizens respond to government and politics. That is, there are government and bureaucratic processes and structures that affect the quality of grassroots activity, associational life, and social capital more generally (see, for example, Skocpol, Ganz, and Munson 2000). And there is evidence that government institutions that treat citizens well encourage political participation and political attitudes supportive of democratic practices.

In this chapter we ask if charter schools have such an effect.[2]

LINKING INSTITUTIONAL STRUCTURE TO POLITICAL BEHAVIOR: THE CASE OF SCHOOLS

All forms of school choice, such as alternative schools, magnet schools, open-enrollment programs, vouchers, and charters, expand the range of options available to parents. Throughout the history of recent choice reforms, two themes have been evident. First, choice has been portrayed as a right that should be made available to everyone (not only to the affluent who have long exercised choice through residential location). This theme was crucial in the adoption of the voucher program in Milwaukee, one of the nation's first. Moe (2000a) finds strong support for this theme in his comprehensive study of attitudes towards vouchers, and it is one of the motivating forces in the current Bush administration's rhetoric for school reform. In addition to this individual-rights theme, as we have seen in earlier chapters, there is also the theme of systemic change, in which school reformers have explicitly coupled choice with a broad challenge to the current system of education. In this view, the marketlike forces unleashed by charter schools and choice will leverage needed improvements in the performance of schools.

The way the broad institutional arrangements of schools affect their performance is a particular concern in the work of John Chubb and Terry Moe, who, in their 1990 book, *Politics, Markets, and America's Schools*, forged a clear link between choice, markets, and the relationships between stakeholders in schools. Chubb and Moe argue that while school reform has often been considered an "insider's game," played by bureaucrats, administrators, teachers, and other school professionals, and fought over what may seem like technical problems (for example, curriculum, testing procedures, or tenure), the bedrock issue in school reform is the issue of governance: who has the right to participate in the decision-making process and at what levels? Chubb and Moe consider this to be a "constitutional" issue because it structures subsequent decisions made by school officials, teachers, parents, and students.

Congruent with this argument, many proposals for reform now seek to rewrite the relationship between stakeholders, building on a widely shared vision emphasizing small, autonomous schools, unburdened by a large administrative structure, and fueled by a desire to bring parents, students, teachers, and administrators into cooperative, supportive relationships. In this vision, parents are given not only the power to choose but are seen as essential to school governance and to the creation of "effective" schools in which the resulting stronger community leads to higher academic performance.

For example, Henderson (1987, 1) argues: "The evidence is now beyond dispute: parent involvement improves student achievement. When parents are involved, children do better in school, and they go to better schools." Similarly, according to Ostrom (1996, 1079): "If students are not actively engaged in their own education, encouraged and supported by their family and friends, what teachers do may make little difference in the skills students acquire." Bryk and his colleagues have repeatedly demonstrated that parents must be involved in schooling to ensure the quality of schools as institutions serving the community. They also show that children from low-income and minority families gain the most from parent involvement (see, for example, Bryk and Schneider 2002; Bryk, Lee, and Holland 1993; or Bryk, Sebring, and Rollow 1998). Clearly, this vision of effective schools means that stakeholders work together to "coproduce" higher-quality education, making the relationship among parents, students, and teachers more cooperative and interdependent (see, e.g., Henig 1994, 187; Ostrom 1996).

While linking the coproduction of education to broader indices of political participation has not been widely investigated, the work on social capital and schools hints at such a link. Indeed, Coleman's (1988) classic article on social capital specifically addressed the question of how effective school communities can create this elusive commodity. Other work has followed Coleman's lead. For example, Schneider, Schiller, and Coleman (1994b) and Astone and McLanahan (1991) examine social capital as a function of the interactions between administrators, teachers, parents, and children. Bryk, Lee, and Holland (1993) identify the "value added" of Catholic schools to a range of outcomes, many of which relate to norms that support participation and political attitudes (also see D. Campbell 2000). Berry, Portney, and Thomson (1993, 294) cite the shift to parental control over local schools in Chicago in the late 1980s as a rare example of a successful attempt to get low-income parents more involved in local public affairs. Carnoy (2000) and Benveniste, Carnoy, and Rothstein (2003) similarly emphasize the importance of schools in fostering social and institutional networks. Schneider and his colleagues (Schneider et al. 1997; Schneider, Teske, and Marschall 2000) show how public-school choice increases the social capital of parents, measured by volunteerism, PTA membership, and sociability.

Clearly, this aspect of the school-reform movement focuses on transforming parents from passive clients of a government service to active partners entitled to a say in how schools are run and how students are taught. Does this in turn create trust and social capital?

CHARTER SCHOOLS AS AN INSTITUTIONAL REFORM THAT CAN BUILD SOCIAL CAPITAL

Why should we expect charter schools to increase the number of parents with higher levels of social capital, trust, and, more generally, attitudes supportive of democratic participation? If Schneider and Ingram are correct that how government policies are implemented "affect[s] people's . . . orientations toward government, and their political participation patterns" (1997, 442) and if, as Soss and others argue, how government agencies treat their clients affects how clients see themselves as citizens, then the fact that charter schools are committed to changing the relationship between parents and schools and making parents more central to the school's educational mission should produce positive changes in parental attitudes and behavior. While much of the research on charter schools has shown that they are not as transformative of the entire system of education as their advocates hoped, there is evidence that charter schools are changing the relationship between the school and the parent. And it is this aspect of change that is central to our argument.

Hill et al. argue that charter schools, freed from many of the bureaucratic rules and regulations governing traditional public schools, have created new key "accountability" relationships with teachers, on whose performance the schools depend, and with families, whom the schools must attract and satisfy (2001, 6). These relationships, according to Hill et al., transform the way in which teachers, administrators, and parents deal with each other. To use Shklar's (1991) terminology, charter schools give parents more "standing" and grant them rights and privileges that accord them first-class citizenship in the school community. More concretely, choice gives parents the authority to make requests and to expect the school to respond appropriately to the needs of individual children (also see Berman et al. 1998). Combined with the fact that charter schools usually offer a smaller, more intimate setting, staffed by people who choose to work in the school, the conditions for stronger ties between parents and the schools exist.

A growing number of studies confirm that charter schools have higher rates of parent involvement than other schools. These higher rates stem from a culture as well as policies that nurture (if not quite force) higher involvement (Corwin and Flaherty 1995; Bryk, Lee, and Holland 1993; Finn et al. 1997). For example, in California, many charter schools use contracts that require parental involvement, including parents' presence at the school. Contracts often include student-attendance requirements as well as parent commitment to provide educational materials at home and to support school codes (Schwartz 1996). According to Miron and Nelson (2000), among Pennsylvania charter schools, half the schools require that parents volunteer, and 25 percent of parents report that they volunteer more than three hours per month. Similarly, Henig et al. (1999) find evidence that public charter schools in Washington, D.C. reach out to parents in similar ways.[3]

Choice may also put pressure on administrators, teachers, and staff to be more "consumer-friendly." As Hassel (1999, 6) writes, "charter schools cannot take their 'customers' for granted. Their very survival depends on the degree to which families believe the schools are responding to family preferences and working hard to provide the education they demand." Teske et al. (2001) found that parents visiting charter schools were, on average, treated better than parents visiting D.C. public schools and that the charter schools treated parental requests for information about programs more seriously and responsively than did staff at the D.C. public schools.

In short, as an institutional reform many advocates argue that charter schools are likely to create a milieu in which parents are better treated and are encouraged to be active "coproducers" of their children's education. Does it follow that this better treatment creates a positive feedback loop generating political attitudes supportive of democratic practices?

To answer this question, we turn again to our survey of parents with children in Washington, D.C. schools. We begin by discussing the particular survey measures that we use to examine this issue.

What to Measure?

Clearly the issues and attendant measures that have been used by researchers looking at how the quality of government services affects citizen attitudes, behavior, and social capital are wide-ranging. In this chapter, we
begin with a set of measures of interpersonal trust. Such trust is essential
not only for improving school performance, especially in inner-city
schools (see, especially, Bryk and Schneider 2000), but, according to
Burns and Kinder (2000), trust provides the foundation for cooperation
and, ultimately, for democratic politics.

While our survey questions draw heavily from Burns and Kinder, other
work also supports our concern for interpersonal trust. Ostrom places
trust at the center of the "core relationships" she argues are essential for
cooperation (1998, especially pages 12–13). Leana and Van Buren (1999,
542) argue that organizational social capital lies in trust and "associabil-
ity"—which they define as "the willingness and ability of individuals to
define collective goals that are then enacted collectively." For Putnam, the
norm of generalized reciprocity helps solve collective-action problems and
creates a viable community with a shared sense of commitment and identity (Putnam 2000; Casella and Rauch 2002). Adler and Kwon argue that
goodwill is central to the concept of social capital, since information,
influence, and solidarity flows from goodwill—and hence the effects of
social capital are based on goodwill (2002, 18). Perhaps most germane
to this study, Bryk and Schneider argue that "a broad base of trust across
a school community lubricates much of a school's day-to-day functioning
. . . and is especially important as we focus on disadvantaged schools"
(2002, 5–6). As noted, Bryk and Schneider link high levels of trust not
only to the smooth operation of the school, but ultimately to academic
performance.

We tailored our questions on the school environment to measure the
foundation of trust and cooperation among parents and between parents
and teachers, reflecting the importance of such relationships to the coproduction of education, which is a hallmark of effective schools. We also
accept Burns and Kinder's argument that trust is rooted in specific practices and dispositions toward neighbors and others in general: that people
earn trust by "keeping promises, by being honest and respectful, and by
being courteous" (2000, 7).

Measuring Trust

To measure levels of trust, we use the following questions, which are
based on measures developed by Burns and Kinder, and modified to fit
the school environment:

Schools Attitudes	Broader Context Attitudes
Teachers/Parents • Respectful • Responsible • Honest	• Trust in government • Understand politics • Well-qualified to participate in politics • Politicians don't care

Figure 11.1. Measures of school and broader-community attitudes used as dependent variables in subsequent analyses.

I'm going to ask you a few questions about the parents of the students who attend your child's school.

- Thinking about those parents, would you say they *treat others with respect* all of the time, most of the time, some of the time, hardly ever, or never?
- What about *irresponsible*? Would you say that *irresponsible* describes these parents extremely well, quite well, not too well, or not well at all?
- Would you say that the word *honest* describes these parents extremely well, quite well, not too well, or not well at all?

In the survey, these same questions were repeated, substituting teachers for parents (the irresponsible question is reverse-coded for subsequent analyses in both cases). We then expand our list of dependent variables to include measures of attitudes for the larger world of politics outside the school.

Figure 11.1 summarizes the indicators of attitude that we measure and use in subsequent analyses. Our measures of broader civic attitudes are a series of questions drawn from the literature on political efficacy (Campbell et al. 1960; Converse 1964, 1975) and includes measures of both "internal" and "external" efficacy (Campbell, Gurin, and Miller 1972). More specifically, we measure the respondent's self-reported trust in government, understanding of politics, belief that she is well-qualified to participate, and agreement with the statement: "I don't think public officials care much what people like me think." Using these measures, we restate the specific questions we posed earlier:

- Do parents who have enrolled their children in charter schools exhibit attitudes more supportive of cooperative behavior within the school?
- Do these school-based norms and behaviors affect parents in other areas of political life?
- Do these attitudes endure over time?

Is There a Charter-School Effect?

As in chapter 9, we must again account for the fact that parents are self-selecting to enroll their children in charter schools and thus that any simple estimates of treatment effects are likely to be biased. Our strategy is to use the propensity-score approach described in chapter 9, combined with the same test of sensitivity to hidden bias introduced by Rosenbaum (2002, 105–38) and discussed by DiPrete and Gangl (2004). As we discussed earlier, we believe this approach is superior to more familiar linear regression models both in adjusting on the observable covariates without strong assumptions and in testing for hidden bias. Furthermore, to address the endogeneity of the "treatment" (that is, enrollment in charter schools) and the response, we once again take advantage of the longitudinal nature of our data to better disentangle cause from effect.

As in chapter 9, we select the 226 (137 charter, 89 DCPS) parents whose child was new to his school in Fall 2001, the time of the first panel interview. We use the same estimated propensity scores we used in that chapter (after multiple imputation of missing values due to both panel attrition and item nonresponse) to match these new charter parents to the new DCPS parents (sampling from the DCPS parents with replacement), and then consider the differences between these matched pairs using the grades assigned by parents in the Spring of 2001, the second panel wave. Once again, after dropping respondents with propensity scores not on the common support and matching with replacement,[4] we have a dataset of either 135 or 136 matched pairs of parents.[5]

We begin our examination of the treatment effect using the propensity-score matching model by estimating the differences in response between the charter parents and their matched noncharter controls on the six school-related attitudes (teachers and parents respectful, responsible, and honest) and the four broader attitudes (trust in government, understanding politics, well-qualified to participate in politics, and politicians don't care) measured at one point in time: the first months of the 2001–2 school year (Wave 1).

Again we use the Wilcoxon signed-rank test for the matched pairs, a nonparametric test which has the added advantage of allowing us to relax the assumption that the outcome measures are continuous. Since the Wilcoxon procedure tests the null of equality of samples but does not produce a point estimate, we also compute the Hodges-Lehmann point estimates of the difference between charter and DPCS parents on each measure (Rosenbaum 2002, 47–50).

As before, we average the results of the point estimates over the five imputed datasets to account for missing values. We also produce averaged *p*-values for the Wilcoxon tests by averaging their approximate *z* scores

TABLE 11.1
The Charter Effect on the Foundations of Trust Is Limited and
There Is Little Evidence of Spillover

	Hodges-Lehmann point estimate	Wilcoxon signed-rank test p	Critical level of Γ
Parents respectful	.2	.15	
Parents responsible	.2	.11	
Parents honest	−.1	.31	
Teachers respectful	.3	.01	1.25
Teachers responsible	.2	.02	1.30
Teachers honest	.1	.09	
Politicians care	−.2	.32	
Understand politics	.1	.13	
Well-qualified to participate	.4	.04	1.24
Trust government	0.0	.19	

Hodges-Lehmann point estimates and Wilcoxon p-values (two-tailed) are averaged over five datasets imputed via predictive mean matching. The Rosenbaum's Γ column provides the values of Γ for which the upper limit of the confidence interval on the p of the signed-rank test is exactly .05. Sample size is 135 or 136 matched pairs due to imputation variability and discarding of observations not on the common support of the estimated propensity score.

(under the large sample assumption of the signed-rank test) following Li, Ragunathan, and Rubin (1991).

We present our results from this set of models in table 11.1. The first column provides the averaged Hodges-Lehman point estimates and the second column gives the averaged p-values of the Wilcoxon test. We find evidence that the charter parents feel their child's teachers to be more respectful ($p = .01$) and more responsible ($p = .02$) than their DCPS counterparts. Arguably, we also find some support that charter parents may find their teachers more honest ($p = .09$) and their fellow parents more responsible ($p = .11$). We also find that charter parents are more likely to report that they feel well qualified to participate in politics ($p = .04$)

The final column of table 11.1 presents the results of our sensitivity test for hidden bias as in chapter 9. Recall that Rosenbaum's Γ (2002, 110–19) is the ratio of the odds that the two cases, matched on the propensity score computed from observable data, will select the treatment. Here, we present the estimated value for Γ at which the signed-rank test is no longer significant at the .05 level (no value is presented if the unadjusted value is not already significant at the .05 level). Thus for the case of the "teachers-respectful" outcome measure, for example, if we hypothesize that there is an unmeasured covariate correlated with both selection to charter schools and the outcome, this covariate would have to be of sufficient size to increase the odds ratio of selecting treatment by 1.25. That is, the charter parent would have to be 1.25 times more likely to choose the charter school due to this hidden bias in order for the Wilcoxon test to fail to reject the null of equivalent samples at the .05 level. As the table shows, we find values of Γ of 1.24 (well-qualified to participate), 1.25 (teachers respectful), and 1.30 (teachers responsible). These values are fairly small (smaller than those we report for the parental satisfaction outcomes in chapter 9), suggesting that hidden bias, if it exists, may perhaps be able to explain at least some of the results. Again it should be emphasized, however, that this test does not allow one to reach conclusions about the *existence* of such bias—only to assess the sensitivity of the results in the case where such an unmeasured covariate exists.

Our results thus appear to indicate that our first question can be answered with a qualified "yes": enrollment in charter schools appears to be associated with at least some of the attitudinal foundation upon which increased civic participation can be built. However, these positive "within-school" attitudes do *not* appear to spill over much to broader domains.[6]

Despite this lack of spillover, the results tell a story supportive of charter schools as an institutional reform that has the *potential* to build social capital and a stronger school-based community.

But Does It Last?

We now turn to an examination of the dynamics of this charter-school effect. A reasonable expectation would be that as a relatively new phenomenon, charter schools may take time to establish a functioning community and work out the "bugs" attendant on any start-up operation. Indeed, Tedin and Weiher (2004) find that it may take as much as three years before social capital starts accumulating as a result of enrollment in charter schools.

To examine the dynamic effects of charter enrollment on school-based and broader civic attitudes, we employ methods similar to those used in our investigation of the dynamics of parent satisfaction in chapter 10. Specifically, we again consider the full four waves of our panel and begin by listwise deleting respondents with any missing values (that is, we consider only complete cases). We once more estimate fixed-effects variance-decomposition models (Plumper and Troeger 2004) in which we regress each outcome measure independently on the following:

- how many years the respondent's child has attended the school, and the square and cube of this amount of time to allow for nonlinearity in this relationship;
- a charter-school indicator, coded 1 if the respondent's child is in a D.C. charter school (this is time-varying in that students may change schools during the panel);
- the interaction of the charter indicator with the time, time-squared, and time-cubed covariates to further capture differences in temporal dynamics between charter and DCPS parents;
- the same vector of demographic, socioeconomic, and attitudinal control variables introduced in chapter 10.

We present the results of the models in table 11.2 (school-community outcomes) and table 11.3 (broader civic outcomes).

As we noted in our discussion of parental satisfaction, it is very difficult to determine the dynamics of the outcome measures by a simple inspection of the tables alone. Accordingly, we again compute predicted values based on our models and present smoothed plots of the expected response levels for charter and DCPS parents, as well as plots of estimated +/− 2 standard errors of the predictions. We present these plots in figures 11.2 and 11.3.

As the figures show, the models predict an interesting variety of trajectories for the various dependent variables. Looking at figure 11.2, for the parents-honest, teachers-respectful, and teachers-responsible measures, the estimated trajectories for DCPS and charter parents appear to be fairly similar (at least up until the five years of attendance mark). For the latter two measures (which are also the school-community attitudes found significant with $p < .05$ in table 11.1), however, the charter parents appear to start at an advantage—and this charter advantage appears to persist. The results for the other outcomes in figure 11.2 suggest that the trajectories for the parents-respectful, parents-responsible, and teachers-honest attitudes may vary, on average, between charter and DCPS parents, with initial declines followed by increases in the latter two measures predicted for charter parents, as opposed to steeper declines over time for the DCPS. However, this difference appears to be reversed for the parents-respectful measure.

In figure 11.3, we present the predictions for the four broader community-attitude measures. For these outcomes, the estimated trajectories for DCPS and charter parents appear to vary both within each measure and across the entire set. For the understand-politics and trust-government responses, the general pattern among charter parents is a decline followed by a steep positive shift in attitude. Predicted responses to the "politicians don't care" item stay approximately constant for the charter parents, and

TABLE 11.2
Parent-School Civics Dynamics (Listwise Deletion)

	Parents respectful	Parents responsible	Parents honest	Teachers respectful	Teachers responsible	Teachers honest
Charter	.27* (.01)	.14* (.03)	.10* (.01)	.21* (.01)	.18* (.03)	.19* (.01)
Time in school	−.02 (.01)	.08* (.03)	.02* (.01)	−.15* (.01)	−.02 (.03)	−.05* (.01)
Time²	.0004 (.005)	−.03* (.009)	.01* (.006)	.04* (.004)	.01 (.01)	.02* (.004)
Time³	.001* (.0003)	.002* (.001)	−.003* (.001)	−.003* (.0003)	−.002* (.001)	−.002* (.000.
Time × charter	−.04* (.02)	−.28* (.05)	−.0001 (.02)	.14* (.02)	−.04 (.05)	.009 (.02)
Time² × charter	.009 (.01)	.07* (.02)	−.03* (.01)	−.11* (.01)	.002 (.02)	−.03* (.008)
Time³ × charter	−.003* (002)	−.002 (.003)	.004* (.001)	.01* (.001)	−.001 (.003)	.006* (.001)
Panel wave	.03* (.005)	−.01 (.009)	.05* (.004)	−.005 (.004)	−.01* (.009)	.006 (.004)
End of year	−.001 (.010)	.04* (.01)	−.01* (.008)	−.10* (.009)	.02 (.02)	−.04* (.008)
Grade level	.0001 (.001)	.01* (.002)	−.003* (.001)	−.01* (.001)	−.01* (.002)	.003* (.001)
< 6 years	−.82* (.05)	.16* (.10)	−.12* (.05)	−.44* (.04)	.04 (.09)	−.04 (.03)
White	.18* (.01)	.29* (.02)	.30* (.01)	.03* (.01)	.09* (.04)	.25* (.01)
Hispanic	.05* (.01)	−.32* (.03)	.05* (.01)	.14* (.01)	.005 (.03)	.04* (.01)
Other Race	.14* (.04)	−.09* (.02)	.006 (.01)	.17* (.01)	−.14 (.03)	.06* (.01)
Years in D.C.	−.0004 (.001)	−.0004 (.002)	.001 (.001)	.004* (.001)	−.002 (.002)	.001* (.000(
In neighbor-hood	−.002* (.001)	.008* (.001)	.001 (.001)	−.001* (.0005)	−.001 (.001)	−.002* (.000·
Church	−.004* (.002)	.007* (.004)	.004* (.002)	−.001 (.001)	.01* (.004)	.004* (.001)
Marital status	.01* (.008)	−.009 (.01)	.13* (.007)	.02* (.007)	.05* (.01)	.03* (.007)
Employed	−.009 (.01)	−.04* (.01)	−.04* (.008)	−.02* (.009)	.02 (.01)	.005 (.008)
Education	.01 (.007)	−.03* (.01)	−.09* (.007)	−.04* (.006)	.08* (.02)	−.05* (.006)
Education²	.00001 (.002)	.003* (.001)	.003* (.0002)	.002* (.0002)	−.002* (.001)	.002* (.000·
DCPS grade	.07* (.005)	−.03* (.007)	.05* (.003)	.03* (.003)	.01 (.008)	.02* (.003)
η	1* (.005)	1* (.009)	1* (.006)	1* (.006)	1* (.01)	1* (.006)
Constant	2.68* (.05)	3.08* (.10)	3.29* (.05)	3.53* (.04)	2.52* (.17)	3.48* (.04)
Number of obs.	1584	1525	1417	1782	1748	1721

* $p < .10$, two-tailed.
Standard errors in parentheses.
Note: Results are coefficients from fixed-effects variance decomposition panel regressions for four waves of panel data, robust standard errors in parentheses, listwise deletion of missing values due to panel attrition and item nonresponse.

TABLE 11.3
Parent Broader-Civics Dynamics (Listwise Deletion)

	Politicians care	Understand politics	Well-qualified	Trust government
Charter	.03 (.09)	−.04 (.04)	−.19* (.10)	−.07* (.01)
Time in school	−.10 (.07)	.05 (.03)	.47* (.07)	.02 (.01)
Time^2	.07* (.02)	−.05* (.01)	−.14* (.02)	.01* (.005)
Time^3	−.008* (.002)	.006* (.001)	.01* (.002)	−.002* (.0004)
Time × charter	.22* (.13)	−.31* (.05)	−.01* (.14)	.10* (.02)
Time^2 × charter	−.18* (.05)	.14* (.02)	.01* (.06)	−.10* (.009)
Time^3 × charter	.02* (.007)	−.01* (.003)	.002 (.009)	.01* (.001)
Panel wave	−.08* (.02)	−.04* (.01)	−.007 (.02)	−.08* (.004)
End of year	.09* (.05)	−.004 (.02)	−.16* (.05)	−.05* (.008)
Grade level	−.03* (.006)	.007* (.002)	.03* (.006)	.02* (.001)
< 6 years	−.31 (.23)	.17 (.11)	.24 (.24)	.28* (.04)
White	.70* (.09)	1.64* (.03)	.36* (.10)	.16* (.01)
Hispanic	.08 (.09)	−.52* (.04)	−.40* (.09)	−.01 (.01)
Other race	.06 (.09)	.14* (.03)	.13 (.09)	−.06* (.01)
Years in D.C.	.009* (.004)	−.003 (.002)	.01* (.004)	−.004* (.0007)
In neighborhood	.002 (.003)	.005* (.001)	−.006* (.003)	−.001* (.0005)
Church	−.03* (.01)	−.007 (.004)	.02* (.01)	.03* (.002)
Marital status	.11* (.04)	.14* (.01)	.01 (.04)	.03* (.007)
Employed	−.07 (.05)	−.11* (.02)	−.10* (.05)	−.06* (.008)
Education	−.14* (.03)	.18* (.02)	.05 (.04)	−.10* (.01)
Education^2	.007* (.001)	−.004* (.001)	.001 (.002)	.004* (.0004)
DCPS grade	.11* (.01)	.007 (.009)	−.02 (.02)	.08* (.003)
η	1* (.01)	1* (.01)	1* (.01)	1* (.005)
Constant	3.27* (.27)	2.73* (.19)	1.76* (.28)	2.79* (.07)
Number of obs.	1788	1836	1822	1789

* $p < .10$, two-tailed. Standard errors in parentheses

Note: Results are coefficients from fixed-effects variance decomposition panel regressions for four waves of panel data, robust standard errors in parentheses, listwise deletion of missing values due to panel attrition and item nonresponse.

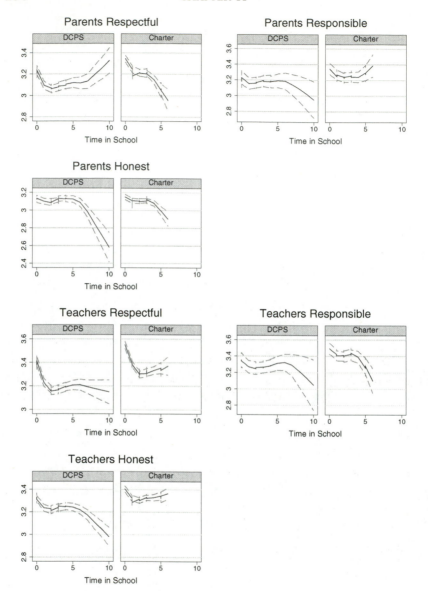

Figure 11.2. The dynamics of school civics (listwise deletion). *Note*: The dark lines are loess-local regressions of predicted values of the dependent variables from the fixed-effects vector decomposition models versus time. The dashed lines are +/– 2 standard errors of the prediction.

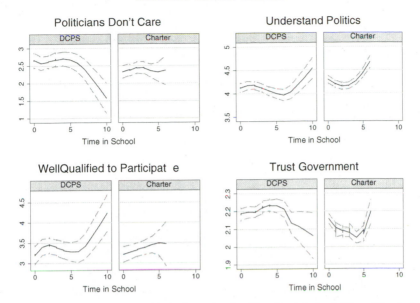

Figure 11.3. The dynamics of broader attitudes (listwise deletion). *Note*: The dark lines are loess-local regressions of predicted values of the dependent variables from the fixed-effects vector decomposition models versus time. The dashed lines are +/– 2 standard errors of the prediction.

the responses to "well-qualified to participate" exhibit a steady increase in the positive direction.

Before we draw any firm conclusions from these models, however, we must again consider the possible biases induced by panel attrition. Accordingly, as in earlier chapters, we employ multiple imputation of the missing values (jointly for both panel attrition and item nonresponse within panel waves), assuming again that the "missingness" is conditional on the observed data (missing at random or MAR in the terminology of missing-data analysis). We then estimate similar panel-data models as those presented above.[7]

We present the results of the models in tables 11.4 (school-community attitudes) and 11.5 (broader attitudes). As the tables show, we still find some support for a charter effect in a handful of the school outcomes, but little for the broader measures. In addition, there are virtually no statistically significant dynamic components in the models (covariates on regressors involving some function of time are in general not statistically different from 0).

These results suggest that the predicted values from these models will not exhibit the same distinct trajectories discussed above. Indeed, as can be seen in figures 11.4 and 11.5, the predicted changes in attitudes over

TABLE 11.4
Parent-School Civics Dynamics (Multiple Imputation)

	Parents respectful	Parents responsible	Parents honest	Teachers respectful	Teachers responsible	Teachers honest
Charter	.14 (.09)	.11 (.10)	.12* (.06)	.21* (.06)	.05 (.09)	.14* (.07)
Time in school	−.08 (.08)	−.02 (.08)	−.03 (.05)	−.09* (.05)	−.07 (.07)	−.05 (.09)
Time²	.007 (.02)	.005 (.02)	.02 (.01)	.01 (.01)	.02 (.02)	.02 (.01)
Time³	.001 (.002)	−.0004 (.002)	−.003* (.002)	−.001 (.001)	−.003 (.004)	−.002 (.001)
Time × charter	−.04 (.11)	−.11 (.11)	−.005 (.07)	−.07 (.07)	.03 (.10)	−.08 (.08)
Time² × charter	.02 (.04)	.05 (.04)	−.01 (.02)	.01 (.02)	.004 (.03)	.02 (.03)
Time³ × charter	−.004 (.004)	−.006 (.004)	.002 (.003)	−.0003 (.003)	−.003 (.004)	−.002 (.003)
Panel wave	.01 (.03)	.001 (.04)	.02 (.02)	−.02 (.02)	−.008 (.03)	.01 (.02)
End of year	−.02 (.06)	−.02 (.06)	−.01 (.04)	−.08* (.04)	−.04 (.06)	−.08* (.04)
Grade level	.009 (.01)	.001 (.009)	.008 (.006)	−.02* (.006)	−.007 (.008)	−.01* (.006)
< 6 years	−.70* (.11)	−.12 (.12)	.15* (.08)	.01 (.08)	−.001 (.11)	.09 (.08)
White	.05 (.14)	.28* (.13)	.22* (.09)	−.02 (.11)	−.04 (.13)	.18* (.11)
Hispanic	−.02 (.12)	−.22 (.14)	.07 (.07)	.06 (.08)	−.02 (.10)	.03 (.08)
Other race	.16 (.11)	−.05 (.13)	.08 (.08)	.12 (.07)	−.05 (.12)	.06 (.08)
Years in D.C.	.001 (.006)	.002 (.006)	.002 (.004)	.002 (.004)	−.001 (.005)	−.0004 (.004)
In neighborhood	.003 (.005)	.009* (.005)	.001 (.003)	.002 (.003)	.001 (.004)	−.002 (.003)
Church	−.007 (.015)	.01 (.01)	.001 (.01)	−.004 (.01)	.009 (.01)	.006 (.01)
Marital status	.03 (.06)	.009 (.06)	.12* (.002)	.02 (.04)	.05 (.05)	.02 (.04)
Employed	−.01 (.07)	−.02 (.02)	−.04 (.04)	−.03 (.05)	.003 (.06)	−.007 (.05)
Education	−.005 (.05)	−.05 (.05)	−.05 (.03)	−.01 (.04)	.06 (.05)	−.01 (.04)
Education²	.001 (.002)	.003 (.002)	.002* (.001)	.001(.002)	−.001 (.002)	.001 (.002)
DCPS grade	.05 (.02)	−.01 (.02)	.05* (.02)	.04* (.02)	.01 (.02)	.04* (.02)
Constant	2.94* (.36)	3.19* (.40)	3.07* (.24)	3.41* (.32)	2.64* (.40)	3.32* (.29)

* $p < .10$, two-tailed.

Note: N = 4,020. Results are coefficients from random-effects panel regressions for four waves of panel data, robust, Li-Raghunathan-Rubin standard errors in parentheses, all results averaged over five multiple-imputed datasets to account for missing values due to panel attrition and item nonresponse.

time are much smoother for the multiple-imputation models, and the standard errors of the predictions are much larger due to the large amount of panel attrition and the subsequent variation across imputed datasets.

The general conclusion that we draw from the predictions shown in these figures is that, after accounting for panel attrition, there is little difference in the evolution of attitudes of school or civic participation between charter-school parents and their traditional peers.

TABLE 11.5
Parent Broader-Civics Dynamics (Multiple Imputation)

	Politicians care	Understand politics	Well- qualified	Trust government
Charter	−.02 (.16)	.08 (.11)	.01 (.21)	.01 (.10)
Time in school	.02 (.12)	.06 (.08)	.21 (.16)	.08 (.09)
Time²	.01 (.03)	−.03 (.02)	−.07 (.05)	−.01 (.02)
Time³	−.003 (.003)	.002 (.002)	.006 (.004)	.001 (.002)
Time × charter	.005 (.17)	−.14 (.12)	−.10 (.23)	−.07 (.12)
Time² × charter	−.009 (.06)	.05 (.04)	.04 (.08)	.005 (.04)
Time³ × charter	.001 (.006)	−.004 (.005)	−.003 (.009)	.002 (.005)
Panel wave	−.11* (.06)	−.04 (.05)	.007 (.08)	−.09* (.03)
End of year	.050 (.10)	.01 (.08)	−.09 (.14)	−.03 (.06)
Grade level	−.01 (.01)	.001 (.01)	−.004 (.02)	.007 (.009)
< 6 years	.32* (.18)	.39* (.13)	.01 (.24)	.11 (.11)
White	.60* (.28)	.18 (.12)	.33 (.31)	.22 (.14)
Hispanic	.09 (.20)	−.48* (.18)	−.44 (.29)	.07 (.13)
Other race	.17 (.22)	.05 (.14)	.003 (.29)	−.03 (.14)
Years in D.C.	.006 (.01)	−.002 (.007)	.01 (.01)	−.003 (.006)
In neighborhood	−.0005 (.008)	.002 (.006)	−.005 (.010)	.001 (.004)
Church	−.01 (.02)	−.007 (.01)	.01 (.03)	.01 (.01)
Marital status	.11 (.10)	.06 (.07)	−.03 (.14)	.03 (.06)
Employed	−.05 (.11)	−.02 (.08)	−.04 (.15)	−.04 (.07)
Education	−.15* (.09)	.17* (.08)	.01 (.12)	−.07 (.05)
Education²	.007* (.004)	−.004 (.003)	.003 (.005)	.002 (.002)
DCPS grade	.10* (.04)	−.002 (.03)	−.01 (.06)	.08* (.02)
Constant	3.26* (.69)	2.75* (.60)	2.40* (.92)	2.64* (.41)

* $p < .10$, two-tailed.

Note: N = 4,020. Results are coefficients from random-effects panel regressions for four waves of panel data, robust, Li-Raghunathan-Rubin standard errors in parentheses, all results averaged over five multiple-imputed datasets to account for missing values due to panel attrition and item nonresponse.

Is the Link between Charter Parents, Civic Participation, and Social Capital Strong Enough?

In the 1800s, Horace Mann argued that public schools were a venue in which the growing number of immigrants to the United States could learn the norms of American civic life and could develop the capacity to be engaged in American democracy. John Dewey also emphasized the impor-

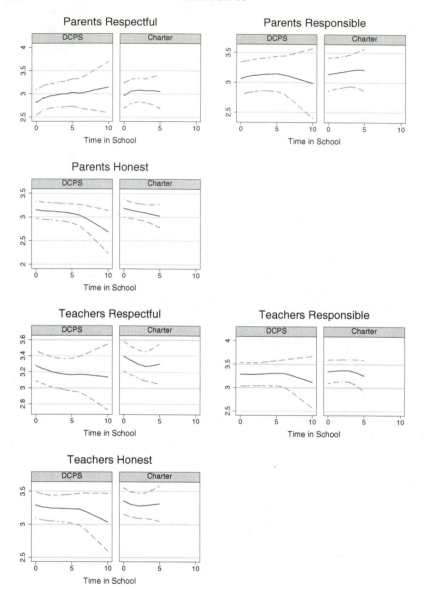

Figure 11.4. The dynamics of school civics (multiple imputation). *Note*: The dark lines are loess-local regressions of predicted values of the dependent variables from random-effects panel-data models versus time. The dashed lines are +/– 2 standard errors of the prediction.

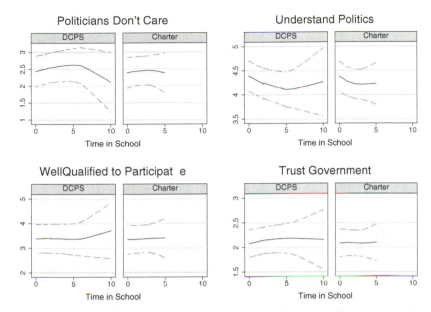

Figure 11.5. The dynamics of broader attitudes (multiple imputation). *Note*: The dark lines are loess-local regressions of predicted values of the dependent variables from random-effects panel-data models versus time. The dashed lines are +/– 2 standard errors of the prediction.

tance of schools as "social centres" (Dewey and Boydston 1976). Indeed, according to David Campbell (2000), linking American public schools to the need to produce "better citizens" became one of the main supports for the rapid expansion of public education in the United States throughout the late nineteenth and early twentieth centuries, and it continues to be one of the expectations vested in today's schools (Henig 1994, 201).

Clearly, creating better citizens is a complex task, but according to Gutmann, one of the defining characteristics of a democratic education is the "ability to deliberate" in a context of "mutual respect" (1987, 46). This perspective is clearly in line with Burns and Kinder's (2000) emphasis on respect and honesty and Putnam's (2000) broad vision of social capital. For these authors, respect for others and mutual trust are essential for the smooth working of democratic societies. For Putnam, in particular, the norm of generalized trust built within social networks people form as they interact in voluntary associations and other settings—including schools— is central. In his view, as trust is built, collaborative effort results, and as successful collaborative efforts move forward more trust is built, creating a virtuous circle.

While much of the argument examining the role of schools in fostering democratic norms and practices focuses on children, we have extended that analysis by examining, to borrow Sapiro's term, schools as venues of "adult political learning" (Sapiro 1994).[8] Many proponents argue that charter schools are creating opportunities for such adult political learning. This argument is supported by empirical evidence showing that many charter schools encourage parents to become integral to the functioning of the school. Proponents further argue that as this fundamental change takes place, parents will learn to respect one another and other members of the school community. In this atmosphere of cooperation and mutual respect, the schools will improve, while at the same time parents will develop the norms essential for democratic participation and a virtuous circle will be built.

Our results indicate that on at least some of the school-related attitudes we measure, parents in charter schools indeed exhibit a stronger foundation for cooperative behavior than do parents in the traditional public schools. Specifically, our evidence suggests that charter schools may present an atmosphere in which parents report strong foundations for higher levels of trust, respect, and cooperative behavior between themselves and their children's teachers.

Unfortunately, these positive findings are offset by another set of results: with one exception, our analysis suggests that the benefits of charter enrollment do not spill over to broader political attitudes. We believe this lack of spillover may be the result of a fundamental characteristic of schools of choice—but one not usually recognized by its adherents.

Recall that many advocates of charter schools and choice more broadly often hold up Catholic schools as exemplars of successful education. While there is debate about exactly how successful Catholic schools really are, the evidence seems to confirm that they do add value for lower-income, inner-city students (such as the students that populate the schools we are studying). Bryk, Lee, and Holland (1993) emphasize the importance of a strong community in creating these results (small school size, an emphasis on academics, and requirements for parental participation are among the other factors that most likely contribute to the success of Catholic schools). But several analysts have argued that choice and the resulting school community create a radically different organizational environment than that found in public schools.

Salganik and Karweit (1982) were among the first to argue that choice ensures a consensus on school goals and high levels of commitment among each of the constituents of the school. In contrast, the public-school environment is more heterogeneous and contested, and the higher levels of conflict and disagreement can reduce the cohesion and "effectiveness" of the school community. This theme was elaborated by Chubb and Moe (1990).

But Benveniste, Carnoy, and Rothstein show an unexpected effect of this difference in community on parent participation. Based on careful observations of a set of schools in California, Benveniste and colleagues argue that "private schools are more likely to define clear boundaries and to stick to the course that the school head and/or the majority on the school governing board deems best for the school, sometime at the cost of shedding dissenters. Public schools do not have this option. They must live with dissent" (2003, 180). The emphasis on exit over voice was also evident in the charter schools in their sample.

Consider how this may lead to a stronger *within*-school community while at the same time leading to the lack of spillover effects: through an emphasis on a clear mission that parents and students acknowledge and through encouraging exit, charter schools can create a relatively homogeneous "voluntary" environment united by a shared sense of mission. In this environment, parents can more easily support staff efforts to educate their children and can enter into "trust relationships" with teachers and staff (Bryk, Lee, and Holland 1993). But this homogeneity has a cost: it can reduce exposure to deliberative processes. Salisbury (1980) shows that citizens who are exposed to more deliberation and discussion are more likely to transfer their participation skills to arenas outside the school. Moreover, the homogeneity of the school may lead to networks of parents linked together by what Granovetter (1973) calls "strong ties." But there is a weakness to strong ties: individuals in networks with strong ties have only limited exposure to new information. Strong ties can define a more satisfying but narrow world.

Together, these processes—greater homogeneity, strong ties to other parents, and the weeding out of dissent—can help create the pattern we observe: strong "internal" communities coupled with no spillover effects to other communities or practices. To use Putnam's terms, school choice may create "bonding" but not "bridging" social capital (2000; also see Putnam 1993).

Fuller, in his discussion of charter schools, observes a similar pattern but has a more alarmist spin. According to Fuller, charter schools can create intense "small, even tribal, public squares bounded by ethnicity, social class, or religion" that can erode "the larger public square" (2000a, 5). We don't know if charter schools are actually leading to an *erosion* of the already depleted stocks of social capital in the inner city that could be used for wider societal goals, but we do see evidence that parents are more involved in these smaller school-based public spheres while at the same time they are not any more likely to participate in the larger public arena.

IS THE GLASS HALF EMPTY OR . . . ?

Like so much research on the relationship between the design of government institutions and individual political behavior, and like so much empirical work on educational reforms, the results we are faced with are
mixed. We can read our results in one of two ways.

On the one hand, on several indicators, charter schools are clearly "better" than traditional public schools and, perhaps more importantly, there
is *no* indicator where charter-school parents view other parents or teachers more negatively than do other parents. Moreover, that these effects
are found at all could be taken as a strong endorsement of charter schools.
Thus, one could argue that the charter-school experiment is "working":
when it comes to building social capital *within* a school, charter schools
are Pareto superior to the traditional public schools we studied. From this
perspective, charter schools already pass one of the most fundamental
tests of policy reform.

On the other hand, the "value added" to social capital by charter
schools is not overwhelming, and, even more problematic, it does not
increase markedly over time—in our dynamic models where we try to
account for panel attrition we find virtually no difference in the trajectories of charter and public parents. Finally, any value added appears to be
limited to the school community with little evidence of spillover effects
from school-based social capital to broader domains. Critics could therefore argue that charter schools represent at best a marginal gain that does
not justify all the money, time, and energy invested in them, at least from
the perspective of building parents' civic capacity.

Finally, there is yet another consideration that may have attenuated the
feedback loop from the schools to broader political practices: in the policy
areas in which a loop has been established by other researchers (mostly
social services such as the former AFDC), the public nature of the service
is clearly evident. In contrast, charter schools, although public schools by
law, may not be recognized as such by all parents—contributing to the
failure of school-related attitudes to spill over to broader political practices. Cities and states seeking to reap the democratic benefits of an increase in school-related social capital may need to embrace these relatively
new institutions more publicly and take credit for their successes.

Do Charter Schools Promote Citizenship
among Students?

THE "COMMON-SCHOOL" MOVEMENT OF THE 1840s placed public schools center stage as the most important provider of civic education in the United States. While the leaders of this movement, "school men" like Horace Mann and Henry Barnard, had a variety of goals for public education (Goldin and Katz 2003), the influx of immigrants to the nation in the second half of the nineteenth century created a perceived need to socialize the newcomers to American values and made citizenship education a central task of the public-school system (Perkinson 1991). Over a century later, schools continue to be seen as important in this endeavor by a large proportion of the American population (see, for example, Moe 2001, 86–91; Hochschild and Scovronick 2003, 9–27), and this attitude is embodied in Macedo's observation that "good citizens are not simply born that way, they must be educated by schools" (2000, 16).

The perceived link between schools and good citizenship also affects policy makers. A body of research suggests that service and activism by students are associated with lifelong civic engagement involving voting, trust in government, and participation in voluntary organizations, so it is probably not surprising that many policy makers and educators now call upon school districts to implement programs requiring students to perform service as a way of building civic capacity and promoting democratic citizenship (see, for example, Youniss, McLellan, and Yates 1997; Jennings 2002; Metz and Youniss 2003; Stewart, Settles, and Winter 1998).

It is also not surprising that citizenship education and the political socialization of American youth is a long-standing topic of interest to an interdisciplinary community of researchers, including philosophers, sociologists, political scientists, psychologists, and scholars of education.[1] However, such interest has been somewhat cyclical. Beginning in the late 1950s with the seminal work of Hyman (1959), the topic attracted considerable research attention, but fell out of favor by the early 1980s. The last decade, however, witnessed a resurgence of interest in the topic (see, for example, Galston 2001; Niemi and Hepburn 1995; Niemi and Junn 1998; Verba, Schlozman, and Brady 1995).

One reason for the renewed interest is the accumulating evidence of a decline in civic participation and political involvement in the United

States, especially among young people. Perhaps the most consistent evidence of this decline has been collected by the Higher Education Research Institute at UCLA's Graduate School of Education and Information Studies. In its repeated surveys of the attitudes of a national sample of college freshman, the study has documented a three-decade-long trend of plummeting political interest. While there was an increase from the record low of 28 percent in 2000, the Fall 2004 study nonetheless found that only one-third of students feel that "keeping up to date with political affairs" is a very important life goal. Political engagement also remains far below the level recorded in the late 1960s, when 60 percent of the 1966 freshmen valued keeping up with politics and one-third of the 1968 freshmen discussed politics frequently.

Political and civic knowledge among students is also abysmally low. The National Assessment of Educational Progress (NAEP) sets the following standards, which seem quite reasonable benchmarks by which to judge citizen knowledge necessary for a functioning democratic society:

> Twelfth-grade students performing at the Proficient level should have a good understanding of how constitutions can limit the power of government and support the rule of law. They should be able to distinguish between parliamentary systems of government and those based on separate and shared powers, and they should be able to describe the structure and functions of American government. These students should be able to identify issues in which fundamental democratic values and principles are in conflict—liberty and equality, individual rights and the common good, majority rule and minority rights, for example, and they should be able to take and defend positions on these issues.[2]

Using these standards, about 75 percent of students at all grades tested were less than "proficient" and over one-third of the graduating seniors who took the exam were below basic—close to totally ignorant of the operations of our government. It is not surprising that Galston finds the results "not encouraging," driving him to the gloomy conclusion: "Whether we are concerned with the rules of the political game, political players, domestic policy, foreign policy, or political geography, student performance is quite low" (2004, 271).

Given this widespread concern, a resurgence in interest in civic education might be expected. But there is an additional impetus—the renewal is driven, at least in part, by proponents of school vouchers (e.g., Greene 1998; Moe 2000b). The push for vouchers (and to a lesser extent, charter schools) has touched off a serious debate about the continued place of the common school in American society and the ability of schools of choice to educate students as citizens.

Democratic political theorists have provided philosophical justification for the public's trust in public schools as the primary socializing agent of American political culture, perhaps none more eloquently than Amy Gutmann (1987). Her argument, generally, is that private schools, particularly religious ones, may not promote the key values of political and religious tolerance. Furthermore, they are likely to be governed by bodies, such as religious orders or boards of trustees, which are not democratically accountable to the general citizenry, thus removing any check on their governance structure or curricula. Finally, in an increasingly multicultural society, some private schools may actually promote cultural or political separatism (Macedo 2000).

Proponents of educational privatization, on the other hand, reject these conclusions. They often argue that the government of public education is dominated by special-interest groups and mired in bureaucracy. This institutional environment hampers civic education and makes it impossible for democratic school-based communities to emerge (Moe 2000b). Their proposed solution is to replace the current institutional arrangement with a market-based approach—often, a universal school-voucher system.

Building on the empirical findings that Catholic schools appear to foster a higher level of civic engagement and volunteerism than their public counterparts (see, e.g., Bryk, Lee, and Holland 1993; Coleman, Hoffer, and Kilgore 1982), voucher proponents argue that the same benefits observed in Catholic schools could be reaped more widely through a universal voucher system; a claim for which there is some empirical support (Belfield 2003; Campbell 2002; Greene 1998).[3]

Our goal in this chapter is to extend this research on citizenship education to include the effects of charter schools on students. As we discuss below, many charter schools appear to offer either explicit curricular reforms or changes in culture and governance that should, in theory, enhance civic education. Despite these expectations, the question of whether charter schools foster civic engagement and democratic norms is an empirical one. To answer this question, we rely on evidence from our telephone survey of seventh–twelfth graders and their parents in Washington, D.C., conducted in the third wave of our study (during the Fall of 2003, as described in chapter 3).

The plan of the chapter is as follows: after a review of the relevant theoretical and empirical literature on civic education, we outline how this scholarship can be applied to charter schools. We then describe our data and our specific measures. Because of the observational nature of our data, as in other chapters, we employ various methods to attempt to remove potential biases caused by the self-selection of parents to charter schools and the attrition of respondents from the panel. After discussing these methods, we then present our results and conclude with some thoughts on both the limits and the implications of our findings.

CREATING CITIZENS

Thomas Jefferson wrote, "Every government degenerates when trusted to the rulers of the people. The people themselves are its only safe depositories. And to render even them safe, their minds must be improved to a certain degree" (1853, 157). More recently but in the same vein, Wolf and Macedo observe:

> Political communities have a significant and legitimate interest in ensuring that children are educated effectively. Democratic societies have a special interest in ensuring that children are prepared for the responsibilities of citizenship. Citizens in a democratic society exercise political power over one another, and to do so responsibly, reflectively, and justifiably they need certain capacities, dispositions, and an adequate grasp of political institutions, history, and the world around them. (2004, 8)

From this perspective, citizenship education is something that empowers people in a democratic republic to function as the ultimate holders of political authority. But what is the content of this education? Not surprisingly, there has been intense debate on this point—a debate that has intensified as the country has become more politically polarized in the last few years.

On one level, the answer to this question is based on the image that individuals have of society and the obligations and rights that citizens have toward the state. One of the main dimensions of this debate is the degree to which individuals believe that it is the obligation of citizens to obey existing laws and authority as compared to the extent to which they should challenge them. The second question is more narrowly tailored around the role of schools in reaching that vision of citizen rights and responsibilities.

Along these lines, Westheimer and Kahne (2004) describe three different "visions" of citizenship: *the personally responsible citizen*; *the participatory citizen*; and *the justice-oriented citizen*. A responsible citizen believes that citizens must be honest, responsible, and law abiding. A participatory citizen is, as the term implies, more active—not only does she enthusiastically participate but she also assumes leadership positions in community organizations and political activities. Westheimer and Kahne compare the personally responsible and participatory citizen using the following example: the personally responsible citizen will contribute food to a food drive, but a participatory citizen helps organize it. Each of these forms of citizenship calls for a different form of education: programs to create personally responsible citizens emphasize good manners, integrity, self-discipline, and hard work, while programs designed to encourage participatory citizens focus on the importance of planning and participating in community programs and in designing programs to help those in need.

Westheimer and Kahne also identify a third type of citizen. These justice-oriented citizens question established systems and seek to change them when these systems produce patterns of injustice. To complete the food drive example, a justice-oriented citizen will ask why people are hungry and seek to identify the root causes of hunger. The education to support this type of citizen would focus on social movements and how to effect systemic change. One of the more contentious dimensions of this type of education is that justice-oriented citizens should learn that citizenship requires government and collective action, rather than emphasizing the individualistic conception of the market (also see Macedo 2000; Gutmann 1987; Barber 1984; for an international perspective see Wolf and Macedo 2004).

Gutmann's influential work, *Democratic Education,* also stresses the importance of questioning authority: "Children must learn not just to *behave* in accordance with authority but to *think* critically about authority if they are to live up to the democratic ideal of sharing political sovereignty as citizens" (1987, 51). She continues: "[A]lthough inculcating character and teaching moral reasoning by no means exhaust the purposes of primary education in a democracy, together they constitute its core purpose: the development of 'deliberative,' or . . . 'democratic' character" (52–53). Gutmann assigns a correspondingly large role to the schools: "[I]f there should be a domain for citizens collectively to educate their children in the democratic virtues of deliberation, then primary schools occupy a large part of that domain, although they do not monopolize it" (53).

Macedo has a similarly expansive view of the role of schools in creating strong democratic citizens—and a view that flies in the face of the drive for vouchers, charter schools, and other forms of choice. Macedo identifies the common school as a venue in which students learn the key ideas central to democratic society:

> The common school ideal stands for educational institutions that contain society's diversity in a tolerant, respectful cooperative context. Common schools remain especially appropriate vehicles for inculcating the civic virtue of mutual respect for those who differ with us in their religious convictions or beliefs about the good life. (2000, 232)

Macedo has not ventured into the design of a curriculum that would maximize mutual respect, but he does argue:

> Civic education is inseparable from education: no teacher could run a class-
> room, no principal could run a school, without taking a stand on a wide
> range of civic values and moral and political virtues. . . . Important moral
> and political values constrain and shape the way we conceive of and advance
> the intellectual enterprise.
>
>   Education and indoctrination are indeed two very different things, but to
> describe classroom learning as "academic" or "intellectual" as opposed to
> "civic" misses the extent to which our conception of learning is infused with
> democratic values. It is quixotic and misguided to think we should, or even
> can, get civic education out of the schools. Civic education is not only legiti-
> mate; it is inescapable. All education, properly undertaken, has a civic element.

Clearly these theorists envision schools occupying a central role in creating citizens who are actively engaged in political discourse and governance. For them, schools are by their very nature indispensable ingredients in building a vibrant civil society in which the democratic rights of
citizens to question the actions of their government is emphasized.

Not surprisingly, this position has not gone unchallenged. Perhaps the
most interesting (and controversial) contemporary alternative vision has
been developed by James Bernard Murphy. In his argument "Against
Civic Education in Public Schools," Murphy argues strongly against civic
education per se. After reviewing many attempts to create civic-education
curricula or practices (most of them egregious examples of ideas sub-
verted for political purposes—including a discussion of Thomas Jefferson's own rather sordid behavior in establishing the curriculum of the
University of Virginia), Murphy argues that "In practice, then, and in
theory, we have compelling evidence that civic education poses a fundamental and permanent threat to both the academic curriculum and to
academic pedagogy" (2004, 248).

Instead, Murphy argues that the correct role ("the inherent moral purpose") for schools is the inculcation of a lifelong love for learning. Murphy argues that schools should impart civic skills, which are just that—
skills—"the trained capacities for deploying civic knowledge in the pursuit of civic goals, such as voting, protesting, petitioning, canvassing, and
debating" (2004, 224). Murphy's argument is consistent with research
showing the relationship between higher levels of formal education and
desirable civic outcomes, such as political participation, tolerance, and
political sophistication (see, e.g., Delli Carpini and Keeter 1996; Verba,
Schlozman, and Brady 1995).

Moreover, for Murphy schools are "relatively weak instruments of civic
education," but he does believe that "schools can play a small though
significant role in teaching civic knowledge and that schools can indirectly
foster civic skills by encouraging extra-curricular participation in student

government and other voluntary organizations" (2004, 225). Murphy's emphasis accords with that of Verba, Schlozman, and Brady, who find that American high schools provide civic education "not by teaching about democracy but by providing hands-on training for future participation" (1995, 376).

How can we make sense of the terms of this debate?

Enslin and White (2002) identify two contrasting research themes—both of which describe a distinction between passive and active citizenship. One theme defines a passive/active dichotomy as the difference between citizens as "passive recipients of rights," and citizens "who are alert to the responsibilities sometimes required by those rights (like, for example, voting, writing to the newspapers, joining protests, etc. . . .)." The second version of this distinction casts passive citizens as "bearers of rights and aware of, and committed to, the related responsibilities," as opposed to citizens "actively virtuous in the public sphere which activity they rate more highly than private concerns" (Enslin and White 2002, 121).

Most work on education for democratic citizenship has focused on the first distinction, identifying the ends of a continuum that stretches between passive and active citizenship and the form of education that matches that conception. We define these ends as follows:

Passive Citizenship defines citizens as passive recipients of rights. Their civic education must consist of sufficient socialization/acculturation so that they are able to recognize the appropriate nation-state or other political entity in which they have membership and be familiar with the rights they (and their fellow citizens) hold under this regime.

Active Citizenship treats citizens as knowledgeable about their rights, but also about their responsibilities as the ultimate repository of political authority. As in the case of passive citizenship, their education must include an understanding of their shared identity. It must also, however, impart the civic skills necessary for participation in the public sphere.

We believe that passive citizenship is insufficient for a vibrant civil society and the vigorous protection of the people's sovereignty. In this we follow Macedo, who argues that we need to create more than the conditions of freedom, order, and prosperity. In addition, he argues that we need to create "the capacities and dispositions conducive to thoughtful participation in the activities of modern politics and civil society" (2000, 10). Therefore, we argue that the role of democratic education should be the creation of active citizens. But if active citizenship is the goal, which civic skills and knowledge should schools teach?

Clearly, the stakes in this debate are high and the debate continues to unfold. But we believe that there are certain aspects of the debate that can be turned into a set of questions that are tractable for empirical analysis.

Given the complexity of the issue, we need to choose a set of values that lie at the bottom of these various arguments. To do so, we build on the work of David Campbell, who in his discussion of the goals of civic education divides political activity into four categories:

- Participation in public-spirited collective action (community service);
- The capacity to be involved in the political process (civic skills);
- An understanding of the nation's political system (political knowledge); and
- A respect for the civil liberties of others (political tolerance).[4] (2002, 3–4)

We accept these as core values that schools can and should further, and, more importantly, that can be empirically studied. In relation to the continuum outlined above, the first two are necessary only for active citizenship, while the latter two categories are necessary for active and passive citizenship.[5] Murphy's argument suggests that schools should concentrate only on the first three categories—but that they should not expect much return from teaching political knowledge and should not even attempt to teach political tolerance.

Our goal in this chapter is to see if charter schools contribute to this set of core values that, despite all the heat that the debate about civic education has generated, virtually all analysts agree are important and good schools can and should further. Before moving on to our empirical analysis, however, we need to take one more diversion.

Do Catholic Schools Provide a Model of Citizen Education?

While democratic theorists support the importance of public schools for civic education, a growing body of empirical evidence supports the claim that private schools do a better job of civic education than their public counterparts. Catholic secondary schools, in particular, have long been thought to promote both the knowledge and attitudes essential for passive citizenship as well as the civic skills needed for active citizenship (Bryk, Lee, and Holland 1993; Coleman and Hoffer 1987). In addition, many believe that Catholic schools promote a particular moral view that encourages political tolerance.

Perhaps the strongest evidence for the benefits of private schooling to citizenship education comes from David Campbell (2002). Using data from both the National Household Education Survey (NHES) and the randomized voucher experiment funded by the Children's Scholarship Fund (Peterson et al. 2002b), Campbell studied the effect of private schooling on his four dimensions of political activity presented above. For knowledge and tolerance (two attributes of passive citizenship),[6] Campbell reports a statistically significant effect for private schools. However, while he finds an effect for Catholic, private-religious (other than Catholic), and private-secular schools on political tolerance, only Catholic schools increase political knowledge. Similarly, for the components of active citizenship, he finds an effect of private schools that appears to be attributable overwhelmingly to Catholic schools.[7]

While non-Catholic private schools may produce some benefits for students, the bulk of the empirical evidence suggests that some combination of characteristics of Catholic education—perhaps the strong sense of community coupled with a firm orientation toward making positive changes in the secular world—gives Catholic schools an advantage in fostering passive *and* active citizenship. Other private schools do not necessarily succeed in improving citizenship education over their public counterparts. However, some would argue that charter schools may represent a "third way" between the overly bureaucratic and special-interest-dominated public schools and the particularistic private sector.

ENTER CHARTER SCHOOLS

Charter schools arguably combine the best of both sectors. They are, in theory, free to innovate; in the context of citizenship education, they can adopt the best practices in civics curricula, as well as encourage or even require extracurricular activities that can build active citizenship.[8] Due to the decentralized nature of their administration, they can also involve parents and students in school governance to an extent not found in traditional public schools (Hill, Pierce, and Gutherie 1997; Hill et al. 2001).[9] Even Macedo, a strong supporter of the common school, sees the virtues of charter schools. Given greater autonomy, including the ability to define specific missions and hire staff committed to that mission, charter schools could become "voluntary communities" built around shared values (Macedo 2000, 265) and thereby replicate the advantages that Catholic schools have in creating higher academic achievement and civic education.

However, and this is critical, charter schools remain *public* schools. They are generally required to serve the entire population of their district (with overenrollment resolved by lottery) instead of particular ethnic or religious minority groups.[10] As public schools of choice, they may encourage participation of parents and students and enhance social capital (Schneider, Teske, and Marschall 2000). As public schools, they may be more likely to educate their students in the foundations of passive citizenship than many private schools. And as public schools, they can continue to serve broader societal goals of openness and tolerance (Macedo 2000, 267).

Fuller presents a strong dissenting viewpoint. He sees charter schools as a "radical decentralization" of authority in which decisions regarding the education of children and the allocation of public resources are entrusted to groups of parents, advocates, and charter school leaders, who push their own particularistic self-interests while neglecting the "common good." Fuller argues that charter-school advocates seek to create isolated ("tribal") communities that "may contribute to the dismantling of the modern state's political foundations." Fuller further argues that under school choice, "the state sanctions the pursuit not of the broad common good but of private interests" (2000b, 25). In short, for Fuller, charter schools threaten not only to displace the "common school" in which students of diverse backgrounds and interests come together in one place to learn tolerance for diversity and respect for their fellow citizens, but also to diminish the civic virtues and democratic practices of students.[11]

Given these claims and counterclaims, we believe that empirically assessing the effect of charter-school enrollment on the active and passive citizenship education of students is an important task for educational policy—a task to which we now turn.

Testing the Effect of Charter Schools on Civic Education

To test the effects of charter schools on citizenship education, we use data from our telephone survey of both charter- and traditional public-school parents and seventh–twelfth grade students conducted in Washington, D.C. in September–October 2003. As readers will recall, the data are drawn from the third wave of the panel survey of parents that we began in the Fall of 2001. The original sample size was 1,012 parents, with approximately half selected by random-digit dialing and the other half, a designed oversample of charter parents, randomly selected from a list. Due to panel attrition, the restriction of student interviews to those in grade levels to seventh–twelfth grade, and the difficulty of convincing parents to allow us to interview their children, we were able to complete only 196 interviews with students. Given the "messy" nature of our data, we again need to address the issues of self-selection to the sample by parents as well as attrition from the panel over time before proceeding with our analysis of the effect of charter enrollment on civic education.

As in other earlier analyses, in this chapter we again use propensity-score matching.[12] In order to reduce the likelihood of self-selection bias on the student outcomes as a result of the decision of parents to enroll their child in a charter school, we first estimate a propensity score for selection to enroll in charter schools for 775 parents in the wave 1, 2001 sample,[13] using a standard maximum-likelihood probit model of the parents' decision to choose with the following covariates:[14]

- A set of three dichotomous variables for self-reported race (Hispanic, white, other, with African American the excluded—and modal—category);
- Residential mobility, as measured by the number of years the person has lived in her current neighborhood and by the years the person has lived in D.C.;
- Respondents' years of schooling and the square of this quantity, to account for possible nonlinearity;
- Respondents' assessment of the general quality of the D.C. public schools, which we include as a control for pretreatment attitudes. This assessment is measured by the grade respondents assigned to the D.C. public schools, using the familiar A, B, C, D, F scale, which we treat here as a continuous 0 (F) to 4 (A) scale;
- Frequency of church attendance (a seven-category measure, again treated as continuous);
- Whether or not the respondent was employed; and
- The respondent's marital status.

The results of the estimation of the model are presented in table 12.1. A small number of the treated observations have propensity scores that are outside the range of untreated scores (i.e., not on the "common support") and we discard these from subsequent analysis.

Our next step is to match the charter parents (the "treatment" group) to the parents in the group of D.C. public school parents who are most similar to them (the "control" group). We use the nearest-neighbor matching method, with a caliper of .01, and allow sampling with replacement from the untreated observations (Becker and Ichino 2002). The result is a new dataset (essentially an integer-weighted adjustment of the original data) consisting of 429 charter parents and their 429 matched noncharter parents. We test the equality of the two samples by comparing the first and second moments of the covariates in the propensity-score model with a series of independent t- and F tests, failing to reject the null of equality at the .05 level for each test. We also conduct the multivariate T^2 test of the joint equality of samples (Hotelling 1931) and fail to reject the null ($p = .27$) of equality of samples.

Panel Attrition and Missing Data

The second major problem in our data is missing data due to high attrition from the first wave to the third wave and due to parents being unwilling to allow their children to be interviewed. From the 858 observations in the dataset created through the matching algorithm, there are only 165 valid students in the sample—81 percent attrition (unit nonresponse).[15] Even within this sample of 165, about 5 percent of the total matrix of

Table 12.1
Results of Propensity-Score Matching Model for Wave 1 Parents

	Coefficient (standard error)
White	−.88* (.23)
Hispanic	−.18 (.17)
Other race	−.11 (.19)
Years lived in neighborhood	.003 (.006)
Years in D.C.	.005 (.009)
Years of education	.50* (.15)
Years of education squared	−.01* (.006)
DCPS grade	−.19* (.03)
Church attendance	−.04* (.01)
Employed	−.08 (.10)
Married	.05 (.09)
Constant	−4.08* (1.07)

* $p < .05$, two-tailed.

Results of probit model with child in charter school as dependent variable. Number of Observations = 775. Log-likelihood of the model is −272.94.

the data is missing as well (item nonresponse). As in other chapters, and following the terminology of Little and Rubin (2002; Rubin 1987), we assume that the data are missing at random (MAR), that is, the "missingness" of any given variable is determined by the observed data, not by any of the missing values themselves or other unmeasured covariates.

To adjust for unit nonresponse, we use the method of propensity weighting (Cassel, Sarndal, and Wretman 1983). That is, we estimate a model predicting the probability of each family unit remaining in the student sample, based on the observed data for the parents in the first wave. Again, we use a maximum-likelihood probit model for dichotomous dependent variables. The model is similar to the propensity-score model reported above, and includes the following covariates:

- A set of two dichotomous variables for self-reported race (Hispanic and other—in wave 3, no white respondents were left in the sample);
- Residential mobility, as measured by the number of years the person has lived in D.C. and by the square of this quantity;
- Respondents' years of schooling and its square;
- The respondent's marital status;
- Whether or not the respondent was employed;
- Frequency of church attendance (a seven-category measure, again treated as continuous);

TABLE 12.2
Results of Propensity-Weighting Model for Unit Nonresponse in Student Sample

	Coefficient (standard error)
Hispanic	−.53 (.33)
Other race	−.93* (.36)
Years in D.C.	−.05 (.06)
Years in D.C. squared	.003 (.003)
Years of education	.03 (.28)
Years of education squared	.001 (.009)
Married	.10 (.10)
Employed	−.27* (.12)
Church attendance	.006 (.02)
School grade	−.51 (.33)
Education × School grade	.01 (.02)
Charter school	1.50* (.67)
Charter × Education	−.08 (.04)
Constant	−2.68 (2.14)

* $p < .05$, two-tailed.

Results of probit model with students observed in sample as dependent variable. Number of Observations = 832. All log-likelihood of the model is −398.40.

- The grade the respondent assigned to her child's school in the first interview. This is a five-category (A, B, . . . F) measure, which we treat here as continuous (A = 4, B = 3, . . . F = 0);
- The interaction of the school grade and her level of education,
- A dichotomous indicator for whether her child was enrolled in a charter school, during the first interview; and
- The interaction of the charter indicator and her level of education.

The results of this model are presented in table 12.2. After estimating the predicted probabilities, we partition the propensities into three adjustment classes and create weights by assigning the inverse of the mean propensity within each to all members. This avoids placing overly large nonresponse weights on observations with an extremely low response propensity (Little and Rubin 2002, 48–49).

To avoid losing any additional observations in subsequent analysis due to item nonresponse, as in earlier chapters we employ multiple imputation (Little and Rubin 2002; Allison 2002; King et al. 2001; Rubin 1987). Here, we impute five complete datasets of 165 observations each using a predictive mean-matching model (Little 1988; Allison 2002, 59–63; Van Buuren, Boshuizen, and Knook 1999) and average the results of the analyses reported below using Rubin's (1987) method. One particular advantage of the partially parametric predictive mean-matching approach over other techniques used in the applied literature is the restriction of imputed values to those observed in the sample.

The Effect of Charter Schools on Citizenship

With these datasets in hand, the only remaining step before we are ready to model the effect of charter enrollment on active and passive citizenship is to construct our measures of the dependent variables. In terms of Campbell's categories, our survey contains questions that attempt to measure community involvement and civic skills (active citizenship), and political tolerance (passive citizenship). We discuss each measure in turn.[16]

COMMUNITY INVOLVEMENT

Our measures of community involvement are student responses to the following questions, each of which asks the student to report the frequency of a given activity over the past school year using four response options (almost every day, once a week, once in a while, and never):

- How often have you participated in school clubs or organizations (like student council, drama club, or others)?
- How often have you participated in church or community youth groups?
- How often have you played team sports?
- How often have you engaged in any community-service activity or volunteer work at your school or in your community?

CIVIC SKILLS

Our civic-skills measure uses students' responses to four yes-or-no questions asking about their behavior in the past year:

- Have you written a letter to a public official, such as the mayor?
- Have you given a speech or an oral report?
- Have you taken part in a debate or discussion in which you had to persuade others of your point of view?
- Have you gone to a community meeting and given comments or a statement?

POLITICAL TOLERANCE

Finally, we asked students two questions aimed at measuring the extent to which they supported basic civil liberties. The first question pertained to free speech and religious tolerance. We asked students:

- If a person wanted to make a speech in your community against churches and religion, do you think he or she should:
  1. Definitely be allowed to speak
  2. Probably be allowed to speak

3. Probably shouldn't be allowed
4. Definitely shouldn't be allowed

Our second question pertained to another dimension of free speech, the flow of information. We asked:

- Suppose a book that most people disapproved of was written, for example, saying that it was all right to take illegal drugs. Should a book like that

  1. Definitely be kept out of a public library
  2. Probably be kept out of a public library
  3. Probably be allowed in a public library
  4. Definitely be allowed in a public library

Although other recent research in this area (e.g., Campbell 2002) has combined measures similar to our survey questions into scales of community involvement, civic skills, and political tolerance, we choose a different approach that retains the ability to focus on the effect of charter schools on the individual measures while accounting for their correlation.[17]

First, for each of the ten outcome measures we estimate independent ordered-probit regressions using the standard maximum-likelihood estimator (Zavoina and McElvey 1975), which is equivalent to a probit model for the dichotomous outcomes. In each case, we regress our indicators of citizenship on the same covariates:

- A dichotomous indicator for charter-school enrollment;
- A measure of the parent's civic engagement;[18]
- The parental response to the two tolerance measures described above;
- The number of students in the school (in hundreds);
- How long (in years) the student has been in the school;
- Frequency of church attendance as reported by the student;
- The student's grade level (7th–12th); and
- The number of close friends in school that the student reports.[19]

The estimation in each case is weighted using the attrition propensity weights discussed above.

Once we have the estimated coefficients and variance-covariance matrix for each of the ordered-probit models, we adjust the latter using a variant of White's (1982) "sandwich" estimator of covariance (Weesie 1999), modeling the joint distribution of the individual model results as a sort of "seemingly unrelated ordered-probit" model to adjust the estimated standard errors, given the likely correlation of our dependent variables. Finally, as discussed above, we repeat the estimation of the full model using each of the five imputed datasets, and average the results, which are presented in tables 12.3a, b, and c.

TABLE 12.3a
The Only Effect of Charter Schools on Community Involvement Is
Community Service / Volunteer Work

Outcome	Covariate	Coefficient estimate	Standard error
Participated in school clubs	Charter enrollment	0.16	0.22
	Parent's civic engagement	−0.01	0.02
	Parent's tolerance (speech)	0.13	0.10
	Parent's tolerance (library)	−0.02	0.09
	Number of students (00's)	−0.009	0.02
	Years at school	0.01	0.07
	Student's church attendance	0.09	0.06
	Grade level	0.02	0.06
	Student's number of close friends	0.18*	0.06
	Cutpoint 1	0.89	0.82
	Cutpoint 2	1.68*	0.82
	Cutpoint 3	2.05*	0.82
Participated in church or Community youth groups	Charter enrollment	−0.04	0.19
	Parent's civic engagement	0.04*	0.01
	Parent's tolerance (speech)	−0.16	0.11
	Parent's tolerance (library)	−0.13	0.09
	Number of students (00's)	−0.02	0.03
	Years at school	0.10	0.06
	Student's church attendance	0.33*	0.06
	Grade level	0.11	0.06
	Student's number of close friends	−0.03	0.05
	Cutpoint 1	1.35	0.91
	Cutpoint 2	2.58*	0.92
	Cutpoint 3	3.70*	0.94
Played team sports	Charter enrollment	−0.14	0.20
	Parent's civic engagement	0.03	0.02
	Parent's tolerance (speech)	−0.14	0.10
	Parent's tolerance (library)	0.09	0.08
	Number of students (00's)	0.042	0.03
	Years at school	−0.04	0.04
	Student's church attendance	0.23*	0.06
	Grade level	0.10	0.06
	Student's number of close friends	−0.01	0.05
	Cutpoint 1	1.88*	0.86
	Cutpoint 2	2.37*	0.86
	Cutpoint 3	2.62*	0.86

TABLE 12.3a (*cont'd*)

Outcome	Covariate	Coefficient estimate	Standard error
Engaged in community service or volunteer work	Charter enrollment	0.72*	0.20
	Parent's civic engagement	0.007	0.02
	Parent's tolerance (speech)	0.25*	0.10
	Parent's tolerance (library)	0.21*	0.10
	Number of students (00's)	0.007	0.03
	Years at school	−0.01	0.05
	Student's church attendance	0.10	0.06
	Grade level	0.23*	0.06
	Student's number of close friends	0.17*	0.05
	Cutpoint 1	4.33*	0.87
	Cutpoint 2	5.89*	0.91
	Cutpoint 3	6.47*	0.93

* $p < .05$, two-tailed.

Results are from a seemingly unrelated ordered-probit model of the probability of selecting the various response categories for each of the 10 outcome measures simultaneously. Model results presented are the average results over five multiple-imputation datasets created by predictive mean matching. The data are also adjusted for possible self-selection to treatment and panel attrition using the models presented in tables 12.1 and 12.2, above. The number of observations is 165.

We find mixed support for a beneficial effect of charter-school enrollment on the civic education of students. In table 12.3a, there is a statistically significant and positive charter effect on the community service/volunteer work outcome ($p < .01$; all values reported are two-tailed), suggesting that, ceteris paribus, charter students are more likely to perform such service. We find no effect, however, on participation in school clubs, church or youth groups, or team sports.

Regarding the estimates of the coefficients on the control variables, the religiosity of the student as measured by frequency of religious-service attendance is a significant predictor of participation in church and youth groups and in team sports ($p < .01$) and perhaps in volunteer work as well ($p = .10$). The number of close friends that the student reports is significantly associated with participation in school clubs ($p < .01$), and parental civic engagement predicts participation in church/youth groups ($p = .01$) and team sports ($p = .10$).

As table 12.3b illustrates, charter enrollment is associated with the enhancement of the civic skills of students. Specifically, we find a statistically significant effect on the probability of taking part in a debate or discussion ($p = .10$, again two-tailed) and making comments or a statement at a community meeting ($p = .09$). The pattern of significance of the control variables is a bit different for these outcomes, with at least one of the parental tolerance measures being a significant predictor for three of the

TABLE 12.3b
Charter Schools Increase Some of the Civic Skills of Students

Outcome	Covariate	Coefficient estimate	Standard error
Written a letter to a public official	Charter enrollment	−0.11	0.26
	Parent's civic engagement	−0.008	0.02
	Parent's tolerance (speech)	0.02	0.13
	Parent's tolerance (library)	0.03	0.10
	Number of students (00's)	−0.01	0.03
	Years at school	−0.02	0.10
	Student's church attendance	−0.21*	0.07
	Grade level	0.14*	0.07
	Student's number of close friends	0.17*	0.07
	Cutpoint 1	1.7*	1.03
Given a speech or oral report	Charter enrollment	−0.35	0.24
	Parent's civic engagement	−0.01	0.02
	Parent's tolerance (speech)	0.17	0.11
	Parent's tolerance (library)	0.20*	0.10
	Number of students (00's)	0.03	0.04
	Years at school	0.07	0.08
	Student's church attendance	0.06	0.08
	Grade level	0.07	0.08
	Student's number of close friends	0.27*	0.07
	Cutpoint 1	1.95	1.27
Taken part in debate or discussion	Charter enrollment	0.41*	0.25
	Parent's civic engagement	−0.01	0.02
	Parent's tolerance (speech)	0.33*	0.12
	Parent's tolerance (library)	0.16	0.11
	Number of students (00's)	0.06	0.04
	Years at school	0.06	0.07
	Student's church attendance	0.23*	0.07
	Grade level	0.17*	0.07
	Student's number of close friends	−0.07	0.14
	Cutpoint 1	3.50*	1.18
Given comments or statement at community meeting	Charter enrollment	0.50*	0.29
	Parent's civic engagement	−0.02	0.03
	Parent's tolerance (speech)	−0.10	0.14
	Parent's tolerance (library)	0.26*	0.11
	Number of students (00's)	−0.02	0.03
	Years at school	0.07	0.07
	Student's church attendance	−0.10	0.08
	Grade level	0.02	0.09
	Student's number of close friends	0.01	0.07
	Cutpoint 1	1.27	1.10

*$p < .10$, two-tailed.

Results are from a seemingly unrelated ordered-probit model of the probability of selecting the various response categories for each of the 10 outcome measures simultaneously. Model results presented are the average results over five multiple-imputation datasets created by predictive mean matching. The data are also adjusted for possible self-selection to treatment and panel attrition using the models presented in tables 1 and 2, above. The number of observations is 165.

TABLE 12.3c
Charter Schools Have No Effect on Student Tolerance

Outcome	Covariate	Coefficient estimate	Standard error
Allow speech against churches and religion	Charter enrollment	0.11	0.21
	Parent's civic engagement	0.01	0.01
	Parent's tolerance (speech)	0.09	0.10
	Parent's tolerance (library)	0.13	0.08
	Number of students (00's)	0.09*	0.03
	Years at school	0.05	0.06
	Student's church attendance	−0.12*	0.07
	Grade level	0.07	0.06
	Student's number of close friends	−0.16*	0.06
	Cutpoint 1	−0.26	0.97
	Cutpoint 2	−0.02	0.96
	Cutpoint 3	1.01	0.94
Allow pro-drug book in library	Charter enrollment	0.17	0.22
	Parent's civic engagement	0.07*	0.01
	Parent's tolerance (speech)	−0.25*	0.12
	Parent's tolerance (library)	0.02	0.08
	Number of students (00's)	−0001	0.02
	Years at school	−0007	0.07
	Student's church attendance	−0.12*	0.06
	Grade level	0.04	0.06
	Student's number of close friends	−0.04	0.06
	Cutpoint 1	−0.04	0.96
	Cutpoint 2	0.60	0.97
	Cutpoint 3	1.15	0.96

* $p < .10$, two-tailed.

Results are from a seemingly unrelated ordered-probit model of the probability of selecting the various response categories for each of the 10 outcome measures simultaneously. Model results presented are the average results over five multiple-imputation datasets created by predictive mean matching. The data are also adjusted for possible self-selection to treatment and panel attrition using the models presented in tables 12.1 and 12.2, above. The number of observations is 165.

four outcome measures (all except writing a letter to a public official). Parent civic engagement, however, does not appear to be a good predictor of the civic-skills measures. Church attendance is also a significant predictor for two of the outcomes, increasing the student's probability of taking part in a public debate or discussion ($p < .01$) but decreasing the probability of writing a letter to a public official ($p < .01$).

The results of the model for our final pair of outcomes, the political-tolerance measures, are presented in table 12.3c. As the table shows, there is no significant charter effect on either of these outcomes. The student's religiosity, however, has a statistically significant and negative effect on both measures ($p = .07$ for each). The parent's civic engagement has a

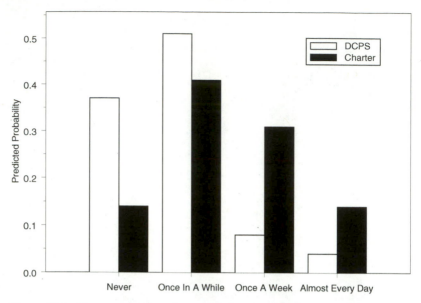

Figure 12.1. Charter-school students participate more often in community service and volunteer work.

positive effect on the "allow drugs book in the library" measure ($p < .01$), but the only significant effect of parental tolerance is negative on this measure ($p = .04$). The size of the school has a positive effect on the religion/speech-tolerance measure ($p < .01$), and the number of close friends has an opposite effect ($p = .02$).

Because it is difficult to interpret the effect size of coefficients in an ordinal regression model due to the model's inherent nonlinearity, we also compute predicted probabilities of the sets of response options for the community service/volunteer work (figure 12.1), participation in a debate or discussion (figure 12.2), and participation in a community meeting (figure 12.3) outcome measures. The predicted probabilities are computed using the estimates from the overall seemingly unrelated ordered-probit model, holding all the covariates at their mean or modal values in sample (varying only the charter indicator). As all three figures illustrate, charter enrollment predicts a substantively significant effect on all of these measures.

Finally, the seemingly unrelated model allows for likelihood-based hypothesis tests across the various submodels. For example, we reject the null that all of the charter-effect coefficients are jointly equal to zero ($p < .01$). Similarly, we reject the null hypotheses that the parental civic engagement, parental political tolerance (speech), student number of close friends, and student church attendance effects are zero for all submodels (all $p < .01$), using a modified Wald test.

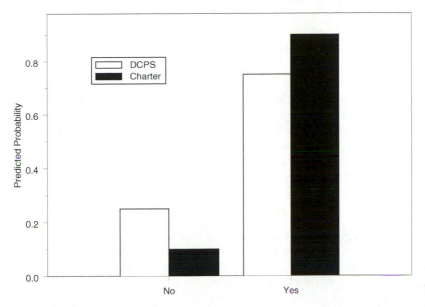

Figure 12.2. Charter students are more likely to report that they have taken part in a debate or discussion.

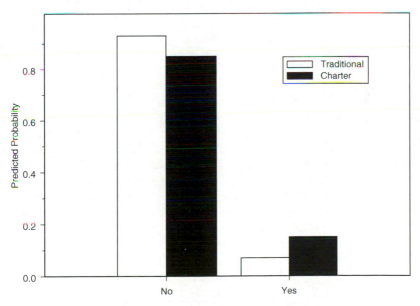

Figure 12.3. Charter students are more likely to report that they have made comments or a statement at a community meeting.

CHARTER SCHOOLS HAVE SOME BENEFICIAL
EFFECTS ON CIVIC EDUCATION

Compared to the traditional public schools, charter schools do a superior job of educating their students in civic skills and getting them to volunteer and to participate in their community. In this respect, then, charter schools appear to perform like private and parochial schools. Given the focus in many charter schools on mandatory service and volunteerism, this result is perhaps not surprising.[20]

In contrast, we find that charter attendance has essentially no effect on political tolerance. Here, charter schools appear to be more similar to magnet schools or traditional public schools than to either non-Catholic religious private schools or their secular or Catholic counterparts. As Campbell notes:

> It is possible that there is some credence to the concern expressed by critics of private education that it has the potential to foster political intolerance. While students in Catholic schools (the most common form of private education) and secular private schools are more politically tolerant than students in assigned public schools . . . America's students in other religious schools— an amalgam of schools sponsored by many different faiths—score lower on the political tolerance index. (2001, 60–61)

Charter schools, then, appear to foster neither the broad civic tolerance of Catholic schools nor the troubling intolerance of non-Catholic religious schools.

Should this mixed result be of concern to educational researchers and the broader public? One response, in line with the philosophical argument put forth by Murphy, is simply "no." Charter schools appear to increase, at least in part, the community involvement and civic skills of their students and thereby conform to Verba, Schlozman, and Brady's emphasis on "hands-on training for future participation" (1995, 376). From this perspective, perhaps this is all that we should expect or want from any of our public schools—and charter schools are doing this part of their job better than their traditional public-school counterparts.

On the other hand, traditional democratic theorists may be concerned with the notion of a publicly funded set of schools that provides their students with the tools of active citizenship but insufficient grounding in the foundations of tolerance needed for the proper use of those tools.

This debate will continue to play out as the charter-school movement continues to transform the nature of the public-school system in the United States.

13

Charter Schools: Hype or Hope?

CHARTER SCHOOLS HAVE BECOME a mainstay of education reform in the United States. There are now over one million students attending over 3,300 charter schools in the vast majority of states throughout the nation. In many states, the number of students enrolled in charter schools is substantial. Arizona, Florida, Michigan, and Texas have over 80,000 charter-school students and California tops the list with over 219,000.[1] Charter schools continue to attract the attention of scholars and policy makers, many of whom support charter schools fervently, and many of whom oppose charter schools with equal passion.

The mantra of today's world of education research is "evidence-based reform"—the desire to find out what really works and then to build schools on a stronger foundation, cutting through the ideologies, the hype, and the (often inflated) hopes that have historically driven so much of the education research and the education-reform "industry." At the same time, the push for charter schools shares a different mantra: that through the expansion of choice and competition, the "magic of the market" can be tapped to enable charter schools to provide better educational alternatives, raise student achievement, and leverage change across the entire system of schooling in the United States.

These two trends—one demanding rigorous evidence and the other demanding more charter schools—may be on a collision course. We believe that the push for charter schools— like so many other school reforms past and present—has been characterized by too many promises that are only, at best, weakly supported by evidence.

As we noted in the opening chapter, even the most basic descriptions of charter schools are often infused with hype. In turn, the creation of charter schools has become more than a reform; it has become a *movement*. Therefore, it is perhaps not surprising that we find charter schools are associated with high hopes on the part of policy makers looking for better schools and trying to avoid infusing large amounts of money into existing (and failing) schools and school bureaucracies. Perhaps even more importantly, the charter-school movement has instilled high hopes among parents who, all too often, rightly feel that their children are being ill served by traditional public schools and who are desperate for better alternatives.

We fear that the hype has inflated student, parental, and societal hope regarding what charter schools can do. And we fear that these hopes will be dashed because the movement has promised more than charter schools as a whole can reasonably deliver.

"FACTS ARE STUBBORN THINGS"

John Adams once observed that "facts are stubborn things." Recall that according to the US Charter Schools web site, charter schools are expected to fulfill the following goals:

- Increase opportunities for learning and access to quality education for all students;
- Create choice for parents and students within the public school system;
- Provide a system of accountability for results in public education;
- Encourage innovative teaching practices;
- Create new professional opportunities for teachers;
- Encourage community and parent involvement in public education;
- Leverage improved public education broadly.

We endorse every one of these goals wholeheartedly and wish that charter schools were unquestionably reaching them. But too many of the facts we have documented in our research suggest that charter schools, on the whole, are falling short, at least as viewed through the eyes of the students and parents who are their customers. And since these facts are indeed stubborn things, we believe that more than a decade into the charter-school "movement," it is time to consider carefully the promise and the limits of charter schools.

Our evidence suggests that wishing that competition and choice will somehow unleash the "magic of the market" that in turn will produce better educational outcomes ignores the extensive infrastructure necessary to make markets work. And the assumption that charter schools are a cure for the ills of urban education flies in the face of the evidence that we (and others) have assembled. With this in mind, we review some of the most important empirical findings of the preceding chapters.

Satisfaction

Many advocates of charter schools believe that school choice will transform the current system of education, improve school performance, increase student achievement, and raise consumer satisfaction. As we noted in chapter 9, higher satisfaction is an outcome that should flow from an expanded system of choice such as that embodied in charter schools, since parents and students get to choose schools that deliver more of what they want from education. In turn, increased satisfaction is one of the most common positive results cited by charter-school advocates to support the push for expanded choice.

Given the importance of this outcome, we spent considerable time and energy exploring parental satisfaction with their children's schools. Reflecting the hopes of parents, their expectations, and their prior beliefs in the quality of charter schools, our empirical analysis showed that charter-school parents *begin* their experience with high evaluations of almost all aspects of their child's school. Charter-school parents are also more likely than parents with children in the traditional schools to overestimate the academic performance of their child's school (see chapter 7; also see Buckley and Schneider 2005). As the reader will further recall from chapter 9, charter-school parents assign higher grades to their children's teachers, principal, and school facilities, and to their school overall. They are also more satisfied with a whole host of other dimensions of their child's educational experience, including school size and the level of discipline. We showed that these differences were remarkably durable in the face of rigorous tests for biases caused by self-selection or by choosers donning "rose-colored glasses."

However, in chapter 10, we found that as experience with the schools accumulates, the charter-school advantage erodes, so that by the end of just a few years, charter-school parents appear on many dimensions to be no more satisfied with their child's school than are their counterparts with children in traditional public schools. We believe that this pattern may result in part as the hopes parents have about the quality of charter schools meet the stubborn facts of urban education.

Larry Cuban has observed, "No sure-fire solutions have yet appeared to reduce the enormous test score gaps. . . . [T]he grim statistics of ghetto life take their toll on schools" (2005, 4). Early in the charter-school movement, Richard Rothstein presciently linked this harsh reality to the future of charter schools as laboratories of innovation: "[A]s charter schools face the same problems regular schools confront, they will find themselves, perhaps to their own astonishment, developing remarkably similar solutions" (1998, 60). To the extent this convergence of solutions happens in response to the stubborn facts of urban life, convergence of parental attitudes across sectors is, perhaps, not surprising.

We also found that the *students* in charter schools, the "customers" with the most direct day-to-day experience with this reform, feel no differently about their schools than their peers in the traditional public schools. They are no more proud of their schools and no less likely to wish they attended a different school than their counterparts in traditional public schools. And peer groups seem to be pretty much the same across the two sectors. In short, if charter schools are supposed to change the dynamic of student life, we found scant evidence of this.

Social Capital and Effective School Communities

We have argued that a good education requires the cooperation of students, parents, and the professional staff of schools. We found, as we did with our satisfaction measures, that charter schools have the *potential* to build strong foundations for school-based social capital and build the cooperative relationships necessary for effective education, but the hope of accumulating social capital over time has not been realized.

We found that on a number of indicators of social capital, charter schools outscored traditional public schools. Of perhaps even more importance, we found *no* indicator where charter-school parents view other parents or teachers in their child's school more negatively than do parents in the traditional public schools. We believe our data present a picture of parents bringing to their schools expectations, hopes, and other raw material that can be tapped to create vibrant communities. Unfortunately, we also found that, by and large, charter schools did not seize this opportunity: over time most of the value added to social capital by charter schools eroded.

We should note that even in the cross-sectional analysis, the charter-school advantage is not large. And the contribution the charter-school experience has to the building of social capital appears to be limited to the school community, with little or no evidence of spillover from school-based social capital to broader domains.

This apparent failure of charter schools to add value is even more disappointing since the smaller size of charter schools gives them an important structural advantage over traditional public schools in building effective school communities. Hallinan (1994) has argued that it is far easier to create a vibrant school community in small schools than larger ones and Hill, Foster, and Gendler (1990) show that creating consensus on educational principles and educational practices is also much easier to do in a small school compared to large ones (also see Wasley et al. 2000; Nathan and Febey 2001, on the advantages of small schools).

Charter schools have other structural advantages over traditional public schools—for example, many have parent contracts requiring parental participation, and others have been granted waivers from broad educational mandates so as to create "niche" schools tightly focused on the needs of their students (Teske, Schneider, and Cassese 2005). But according to our data, even with these advantages, charter schools experienced only a small and transient advantage over the traditional public schools in generating school-based social capital.

Building Good Citizens

Another outcome we studied was the differential ability of schools to create the foundations for citizenship. In this phase of our study, we found differences between students in the charter schools and in the traditional public schools in terms of instilling democratic values, skills, or confidence. All these differences favored charter schools; however, they were small in magnitude and not found across all measures. And while many advocates argue that charter schools will be able to create an atmosphere that produces the same kinds of gains that have often been found among students in Catholic schools, our evidence did not support this hope.

We have argued that charter-school "customers" constitute a core constituency for the future of the charter-school movement. However, if charter-school parents are no more satisfied with their schools than traditional-school parents, then they might not provide a strong foundation to help charter schools weather the storms and controversies that will inevitably confront those schools in the future. And if charter schools are not nurturing social capital among parents that can then translate into broader political practices, these parents will fail to develop the political skills to protect charter schools in the face of inevitable challenges.

Thus, the failure of charter schools to fully develop the civic capacity of their constituent consumers may present problems for the movement—and, perhaps, for school reform in general. Braatz and Putnam argue that "revitalizing American civic engagement may be a prerequisite for revitalizing American education" (1998, 37). Clarence Stone similarly argues that "the connections between the level of civic capacity and degree of effort at education improvement seems quite solid" (1998, 261). From this perspective, education reform can succeed only if there is long-term political engagement by parents who are drawing on a healthy stock of civic capacity. This is particularly important because the political cycle is short, and most politicians cannot wait for systemic education reform to work. Therefore, building strong constituent support and keeping politicians engaged over the long haul is essential to success (Sexton 2004; Hess 1999). Put these observations together and we can see that the failure of charter schools to build civic capacity may reduce one of the pillars necessary to support charter schools and perhaps other future educational reforms in the turbulent world of American education policy.

Achievement

This book is not about test scores as measures of academic achievement. However, we did touch on this issue in chapter 4, where we waded into the tempest over the extent to which charter-school students are easier or harder to educate than students in traditional public schools. We showed that on a variety of indicators, there are few consistent differences between the inherent ease (or difficulty) of educating students in either sector, at least among students in Washington, D.C. For us, this means that the fights we have observed over test scores in which partisans say that because charter-school students are harder to educate, we should expect lower scores, and in which charter-school opponents say that the charters' test scores should be higher as the result of cream skimming, are not useful.

Clearly, some schools (regardless of sector) have harder-to-educate students, but others don't. It is the composition of *individual* schools, not the overall composition of the sectors, that matters for helping us identify which schools add value. Below, we return to the importance of moving beyond the "main effects" of charter schools to get inside the school to learn what works and what doesn't.

"FIRST, DO NO HARM"

If these comments seem critical, they are perhaps a reaction to the hype that has surrounded the creation and growth of charter schools. To be fair, on *every one* of the numerous comparisons we conducted throughout our research, charter schools *never* fared worse than the traditional public schools—and they quite often did better. While we do not study achievement scores, the same could probably be said of what we know about test scores. For example, according to the National Center for Education Statistics analysis reported in *Results From the NAEP 2003 Pilot Study*, "for students from the same racial/ethnic backgrounds, reading and mathematics performance in charter schools did not differ from that in other public schools" (NCES 2005).

Couple the comparisons we have presented in this book with these NAEP data on achievement and it seems that, on the whole, charter schools pass the most fundamental test of policy analysis that we discussed in chapter 1: they are Pareto superior. But before accepting that as an endorsement of charter schools, we ask a simple question: *Given the promises put forth by the charter-school movement, is it really sufficient to endorse charter schools because they pass such a minimum test?* For us, the answer lies at the crux of the seemingly endless debates between the proponents and the opponents of charter schools.

Building Markets for Education

In chapter 1, we argued that charter schools were created to increase competition and choice, fundamental building blocks of a market for schools, from which greater accountability and higher achievement should flow. In chapters 6–8, we explored the role of parents as consumers, highlighting some of the conditions that are needed to support choice. We found mixed evidence of the ability of parents to exercise choice and to use market forces to improve schools. Perhaps most importantly, we documented the importance of race in how parents shop for schools. That parents weigh the racial composition of schools heavily when choosing their children's school should come as no surprise given how segregated schools are; however, survey evidence has consistently indicated the importance of academic performance and teacher quality in parent choice and dismissed the importance of race. Our evidence, consistent with the handful of existing studies focused on actual parental behavior, showed that while parents will hardly ever say that they care about race when choosing schools, their behavior shows the opposite.

Our data also documented other patterns in parental search procedures—some of them supportive of the idea that parents can effectively shop for schools and others less so. Following Schneider, Teske and Marschall (2000), we relied on the idea of the marginal consumer to help explain how the market for schools might still work given so little active shopping by parents and given that they have so little accurate information. Using different methods and measurements than Schneider and colleagues, we explored the idea that a small number of parents with effective search procedures can make choices that could lead to better schools overall.

Of perhaps greater importance, we also documented the fact that good information about alternative schools *does* increase the propensity of parents to change schools. So, theoretically, better modes of disseminating information could increase the quality of parental choice and could increase the pressure on schools to improve.

However, we identified two problems with this argument. First, among the parents of Washington, D.C., where there is probably more choice than in any other city in the country, most parents did not have very good information about their schools—and our efforts to disseminate more information (via our web site DCSchoolSearch.com) were less than successful. In short, while more information can encourage more shopping, getting that information into the hands of parents is not easy.

Policy makers face the same difficulties as researchers in trying to disseminate information about schools. Sexton describes the barriers to effective parental involvement in the schools when he documents the mobilization strategy the Pritchard Committee used in Kentucky to increase parental involvement with the public schools (2004, 103–4):[2] The barriers the Pritchard Committee identify and the logic of their intervention should come as no surprise to the reader:

- High achievement requires outside pressure and assistance, particularly from families;
- The most credible communication with the public about school reform is one-on-one communication. And the most common form of one-on-one communication is between parents and teachers. This is the main source of information about education and reform;
- Useful communication between parents and teachers is inhibited by such well-known barriers as school schedules or educational jargon;
- This communication is also limited by how little information parents have about schools—they know very little about their child's academic achievement except what they see in school report cards and hear in conferences. They need more information to act effectively.

The Pritchard Committee devoted a considerable number of resources to informing parents about many aspects of school achievement through "specially prepared user-friendly reports" on their child's school. This data, reported by race, SES, and gender, according to Sexton, allowed parents to understand better the performance of the school and its students. This was a time-consuming and resource-intensive process, but in so doing, Sexton argues that the amount of information put in the hands of parent/consumers increased, allowing parents to pressure schools to perform better.[3]

In addition to the obstacles to the flow of information, we identified a second problem that may be hardwired into the architecture of the human mind—"hot cognition." Relying particularly on the work of the noted political psychologist Milton Lodge, we argued that, due to entrenched opinions or biases, even the most skilled consumer might perceive information in an inaccurate fashion. Indeed, given the hype and the hope surrounding charter schools, it is not hard to envision how hot cognition and its "cousin," motivated reasoning, could help explain the initial high expectations and evaluations that parents assign to the charter schools. These same mechanisms can also help explain why repeated exposure to the reality of the school may lead, albeit slowly, to an updated evaluation that is more realistic and more grounded in empirical reality. Among the most important implications of these studies is that getting good information out to consumers is important, but getting it to them is difficult, and predicting how such information will be used is no easy task.

DCSchoolSearch.com was our effort to provide more information and make it more accessible to parents facing an ever-expanding array of school choices. However, as we documented in chapter 5, this was a difficult undertaking and the lessons to be learned further highlight the hard work of building the foundations for choice (also see Schneider and Buckley 2000; Schneider 2001). Thus, despite the evidence that information matters, and despite the importance of information to any theory of markets, we believe that choice and charter-school advocates have still not addressed the issue of the flow of information adequately.

Indeed, we think that charter-school proponents have in general not paid enough attention to the fact that markets do not spring up instantaneously; rather, as economic historians, such as Douglass North, and as political scientists concerned with institutions, such as Eleanor Ostrom, have shown, perhaps the real magic of markets is that they exist at all (Eggertsson 1994; North 1990; Ostrom 1990; Alston et al. 1996).

We think that analysts need to identify more thoroughly the basic building blocks of education markets and the kinds of rules, regulations, and supports policy makers need to institute to make choice work. Henig (1994) argued that we have to move beyond the market metaphor when thinking about school choice. We agree, but we also believe that the challenge he laid down has not been adequately addressed.

An Equity/Efficiency Trade-Off?

Some of our findings also highlight an equity/efficiency trade-off that is built into the market for schools. We need to be particularly concerned how, to use Arthur Okun's (1975) term, this "big trade-off" plays out, given the particular importance of schooling in a democracy committed to equality of access and opportunity.

Many advocates believe that choice can pressure schools to deliver better education more efficiently. Moreover, in a system of choice, parents should be able to place their children in schools that emphasize the aspects of education they embrace. Clearly these gains are desirable. But if, as our data indicate, many parents' decisions are likely to be influenced by race, then a "pure" open marketlike choice plan for schools can increase segregation.

Moreover, stratification can also increase if parents with higher levels of education are more likely to exercise choice than less-educated parents and are more likely to engage in higher-quality search activity to gather information about their options. Given the importance of good information to school choice, and given its unequal distribution, special efforts must clearly be made to increase the flow of information to lower-status parents.

Combining the inequality in access to information with the deep-seated concern for the racial composition of schools evident in parent search behavior leads us to a complicated conclusion about markets and school choice. While we believe that the market mechanisms built into expanded choice can increase efficiency, we have two fundamental concerns.

First, at the level of parent behavior, we are concerned that unregulated choice may increase the importance of student demographics in the choice behavior of parents, including the choices of more highly educated marginal consumers who are essential for the effectiveness of any option-demand system—including charter schools.

Second, this shopping behavior could have adverse affects on academic achievement through the composition and pressure of peer groups that are created within schools. In recent years, a body of work has begun to document the importance of peers in learning outcomes.[4] According to Hanushek, Kain, Markman, and Rivkin: "The peer group composition of schools is undeniably important in the minds of parents as well as policy makers at the local, state, and federal level." While they believe that much is left to be learned about how peer groups affect learning outcomes, they argue that the "most common perspective is that peers, like families, are sources of motivation, aspirations, and direct interactions in learning" (2003, 3). What happens within schools if the students who are available to create peer groups in schools are assembled through family decisions that are more attuned to race or class than to academic performance?

One possibility is an adverse outcome at the level of the schools: to the extent that choice is driven by demographics rather than academics, unfettered choice may actually *decrease* the pressure on schools to improve their academic performance and one of the most basic promises of choice may dissipate.

We believe that the task facing advocates of choice is to design a system that can produce a socially acceptable trade-off between a more efficient school system and one that mixes together children of different races and classes. While less theoretically elegant and ideologically appealing than proposals for unrestricted choice, racial and income requirements can be introduced and enforced in choice plans. Indeed, "controlled choice" has been implemented in a number of cities and school districts and is common in admissions decisions to magnet schools (see, e.g., Henig 1994, 1996). However, controlled choice plans all impose regulations that limit choice and may therefore fail to attract the passionate support of the most ardent (and pro-market) proponents of choice. In every market, we have to strike a balance between equity and efficiency—and the market for schools is no different.

Who Chooses Whom?

Like most researchers, we have gone about our analysis with the implicit assumption that the driving force in this market for schools are the consumers of education, the parents and their children who have a growing number of schools from which to choose. Indeed, when researchers talk about school choice, they almost always mean the process of how students and parents as *consumers choose schools*. But schools are not passive actors in the choice process, and researchers have all too often neglected the fact that *schools choose students*. Ignoring this aspect of the "market" can lead to big holes in our understanding of how charter schools actually operate and the outcomes we observe.

There are a number of studies that are beginning to fill this hole. Amy Stuart Wells et al., in a descriptive study of ten California school districts, argues that charter schools have considerable freedom "to choose which parents and students will attend. Through various mechanisms such as enrollment, recruitment, and requirements, charter schools have more power than most public schools to shape their educational communities. . . . Our data indicate that powerful self-selection is taking place in many charter schools, both in terms of families choosing schools and schools choosing families" (1998, 42).

Bifulco and Ladd (2004) also present evidence showing how charter schools actively shape their student (and parent) population. Using data from the Schools and Staffing Survey, they show that parental involvement is higher in charter schools than in observationally similar public schools. However, they find that the specific programmatic characteristics of charter schools are not linked to active school communities; rather, charter schools tend to locate in areas with above-average proportions of involved parents—through their locational choices, charter schools are choosing students (also see Carnoy et al. 2005). Researchers in other countries with choice systems have paid more attention to this issue and have demonstrated how schools use a variety of mechanisms to shape the student body they want (on Chile, see Parry 1996 or Gauri 1998; on New Zealand, see Fiske and Ladd 2000).

In a perfect market, producers are "price takers, not price makers." Yet in the imperfect market of school choice, schools may have far more latitude to be strategic actors. Clearly, further research needs to be undertaken about the extent of such strategic behavior and its consequences.

BACK TO FUNDAMENTALS

If schooling has always been about the "three R's," we have argued that the debate over charter schools is about "three C's": competition, choice, and community. By embracing these factors, proponents of choice argue that schools will earn two A's, increasing accountability and achievement. As we conclude this book, we return to these fundamentals.

Clearly in many cities and states across the nation, charter schools have increased competition and choice. They have not necessarily created stronger communities, although we believe they have the potential to do so. We believe that many parents walking through charter-school doors *want* to participate and *want* to join in a more effective school community. Charter schools (indeed all schools) need to figure out how to tap this source of energy and concern to build stronger communities and through these more effective communities, achieve better student outcomes.

What about the two "A's" of accountability and achievement? Parents are in some ways the ultimate source of accountability—they increasingly have the power to vote with their feet. However, even in Washington, D.C. with its large concentration of students in charter schools, good schools are in short supply and even mediocre charter schools have waiting lists. Ultimately, we cannot expect parents to exercise choice and enforce accountability without a supply of better schools.

The issue of how charter schools affect achievement will continue to be debated. Our study was not designed to address this issue directly. We know what the study to address this question should look like: longitudinal student-level data collected from individual students who are randomly assigned to charter schools or traditional public schools by lotteries executed in the face of oversubscription to the charter schools. The U.S. Department of Education, through its Institute for Education Sciences, has recently launched two studies with these design characteristics. That's the good news. The bad news is that it will take three to five years before we have even preliminary data on the effects of charter schools on academic achievement (measured by test scores). It will take even longer for us to learn whether charter schools affect the other things we really want schools to deliver (advanced degrees, better jobs, higher income, less crime, and so on), for which test scores are only a surrogate. Moreover, if the debate over the data about voucher programs that used random assignment is any indicator, even when these data are released, it will take years of intense analysis and contentious reanalysis before consensus emerges on how much charter schools contribute.

Getting inside the Black Box

As we await those results, we believe that there are factors that the research and policy community must think about more carefully, factors that can help us understand how choice and charters can work better, and factors that we believe future studies must consider. Bulkley and Fisher observed in 2002 that we know much more about how charter schools are organized and governed than about what happens inside charter schools and their classrooms—and not all that much has changed since. We believe this must change, and thus, we issue a final challenge to the next generation of research. In this we are following the argument of Cohen, Raudenbush, and Ball, who believe that for education researchers the "overarching research question cannot be 'Do resources matter?' . . . The overarching question must be 'What resources matter, how, and under what circumstances?' " (2003, 134). To translate this charge into the issue we have studied in this book, the question is no longer "Does choice matter?" rather we must move on to ask, "What do schools do in response to choice, and do those responses matter?"

To return to the language of "treatment" we have used throughout this book, we need to recognize that neither charter schools nor traditional public schools are homogeneous treatments. The debate about charter schools up to now (and including our work) has overwhelmingly focused on the overall (or "main") effect of charter schools on outcomes. This is a perfectly reasonable first step, since it tells policy makers whether or not charter schools are a dangerous reform that must be stopped or a reform that is so unquestionably good that we must push further ahead. Unfortunately, the results of most policy reforms, perhaps especially those in the field of education, hardly ever point unambiguously to either outcome.

We have found that *on average* charter schools do no harm and in fact have the potential for doing good in many critical areas such as building social capital, increasing customer satisfaction, and enhancing the civic skills of students. With this base established, we believe that the research community needs to move on to identifying the factors that translate the potential of charter schools into reality. We have plenty of evidence that charter schools are not a homogeneous treatment and therefore getting inside the black box to identify what works is essential. We need to cut through the hype surrounding the charter-school movement to identify the programs, structures, and practices that increase accountability and achievement. We then need to test what works through a variety of methods and in a variety of settings. It is only by so doing that we can ensure the hopes that parents now bring to the schools, hopes that are now all too often unrealized, can be translated into reality.

Some Charter Schools Don't Make the Grade

Indeed, even a quick peek inside the black box shows a range of schools delivering vastly different products and with vastly different levels of success. Consider the charter schools in Washington, D.C. alone, among which there are clear success stories but also clear failures.

About 15 percent of the charter schools that have opened in the city (and, indeed, in the nation) have already closed their doors. While it is better to close bad schools than to let them run on and on, this high failure rate may be indicative of other problems that affect parental evaluations of the schools and the quality of the education parents' children are receiving. A scan of local newspapers and media produces a smorgasbord of stories of mismanaged charter schools. We begin with the some of the sadder stories chalked up by the D.C. charter school movement.

THE VILLAGE LEARNING CENTER

In November 2003, Desmond Kirk Pierre-Louis, the director of the Village Learning Center in Northeast Washington, was arrested for sexually assaulting a fourteen-year-old boy who spent several weekends at his home (Pierre-Louis was a respite foster parent). The school had a history of problems, including problems paying its lease and neglecting to pay federal taxes on teachers' salaries. In addition to fiscal mismanagement (and probably not surprising given that mismanaging money often goes hand in hand with mismanaging children), test scores at the Village Learning Center fell below the requirements of the No Child Left Behind Act. The school was also charged with hiring teachers without college degrees (that allegation, unlike several others, could not be substantiated). In the Spring of 2004, the Board of Education voted to close the school when a city audit found that the school spent hundreds of thousands of dollars on leased space it did not occupy, credit card charges for apparel and gifts, and loan repayments that lacked documentation.

THE ASSOCIATES FOR RENEWAL IN EDUCATION (ARE) PUBLIC CHARTER SCHOOL

The Public Charter School Board closed the Associates for Renewal in Education (ARE) Public Charter School in June 2003 for failing to improve attendance and failing to provide federally required special education services. This closure culminated a two-year review of its special education program that showed only four of its thirteen special education students had up-to-date individualized education plans (IEPs). The review also showed that the ARE School failed to provide paperwork to monitors who were legally charged with determining whether students were receiving required speech and language services or counseling.

THE MECHANICAL, INDUSTRIAL, TECHNICAL PUBLIC CHARTER SCHOOL

Just months before the scheduled opening of the Mechanical, Industrial, Technical Public Charter School in Northeast Washington, it became publicly known that Mary Anigbo, a former charter-school principal, was president of the board of trustees. The problem was that Ms. Anigbo was convicted in 1997 of assaulting a newspaper reporter and two police officers.

The bad news is that these events happened, but the good news is that these schools were closed down (or in the case of Mechanical, never opened). Unfortunately, these closures were sparked by egregious management behavior and not by the failure of the schools to meet high academic standards. However, and this is fundamentally important, as more charter schools reach the end of their contracts and as charter schools garner attention as a popular reform strategy, there is evidence that closures are increasingly driven by concern over low academic performance (Gau 2006). This is a marked change from earlier practices.[5]

Some Charter Schools Do Fulfill the Vision

While it may seem as though we are ending this book on a critical note, there are in fact reasons for hope. In our research, we have encountered some wonderful charter schools doing wonderful things. We highlight just a few.

CAPITAL CITY PUBLIC CHARTER SCHOOL

Capital City Public Charter School was founded in 2000 by a group of D.C. public school parents. Its first home was above a CVS Drugstore, although it has since moved to a better facility. Like many other charter schools in the district, the school is small, enrolling around 240 students in kindergarten through grade 8. It is also diverse: about half African American, a fifth Hispanic/Latino, and the rest Caucasian. Most of the students come from low-income families and about half receive reduced-price or free lunch.

Capital City is also one of the highest performing charter schools in the city: in recent years, about two-thirds of its students scored at or above the proficient level on the SAT-9 reading test and a slightly lower proportion reached the same level on the SAT-9 math test. According to the D.C. Public Charter School Board, students at Capital City improved in every measure in both reading and mathematics in 2004. The gain scores indicate that a large percentage of students improved by at least one year in math, while the majority made the expected progress in reading. Given these numbers, it's not surprising that Capital City is popular: in some years the ratio of applications to acceptances is a 10 to 1, about the same as an elite Ivy League university, and over 90 percent of the students reenroll.

KIPP DC: KEY (KNOWLEDGE EMPOWERS YOU) ACADEMY PUBLIC CHARTER SCHOOL

Opened in 2001, the KEY middle school affiliated with the national KIPP (Knowledge Is Power Program) Foundation. The foundation recruits, trains, and supports outstanding teachers to open college-preparatory public schools in high-need communities. It helps arrange for facilities and operating contracts while training school leaders. Recruited from some of the nation's top universities, KIPP principals enroll for a year's intensive training at the UC Berkeley Haas School of Business, where they learn how to manage a school budget, how to recruit students and teachers, and how to choose academic programs.

The defining characteristic of the school is the high expectations it has for its students and the intensity of the instruction it uses to get students to meet those expectations. There are strict codes of behavior, such as wearing the school uniform properly, walking in quiet, single-file lines, displaying correct gestures while listening, even not eating candy. In fact, the intense boot-camp approach sets the academy apart from the rest of the charter schools. It also holds classes six days a week, eleven months a year. The school day is much longer than at most public schools. Students go home at 5 p.m., with one to two hours of homework left to complete—and the school gives all its teachers cell phones so that they can answer students' questions at night.

The school also emphasizes teaching "character" as well as academics. For instance KIPP students can earn weekly "paychecks" based on behavior, which can be spent in the student store. In contrast, students who have misbehaved write letters of apology to other students. The atmosphere is such that being smart is socially desirable, counteracting the adverse peer-group effects found in many schools.

The success of the school's boot-camp approach is in part due to its success in getting parents involved in their children's education. The parents sign an agreement to check homework, to read to their child every night, and to limit the amount of TV they watch.

The school's approach seems to work. In 2004, 70 percent of the students scored at the proficient level on the SAT-9 reading test and an incredible 97 percent reached the same level in math.

The record of high student achievement has attracted some large donors. The KIPP DC: KEY Academy gets 18 percent of its operating funds from outside sources, including federal and private grants, enough to pay high rent on its new building. With good physical facilities, and more resources to expend per student, the Academy's success in educating its 242 (100 percent African American) students, who mostly come from low-income families, convinced the Public Charter School Board to approve the KIPP Academy's request to open two new middle schools.

KIPP also provides evidence of how competition from successful charter schools can leverage change: as of this writing, the D.C. Board of Education is likely to approve a plan by which KIPP DC and a D.C. public school will provide K–8 education in the same school building, with KIPP in charge of grades 5–8. The partnership proposal specifically states: "This partnership would enable DCPS to incorporate effective strategies being used in charter schools and integrate these best practices into the broader public school system."

Using Entrepreneurship to Fix Facilities

We also discovered how the challenges of creating and maintaining charter schools can mobilize entrepreneurs to attempt things that they would never attempt in a large bureaucratic system such as the traditional D.C. public schools. We highlight one of the most interesting charter-school leaders we have met in Washington. And we focus on how this entrepreneurial leader is addressing the perennial challenge of poor facilities facing charter schools.

JOSH KERN AND THE THURGOOD MARSHALL ACADEMY

Located in the poor southeastern quadrant of Washington, D.C., the Thurgood Marshall Academy (TMA), a small high school currently with fewer than 350 students, was founded by a group of students from Georgetown University Law Center Street Law Clinic, who, as part of the law school's clinic requirements, taught in neighborhood public schools. Based on their experience, these law students developed a proposal for the TMA charter school and submitted it to the Public Charter School Board in the Spring of 2000. The plan was quickly approved.

Since opening its doors in a temporary facility in 2001, the Thurgood Marshall Academy had been actively searching for a facility that would accommodate the school at full capacity of 300 students. In October 2003, the District of Columbia agreed to sell the Nichols Avenue School property at 2427 Martin Luther King, Jr. Avenue, SE to the TMA.

Using his skills, his vision and his entrepreneurship, Josh Kern, one of the members of the original group of law students and now TMA's president, set about securing the money to turn this abandoned DCPS building into a modern educational facility. As of this writing, using his legal, financial, political, and entrepreneurial skills, Kern has secured the following:

- A $1 million line-item federal appropriation. Kern won this appropriation with the help of Andrew Rosenberg, a lobbyist. The appropriation was championed by Senator Mary Landrieu from Louisiana, who is the ranking member of the D.C. Appropriations Committee and a powerful force in D.C. politics.
- A $1 million "city build" grant. This is money from the federal government that is funneled through the city. TMA was one of only five schools to get this grant to promote community-based schools.
- A $1.5 million allocation through the D.C. Office of Property Management.
- A $1 million low-interest-rate loan from Building Hope, a 501(c)(3) offshoot of Sallie Mae.

- A $2 million low-interest-rate loan through the D.C. Office of Banking and Finance.
- A $1 million Qualified Zone Academy Bond, a highly subsidized bond that is used to promote revitalization in targeted areas.[6]
- An $8 million construction loan.

According to Kern, the $11 million of borrowed funds will be replaced by permanent financing using New Market Tax Credits (these were created in 2000 and provide private investors with federal-tax credits when they invest in projects in targeted low-income areas).

In addition to raising funds for the renovation and addition to the old Nichols Avenue school, the TMA has engaged in extensive fund-raising activities to support its academic programs. In order to meet the specific programmatic needs of its student body, TMA raises and spends $4,000 more on each student than it can get from local public funds. These additional funds come from federal and foundation grants, fund-raising events, and individual contributions.

It is the relative autonomy given to charter schools that allowed Kern to tap all these diverse sources of money to create what everyone believes will be a first-class school facility.

IS THE GLASS HALF FULL OR HALF EMPTY?

Carnoy et al. observe that the freedom inherent in charter schools is no *guarantee* of success; rather, it provides the "opportunity" for both great success and spectacular failures: "Freed from bureaucratic regulations and union rules, many of the best educators can design excellent charter schools. But freed from these rules, many of the worst educators can design terrible schools" (2005, 118).

Given this inevitable variation, we can cherry-pick success stories, such as KIPP, and we can, and should, admire the entrepreneurial talents let loose by the charter-school movement embodied in Josh Kern. These stories show how some charter schools can fulfill the promises of the "movement." Alternatively, we can harp on the bad news of charter schools and the intense disruptions to student lives when charter schools close their doors. We could also highlight the fact that far too many charter schools fail to deliver on the innovative and successful education they have promised.

Charter schools are now stubborn facts on the ground. While both criticism and compliments will no doubt accrue simultaneously and while the proponents and the opponents of charter schools will continue to pick and choose which of criticisms and which compliments they emphasize, perhaps the most reasonable position is a pragmatic middle ground emerging among those who are working among charter schools on a day-to-day basis. As Robert Cane, the Executive Director of Friends of Choice in Urban Schools has put it: "When you open up charter schools you provide choices for parents, opportunities for teachers, and better schooling right now to some kids, rather than making them wait for yet another system-wide overhaul. You hope the traditional public schools will follow your lead, but it's beyond your control."[7]

How these pluses and minuses eventually balance out (and how charter schools will be evaluated in the long run) depends on hard work by students, parents, policy makers, and researchers. While parents must exercise their expanded power to hold charter schools accountable from the bottom, these schools must also be held accountable from the top, by serious efforts to gather evidence about what works and for whom.

Finally, the absence of consistent indictors of charter-school success also should lead us to think more carefully about what is needed to support effective school choice.

Chubb and Moe (1990) set much of the terms of the present debate concerning school choice by linking the failure of traditional public schools to both the intrusion of democratic politics into school policy and to the power of teacher unions (and other education-oriented organizations) to thwart educational improvement. Chubb and Moe advocated school choice (specifically vouchers) as a way to undermine the self-serving interests of these powerful groups. While charter schools do not embody marketlike mechanisms to the extent that a fully developed voucher system would, charter schools are schools of choice and many have considerable freedom from local school boards and the constraints of union contracts with teachers. If simply unleashing choice and market forces was all that was required, then the results we observe for charter schools should be uniformly better. The problems facing charter schools (which all too often mirror the problems of traditional public schools serving the same communities) suggest that more is at work than simply too much bureaucracy and not enough market competition.

Yes, markets are beautiful things, but they don't work without lots of information, without a developed infrastructure, and without an adjudicating and enforcement authority. And charter schools won't work without the corresponding mechanisms necessary to support school choice in an ever-expanding market for education.

Of course, none of this is as easy as venturing forth to slay the dragon of low-performing public schools waving a flag emblazed with the slogan "Markets Work!"

NOTES

1. These numbers come from the Center for Education Reform, which keeps a running total—and they change frequently. These were downloaded from the center's web site: http://www.edreform.com/index.cfm?fuseAction=state StatChart&psectionid=15&cSectionID=44 (accessed April 4, 2006).

2. The reader is referred to Hill, Pierce, and Guthrie 1997; Hill and Lake 2002; Hassel 1999; Gill et al. 2001; Cookson and Berger 2002.

3. As noted later, it is hard to estimate the rate at which charters are not renewed, but it is probably in the 10–15 percent range.

4. http://www.uscharterschools.org/pub/uscs_docs/o/index.htm (accessed April 4, 2006).

5. Assuming of course that costs do not increase—but most charter schools are funded at the same (or at a lower) level as traditional public schools.

6. The extensive information requirements of the No Child Left Behind Act may dramatically change this.

7. David Tyack is probably the most articulate researcher of the history and status of the common school in the United States. See, for example, Tyack 2004.

8. Cuban (2004) does an excellent job exploring the relationship among education, the economy, and democracy; he also roots the charter-school movement in the historic social and political beliefs about these relationships.

9. In his study of the belief systems of modern economics and their similarity to theology, economist Robert Nelson further suggests that the very market mechanism itself (and not just its application to education), "is best understood as a compelling metaphor for its time designed to attract converts to a new understanding of the progressive gospel of efficiency" (2001, 58).

10. For an accessible introduction to this idea see, for example, Weimer and Vining 2004.

11. Of course, there are noneconomic ways of securing this outcome—compulsory attendance laws try to ensure that all people in the United States have at least a minimum level of education.

12. As noted below in chapters 11 and 12, similar arguments have been leveled against charter schools.

13. On the nature of goods, see, for example, Weimer and Vining 2004, especially chap. 5.

14. On the importance of financing facilities and the extent of inequalities, see the 2005 Thomas B. Fordham Institute Report entitled "Charter School Funding: Inequities Next Frontier," http://www.edexcellence.net/institute/charterfinance/ (accessed April 4, 2006).

15. One of the best-known EMOs is the Edison Corporation. The performance of Edison schools (as well as the corporation's financial well-being) has been sub-

ject to intense debate. Miron and Applegate find "that students in schools operated by Edison—while they often start at levels below national norms and district
averages—progress at rates comparable to students in other district schools. This
conclusion indicates that the expectations of district and charter school boards
that contract with Edison as well as the expectations of parents who enroll their
children in an Edison school are not being met" (2000, 26).

16. For a contrary view, see Levin and Driver (1997), who argue that a national
voucher program might increase expenditures of public education by as much as
25 percent.

17. These data come from the CER's 8th ed. of *Charter School Laws across
the States: Ranking and Scorecard*, http://edreform.com/_upload/charter_school
_laws.pdf (accessed April 4, 2006).

18. Figlio and Lucas (2004) provide further evidence on this point.

19. The importance of this dimension was highlighted by the uproar set off by
an AFT report in August 2004 arguing that NAEP scores showed that charter
schools were underperforming, compared to traditional public schools. See for
example the special issue of *AFT's Closer Look* devoted explicitly to the debate
(http://www.aft.org/pubs-reports/closer_look/082704.htm#Bookmark1). The AFT
report made the front page of the *New York Times* with almost instantaneous
rebuttals by charter-school advocates. For a taste of the debate see, for example,
Amy Stuart Wells, "Charter Schools: Lessons in Limits," *Washington Post*, December 29, 2004; Paul Hill, "Assessing Student Performance in Charter Schools:
Why Studies Often Clash and Answers Remain Elusive," *Edweek*, January 12,
2005; or Carnoy et al. 2005.

20. Not surprisingly, given the number of charter schools and their importance,
other authors have developed different sets of criteria for evaluation. For example,
Gill et al. (2001) provide an extensive discussion of the criteria to evaluate charter
schools, including academic achievement, choice, access, integration, and civic
socialization. Note that our criteria map fairly well onto the criteria proposed by
Levin, which include choice, productive efficiency, equity, and social cohesion
(Levin 2002; Levin and Belfield 2003). Also see National Working Commission
on Choice in K-12 Education (2003).

21. According to the Center for Education Reform, Washington ranked third
in the nation in terms of the strength of its chartering law.

22. Some new longitudinal studies are being launched, funded by the Institute
for Education Science in the U.S. Department of Education, but the results of these
will not be available for years.

CHAPTER 2

THE EVOLUTION OF CHARTER-SCHOOL CHOICE
IN THE DISTRICT OF COLUMBIA

1. The SEO was established under the Office of the Mayor on October 1, 2000,
as required by the State Education Office Establishment Act of 2000.

2. These data come from the *DC Public School and Public Charter School
Capital Budget Project, Task 3 Report*, prepared for the Office of the Mayor and

city administrator, Washington, D.C., by the Brookings Greater Washington Research Program and the 21st Century School Fund on November 30, 2004.

3. While Arizona's population of 5.1 million is larger than the 2.7 million in Kansas, even adjusting for this difference would hardly dent the difference in the size of the charter sector in the two states. These data were obtained from the Center for Education Reform website, http://www.edreform.com/index.cfm?fuseAction=stateStatChart&psectionid=15&cSectionID=44 (accessed April 13, 2006).

4. These data were downloaded from the Center for Education Reform web site, http://www.edreform.com/_upload/ranking_chart.pdf (accessed April 13, 2006).

5. Indeed, the Edison Corporation manages several schools in D.C.

6. In fairness to the Board of Education, in response to past criticisms they have in fact tightened their review process and, as noted above, their acceptance rate for the last few years has fallen, so that it is actually lower than the Public Charter School Review Board. Of course, this could also signify a growing concern among the members of the Board about the rapid and continuing growth of their charter school competitors.

7. There is anecdotal evidence that charter schools can and do manipulate these seemingly impartial processes to shape their student body. One procedure that has been noted is for a charter school to announce an early cutoff for admissions application and not advertise this deadline widely. Once the deadline has passed, and the school has filled up its class with its targeted population, if there are remaining seats, then the admissions process is reopened and the formal processes are followed.

8. There are serious debates about whether or not reimbursement of average per-pupil expenditure for operating costs is fair. Much of this argument revolves around the extent to which the charter schools and the traditional public schools educate the same types of students. The equal funding is fair only if the same services and types of students are enrolled in both sectors. We do not, however, address one other possible difference in the population served—and the attendant costs. Many argue that, among special education students, on average, charter schools do not serve the moderately or severely handicapped students, serving instead the less expensive learning-disabled students. To the extent this is true, paying average costs to the charter schools actually creates a fiscal advantage. We address much of this issue in chapter 4.

9. These data were provided by the Office of the Mayor and the D.C. Chief Financial Officer.

10. The surveys were conducted mostly by e-mail in the Spring of 2004. Principals were e-mailed several requests to participate in this online survey. These e-mail requests were followed up by faxes and telephone calls. Consequently, response rates were still low. In turn, we present this data as indicative, not definitive.

11. In chapters 9 and 10, we show that this differential is also evident among parents in the two sectors.

12. Alternative accountability plans are put in place for IEP/NEP/LEP students.

13. For more on the closing of charter schools, see Teske, Schneider, and Cassese 2005, and Hassel and Batdorff 2004.

14. The CER numbers are often subject to criticism. For example, their closure rates include voluntary closures, and, in some cases, schools that were authorized, but never were actually launched.

15. See the editorial on May 3, 2004, entitled "The Mayor Tries Again."

16. If Williams succeeds, D.C. will be joining a growing list of big-city school systems under mayoral control. New York, Boston, Chicago, Cleveland, and Detroit are on the growing list of big cities that have put mayors in charge of their schools.

CHAPTER 3
THE PANEL STUDY

1. As explained below, we drew a sample of about one thousand D.C. parents and interviewed them about their attitudes and behavior toward the schools in which one of their children was enrolled. These parents became part of the "panel" that we then sought to reinterview on three more occasions. We present more details of this process and the parents we interviewed throughout this chapter.

2. We should note that we chose to interview only students who were in grade 7 or above, both because younger students are more difficult to interview by telephone, and because our focus with this student population is on civic education and participation. We use these student data at several points in the book, and they are the focal point of chapter 12, where we study charter schools as a venue of civic education.

3. See the appendix to this chapter for information on all four waves of the survey, including technical information on how the sample was constructed, how the surveys were conducted and response rates.

4. As noted in the appendix, if the parent was selected from a list of parents we obtained from the D.C. charter schools, we focused the interview on that child's school. If the parent was from our random digit dialing and if the parent had more than one child in the public schools, we asked the parent to talk about the child whose birthday was next, to ensure randomization. The survey wording was identical for both sets of parents, and the study was clearly identified as research not associated with or affiliated with either the District or the charter schools.

5. The U.S. Department of Education has recently funded several randomized field trials to better identify the effects of charter schools. However, the results of these studies will not be available for several years.

6. There is considerable debate about the use of experiments in education research. See, for example, Cook 2002.

7. There is one exception to this. In chapter 9, where we study parental satisfaction with their schools, we look at a set of parents who tried to enroll their child in a charter school but lost the lottery. In one set of analyses in that chapter we use parents who were "lotteried out" of charter schools as a naturally occurring control group for charter parents.

8. This is essentially Moe's position vis-à-vis vouchers (see Moe 2001), which relies on some regulation, but mostly emphasizes the importance of market forces in fostering innovation and accountability.

9. See Schneider 1999 for details on how difficult it was to gather the school-level data used in the web site.

10. The pattern of attrition between panels is complex. For example, when we undertook Wave 3, we decided to contact everyone in Wave 1, regardless of whether or not they were in Wave 2. We were able to reinterview 96 parents who were in Wave 1 but were not in Wave 2.

11. Nomenclature is always an interesting issue in discussing charter schools. Charter schools *are* public schools and in Washington, D.C. about half are chartered by the D.C. public school system. However, in this book, when we use the term DCPS we are referring to "traditional" (noncharter) schools run by the D.C. public school system. Also, when we talk about "charter parents" we are clearly referring to parents whose children attend D.C. charter schools (likewise "DCPS parents" refers to parents with children in traditional D.C. public schools).

12. When asked to mention the things they think are most important in terms of education, while only a small percentage of parents in either sector mention "values," twice as many (6 percent) of charter-school parents as DCPS parents volunteered values as important.

13. As with our discussion of demographics, we concentrate on Wave 1 data, because it is the most representative of the entire D.C. population and has not been affected by differential attrition. We look at the over-time data in later chapters.

14. The first question asked for a simple count for the number of people whom they talked with about schools in the last six months, while the follow-up questions asked specifically about the (up to three) people they talk to the most about their child's school—a question designed to tap into real networks in which education is frequently discussed.

15. In chapter 9, we report parental grades for a set of specific school characteristics. In chapter 10, we report patterns over time.

CHAPTER 4
ARE CHARTER-SCHOOL STUDENTS HARDER TO EDUCATE THAN
THOSE IN THE TRADITIONAL PUBLIC SCHOOLS?

1. This is evident in the intense debate that has surrounded the randomized field trials of private voucher programs (for example, see Barnard et al. 2003; Krueger and Zhu 2004).

2. The essence of these findings has been confirmed by an analysis conducted by the National Center for Education Statistics, "A Closer Look at Charter Schools Using Hierarchical Linear Modeling." U.S. Department of Education Institute of Education Sciences, NCES 2006–460.

3. A typology of the criticisms leveled at the report, along with a response from the authors, is available at http://www.aft.org/pubs-reports/closer_look/082704.htm#Bookmark6.

4. The AFT report did try to control for some factors that may reflect educability, such as free and reduced price lunch percentage and some other demographic indicators, such as race and ethnicity, but the data they had were limited by the NAEP "data tool" they used and their analysis was basically descriptive, leaving the report open to this charge.

5. Simpson's paradox (Simpson 1951; Blyth 1972) usually refers to the extreme case in which a relationship between variables at one level of aggregation is reversed for every subunit at a lower level of aggregation (see Pearl 2000; 173–200 for a description and illustration).

6. See chapter 3 for further examination of this point.

7. While the racial distribution across schools is often used as a further indicator of the challenges schools face in educating their students, this measure has little meaning in Washington, D.C., where the overwhelming majority of students are African American.

8. Our data for the DCPS come from a variety of sources. For our measure of free/reduced price lunch, we obtained data from the DCPS Division of Food and Nutrition Services. Data on the proportion of special education students is from the DCPS web site (http://www.k12.dc.us/dcps/offices/facts1.html#14), and our data on English language learners was obtained from the DCPS Office of Bilingual Education. There are two chartering authorities in D.C., so our data on the charters comes from either the D.C. Public Charter School Board School Performance Reports or the D.C. Board of Education charter school web site (http://www.dcboecharters.org/charter_schools.htm). We should note that procedures used by schools in identifying eligibility for free or subsidized school lunches make this a biased measure. Small schools and charter schools may be particularly prone to "help" their students and parents fill out and return forms more than large schools and public ones. This may help explain part of the results we report below in which so many of the charters indicate a higher free/reduced price lunch relative to DCPS. All of our data are available on request.

9. This difference arises in that, instead of point estimates for the parameters of interest, the Bayesian result is the aforementioned posterior distribution for the parameters. That is, parameters are treated as random variables instead of fixed but unknown quantities. The reader interested in more detail about Bayesian methods should consult an accessible text such as Carlin and Louis 2000 or Gill 2002.

10. A Jeffreys prior is an often desirable way to express prior ignorance because it is invariant to the scale of the unknown estimands. It thus can be used regardless of what scale we choose to measure the unknown parameters (Lee 1997, 87–88). Graphically, the Jeffreys prior for the beta distribution is in the shape of a "U" with asymptotes at 0 and 1.

11. For completeness, we also estimated models separately by level of school (elementary, middle, secondary), with the appropriate DCPS comparison proportion also computed by level. The inferential results are the same as those reported later in the chapter.

12. Our mixture model, which is adapted from a model used by Laird (1982) to model batting averages for major league baseball, employs the specification discussed in Congdon (2001, 217–8).

13. Here our choice of prior is constrained from being completely uninformative by technical issues of estimation (and the fact that the choice of $K = 2$ itself reflects a fairly strong prior assumption). The fundamental problem is specifying the model in such a way that the computer will allow each school to have a probability of membership in each subpopulation, and not get "trapped" in a particular category. Again we follow the implementation of Congdon (2001, 217–18).

14. The results presented are computed using 20,000 MCMC iterations after discarding 180,000 as burn-in. Visual inspection of estimated posterior distributions and autocorrelations, as well as the Geweke (1992) and the Heidelberger and Welch (1983) diagnostics do not suggest nonconvergence. WinBUGS code for the models estimated is available upon request.

15. The survey design is described at length in chapter 3.

16. About 4.6 percent of the data are missing due to item nonresponse.

17. The results presented are computed using 200,000 MCMC iterations after discarding 600,000 as burn-in. Visual inspection of estimated posterior distributions and autocorrelations, as well as the Geweke (1992) and the Heidelberger and Welch (1982) diagnostics do not suggest nonconvergence. WinBUGS code for the models estimated, as well as full posterior results for the other parameters (e.g., the estimated weights and precisions), is available upon request.

18. Carnoy et al. 2005, chap. 5, discuss both cross-sectional and value-added measures and review many of the extant studies of student achievement using these measures.

19. We use the method of Mahalanobis metric matching (Rubin 1973, 1979, 1980; Leuven and Sianesi 2003) to identify "neighbors."

20. Keep in mind the discussion in note 8 above, that is, charter schools may be particularly prone to "help" their students and parents fill out and return free/reduced price lunch forms compared to public schools.

CHAPTER 5
SHOPPING FOR SCHOOLS ON THE INTERNET USING DCSCHOOLSEARCH.COM

1. We should note that in the last few years, the administration of the D.C. Public Schools has changed, and the hostility we encountered has been replaced by a commitment to greater transparency. Indeed, under the present administration, the city and the State Office of Education have taken over the responsibility of keeping DCSchoolSearch.com up and running.

2. For essentially static information see, for example, Virginia's at http://www.pen.k12.va.us/VDOE/src/vasrc-reportcard-intropage.shtml. For an example of simply posting PDF files, see New York's at http://www.emsc.nysed.gov.

3. The Digital Divide Network provides a useful overview of ongoing issues concerning patterns of IT usage: http://www.digitaldividenetwork.org/.

4. Others are also recognizing the declining importance of access and are emphasizing new issues. Most notably, DiMaggio et al. 2001 articulate a research agenda that recognizes that reducing inequalities in access by itself will not lead to the demise of the digital divide.

5. There is no information on private schools in the site, in part because gathering such information is so difficult. The Washington Scholarship Fund, a privately financed voucher program, enrolled students in about 120 private schools for the 2001–2 academic year, covering about one-tenth the number of children in charter schools but about three times as many schools. Getting information about these schools is extremely difficult. The *Washingtonian* magazine's "Annual Guide to Private Schools in Washington" (http://www.washingtonian.com/schools/private/2005/main.html), for example, provides information on school size and tuition ranges, but each school would need to be contacted directly to get numbers on racial and economic demographics of their student population as well as test scores (assuming that they would even provide it). Given the size of this task, we did not collect information on private schools.

6. For a comparison of DCSchoolSearch.com to other Internet-based school sites, see Schneider and Buckley 2000.

7. The visual design of the site changed dramatically when it was taken over by the city, also reflecting the evolution of Internet graphic design in general and the desire to make the site have the same look and feel as other D.C. government web sites.

8. We discuss various decision-making theories and the use of information boards in the next section of the book.

9. Examples of this trend are wide-ranging, including the work of the firm Knowledge Networks, which started off as a public opinion survey using Web TV and became a marketing research team (http://www.intersurvey.com); Alvarez and Sherman's work at CalTech, which focuses on developing Internet-based survey research methodologies (http://survey.caltech.edu/); John Robinson's work at the University of Maryland tracking time use on the net; Shanto Iyengar's work on Internet-based experiments, and so on. Most of this work is focused on political opinion and attitudes.

10. Note that we did not ask questions about the age of the site visitor. Studies have shown that age strongly affects the use of the Internet and attitudes about electronic government (see, for example, Bimber 2001; Tolbert et al. 2002). It is likely that over time, as a new generation of Americans comes of age, the fact that they will have been raised with the Internet will transform the unequal patterns we, and others, have observed.

11. Our numbers look fairly similar to those reported by GreatSchools.net, a very large Internet-based school-information site, during the same time period. According to their web site, 71 percent of their visitors have household incomes of $50,000 or more and 90 percent have some college education. Similar to our experience, 70 percent of GreatSchools users are parents.

CHAPTER 6
WHAT DO PARENTS WANT FROM SCHOOLS? IT DEPENDS ON HOW YOU ASK

1. About 10 percent of responses did not fall into any of these categories, representing an amorphous set of characteristics. Here, we focus on the major categories. In addition, while we have panel data, we report only responses from the

first wave. There are very few differences over time, and the patterns we discuss here are repeated in the data we collected in subsequent waves.

2. Since we are assuming lower scores actually were given to attributes that the respondent liked most, we have reversed the order displayed by subtracting the observed mean from 6, which was the highest observed mean +1. Thus, following the other charts in this chapter, the higher the bar, the more the attribute was liked by the respondent.

3. There is a problem that flows from using a web-based research tool to precisely identify parental preferences. In a laboratory setting, stimuli can be narrowly crafted and responses therefore more highly calibrated, but DCSchoolSearch.com was designed both as an information tool to help parents find appropriate schools for their children and as a research tool. Because it was based on real data and faced the limits of the Internet, the stimuli presented by the site are much "messier" than in a laboratory setting. For example, there are differences in the quality of the data—locational data, test-score data, and racial data are centrally collected and easily understood, but other data, on such things as extended-day programs, student/teacher ratios, or other measures of teacher quality are harder to collect and verify. Search patterns may be biased by the a priori beliefs that parents have in the validity of the data. In addition, not each "page" of the site was identical—some contained more information than others. This too may have produced some bias, but limiting the analysis to the initial stages of search should limit this problem (visitors do not yet know much of the details about each page—they only know the titles).

4. The differences displayed in these figures are significant at the .01 level, two-tailed.

5. We examine median values in the figure instead of means because the data for all three covariates are highly skewed. Nevertheless, similar results are obtained using means.

CHAPTER 7
SCHOOL CHOICE AND THE IMPORTANCE OF PARENTAL INFORMATION

1. There are clearly many indicators that could be used to test knowledge (see Schneider, Teske, and Marshall 2000). As noted, we concentrate on test scores, since the current debate about choice and accountability, especially after the passage of the No Child Left Behind Act, focuses so tightly on student achievement as measured by standardized tests.

2. In this analysis of parent accuracy, we began with 652 parents, losing the third that gave no answer. We lost further respondents due to missing values in reported test scores from the schools and in a few cases, an inability to place the student in a school. Ultimately, we were left with 518 observed values.

3. Elsewhere, we have shown in more detail that this higher error-rate bias is in part a result of the greater propensity of charter parents to overestimate the performance of their child's school compared to parents whose children are in traditional public schools (Buckley and Schneider 2005).

296 NOTES TO CHAPTER 8

4. See, for example, the work of Burt (1992) or Granovetter (1973). On political networks see, for example, Mutz (2002), Huckfeldt and Sprague (1995), or La Due Lake and Huckfeldt (1998). On networks for information about schools see Schneider et al. (1998).

5. Kelling's work has been adopted by many urban police departments that have increased their pursuit of minor crimes, in order to nurture more vibrant urban life, which in turn supports stronger communities that deter crime.

6. The work has many foundations. See, for example, Hogarth 2001 and LeDoux 1998. Also see the work of Fazio and his colleagues, such as Fazio et al. 1986; Fazio and Williams 1986; and Schuette and Fazio 1995.

7. See Lin (2001) on the importance of networks in defining social capital.

CHAPTER 8
HOW DO PARENTS ACCESS AND PROCESS INFORMATION ABOUT SCHOOLS?

1. For an explication and comparison of no fewer than fourteen of these theories, see Cooksey 1996.

2. Cooksey and others have disagreed with this broadly inclusive definition of behavioral-decision theory, but it is a useful and well-recognized one (see Beach and Mitchell 1998; Lau and Levy 1998).

3. While Jones explores deeply the relationship between bounded rationality and institutional development, the concept of bounded rationality has informed many different research questions in political science and public administration, most notably budgeting (e.g., Wildavsky) and organizational-decision making (e.g., March).

4. A variety of studies using "microworlds," computer-simulated complex decision environments that strive to approximate real-world decision problems, finds strong evidence that experienced, expert decision makers, "are more likely to spend more time in the phase of initial orientation and goal elaboration, to think in causal nets and not in causal chains, to consider possible side effects, to acquire more knowledge, to exhibit more concerted decision making behavior, and to achieve higher levels of performance" (Rigas and Brehmer 1999, 58).

5. Researchers have long argued that education is indeed such a good. In the literature on the choice of private over public schooling, dimensions such as relative or absolute academic performance (Buddin, Cordes, and Kirby 1998; Lankford and Wykoff 1992; Moe 2000a; cf. Smith and Meier 1995), racial composition (Clotfelter 1976; Lankford, Lee, and Wykoff 1995), values (Schneider, Teske, and Marschall 2000), and religious affiliation (Long and Toma 1988; Moe 2000a) have all been found to be salient to choosing parents. Similarly, recent work on the motivations of parents using newer forms of option-demand school choice within the public system or at public expense have identified academic performance (Dhami, Hertwig, and Hoffrage 2004; Finn, Manno, and Vanourek 2000; Greene, Howell, and Peterson 1998; Moe 2000a; Schneider, Teske, and Marschall 2000) and race (Henig 1994) as important factors. Additional dimensions on which parents in the public sector may evaluate schools include proximity to

home, physical safety, the availability of extended-day programs, and particular programmatic innovations (Teske et al. 2001).

6. On other occasions, such as a mail survey of research psychologists (Kahneman, Slovic, and Tversky 1982), settings were uncontrolled.

7. Representative design is also referred to as "neo-Brunswikian," after pioneering psychologist Egon Brunswik's (1952) work on ecological models and representative design. According to Dhami, Hertwig, and Hoffrage: "Egon Brunswik argued that psychological processes are adapted to environmental properties. He proposed the method of representative design to capture these processes and advocated that psychology be a science of organism-environment relations. Representative design involves randomly sampling stimuli from the environment or creating stimuli in which environmental properties are preserved. This departs from systematic design" (2004, 960).

8. There is a long-standing debate over the use of "direct" versus "indirect" methods for studying the evaluations of attributes in a choice situation (see, for example, Adamowicz, Louviere, and Williams 1994; Cummings et al. 1986; Mitchell and Carson 1989).

9. Note that in contrast to the traditional decision board in which the alternatives are usually limited to a set constructed by the researcher, in DCSchoolSearch the set of alternatives is dynamically constructed (as the representative-design approach requires) by the parent and presents real-world alternatives.

10. See Schneider and Buckley (2000) for a more detailed description of creating school-based Internet sites and the joys (and horrors) of researching school-choice behavior on the Internet.

11. We experimented with a range of cut-offs above and below the "natural" cut point of 50 percent of the tabs. The results we report below are robust from about one-third to all of the available information.

12. Again, see Schneider and Buckley 2000.

13. We operationalize the idea of the marginal consumer below.

14. The marginal-consumer variable was created by using the iterated-principal factor method to analyze the correlation matrix of the variables. Factors then underwent varimax rotation and the logical factor with positive loading on all six variables was selected and scored to create the final continuous variable.

15. Another possibility, from the literature on motivated reasoning, is confirmatory search bias (see, for example, Lodge and Taber 2000). According to this theory, some searchers (perhaps those with strong preferences for their current school or a well-known alternative) will "search" only for information that bolsters their prejudices. While we believe that this is an accurate description of human behavior, we do not think that it represents a confound to our hypothesis. For one thing, unlike psychological experiments set up to gauge the effects of motivated reasoning, DCSchoolSearch does not offer information that appears to come from sources of varying ideological polarity (such as education unions or choice activists). This alone greatly limits the ability for motivation to affect search. Of course, we cannot accurately determine the extent to which any particular piece of information is attended to in the minds of the subjects, but we believe that this ultimately has no effect on our hypothesis.

16. Our dependent variable is coded from dichotomous responses to the survey question: "Because of the information you got through DCSchoolSearch.com, have you actually tried to change your child's school?"

17. In the analysis presented below, we transform both the number of total actions (which ranges from 2 to 1,350 in sample) and the number of searches per school (1 to 39 in sample) by taking the natural logarithm of both. The correlation between the two untransformed variables is 0.004 and the correlation between the logged variables is still only 0.23, suggesting that these two measures are (as expected) capturing different characteristics of search.

18. One possible interpretation of this result is that searches per school is a measure, to an extent, of the quality of search (more precisely, of its compensatory nature—a search's ability to trade off in different areas to allow the proper ranking of almost-matched alternatives). Our dependent variable does not take quality into account. We do not attempt to measure whether the parent is making the "right" choice, either based on an "objective" comparison of her stated preferences and her choice's attributes or on a subjective evaluation by the parent after choosing. So while we find that, on average, more information increases the probability of changing schools, we cannot be sure that the new school chosen is a better fit for parent and student.

CHAPTER 9
SATISFACTION WITH SCHOOLS

1. Fundamental to our panel design is the idea that the effects of choice are dynamic and that therefore time matters. When we start exploring the effects of charter schools over time, we need to explore alternative methods for addressing dynamic effects, especially given the difficult nature of our panel—and we put the discussion of those problems and models off until the next chapter.

2. This argument is central to Moe's analysis of vouchers (2001); also see Stone (1998) on the importance of building civic capacity to sustain school reform.

3. Many of the factors discussed here are associated with choice in general, and have not been developed specifically for charter schools as a form of choice—but clearly apply to the charter-school option as well.

4. We explore these issues in more detail in chapter 11.

5. This notion that "consumers" of education will have more voice has long been a centerpiece of the market model of schooling (e.g., Chubb and Moe 1990). However, as Benveniste, Carnoy, and Rothstein (2003, chap. 3) point out, public schools cannot necessarily take their clientele for granted, either, since parents as citizens have numerous rights in regards to their child's school and recourse to the legal system if they are infringed. Indeed this debate about the relative efficacy of parent-citizens versus parent-consumers is at the very core of the theoretical arguments over school choice (see, especially, Henig 1994).

6. The survey data are weighted for probability of inclusion and poststratified on charter enrollment due to intentional oversampling of this subpopulation, as described in chapter 3. All the figures, tables, and models estimated below use the same weights.

7. We use the one-to-one matching algorithm in the software provided by Leuven and Sianesi (2003). Note also that in this analysis we are assuming a simple, additive treatment effect and that the stable unit treatment value assumption (SUTVA—that the treatment status of one unit does not affect the assignment to treatment of other units).

8. We construct this measure by comparing each matched pair on each of the four outcome measures. If the charter parent has a higher response than the control, we add 1 to the measure; we subtract 1 if the control parent's outcome is larger. The final measure thus ranges between –4 and 4.

9. There have been well-known and very intense debates about how well this design has been implemented and about the effects of vouchers (e.g., Krueger and Zhu 2004; Barnard et al. 2003). In addition, others have criticized randomized trials as introducing new biases and complication to policy evaluation (e.g., Hanushek 1999 on class-size experiments in education and Heckman and Smith 1995 on "randomization bias" in social experiments in general).

10. As noted earlier, as of this writing, the U.S. Department of Education is in the process of launching such a study. The results of this study will not be available for several years.

11. One of the least discussed aspects of many school-choice programs is the extent to which *schools choose students* as compared to the more frequently asked question of how *students choose schools*. There is some anecdotal evidence that more than the luck of the draw is involved in the selection process. For example, some charter schools have been accused of announcing very short deadlines for applications (and then recruiting the students they want to apply before the deadline). When all these desired students are signed on, the school then extends the deadline (if there are seats left over) and conducts the mandated lottery. One consequence is that the parents who have lost the lottery may actually learn that the deck was stacked against them, causing them to evaluate the schools in which their children remain even more negatively. See Fetterman (1982) and Fiske and Ladd (2000, 285–86). We discuss this point further in the concluding chapter.

12. We asked parents how satisfied they were to the attention of the school to "values" without defining the term. C.S. Lewis, in his *Studies in Words*, identified "the tendency of words to become less descriptive and more evaluative . . . and to end up by being purely evaluative—useless synonyms for good and for bad" (1960, 7–8). We believe that the term "values" clearly central to many political debates (including that over schools) has such an evaluative component. In turn, we know that the term is essentially undefined—but has strong emotional connotations, as evidenced in the 2004 presidential election campaign.

13. Cotton 2001 presents an excellent review of the literature examining the effects of small learning communities.

14. These differences will most likely not endure over time. Many of the differences are the result of the newness of charter schools, many of which are just ramping up to full size, often by adding grade levels.

15. The preference for smaller classes is being codified in law: nearly half the states have enacted legislation and are spending hundreds of millions of dollars each year to reconfigure school buildings to reduce the student-teacher ratio to twenty or fewer students per teacher (Magnuson 2000).

16. Appendix 9.1 gives more details on the CHOPIT model.

17. The subset of data used in this analysis is from the second wave of the telephone survey, with a sample size of 374 (after loss due to panel attrition and listwise deletion of missing responses). Two hundred of the parents in the sample have a child in a charter school.

18. These are the data we analyzed earlier in the chapter.

19. The order in which the three sets of vignettes was presented was randomized as was the order of the three alternatives.

20. An interesting aside: we asked parents to grade other services, including the parks and the quality of garbage pickup. There was a difference in the pattern of evaluations, with charter-school parent evaluations significantly lower than DCPS parents. For example, while 19 percent of DCPS parents assigned the D.C. parks a grade of A, less than 14 percent of charter parents did so. Similarly, 25 percent of DCPS parents assigned a grade of A to the quality of garbage pickup, higher than the 21 percent of charter parents who did so. The grey-colored glasses charter parents wear when it comes to schools may also be reflected in their evaluation of other municipal services as well.

21. For the agree/disagree questions, we read students a four-point scale: agree strongly, agree somewhat, disagree somewhat, and disagree strongly. They had the option to say that they didn't know or that they neither agreed nor disagreed. For the questions pertaining to satisfaction with discipline and values, we used a four-point scale, and we report the percent that were very satisfied. They also had the option of saying they were neither satisfied nor dissatisfied.

22. As elsewhere in this book, these predicted response probabilities are generated via stochastic simulation holding all other covariates at their mean or modal values.

Chapter 10
Will You Still Love Me Tomorrow? Parental Satisfaction over Time

1. For a discussion of different types of goods, see, for example, Weimer and Vining 2004. Some might argue that education could even be categorized as a "postexperience" good—one whose worth cannot be determined until long after consumption (i.e., when one's lifetime earnings are tallied).

2. Note that, in addition to the fixed-effects vector-decomposition models, we also estimated a variety of more traditional fixed- and random-effects specifications, including a generalized estimating-equations model with an unstructured-covariance matrix. The substantive findings reported in this chapter remain largely unchanged.

3. For the first and second stages of all models, we reject the omnibus F test of all coefficients jointly equal to 0 and an F test that all unit effects equal zero (all $p < .05$), except for the school-size case, where the p for the first stage omnibus F test is about .17. This suggests, as table 10.1 shows, that the time-varying predictors of satisfaction with school size jointly are poor predictors of the outcome. Adjusted R^2 for all eight third-stage models range between about .60 and .71.

4. A key difference between the models is that, instead of adjusting the sample through propensity-score matching, discarding the parents not new to their school, and testing the hypothesis of the charter effect nonparametrically, here the treatment effect is estimated conditional on the unit fixed effects and the parametric specification of the linear model.

CHAPTER 11
BUILDING SOCIAL CAPITAL IN THE NATION'S CAPITAL:
CAN SCHOOL CHOICE BUILD A FOUNDATION FOR COOPERATIVE BEHAVIOR?

1. Mettler and Soss (2004) provide an excellent overview of the various strains of policy feedback research.

2. For an interesting look at this argument in reverse, see the work of Fischel (2001), who argues that voters have consistently rejected school-voucher referenda because they fear the loss of community-specific social capital.

3. It is possible that these contracts and demands on parents act as a screening mechanism by which charter schools try to select parents with a propensity for greater involvement in the school. However, while, as noted, many charter schools do indeed have formal contracts, Henig's work and our own observations suggest that the charter schools in our study are engaged more in outreach activities than in enforcing contracts. This probably reduces the likelihood of charter schools "cherry picking" parents and students.

4. "Common support" simply means that if some people have such a high (or low) probability of being charter parents that there is no one in the control group who can match them, we drop them from the analysis.

5. As in chapter 9, the sample size varies slightly over imputed datasets due to imputation variability and the discarding of units with estimated propensity scores off of the common support.

6. The tensions between a tight focus within schools of choice and how that might affect broader attitudes and behaviors has been explored by Fuller (2000b) and Fischel (2001).

7. Here we use the Bayesian multivariate normal imputation model as described in chapter 8. Since this produces continuous (real-valued) imputed values for the missing data, we estimate the panel models using a random-effects specification as opposed to the fixed-effects vector-decomposition models used above.

8. This may be a liberal "borrowing": Sapiro's analysis is more a general piece on adult political learning focusing on the timing and sequence of political socialization over a lifetime, but the term fits our argument—and the concept that Sapiro studies is related to the idea we explore here.

CHAPTER 12
DO CHARTER SCHOOLS PROMOTE CITIZENSHIP AMONG STUDENTS?

1. The terminology used in the literature varies across and within disciplines. The term "citizenship education," borrowed from the philosophy of education,

is roughly synonymous with the "civic education" or "democratic education" described by political theorists. We use these terms interchangeably. Psychologists and empirical political scientists also frequently refer to "political socialization," a term that connotes an interest in the "process of inducting youth into the political culture" (Ehman 1980, 99). While citizenship/civic education certainly has more normative overtones than political socialization, there is nonetheless substantial overlap. Note also that our focus here is on K–12 education and our empirical evidence is from secondary schools.

2. For a definition of the various levels of proficiency see the "The NAEP Civics Achievement Level," http://nces.ed.gov/nationsreportcard/civics/achieveall .asp.

3. For an international perspective on these issues see the papers in Macedo and Wolf (2004), and in particular the one by Harris.

4. This set of components seems fairly consensual. See, for example, Branson 1998.

5. Neither set, however, is sufficient. All citizens must also possess more basic academic skills as well, such as reading ability, mathematics skills, and some knowledge of science (Galston 2001).

6. Campbell himself does not use this distinction.

7. For more on the role of more fundamentalist Christian schools on inculcating civic virtues see Godwin, Godwin, and Martinez-Ebers 2004.

8. The extent to which charter schools actually do innovate, however, has been questioned (see, for example, Teske et al. 2001; Lubienski 2003).

9. But see Benveniste, Carnoy and Rothstein (2003) for a contrary view.

10. There is some concern in the literature that charter schools will "skim the cream" off of the student population. Lacireno-Paquet et al. (2002), however, find this to be a problem of limited extent. We discuss this issue at greater length in chapter 4.

11. For a critical appraisal of the "common school," see Glenn (1988).

12. As a reminder to the reader, the logic underlying this method is to construct, from quasi-experimental data, a new variable (the propensity score) that summarizes pretreatment characteristics of each respondent. Based on these propensity scores, a treatment group and a matched control group are created and the size and significance of the treatment effect can be estimated using these groups.

13. This number is lower than the original 1,012 due primarily to the a priori removal of parents with children in grades K–6 and also due to listwise deletion of cases with missing values on any of the covariates in the propensity-score model.

14. We also employ the same poststratification weight (Little 1993) to adjust the propensity-score estimation for the designed charter oversample that we use elsewhere and discuss in chapter 3.

15. This number is 165 instead of 196 due to the discarding of parents not on the common support of the propensity-score model.

16. Our research questionnaire, unfortunately, did not include any measures of political knowledge.

17. Another reason for this is that the individual measures do not scale particularly well. Using Mokken's nonparametric item-response model for scaling ordinal items (Hemker, Sijtsma, and Molenaar 1995; Mokken 1971), we find a scala-

bility coefficient (*H*) of slightly less than .3 for each of the three groups of measures, although some restricted sets of items yield *H*'s of about .4.

18. This measure is constructed similarly as a Mokken scale (*H* = .379) by adding the polytomous responses to nine questions asking parents whether they are frequent volunteers at school events, if they are PTA members, how many organizations, clubs, or groups they are members of, how confident they are in their ability to write a letter to a public official clearly stating their opinion, how confident they are in making a statement at a public meeting, how often they attend events at their child's school, how often they talk to politicians at any level, the number of discussants they converse with about their child's education regularly, and the extent to which they agree that they are well qualified to participate in politics.

19. We include this in response to the criticism of Portes (1998) that the empirical literature on social capital generally fails to deal with the potential confound of sociability, although there is the possibility of endogeneity, particularly in the case of the groups/clubs-membership outcome.

20. In our data, for example, we find that volunteer activity among charter schools is 35 percent more likely to be a result of mandatory school programs than in the case of students in the traditional public schools.

CHAPTER 13
CHARTER SCHOOLS: HYPE OR HOPE?

1. These data are from the Center for Education Reform as of April 30, 2006. The CER keeps a running total that can be downloaded from their website, http://www.edreform.com/index.cfm?fuseAction=stateStatChart&psectionid=15&cSectionID=44.

2. The Pritchard Committee was formed in the late 1990s to monitor and work toward improving the quality of education in the state of Kentucky. Its influential report "Teaching for Kentucky's Future" was issued in October 1999; in it researchers documented the positive impact that high-quality teaching has on academic performance and identified a host of mechanisms for improving the schools. Kentucky has ranked high on academic improvement in recent years: Quality Counts 2004, for instance, gave Kentucky the third highest score in the nation for teaching quality. Similarly, Kentucky earned a fifth-place ranking in the National Council on Teacher Quality's evaluation of twenty states. Not surprisingly, the Pritchard Committee has gained national visibility for its thoughts on effective school reform.

3. Much of the data (and the groups for which the data were reported) resemble the reporting requirements of the No Child Left Behind Act. However, how to present these data to increase their usefulness to parents is still a major issue.

4. There are at least two major lines of research, which seem to be conducted independently of one another. One, mostly by psychologists and scholars of learning, emphasizes the effects of cooperative learning on the academic achievement of students (see for example, Antil et al. 1998; Tateyama-Sniezek 1990; Slavin 1996; McMaster and Fuchs 2002). The other (and shorter) line of research has

been conducted by economists and sociologists and is exemplified by the work of Epple and Romano 1998; Hanushek et al. 2003; Hoxby 2000a; Zimmer and Toma 2000; McEwan 2003; Willms n.d.

5. The emphasis on management failure is clear in D.C. Most of the charters that closed during our study were closed for financial reasons and, indeed, under D.C. law a charter school cannot be closed for academic reasons until it has completed five years—the amount of time lawmakers thought the schools needed to get established. Many believe that in D.C., as elsewhere, the charter schools will be held more accountable on the basis of academic performance. Whether or not fewer charter schools will succumb to bad management remains to be seen.

6. Qualified Zone Academy Bonds (QZABs) are a relatively new financing instrument that can be used to fund school renovations and repairs as well as other improvements. The federal government covers, on average, all of the interest on these bonds, thus enabling schools to save up to 50 percent of the costs of these qualified projects. The interest payment is a tax credit, in lieu of cash, provided to financial institutions that hold the bonds.

7. Private correspondence, May 1, 2006.

REFERENCES

Abernathy, Scott. 2004. "School Choice and Democratic Participation." Ph.D. diss., Princeton University.

Ackerman, Frank. 2004. "Priceless Benefits, Costly Mistakes: What's Wrong with Cost-Benefit Analysis." *Post-Autistic Economics Review* 25:2–7.

Adamowicz, Wiktor, Jordan J. Louviere, and Michael Williams. 1994. "Combining Revealed and Stated Preference Methods for Valuing Environmental Amenities." *Journal of Environmental Economics and Management* 26:271–92.

Adler, Paul S., and Seok-Woo Kwon. 2002. "Social Capital: Prospects for a New Concept." *Academy of Management Review* 27 (1): 17–40.

Akerlof, George A. 1970. "Market for Lemons—Quality Uncertainty and Market Mechanism." *Quarterly Journal of Economics* 84:488–500.

Aldrich, John. 1993. "Rational Choice and Turnout." *American Journal of Political Science* 37:246–78.

Allison, Paul. S. 2002. *Missing Data*. Thousand Oaks, Calif.: Sage.

Alston, Lee J., Thrainn Eggertsson, Douglass North, and Randall Calvert. 1996. *Empirical Studies in Institutional Change*. Cambridge: Cambridge University Press.

Amemiya, Takeshi, and Thomas E. MaCurdy. 1986. "Instrumental-Variable Estimation of an Error-Components Model." *Econometrica* 54 (4): 869–80.

Amrein, Audrey L., and David C. Berliner. 2002. "High-Stakes Testing, Uncertainty, and Student Learning." *Education Policy Analysis Archives* 10 (18); http://epaa.asu.edu/epaa/v10n18.

Antil, Laurence R., Joseph R. Jenkins, Susan K. Wayne, and Patricia F. Vadasy. 1998. "Cooperative Learning: Prevalence, Conceptualizations, and the Relation between Research and Practice." *American Educational Research Journal* 35 (3): 419–54.

Apple, Michael W. 2001. *Educating the "Right" Way: Markets, Standards, God, and Inequality*. New York: Routledge.

Arbuthnott, J. 1710. "An Argument for Divine Providence, Taken from the Constant Regularity Observ'd in the Births of Both Sexes." *Philosophical Transactions* 27:186–90.

Armor, David J., and Brett M. Peiser. 1998. "Interdistrict Choice in Massachusetts." In *Learning from School Choice*, ed. P. E. Peterson and B. C. Hassel. Washington, D.C.: Brookings Institution Press.

Ascher, Carol, Norm Fruchter, and Robert Berne. 1996. *Hard Lessons: Public Schools and Privatization*. New York: Twentieth Century School Fund Press.

Ashenfelter, Orley. 1978. "Estimating the Effect of Training Programs on Earnings." *Review of Economics and Statistics* 60 (1): 47–57.

Astone, Nan Marie, and Sara S. McLanahan. 1991. Family-Structure, Parental Practices and High-School Completion. *American Sociological Review* 56 (3): 309–20.

Austen-Smith, David and William Riker. 1987. "Asymmetric Information and the Coherence of Legislation." *American Political Science Review* 81:897–918.

Baltagi, Badi H. 2001. *Econometric Analysis of Time Series Data.* Chichester, England: John Wiley.

Barber, Benjamin. 1984. *Strong Democracy: Participatory Politics for a New Age.* Berkeley: University of California Press.

Barnard, John, Constantine E. Frangakis, Jennifer L. Hill, and Donald B. Rubin. 2003. "Principal Stratification Approach to Broken Randomized Experiments: A Case Study of School Choice Vouchers in New York City." *Journal of the American Statistical Association* 98 (462): 299–311.

Bartels, Larry. 1996. "Uninformed Votes: Information Effects in Presidential Elections." *American Journal of Political Science* 40:194–230.

Baumgartner, Frank R., and Bryan D. Jones. 1993. *Agendas and Instability in American Politics.* Chicago: University of Chicago Press.

Beach, Lee Roy. 1990. *Image Theory: Decision Making in Personal and Organizational Contexts.* Chichester, England: Wiley.

Beach, Lee Roy and Terence R. Mitchell. 1987. "Image Theory: Principles, Goals and Plans in Decision Making." *Acta Psychologica* 66:201–20.

———. 1998. "The Basics of Image Theory." In *Image Theory: Theoretical and Empirical Foundations,* ed. L. R. Beach. Mahwah, N.J.: Lawrence Erlbaum Assoc.

Becker, Sascha O., and Andrea Ichino. 2002. "Estimation of Average Treatment Effects Based on Propensity Scores." *Stata Journal* 2 (4): 358–77.

Belfield, Clive. 2003. "Democratic Education across School Types: Evidence from the NHES99." Occasional Paper No. 73. National Center for the Study of Privatization in Education, Teachers College, Columbia University.

Belsley, Timothy, and Anne Case. 2000. "Unnatural Experiments? Estimating the Incidence of Endogenous Policies." *Economic Journal* 110:F672–94.

Benveniste, Luis, Martin Carnoy, and Richard Rothstein. 2003. *All Else Equal: Are Public and Private Schools Different?* New York: RoutledgeFarmer.

Berman, Paul, Beryl Nelson, John Ericson, Rebecca Perry, and Debra Silverman. 1998. *A Study of Charter Schools: Second Year Report.* Washington, D.C.: U.S. Department of Education, Office of Educational Research and Improvement.

Berry, Jeffrey, Kent Portney, and Ken Thomson. 1993. *The Rebirth of Urban Democracy.* Washington, D.C.: Brookings Institution Press.

Berry, John, and Ed Kellery. 2003. *The Influentials: One American in Ten Tells the Other Nine How to Vote, Where to Eat, and What to Buy.* New York: Free Press.

Bertrand, Marianne, Esther Duflo, and Sendhil Mullainathan. 2004. "How Much Should We Trust Differences-in-Differences Estimates?" *Quarterly Journal of Economics* 119 (1): 249–75.

Bettman, James. 1986. "Consumer Psychology." *Annual Review of Psychology* 37:257–89.

Betts, Julian, and Darlene Morell. 1999. "The Determinants of Undergraduate Grade Point Average: The Relative Importance of Family Background, High

School Resources, and Peer Group Effects." *Journal of Human Resources* 34 (2): 268–93.

Bifulco, Robert, and Helen Ladd. 2004. "Institutional Change and Coproduction of Public Services: The Effect of Charter Schools on Parental Involvement." Unpublished Manuscript.

Bimber, Bruce. 1998. "The Internet and Political Transformation: Populism, Community, and Accelerated Pluralism." *Polity* 31:133–60.

———. 1999. "The Internet and Citizen Communication with Government: Does the Medium Matter?" *Political Communication* 16:409–28.

———. 2000. "The Study of Information Technology and Civic Engagement." *Political Communication* 17:329–33.

———. 2001. "Information and Political Engagement in America: The Search for Effects of Information Technology at the Individual Level." *Political Research Quarterly* 54:53–67.

Bishop, John H. 1999. "Nerd Harassment, Incentives, School Priorities, and Learning." In *Learning and Earning: How Schools Matter*, ed. by Susan E. Meyer and Paul Peterson. Washington D.C.: Brookings Institution.

Bloch, Peter, Daniel Sherrel, and Nancy Ridgway. 1986. "Consumer Search: An Extended Framework." *Journal of Consumer Research* 13:119–26.

Blyth, C. R. 1972. "On Simpson's Paradox and the Sure-Thing Principle." *Journal of the American Statistical Association* 67:364–66.

Bohrnstedt, George W., and Brian M. Stecher. 2000. "Class Size Reduction in California: A Summary of the 1998–1999 Evaluation Findings." Paper No. RP901/3. RAND Corporation, Santa Monica, Calif.

Braatz, Jay, and Robert Putnam. 1998. "Community-Based Social Capital and Educational Performance: Exploring New Evidence." Harvard University Graduate School of Education and Kennedy School of Government.

Brandl, John E. 1998. "Civic Values in Public and Private Schools." In *Learning from School Choice*, ed. Paul E. Peterson and Bryan C. Hassell. Washington, D.C.: Brookings Institution Press.

Branson, Margaret S. 1998. "The Role of Civic Education." Center for Civic Education, Calabasas, Calif. http://www.civiced.org/articles_role (accessed December 10, 2005).

Brawner, Marilyn R. 1973. "Migration and Educational Achievement of Mexican Americans." *Social Science Quarterly* 53:727–37.

Brent, George, and Nicholas DiObilda. 1993. "Effects of Curriculum Alignment versus Direct Instruction on Urban Children." *Journal of Educational Research* 86:333–38.

Brewer, K.R.W. 1963. "Ratio Estimation and Finite Populations: Some Results Deducible from the Assumption of an Underlying Stochastic Process." *Australian Journal of Statistics* 15:145–52.

Bridge, Gary. 1978. "Information Imperfections: The Achilles' Heel of Entitlement Plans." *School Review* 86:504–29.

Bridge, Gary R., and Julie Blackman. 1978. *A Study of Alternatives in American Education.* Family Choice in Schooling Series, vol. 4. Santa Monica, Calif.: RAND.

Brookings Greater Washington Research Program and 21st Century School Fund. 2004. *DC Public School And Public Charter School Capital Budget Project. Task 3 Report.* Washington, D.C.: Brookings Institution.

Brooks-Gunn, Jeanne, Greg J. Duncan, and J. L. Aber. 1997. *Neighborhood Poverty.* New York: Russell Sage Foundation.

Brown, Heath, Jeffrey Henig, Natalie Lacireno-Paquet, and Thomas Holyoke. 2003. "Scale of Operations and Locus of Control in Market- vs. Mission-Oriented Charter Schools." Presented at the Annual Research Conference of the Association of Public Policy and Management, Washington, D.C.

Bryk, Anthony. S., Valerie. E. Lee, and Peter. B. Holland. 1993. *Catholic Schools and the Common Good.* Cambridge, Mass.: Harvard University Press.

Bryk, Anthony S., and Barbara Schneider. 2002. *Trust in Schools.* New York: Russell Sage Foundation.

Bryk, Anthony S., Penny A. Sebring, and Sharon G. Rollow. 1998. *Charting Chicago School Reform: Democratic Localism as a Lever for Change.* Boulder, Colo.: Westview Press.

Bryson, Alex, Richard Dorsett, and Susan Purdon. 2002. "The Use of Propensity Score Matching in the Evaluation of Active Labour Market Policies." Working Paper No. 4, Policy Studies Institute, U.K. Department of Work and Pensions.

Buckley, Jack, and Mark Schneider. 2003. "Making the Grade: Comparing D.C. Charter Schools to Other D.C. Public Schools." *Educational Evaluation and Policy Analysis* 25(2).

———. 2004. "Charter Schools as a Tool to Reform Local Schools by Transforming Governance." In *Metropolitan Governance*, ed. R. C. Feiock, 183–211. Washington, D.C.: Georgetown University Press.

———. 2005. "School Choice, Parental Information, and Tiebout Sorting: Evidence from Washington, D.C." Paper presented at the Lincoln Institute for Land Policy and the Rockefeller Center for Public Policy and Social Sciences Tiebout at 50 Conference. Hanover, N.H. June 26–28.

Buddin, Richard J., Joseph J. Cordes, and Sheila Nataraj Kirby. 1998. "School Choice in California: Who Chooses Private Schools?" *Journal of Urban Economics* 44:110–34.

Bulkley, Katrina, and Jennifer Fisher. 2002. "A Decade of Charter Schools: From Theory to Practice." *CPRE Policy Briefs*, April.

Burns, Nancy, and Donald Kinder. 2000. "Social Trust and Democratic Politics." Report to the National Election Studies Board, Based on the 2000 NES Special Topic Pilot Study. ftp://ftp.nes.isr.umich.edu/ftp/resourcs/psreport/2000pilot/burns2000.pdf (accessed May 22, 2003).

Burt, Ronald S. 1992. *Structural Holes: The Social Structure of Competition.* Cambridge, Mass.: Harvard University Press.

Burtless, Gary, ed. 1996. *Does Money Matter? The Effect of School Resources on Student Achievement and Adult Success.* Washington, D.C.: Brookings Institution Press.

Campbell, Andrea L. 2000. "The Third Rail of American Politics: Senior Citizen Activism and the American Welfare State." Ph.D. diss., University of California, Berkeley.

Campbell, Angus, Philip E. Converse, Warren E. Miller, and Donald E. Stokes. 1960. *The American Voter*. New York: John Wiley.

Campbell, Angus, Gerald Gurin, and Warren E. Miller. 1972. *The Voter Decides*. Westport, Conn.: Greenwood.

———. 2002. "The Civic Side of School Reform: How Do School Vouchers Affect Civic Education?" Working Paper No. 4., Program In American Democracy, University of Notre Dame.

———. 2001. "Bowling Together: Private Schools, Serving Public Ends." *Education Next*, Fall, 55–61.

Campbell, David E. 2000. "Making Democratic Education Work: Schools, Social Capital And Civic Education." Harvard University Program on Education Policy and Governance.

Carlin, Bradley P., and Thomas A. Louis. 2000. *Bayes and Empirical Bayes Methods for Data Analysis*. 2nd ed. Boca Raton, Fla.: CRC/Chapman and Hall.

Carnegie Foundation for the Advancement of Teaching. 1992. *School Choice*. Menlo Park, Calif.: Carnegie Foundation for the Advancement of Teaching.

Carnoy, Martin. 2000. *Sustaining the New Economy: Work, Family, and Community in the Information Age*. Cambridge, Mass.: Harvard University Press.

Carnoy, Martin, Rebecca Jacobsen, Lawrence Mishel, and Richard Rothstein. 2005. *The Charter School Dust-Up: Examining the Evidence on Enrollment and Achievement*. New York: Teachers College Press.

Carver, Rebecca L., and Laura H. Salganik. 1991. "You Can't Have Choice Without Information." *Equity and Choice* 7 (2–3): 71–75.

Cassel, C. M., C. E. Sarndal, and J. H. Wretman.1983. "Some Uses of Statistical Models In Connection with the Nonresponse Problem." In *Incomplete Data in Sample Surveys*, vol. 3, *Symposium on Incomplete Data, Proceedings*, ed. W. G. Madow and I. Olkin. New York: Academic Press.

Casella, Alessandra, and James E. Rauch. 2002. "Anonymous Market and Group Ties in International Trade." *Journal of International Economics* 58 (1): 19–47.

Center for Education Reform. 2004. *Charter Achievement Questioned . . . and Answered*. Washington, D.C.: Center for Education Reform.

———. 2006. "Charter Schools." http://www.edreform.com/index.cfm?fuseAction =stateStatsandpSectionID=15andcSectionID=44 (accessed April 26, 2006).

Chatterji, Madhabi. 2004. "Good and Bad News About Florida Student Achievement: Performance Trends on Multiple Indicators Since Passage of the A+ Legislation." Arizona State University, Education Policy Studies Laboratory.

Chubb, John E., and Terry. M. Moe. 1990. *Politics, Markets, and America's Schools*. Washington, D.C.: Brookings Institution Press.

Cleveland, Warren S. 1979. "Robust Locally Weighted Regression and Smoothing Scatterplots." *Journal of the American Statistical Association* 74:829–36.

Clotfelter, Charles T. 1976. "Detroit Decision and White Flight." *Journal of Legal Studies* 5:99–113.

Cobb, Casey D., and Gene V. Glass. 1999. "Ethnic Segregation in Arizona Charter Schools." *Education Policy Analysis Archives* 7(1), http://epaa.asu.edu/epaa/ v7n1/ (accessed March 1, 2003).

Cochran, W. G. 1946. "Relative Accuracy of Systematic and Stratified Random Samples for a Certain Class of Populations." *Annals of Mathematical Statistics* 17:164–77.

Cohen, David K., Stephen W. Raudenbush, and Deborah Loewenberg Ball. 2003. "Resources, Instruction, and Research." *Educational Evaluation and Policy Analysis* 25(2): 119–42.

Cohen, Joel, and Dipankar Chakrovarti. 1990. "Consumer Psychology." *Annual Review of Psychology* 41:243–88.

Coleman, James S. 1961. *The Adolescent Society: The Social Life of the Teenager and its Impact on Education*. New York: Free Press.

Coleman, James S. 1988. "Social Capital in the Creation of Human Capital." *American Journal of Sociology* 94:S95-S120.

Coleman, James S., and Thomas Hoffer. 1987. *Public and Private High Schools: The Impact of Communities*. New York: Basic Books.

Coleman, James S., Thomas Hoffer, and Sally Kilgore. 1982. *High School Achievement: Public, Catholic, and Private Schools Compared*. New York: Basic Books.

Congdon, Peter. 2001. *Bayesian Statistical Modeling*. Chichester, England: John Wiley.

Converse, Philip E. 1964. "The Nature of Belief Systems in Mass Publics." In *Ideology and Discontent*," ed. D. Apter. New York: John Wiley.

———. 1975. "Public Opinion and Voting Behavior. In *Handbook of Political Science*," ed. F. I. Greenstein and N. W. Polsby. Reading, Pa.: Addison Wesley.

———. 1990. "Popular Representation and the Distribution of Information." In *Information and Democratic Processes*, ed. J. A. Ferejohn and H. Kuklinski. Urbana: University of Illinois Press.

Cook, Thomas. 2002. "Randomized Experiments in Educational Policy Research." *Educational Evaluation and Policy Analysis* 24:175–99.

Cooksey, Ray W. 1996. *Judgment Analysis: Theory, Methods and Applications*. San Diego, Calif.: Academic Press.

Cookson, Peter W. 1992. *The Choice Controversy*. Newbury Park, Calif.: Corwin Press.

Cookson, Peter, and Kristina Berger. 2002. *Expect Miracles: Charter Schools and the Politics of Hope and Despair*. Boulder, Colo.: Westview Press.

Coons, John E, and Stephen D. Sugarman. 1978. *Education by Choice: The Case for Family Control*. Berkeley: University of California Press.

Cortes, Ernesto J., Jr. 1996. "Community Organization and Social Capital." *National Civic Review* 85 (Fall): 49–53.

Corwin, Ronald, and John Flaherty, eds. 1995. *Freedom and Innovation in California's Charter Schools*. San Francisco, Calif.: WestEd.

Cotton, Kathleen. 1996. "School Size, School Climate, and Student Performance." Northwest Regional Education Laboratory, http://www.nwrel.org/scpd/sirs/10/c020.html (accessed July 3, 2002).

———. 2001. *New Small Learning Communities: Findings from Recent Research*. Portland, Ore.: Northwest Regional Education Laboratory. http://www.nwrel.org/scpd/sirs/nslc.pdf. (accessed July 3, 2002).

Cuban, Larry. 2004. *The Blackboard and the Bottom Line: Why Schools Can't Be Businesses.* Cambridge, Mass.: Harvard University Press.

Cummings, R., D. Brookshire, and W. Schulze. 1986. *Valuing Environmental Goods: An Assessment of the Contingent Valuation Method.* Totowa, N.J.: Rowman and Allanheld.

Dahlberg, L. 2001. "The Habermasian Public Sphere Encounters Cyber-Reality." Paper presented at EURICOM Colloquium, Piran.

DC Appleseed Center. 2001. *Charter Schools in the District of Columbia: Improving Systems for Accountability, Autonomy, and Competition.* Washington, D.C.: DC Appleseed Center.

Dehejia, Rajeev H., and Sadek Wahba. 1999. "Causal Effects in Nonexperimental Studies: Reevaluation of the Evaluation of Training Programs. *Journal of the American Statistical Association* 94:1043–62.

———. 2002. "Propensity Score Matching Methods for Non-Experimental Causal Studies." *Review of Economics and Statistics* 84:151–61.

Delli Carpini, Michael X., and Scott Keeter. 1996. *What Americans Know about Politics and Why it Matters.* New Haven: Yale University Press.

Dewey, John, and Jo Ann Boydston. 1976. *The Middle Works, 1899–1924.* Carbondale: Southern Illinois University Press.

Dhami, Mandeep K., Ralph Hertwig, and Ulrich Hoffrage. 2004. "The Role of Representative Design in an Ecological Approach to Cognition." *Psychological Bulletin* 130:959–88.

DiMaggio, Paul, Eszter Hargittai, W. Russell Neuman, and John P. Robinson. 2001. "Social Implications of the Internet." *Annual Review of Sociology* 27:307–36.

DiPrete, T. A., and M. Gangl. 2004. "Assessing Bias in the Estimation of Causal Effects: Rosenbaum Bounds on Matching Estimators and Instrumental Variables Estimation with Imperfect Instruments." Discussion paper SP I 2004–101. Wissenschaftszentrum Berlin für Sozialforschung.

Dowding, Keith, Peter John, and Stephen Biggs. 1994. "Tiebout: A Survey of the Empirical Literature." *Urban Studies* 31:767–97.

Downs, Anthony. 1957. *An Economic Theory of Democracy.* New York: Harper Collins.

Driscoll, Mary. 1993. "Choice, Achievement, and School Community." In *School Choice: Examining the Evidence*, ed. Edith Rassell and Richard Rothstein. Washington, D.C.: Economic Policy Institute.

Duke, David, and Sara Trautvetter. 2001. "Reducing the Negative Effects of Large Schools." National Clearinghouse for Educational Facilities, http://www.edfacilities.org/pubs/size.html (accessed July 3, 2002).

Edwards, Ward. 1954. "The Theory of Decision Making." *Psychological Bulletin* 51:380–417.

Efron, Bradley, and Robert J. Tibshirani. 1996. *An Introduction to the Bootstrap.* Boca Raton, Fla.: Chapman and Hall.

Egelson, Paula, Patrick Harman and Charles M. Achilles. 1996. *Does Class Size Make a Difference? Recent Findings from State and District Initiatives.* ED 398644.Washington, D.C.: ERIC Clearinghouse.

Eggertsson, Thrain. 1994. *Economic Behavior and Institutions: Principles of Neo-institutional Economics*. Cambridge: Cambridge University Press.

Ehman, Lee H. 1980. "The American School in the Political Socialization Process." *Review of Educational Research*, 50 (1): 99–119.

Elmore, Richard F. 1991. "Public School Choice as a Policy Issue." In *Privatization and Its Alternatives*, ed. William T. Gormley, 55–78. Madison: University of Wisconsin Press.

Elmore, Richard. F., C. H. Abelmann, and Susan H. Furhman. 1996. "The New Accountability in State Education Reform: From Process to Performance." In *Holding Schools Accountable: Performance-Based Reform in Education*, ed. H. F. Ladd, 65–98. Washington, D.C.: Brookings Institution Press.

Enslin, Penny, and Patricia White. 2002. "Democratic Citizenship." In *The Blackwell Guide to the Philosophy of Education*, ed. N. Blake, P. Smeyers, R. Smith, and P. Standish. Oxford: Blackwell.

Epple, Dennis, and Roberta E. Romano. 1998. "Competition between Private and Public Schools, Vouchers, and Peer-Group Effects." *American Economic Review* 88 (1): 33–62.

Ericsson, Anders K., and Herbert A. Simon. 1984. *Protocol Analysis: Verbal Reports as Data*. Cambridge, Mass.: MIT Press.

Erikson, Donald. 1982. "The British Columbia Story: Antecedents and Consequences of Aid to Private Schools." Institute for the Study of Private Schools, Los Angeles.

———. 1986. "Choice and Private Schools: Dynamics of Supply and Demand." In *Private Education: Studies in Choice and Public Policy*, ed. Daniel C. Levy. New York: Oxford University Press.

Fazio, Russell. H., David M. Sanbonmatsu, Michael C. Powell, and Frank R. Kardes. 1986. "On the Automatic Activation of Attitudes." *Journal of Personality and Social Psychology* 50:229–38.

Fazio, Russell H., and Carol J. Williams. 1986. "Attitude Accessibility as a Moderator of the Attitude-Perception and Attitude-Behavior Relations—an Investigation of the 1984 Presidential Election." *Journal of Personality and Social Psychology* 51:505–14.

Feick, Lawrence F, and Linda L. Price. 1987. "The Market Maven: A Diffuser of Marketplace Information." *Journal of Marketing* 51:83–97.

Ferguson, Ronald F. 1991. "Paying for Public Education: New Evidence on How And Why Money Matters." *Harvard Journal on Legislation*, 28 (2): 465–98.

Ferguson, Ronald F., and Helen Ladd. 1996. "Additional Evidence on How and Why Money Matters: A Production Function Analysis of Alabama Schools." In *Holding Schools Accountable: Performance-Based Reform in Education*, ed. Helen F. Ladd. Washington, D.C.: Brookings Institution Press.

Fetterman, David M. 1982. "Ibsen's Baths: Reactivity and Insensitivity (A Misapplication of the Treatment-Control Design in a National Evaluation)." *Educational Evaluation and Policy Analysis* 4 (3): 261–79.

Figlio, David, and Lawrence S. Getzler. 2002. "Accountability, Ability and Disability: Gaming the System." NBER Working Paper No. 9307.

Figlio David, and Mel Lucas. 2004. "What's in a Grade? School Report Cards and the Housing Market," *American Economic Review* 94 (3): 591–604.

Finn, Chester E. 2003. "The Least-Known Side of Charter Schools." *Education Gadfly* 3 (20), June 5, http://www.fordhaminstitute.org/institute/gadfly/issue.cfm?id=25&edition=.

Finn, Chester E., Jr., Bruno V. Manno, Louann A. Bierlein, and Gregg Vanourek. 1997. *Charter Schools in Action: Final Report*. Washington, D.C.: Hudson Institute.

Finn, Chester E., Jr., Bruno V. Manno, and Gregg Vanourek. 2000. *Charter Schools in Action*. Princeton, N.J.: Princeton University Press.

———. 2001. "Getting Charter Schools Started: Seven Songs of Woe and Ways to Overcome Them." *Texas Education Review* (Winter).

Fischel, William A. 2001. *The Homevoter Hypothesis: How Home Values Influence Local Government Taxation, School Finance, and Land-Use Policies*. Cambridge, Mass.: Harvard University Press.

Fiske, Edward B., and Helen F. Ladd. 2000. *When Schools Compete: A Cautionary Tale*. Washington, D.C.: Brookings Institution Press.

Fiske, Susan T., and Shelley E. Taylor. 1991. *Social Cognition*. New York: McGraw-Hill.

Fitchen, Janet M. 1994. "Residential Mobility among the Rural Poor." *Rural Sociology* 59 (3): 416–36.

Folger, John, and Carolyn Breda. 1989. "Evidence From Project STAR about Class Size And Student Achievement." *Peabody Journal of Education* 67 (1): 17–33.

Ford, J. Kevin, Neal Schmitt, Susa L. Schectman, Brian M. Hults, and Mary L. Doherty. 1989. "Process Tracing Methods: Contributions, Problems and Neglected Research Questions." *Organizational Behavior and Human Decision Processes* 43:75–117.

Fossey, Richard. 1994. "Open Enrollment in Massachusetts: Why Families Choose." *Educational Evaluation and Policy Analysis* 16 (3): 320–34.

Fowler, William. J., Jr., and Herbert J. Walberg, 1991. "School Size, Characteristics, and Outcomes." *Educational Evaluation and Policy Analysis* 13 (2): 189–202.

Friedman, Milton. 1955. "The Role of Government in Education." In *Economics and the Public Interest*, ed. R. A. Solo. New Brunswick, N.J.: Rutgers University Press.

———. 1962. *Capitalism and Freedom*. Chicago: University of Chicago Press.

Frisch, Deborah, and Robert T. Clemen. 1994. "Beyond Expected Utility: Rethinking Behavioral Decision Research." *Psychological Bulletin* 116:46–54.

Fukuyama, Francis. 1995. *Trust: The Social Virtues and the Creation of Prosperity*. New York: Free Press.

Fuller, Bruce. 2000a. "Introduction: Growing Charter Schools, Decentering the State." In *Inside Charter Schools: The Paradox of Radical Decentralization*, ed. Bruce Fuller, 1–11. Cambridge, Mass.: Harvard University Press.

Fuller, Bruce. 2000b. "The Public Square, Big or Small? Charter Schools in Political Context." In *Inside Charter Schools: The Paradox of Radical Decentralization*, ed. Bruce Fuller, 12–65. Cambridge, Mass.: Harvard University Press.

Galston, William A. 2001. "Political Knowledge, Political Engagement, and Civic Education." *Annual Review of Political Science* 4:217–34.

Galston, William A. 2004. "Civic Education and Political Participation." *PS— Political Science & Politics* 37:263–266.

Gau, Rebecca. 2006. *Trends in Charter School Authorizing.* Washington, D.C.: Thomas B. Fordham Institute.

Gauri, Varun. 1998. *School Choice in Chile: Two Decades of Educational Reform.* Pittsburgh, Pa.: University of Pittsburgh Press.

Gelman, Andrew, John B. Carlin, Hal S. Stern, and Donald B. Rubin. 1995. *Bayesian Data Analysis.* London: Chapman and Hall.

Geweke, J. 1992. "Evaluating the Accuracy of Sampling-Based Approaches to Calculating Posterior Moments." In *Bayesian Statistics 4*, ed. J. M. Bernardo, J. O. Berger, A. P. Dawid, and A. F. M. Smith, 169–93. Oxford: Clarendon Press.

Gilens, Martin. 2001. "Political Ignorance and Collective Policy Preferences." *American Political Science Review* 95:379–96.

Gill, Brian P., and S. L. Schlossman. 2003. "A Nation at Rest: The American Way of Homework." *Educational Evaluation and Policy Analysis* 25 (3): 319–37.

Gill, Brian P., P. Michael Timpane, Karen E. Ross, and Dominic J. Brewer. 2001. *Rhetoric versus Reality: What We Know and What We Need to Know about Vouchers and Charter Schools.* Santa Monica, Calif.: Rand Corporation.

Gill, Jeff. 2001. "Whose Variance Is It Anyway? Interpreting Empirical Models with State-Level Data." *State Politics and Policy Quarterly* 1 (3): 318–39.

———. 2002. *Bayesian Methods: A Social and Behavioral Sciences Approach.* Boca Raton, Fla.: CRC / Chapman and Hall.

Gladwell, Malcolm. 2000. *The Tipping Point.* Boston: Back Bay Books.

Glazerman, Steven. 1997. "A Conditional Logit Model of Elementary School Choice: What Do Parents Value?" University of Chicago, Harris School of Public Policy.

Glenn, Charles. 1988. *The Myth of the Common School.* Amherst: University of Massachusetts Press.

Godwin, R. Kenneth, Jennifer W. Godwin, and Valerie Martinez-Ebers. 2004. "Civic Socialization in Public and Fundamentalist Schools." *Social Science Quarterly* 85 (5): 1097–111.

Goldhaber, Dan D., and Emily Anthony. 2003. "Indicators of Teacher Quality. ERIC Digest." ERIC Clearinghouse on Urban Education, New York.

Goldhaber, Dan D., and Eric R. Eide. 2003. "Methodological Thoughts on Measuring the Impact of Private Sector Competition on the Educational Marketplace." *Educational Evaluation and Policy Analysis* 25 (2): 217–32.

Goldin, Claudia, and Lawrence F. Katz. 2003. "The 'Virtues' of the Past: Education in the First Hundred Years of the New Republic." Working Paper 9958. National Bureau of Economic Research, Cambridge, Mass.

Goldring, Ellen B., and Rina Shapira. 1993. "Choice, Empowerment, and Involvement: What Satisfies Parents?" *Educational Evaluation and Policy Analysis* 15:396–409.

Goldsmith, Ronald E., Leisa R. Flynn, and Elizabeth B. Goldsmith. 2003. "The Market Maven." *Journal of Marketing Theory and Practice* 11:54–64.

Gormley, William, and David L. Weimer. 1999. *Organizational Report Cards.* Cambridge, Mass.: Harvard University Press.

Government Accountability Office. 2003. *Charter Schools: New Charter Schools across the Country and in the District of Columbia Face Similar Start-Up Challenges.* Washington, D.C.: GAO.

Granovetter, Mark. 1973. "Strength of Weak Ties." *American Journal of Sociology* 78:1360–80.

Greenberger, Scott. 2004a. "House Targets Charter Schools, Seeks Moratorium on New Approvals." *Boston Globe*, April 29, 3rd ed., sec. B.

———. 2004b. "Romney Backed on Charter Schools, Veto Sustained on Moratorium." *Boston Globe*, July 21, sec. A.

Greene, Jay P. 1998. "Civic Values in Public and Private Schools." In *Learning from School Choice*, ed. P. E. Peterson and B. Hassel. Washington, D.C.: Brookings Institution Press.

———. 2000a. "The Effect of School Choice: An Evaluation of the Charlotte Children's Scholarship Fund." Manhattan Institute Civic Report 12, http://www.manhattan-institute.org/html/cr_12a.htm (accessed May 26, 2005).

———. 2000b. "Civic Education (Book Reviews)." *Social Science Quarterly* 81 (2): 696–98.

Greene, Jay P., William G. Howell, and Paul E. Peterson. 1998. "Lessons from the Cleveland Scholarship Program." In *Learning from School Choice*, ed. P. E. Peterson and B. C. Hassel. Washington, D.C.: Brookings Institution Press.

Greenwald, Rob, Larry. V. Hedges, and Richard D. Laine. 1996. "The Effect of School Resources on Student Achievement." *Review of Educational Research* 66 (3): 361–96.

Gutmann, Amy. 1987. *Democratic Education.* Princeton, N.J.: Princeton University Press.

Hahn, G. 2000. "Weighting GLMs—Solution." *BUGS Archives* 110, http://www.jiscmail.ac.uk/cgi-bin/wa.exe?A2=ind00&L=BUGS&P=R7919&I=-3 (accessed December 10, 2005).

Hale, Matthew, Juliet Musso and Christopher Weare. 1999. "Developing Digital Democracy: Evidence from California Municipal Web Pages." In *Digital Democracy*, ed. B. N. Hague and B. D. Loader, 96–115. London: Routledge.

Hallinan, Maureen T., ed. 1994. *Restructuring* Schools. New York: Plenum Press.

Hammond, Kenneth R., Thomas R. Stewart, Berndt Brehmer, and Do Steinmann. 1975. "Social Judgment Theory." In *Human Judgment and Decision Processes*, ed. M. Kaplan and S. Schwartz. New York: Academic Press.

Haney, Walt. 2000. "The Myth of the Texas Miracle in Education." *Educational Policy Analysis Archives* 8 (41), http://epaa.asu.edu/epaa/v8n41/ (accessed January 12, 2004).

Hanushek, Eric A. 1997. "Assessing the Effects of School Resources on Student Performance: An Update." *Educational Evaluation and Policy Analysis* 19:141–64.

———. 1999. "Some Findings from an Independent Investigation of the Tennessee STAR Experiment and from Other Investigations of Class Size Effects." *Educational Evaluation and Policy Analysis* 21 (2): 143–63.

Hanushek, Eric A., John F. Kain, Jacob M. Markman, and Steven G. Rivkin. 2003. "Does Peer Ability Affect Student Achievement?" *Journal of Applied Econometrics* 18 (5): 527–44.

Hartley, H. O., and R. L. Sielken. 1975. "A 'Super-Population Viewpoint' for Finite Population Sampling." *Biometrics* 31:411–22.

Hassel, Bryan C. 1999. *The Charter School Challenge.* Washington, D.C.: Brookings Institution Press.

Hassel, Bryan, and Meagan Batdorff. 2004. *High-Stakes: Findings from a National Study of Life-or-Death Decisions by Charter School Authorizers.* Chapel Hill, N.C.: Public Impact.

Hausman, Jerry A. and William E. Taylor. 1981. "Panel Data and Unobservable Individual Effects." *Econometrica* 49:1377–98.

Heckman, James J. 1979. "Sample Selection Bias as a Specification Error." *Econometrica* 47:153–61.

Heckman, James J., Hidehiko Ichimura, and Petra E. Todd. 1997. "Matching as an Econometric Evaluation Estimator: Evidence from Evaluating a Job Training Program." *Review of Economic Studies* 64:605–54.

Heckman, James J., and Jeffrey A. Smith. 1995. "Assessing the Case for Social Experiments." *Journal of Economic Perspectives* 9:85–110.

Heidelberger, P., and P. D. Welch. 1983. "Simulation Run Length Control in the Presence of an Initial Transient." *Operations Research* 21:1109–44.

Hemker, Bas T., Klass Sijtsma, and I. W. Molenaar. 1995. "Selection of Unidimensional Scales From a Multidimensional Item Bank in the Polytomous Mokken IRT Model." *Applied Psychological Measurement* 19 (4): 337–52.

Henderson, Anne T., ed. 1987. *The Evidence Continues to Grow: Parent Involvement Improves Student Achievement: An Annotated Bibliography.* Columbia, Md.: National Committee for Citizens in Education.

Henig, Jeffrey R. 1990. "Choice in Public Schools: An Analysis of Transfer Requests among Magnet Schools." *Social Science Quarterly* 71 (1): 69–82.

———. 1994. *Rethinking School Choice: Limits of the Market Metaphor.* Princeton, N.J.: Princeton University Press.

———. 1996. "The Local Dynamics of Choice: Ethnic Preferences and Institutional Responses." In *Who Chooses? Who Loses? Culture, Institutions and the Unequal Effects of School Choice,* ed. B. Fuller, R. F. Elmore, and G. Orfield. New York: Teachers College Press.

Henig, Jeffrey, Thomas T. Holyoke, Natalie Lacireno-Paquet, and Michele Moser. 2001. *Growing Pains: An Evaluation of Charter Schools in the District of Columbia, 1999–2000.* Washington, D.C.: Center for Washington Area Studies, George Washington University.

Henig, Jeffrey, and Jason MacDonald. 2002. "Locational Decisions of Charter Schools: Probing the Market Metaphor." *Social Science Quarterly* 83 (4): 962–80.

Henig, Jeffrey, Michele Moser, Thomas T. Holyoke, and Natalie Lacireno-Paquet. 1999. *Making a Choice, Making a Difference? An Evaluation of Charter Schools in the District of Columbia.* Washington, D.C.: Center for Washington Area Studies, George Washington University.

Hess, Frederick. 1999. *Spinning Wheels: The Politics of Urban School Reform.* Washington, D.C.: Brookings Institution Press.

Hill, Paul, Gail E. Foster, and Tamar Gendler. 1990. *High Schools with Character.* Santa Monica, Calif.: RAND Corporation.

Hill, Paul, and Robin Lake. 2002. *Charter Schools and Accountability in Public Education.* Washington, D.C.: Brookings Institution Press.

Hill, Paul, Robin Lake, Mary Beth Celio, Christine Campbell, Paul Herdman, and Katrina Bulkley. 2001. *A Study of Charter School Accountability: National Charter School Accountability Study.* Washington, D.C.: U.S. Department of Education, Office of Educational Research and Improvement.

Hill, Paul, Lawrence C. Pierce, and James W. Guthrie. 1997. *Reinventing Public Education.* Chicago: University of Chicago Press.

Hirano, Keisuke, and Guido Imbens. 2001. "Estimation of Causal Effects Using Propensity Score Weighting: An Application to Right Heart Catheterization." *Health Services and Outcomes Research Methodology* 2:259–78.

Hirschman, Albert O. 1970. *Exit, Voice, and Loyalty.* Cambridge, Mass.: Harvard University Press.

Hochschild, Jennifer, and Nathan Scovronick. 2003. *The American Dream and the Public Schools.* New York: Oxford University Press.

Hoffer, Thomas, Andrew M. Greeley, and James S. Coleman. 1985. "Achievement Growth in Public and Catholic Schools." *Sociology of Education* 58:74–97.

Hogarth, Robin M. 1987. *Judgment and Choice: The Psychology of Decision.* Chichester, England: John Wiley.

Hogarth, Robin M. 2001. *Educating Intuition.* Chicago: University of Chicago Press.

Holland, Paul W., and Howard Wainer. 1993. *Differential Item Functioning.* Hillsdale, N.J.: Lawrence Erlbaum.

Holyoak, K. J., and B. A. Spellman. 1993. "Thinking." *Annual Review of Psychology* 44:265–315.

Honaker, James, Anne Joseph, Gary King, Kenneth Scheve, and Naunihal Singh. 1999. "Amelia: A Program for Missing Data." Harvard University, Center for Basic Research in the Social Sciences.

Hotelling, Harold. 1931. "The Generalization of Student's Ratio." *Annals of Mathematical Statistics* 2:360–78.

Howell, William. 2004a. "Dynamic Selection Effects in Urban, Means-Tested School Voucher Programs." *Journal of Policy Analysis and Management* 22:225–50.

———. 2004b. "Parents, Choice, and Some Foundations for Education Reform in Massachusetts." Pioneer Institute for Public Policy, Boston, Mass.

Howell, William G., and Paul E. Peterson. 2000. "School Choice in Washington, D.C.: An Evaluation after One Year." Program on Education Policy and Governance, Harvard University.

———. 2002. *The Education Gap: Vouchers and Urban Schools.* Washington, D.C.: Brookings Institution Press.

Howell, William G., Paul E. Peterson, and Martin R. West. 2004. "Dog Eats AFT Homework." *Wall Street Journal,* August 18.

Howley, Charles, Martin Strange, and Richard Bickel. 2000. "Research about School Size and School Performance in Impoverished Communities." ERIC Clearinghouse on Rural Education and Small Schools, December.

Hoxby, Caroline M. 1997. "Does Competition among Public Schools Benefit Students and Taxpayers?" NBER Working Paper Series, no. 4978. National Bureau of Economic Research, Cambridge, Mass.

———. 2000a. "Peer Effects in the Classroom." NBER Working Paper Series, no. 7867. National Bureau of Economic Research, Cambridge, Mass.

———. 2000b. "The Effects of Class Size on Student Achievement: New Evidence from Population Variation." *Quarterly Journal of Economics* (November): 1239–84.

———. 2000c. "Does Competition among Public Schools Benefit Students and Taxpayers?" *American Economic Review* 90:1209–38.

———. 2003. "School Choice and School Productivity: Could School Choice Be a Tide that Lifts all Boats?" In *The Economics of School Choice*, ed. Caroline M. Hoxby, 287–341. Chicago: University of Chicago Press.

———. 2004. "A Straightforward Comparison of Charter Schools and Regular Public Schools in the United States," http://post.economics.harvard.edu/faculty /hoxby/papers/hoxbycharters.pdf (accessed September 10, 2004).

Hsu, Spencer S., and Justin Blum. 2004. "D.C. School Vouchers Win Final Approval." *Washington Post*. January 23.

Huber, P. J. 1967. "The Behavior of Maximum-Likelihood Estimates Under Non-Standard Conditions." In *Proceedings of the Fifth Berkeley Symposium on Mathematical Statistics and Probability*, 221–23. Berkeley: University of California Press.

Huckfeldt, Robert, and John Sprague. 1995. *Citizens, Politics and Social Communication*. New York: Cambridge University Press.

Huerta, Luis A. 2000. "Losing Public Accountability: A Home Schooling Charter." In *Inside Charter Schools: The Radical Paradox of Decentralization*, ed. Bruce Fuller, 177–202. Cambridge, Mass.: Harvard University Press.

Hyman, Herbert H. 1959. *Political Socialization*. Glencoe, Ill.: Free Press.

Ingersoll, Gary M., James P. Scamman, and Wayne D. Eckerling. 1989. "Geographic Mobility and Student Achievement in an Urban Setting." *Educational Evaluation and Policy Analysis* 11 (2): 143–49.

Ingram, Helen, and Anne L. Schneider. 1995. "Social Construction (Continued)—Response." *American Political Science Review* 89 (2): 441–46.

Jackman, Simon. 2000. "Estimation and Inference via Bayesian Simulation." *American Journal of Political Science* 44 (2): 375–404.

Jacob, Brian, and Steven Levitt. 2003. "Rotten Apples: An Investigation of the Prevalence and Predictors of Teacher Cheating." NBER Working Paper no. w9413. National Bureau of Economic Research, Cambridge, Mass.

Janis, Irving L. 1989. *Crucial Decisions: Leadership in Policymaking and Crisis Management*. New York: Free Press.

Janis, Irving L., and Leon Mann. 1977. *Decision Making: A Psychological Theory of Conflict, Choice and Commitment*. New York: Free Press.

Jefferson, Thomas. 1853. *Notes on the State of Virginia*. Richmond, Va.: J. W. Randolph.

Jeffreys, Harold. 1946. "An Invariant Form for the Prior Probability in Estimation Problems." *Proceedings of the Royal Society* A 186:453–61.

Jennings, M. Kent. 2002. "Generation Units and the Student Protest Movement in the United States: An Intra- And Intergenerational Analysis." *Political Psychology* 23:303–24.

Johnson, Kirk. 2000. "Do Small Classes Influence Academic Achievement? What the National Assessment of Educational Progress Shows." Center for Data Analysis Report 00–07. Heritage Foundation, Washington, D.C.

Jones, Bryan D. 2001. *Politics and the Architecture of Choice*. Chicago: University of Chicago Press.

Kahneman, Daniel, Paul Slovic, and Amos Tversky. 1982. *Judgment under Uncertainty: Heuristics and Biases*. New York: Cambridge University Press.

Kahneman, Daniel, and Amos Tversky. 1979. "Prospect Theory: An Analysis of Decision under Risk." *Econometrica* 47:263–91.

Kane, Thomas. J., and Douglas O. Staiger. 2002. "The Promise and Pitfalls of Using Imprecise School Accountability Measures." *Journal of Economic Perspectives* 16 (4): 91–114.

Kardes, Frank R. 1994. "Consumer Judgment and Decision Processes." In *Handbook of Social Cognition*, ed. R. S. Wyer and T. K. Srull. Hillsdale, N.J.: Lawrence Erlbaum.

Katona, George, and Eva Mueller. 1955. "A Study of Purchase Decisions in Consumer Behavior." in *Consumer Behavior*, ed. L. Clark. New York: NYU Press.

Keeney, Ralph L., and Howard Raiffa. 1976. *Decisions with Multiple Objectives: Preferences and Values Tradeoffs*. New York: John Wiley.

Kelling, George, and Catherine Coles. 1996. *Fixing Broken Windows: Restoring Order and Reducing Crime in Our Communities*. New York: Free Press.

Kelling, George, and James Q. Wilson. 1982. "Broken Windows: The Police and Neighborhood Safety." *Atlantic Monthly*, March.

Kinder, Donald R. 1998. "Opinion and Action in the Realm of Politics." In *Handbook of Social Psychology*, ed. Daniel T. Gilbert, Susan T. Fiske, and Gardner Lindzey. New York: McGraw-Hill.

King, Gary, James Honaker, Anne Joseph, and Kenneth Scheve. 1998. "Listwise Deletion is Evil: What to Do about Missing Data in Political Science," http://polmeth.wustl.edu/retrieve.php?id=301 (accessed September 15, 2000).

King, Gary, Michael Tomz, and Jason Wittenberg. 2000. "Making the Most of Statistical Analyses: Improving Interpretation and Presentation." *American Journal of Political Science* 44:347–61.

King, Gary, James Honaker, Anne Joseph, and Kenneth Scheve. 2001. "Analyzing Incomplete Political Science Data: An Alternative Algorithm for Multiple Imputation." *American Political Science Review* 95 (1): 49–69.

King, Gary, Christopher J. L. Murray, Joshua A. Salomon, and Ajay Tandon. 2003. "Enhancing the Validity and Cross-Cultural Comparability of Survey Research." *American Political Science Review* 97 (4): 567–84.

Klein, Gary A. 1993. "A Recognition-Primed Decision (RPD) Model of Rapid Decision Making." In *Decision Making in Action: Models and Methods*, ed. G. A. Klein, R. Calderwood, J. Orasanu, and C. E. Zsambok. Norwood, N.J.: Ablex.

Kleitz, Bretten, Gregory R. Weiher, Kent Tedin, and Richard Matland. 2000. "Choices, Charter Schools, and Household Preferences." *Social Science Quarterly* 81 (3): 846–54.

Kolderie, Ted. 1990. *Beyond Choice to New Public Schools: Withdrawing the Exclusive Franchise in Public Education.* Washington, D.C.: Progressive Policy Institute.

Koppich, Julia, Patricia Holmes, and Margaret L. Plecki. 1998. *New Rules, New Roles? The Professional Work and Lives of Charter School Teachers.* Washington, D.C.: National Education Association.

Krueger, Alan B. 2000. "Economic Considerations and Class Size." Working Paper No. 447. Princeton University, Industrial Relations Section, http://netec.mcc.ac.uk/WoPEc/data/Papers/fthprinin447.html, (accessed July 3, 2002).

Krueger, Alan B. and Diana M. Whitmore. 2000. "The Effect of Attending a Small Class in the Early Grades on College-Test Taking and Middle School Test Results: Evidence from Project Star." NBER Working Paper No. w7656. National Bureau of Economic Research, Cambridge, Mass.

Krueger, Alan B., and Pei Zhu. 2004. "Another Look at the New York City School Voucher Experiment." *American Behavioral Scientist* 47:658–98.

Kucsova, Simona, and Jack Buckley. 2004. "The Effect of Charter School Legislation on Market Share." *Educational Policy Analysis Archives* 12 (66), http://epaa.asu.edu/epaa/v12n66/ (accessed January 1, 2005).

Kuklinski, James H., and Norman L. Hurley. 1994. "On Hearing and Interpreting Political Messages: A Cautionary Tale of Citizen Cue-Taking." *Journal of Politics* 56:729–51.

Kuklinski, James H., and Paul J. Quirk. 1998. "Just the Facts, Ma'am: Political Facts and Public Opinion." *Annals of the American Academy of Political and Social Science* 560:143–54.

———. 2000. "Reconsidering the Rational Public: Cognition, Heuristics, and Mass Opinion." In *Elements of Reason: Understanding and Expanding the Limits of Political Rationality*, ed. A. Lupia, M. McCubbins, and S. Popkin. London: Cambridge University Press.

Kuklinski, James H., Paul J. Quirk, David Schwieder, and Robert E. Rich. 1996. "Misinformation and the Currency of Citizenship." Paper presented at the Annual Meetings of the American Political Science Association. San Francisco.

Lacireno-Paquet, Natalie, Thomas T. Holyoke, Michele Moser, and Jeffrey R. Henig. 2002. "Creaming versus Cropping: Charter School Enrollment Practices in Response to Market Incentives." *Educational Evaluation and Policy Analysis* 24 (2): 145–58.

Ladd, Helen. 2001. "School-Based Accountability Systems: The Promise and the Pitfalls." *National Tax Journal* 54 (2): 385–400.

La Due Lake, Ronald, and Robert Huckfeldt. 1998. "Social Capital, Social Networks and Political Participation." *Political Psychology* 19:567–84.

Laird, N. 1982. "Empirical Bayes Estimates Using the Nonparametric Maximum Likelihood Estimate for the Prior." *Journal of Statistical Computation and Simulation* 15: 211–20.

Lalonde, Robert. 1986. "Evaluating the Econometric Evaluations of Training Programs with Experimental Data." *American Economic Review* 76: 604–20.

Lankford, R. Hamilton, E. S. Lee, and James H. Wykoff. 1995. "An Analysis of Elementary and Secondary School Choice." *Journal of Urban Economics* 38:236–51.

Lankford, R. Hamilton, and James H. Wykoff. 1992. "Primary and Secondary School Choice among Public and Religious Alternatives." *Economics of Education Review* 11:31–37.

Lau, Richard R., and Jack S. Levy. 1998. "Contributions of Behavioural Decision Theory to Research in Political Science." *Applied Psychology* 47:29–44.

Lazarsfeld, Paul Felix, Bernard Berelson, and Hazel Gaudet. 1944. *The People's Choice: How the Voter Makes Up His Mind in a Presidential Campaign.* New York: Duell, Sloan and Pearce.

Leach, C. 1991. "Nonparametric Methods for Complex Data Sets." In *New Developments in Statistics for Psychology and the Social Sciences*, vol. 2, ed. P. Lovie and A. D. Lovie. London: British Psychological Society and Routledge.

Leana, Carrie R., and Harry J. Van Buren. 1999. "Organizational Social Capital and Employment Practices." *Academy of Management Review* 24 (3): 538–55.

LeDoux, Joseph. 1998. *The Emotional Brain.* New York: Simon and Schuster.

Lee, E. S. 1951. "Negro Intelligence and Selective Migration: A Philadelphia Test of the Klineberg Hypothesis." *American Sociological Review* 16:227–33.

Lee, Peter M. 1997. *Bayesian Statistics: An Introduction.* 2nd ed. London: Arnold.

Lee, Valerie E., and Susanna Loeb. 2000. "School Size in Chicago Elementary Schools: Effects on Teachers' Attitudes and Students' Achievement." *American Educational Research Journal* 37 (4): 907–45.

Lee, Valerie E., and Julia Smith. 1997. "High School Size: Which Works Best, and for Whom?" *Educational Evaluation and Policy Analysis* 19 (3): 205–27.

Legislative Office of Education Oversight. 2003. *Community Schools in Ohio: Final Report on Student Performance, Parent Satisfaction, and Accountability.* Columbus, Ohio: State of Ohio.

Leuven, E., and B. Sianesi. 2003. "PSMATCH2: STATA Module to Perform Full Mahalanobis and Propensity Score Matching, Common Support Graphing, and Covariate Imbalance Testing, Version 1.2.3," http://ideas.repec.org/c/boc/bocode/s432001.html (accessed August 15, 2004).

Levi, Margaret. 1996. "Social Capital and Unsocial Capital: A Review Essay of Robert Putnam's *Making Democracy Work.*" *Politics and Society* 24:45–55.

Levin, Henry M. 1989. *The Theory of Choice Applied to Education.* No. 89-CERAS-10. Stanford, Calif.: Stanford University School of Education.

———. 1991. "The Economics of Educational Choice." *Economics of Education Review* 10 (2): 137–58.

———. 2002. "A Comprehensive Framework for Evaluating Educational Vouchers." *Educational Evaluation and Policy Analysis* 24 (3): 159–74.

Levin, Henry M., and Clive R. Belfield. 2003. *The Marketplace in Education.* New York: National Center for the Study of Privatization in Education, Teachers College, Columbia University.

Levin, Henry M., and Cyrus E. Driver. 1997. "The Costs of an Educational Voucher System." *Education Economics* 5 (3): 265–83.

Levine, Charles. 1984. "Citizenship and Service Delivery: The Promise of Coproduction." *Public Administration Review* 44 (March): 178–87.

Levinson, Meira. 1999. *The Demands of Liberal Education*. Oxford: Oxford University Press.

Lewis, C. S. 1960. *Studies In Words*. Cambridge: Cambridge University Press.

Li, K., T. Ragunathan, and D. B. Rubin. 1991. "Large Sample Significance Levels from Multiply-Imputed Data Using Moment-Based Statistics and an F Reference Distribution." *Journal of the American Statistical Association* 86:1065–73.

Lin, Nan. 2001. *Social Capital: A Theory of Social Structure and Action*. Cambridge: Cambridge University Press.

Lindblom, Charles E. 1959. "The Science of Muddling Through." *Public Administration Review* 19:79–88.

Lipsey, Richard G., and Kevin Lancaster. 1956. "The General Theory of Second Best." *Review of Economic Studies* 24 (1): 11–32.

Little, Roderick J. 1988. "Missing Data in Large Surveys (with Discussion)." *Journal of Business and Economic Statistics* 6:287–301.

Little, Roderick J. 1993. "Post-Stratification: A Modeler's Perspective." *Journal of the American Statistics Association* 88:1001–12.

Little, Roderick J., and Donald B. Rubin. 2002. *Statistical Analysis with Missing Data*. 2nd ed. New York: John Wiley.

Lodge, Milton, and Marco Steenbergen. 1995. "The Responsive Voter: Campaign Information and the Dynamics of Candidate Evaluation." *American Political Science Review* 89:309–26.

Lodge, Milton, and Charles Taber. 2000. "Three Steps Toward a Theory of Motivated Political Reasoning." In *Elements of Reason: Understanding and Expanding the Limits of Political Rationality*, ed. A. Lupia, M. McCubbins, and S. Popkin. London: Cambridge University Press.

Long, James E., and Eugenia F. Toma. 1988. "The Determinants of Private School Attendance 1970–1980." *Review of Economics and Statistics* 70:351–57.

Lopez, Alejandra, Amy Stuart Wells, and Jennifer Jellison Holme. 2002. "Creating Charter School Communities: Identity Building, Diversity, and Selectivity." In *Where Charter School Policy Fails: The Problems of Accountability and Equity*, ed. Amy Stuart Wells, 129–58. New York: Teachers College Press.

Lowi, Theodore J. 1964. "American Business, Public Policy, Case Studies and Political Theory." *World Politics* 16:677–715.

Lubell, Mark, Mark Schneider, John T. Scholz, and Mihriye Mete. 2002. "Watershed Partnerships and the Emergence of Collective Action Institutions." *American Journal of Political Science* 46 (1): 148–63.

Lubienski, Christopher. 2003. "Innovation in Education Markets: Theory and Evidence on the Impact of Competition and Choice in Charter Schools." *American Educational Research Journal* 40 (2): 395–443.

Lupia, Arthur, 1994. "Short Cuts versus Encyclopedias: Information and Voting Behavior in California Insurance Reform Election." *American Political Science Review* 88:63–76.

Lupia, Arthur, and Mathew D. McCubbins. 1998. *The Democratic Dilemma: Can Citizens Learn What They Need to Know?* Cambridge: Cambridge University Press.

————. 2000. "The Institutional Foundations of Political Competence." In *Elements of Reason*, ed. A. Lupia, M. McCubbins, and S. Popkin, 47–66. New York: Cambridge University Press.

Macedo, Steven. 2000. *Diversity and Distrust: Civic Education in a Multicultural Democracy*. Cambridge, Mass: Harvard University Press.

————. 2004. "Crafting Good Citizens." *Education Next*, http://www.education next.org/20042/10.html (accessed November 16, 2004).

MaCurdy, Thomas, Thomas A. Mroz, and R. Mark Gritz. 1998. "An Evaluation of National Longitudinal Survey of Youth." *Journal of Human Resources* 33 (2): 345–436.

Maddala, G. S. 1983. *Limited-Dependent and Qualitative Variables in Econometrics*. Cambridge: Cambridge University Press.

Magnuson, Peter. 2000. "Does Size Really Matter? The Debate Over Class Size." *National Association of Elementary School Principals Communicator*, December, 1–2, http://www.naesp.org/ContentLoad.do?contentId=160 (accessed November 12, 2004).

Maranto, Robert, Scott R. Milliman, Frederick Hess, and April W. Gresham, eds. 1999. *School Choice in the Real World: Lessons from Arizona Charter Schools*. Boulder: Westview.

March, James G. 1994. *A Primer on Decision Making: How Decisions Happen*. New York: Free Press.

Marschall, Melissa. 2004. "Citizen Participation and the Neighborhood Context: A New Look at the Coproduction of Local Public Goods." *Political Research Quarterly* 57 (2): 231–44.

Matthews, Jay. 2004. "Are Charter Schools Any Good?" *Washington Post*, October 28, http://www.washingtonpost.com/wp-dyn/articles/A18571–2004Nov2 .html.

McEwan, Patrick. J. 2000. "The Potential Impact of Large-Scale Voucher Programs." *Review of Educational Research* 70:103–49.

————. 2003. "Peer Effects on Student Achievement: Evidence from Chile." *Economics of Education Review* 22 (2): 131–41.

McMaster, Kristen N., and Douglas Fuchs. 2002. Effects of Cooperative Learning on the Academic Achievement of Students with Learning Disabilities: An Update of Tateyama-Sniezek's Review. *Learning Disabilities Research and Practice* 17:107–17.

Meier, Kenneth J., Robert D. Wrinkle, and James L. Polinard. 2000. "Bureaucracy and Organizational Performance: Causality Arguments about Public Schools." *American Journal of Political Science* 44:590–603.

Mettler, Susan. 2002. "Bringing the State Back in to Civic Engagement: Policy Feedback Effects of the GI Bill for World War II Veterans." *American Political Science Review* 96 (2): 351–65.

Mettler, Susan, and Joe Soss. 2004. "The Consequences of Public Policy for Democratic Citizenship: Bridging Policy Studies and Mass Politics." *Perspectives on Politics* 2 (1): 55–73.

Metz, Edward, and James Youniss. 2003. "A Demonstration that School-Based Required Service Does Not Deter—but Heightens—Volunteerism." *PS—Political Science & Politics* 36:281–86.

Minkoff, Debra C. 1997. "Producing Social Capital—National Social Movements and Civil Society." *American Behavioral Scientist* 40 (5): 606–19.

Mintrom, Michael. 1997. "Policy Entrepreneurs and the Diffusion of Innovation." *American Journal of Political Science* 41 (3): 738–70.

Miron, Gary, and Brooks Applegate. 2000. *An Evaluation of Student Achievement in Edison Schools Opened in 1995 and 1996.* Kalamazoo, Mich.: Evaluation Center, Western Michigan University.

Miron, Gary, and Christopher Nelson. 2000. *Autonomy in Exchange for Accountability: An Initial Study of Pennsylvania Charter Schools.* Kalamazoo, Mich.: Evaluation Center, Western Michigan University.

———. 2002. *What's Public About Charter Schools? Lessons Learned about Accountability and Choice.* Thousand Oaks, Calif.: Corwin Press.

Mitchell, Robert C., and Richard T. Carson. 1989. *Using Surveys to Value Public Goods: The Contingent Valuation Method.* Washington, D.C.: RFF Press.

Moe, Terry M. 1995. "Private Vouchers." In *Private Vouchers,* ed. T. Moe. Stanford, Calif.: Hoover Institute Press.

———. 2000a. "The Attraction of Private Schools." Harvard University Program on Education Policy and Governance.

———. 2000b. "The Two Democratic Purposes of Education." In *Rediscovering the Democratic Purposes of Education* ed. L. M. McDonnell, P. M. Timpane, and R. Benjamin. Lawrence: University Press of Kansas.

———. 2001. *Schools, Vouchers, and the American Public.* Washington, D.C.: Brookings Institution Press.

Mokken, R. J. 1971. *A Theory and Procedure of Scale Analysis.* New York: De Gruyter.

Molnar, Alex, Philip Smith, John Zahorik, Amanda Palmer, Anke Halbach, and Karen Ehrle. 1999. "Evaluating the SAGE Program: A Pilot Program in Targeted Pupil-Teacher Reduction in Wisconsin." *Educational Evaluation and Policy Analysis* 21:165–77.

Mooney, Christopher Z., and Robert D. Duval. 1996. *Bootstrapping: A Nonparametric Approach to Statistical Inference.* Newbury Park, Calif.: Sage.

Montgomery, H. 1983. "Decision Rules and the Search for Dominance Structure: Towards a Process Model of Decision Making." In *Analyzing and Aiding Decision Processes,* ed. P. C. Humphreys, O. Svenson, and A. Vari. Amsterdam: North-Holland.

Mosteller, Frederick. 1995. "The Tennessee Study of Class Size in the Early Grades." *Future of Children* 5:113–27.

Munger, Michael C. 2000. *Analyzing Policy: Choices, Conflicts, and Practice.* New York: Norton.

Murphy, James B. 2004. "Against Public Schooling." *Social Philosophy and Policy* 21 (1): 221–65.

Musso, Julliet, Christopher Weare, and Matt Hale. 2000. "Using Web Technology for Governance Reform." *Political Communication* 17:1–17.

Mutz, Diana. 2002. "The Consequences of Cross-Cutting Networks for Political Participation." *American Journal of Political Science* 46:838–55.

Mutz, Diana C. and Jeffery J. Mondak. 2006. "The Workplace as a Context for Cross-cutting Political Discourse." *Journal of Politics* 68 (1).

Nathan, Joe 1996. *Charter Schools: Creating Hope and Opportunity for American Education.* San Francisco, Calif.: Jossey-Bass.

Nathan, Joe, and Karen Febey. 2001. *Smaller, Safer, Saner, Successful Schools.* Washington, D.C.: National Clearinghouse For Educational Facilities, http://www.edfacilities.org/pubs/saneschools.pdf (accessed July 3, 2002).

National Center for Education Statistics. 2005. *Results from the NAEP 2003 Pilot Study.* Washington, D.C.: National Center for Education Statistics, U.S. Department of Education.

National Working Commission on Choice in K-12 Education. 2003. *School Choice: Doing It the Right Way Makes a Difference.* Washington D.C.: Brookings Institution. http://www.brookings.edu/dybdocroot/gs/brown/20031116 schoolchoicereport.pdf (accessed January 3, 2005).

Nechyba, Thomas. 1996. "Public School Finance in a General Equilibrium Tiebout World: Equalization, Peer Effects, and Private School Vouchers." NBER Working Paper 5642. National Bureau of Economic Research, Cambridge, Mass.

Nelson, F. Howard, Bella Rosenberg, and Nancy Van Meter. 2004. *Charter School Achievement on the 2003 National Assessment of Educational Progress.* Washington, D.C.: American Federation of Teachers. http://www.aft.org/pubs-reports/downloads/teachers/NAEPCharterSchoolReport.pdf.

Nelson, Robert H. 2001. *Economics as Religion: From Samuelson to Chicago and Beyond.* University Park: Pennsylvania State University Press.

Newman, Maria. 1999. "State Plans Return of Jersey City Schools to Local Control." *New York Times,* May 27.

New Mexico State University Center for Entrepreneurship. 2003. "Market Mavens."

Niemi, Richard, and Mary Hepburn. 1995. "The Rebirth of Political Socialization." *Perspectives on Political Science* 24:7–16.

Niemi, Richard G., and Jane Junn. 1998. *Civic Education: What Makes Students Learn?* New Haven: Yale University Press.

North, Douglass Cecil. 1990. *Institutions, Institutional Change, and Economic Performance: The Political Economy of Institutions and Decisions.* Cambridge: Cambridge University Press.

Okun, Arthur. 1975. *The Big Trade-Off: Efficiency and Equity.* Washington, D.C.: Brookings Institution Press.

Ostrom, Elinor. 1990. *Governing the Commons: The Evolution of Institutions for Collective Action.* Cambridge: Cambridge University Press.

———. 1996. "Crossing the Great Divide: Coproduction, Synergy, and Development." *World Development* 24 (6): 1073–87.

———. 1998. "A Behavioral Approach to the Rational Choice Theory of Collective Action." *American Political Science Review* 92 (1): 1–22.

Palmer, Louann Bierlein, and Rebecca Gau. 2003. *Charter School Authorizing: Are States Making the Grade?* Washington D.C.: Thomas P. Fordham Institute.

Parry, T. R. 1996. "Will Pursuit of Higher Quality Sacrifice Equal Opportunity in Education? An Analysis of the Education Voucher System in Santiago." *Social Science Quarterly* 77 (4): 821–41.

Payne, John. 1976. "Task Complexity and Contingent Processing in Decision Making: An Information Search and Protocol Analysis." *Organizational Behavior and Human Performance* 16:366–87.

Payne, John W., James R. Bettman, and Eric J. Johnson. 1993. *The Adaptive Decision Maker*. New York: Cambridge University Press.

Pearl, Judea. 2000. *Causality: Models, Reasoning, and Inference*. Cambridge: Cambridge University Press.

Perkinson, Henry J. 1991. *The Imperfect Panacea: American Faith in Education 1865–1990*. 3rd ed. New York: McGraw-Hill.

Peterson, Paul E. 1998. "School Choice: A Report Card." In *Learning from School Choice*, ed. P. E. Peterson and B. Hassel, 17–19 Washington, D.C.: Brookings Institution Press.

Peterson, Paul E., and David E. Campbell. 2001. *Charters, Vouchers, and Public Education*. Washington D.C.: Brookings Institution Press.

Peterson, Paul E., and William G. Howell. 2003. "Latest Results from the New York City Voucher Experiment." Paper presented at the Annual Meeting of the Association of Public Policy and Management, Washington, D.C., November.

Peterson, Paul E., William G. Howell, Patrick J. Wolf, and David E. Campbell. 2002a. *The Education Gap: Vouchers and Urban Schools*. Washington D.C.: Brookings Institution Press.

———. 2002b. "School Vouchers and Academic Performance: Results from Three Randomized Field Trials." *Journal of Policy Analysis and Management* 21 (2): 191–217.

Piattelli-Palmarini, Massimo. 2000. "The Metric of Open-Mindedness." *Natural Language & Linguistic Theory* 18:859–62.

Plumper, Thomas, and Vera E. Troeger. 2004. "The Estimation of Time-Invariant Variables in Panel Analyses with Unit Fixed Effects." Max Planck Institute for Research into Economics Systems, Jenna, Germany.

Popkin, Samuel. 1994. *The Reasoning Voter: Communication and Persuasion in Presidential Campaigns*. 2nd ed. Chicago: University of Chicago Press.

Porter, Michael. 1980. *Competitive Strategy*. New York: Free Press.

Portes, Alejandro. 1998. "Social Capital: Its Origins and Applications in Modern Sociology." *Annual Review of Sociology* 24:1–24.

Prais, S. J., and Christopher B. Winsten. 1954. "Trend Estimators and Serial Correlation." Discussion Paper No. 383. Cowles Commission, Chicago.

Price, Vincent, and John Zaller. 1993. "Who Gets the News? Alternative Measures of News Reception and Their Implications for Research." *Public Opinion Quarterly* 57:133–64.

Public Agenda. 1999. "On Thin Ice: How Advocates and Opponents Could Misread the Public's Views On Vouchers and Charter Schools." Public Agenda, New York.

Public Charter School Board. 2004. *Annual Report 2004*. Washington, D.C.: D.C. Public Charter School Board.

Public Policy Forum. 1998. *Choice School Accountability*. Milwaukee: Public Policy Forum.

Puhani, Patrick A. 2000. "The Heckman Correction for Sample Selection and Its Critique—A Short Survey." *Journal of Economic Surveys* 14:53–68.

Putnam, Robert D. 1993. *Making Democracy Work: Civic Traditions in Modern Italy*. Princeton, N.J.: Princeton University Press.

———. 1995. "Bowling Alone: America's Declining Social Capital." *Journal of Democracy* 6 (1): 65–78.

———. 2000. *Bowling Alone: The Collapse and Revival of American Community*. New York: Simon and Schuster.

Rabe-Hesketh, Sophia, and Anders Skrondal. 2002. "Estimating Chopit Models in gllamm: Political Efficacy Example from King et al. (2002)." Institute of Psychiatry, King's College, London.

Ravitch, Diane. 1996. "The Facts About Catholic Education." *Wall Street Journal*, October 1.

Raywid, Mary Anne. 1989. *The Mounting Case for Schools of Choice*. Fastback #283. Bloomington, Ind.: Phi Delta Kappan Education Foundation.

Research Policy Practice International. 2001. *The State of Charter Schools 2000: Fourth-Year Report*. Washington, D.C.: U.S. Department of Education.

Rhoads, Steven. 1985. *The Economist's View of the World: Government, Markets and Public Policy*. New York: Cambridge University Press.

Rigas, Georgios, and Berndt Brehmer. 1999. "Mental Processes in Intelligence Tests and Dynamic Decision Making Tasks." In *Judgment and Decision Making: Neo-Brunswikian and Process-Tracing Approaches*, ed. P. Juslin and H. Montgomery. Mahwah, N.J.: Lawrence Erlbaum.

Riker, William. 1982. *Liberalism Against Populism*. Prospect Heights, Ill.: Waveland Press.

———. 1984. "The Heresthetics of Constitution-Making." *American Political Science Review* 78:1–16.

Rofes, Eric. 1998. *How Are School Districts Responding to Charter Laws and Charter Schools?* Berkeley: University of California, School of Education, Policy Analysis for California Education.

Rose, Lowell C., and Alec M. Gallup. 2005. "The 37th Annual Phi Delta Kappa / Gallup Poll of the Public's Attitudes Toward The Public Schools." *Phi Delta Kappan*, September, http://www.pdkintl.org/kappan/k0509pol.pdf (accessed December 15, 2005).

Rosen, Emanual. 2000. *The Anatomy of Buzz*. New York: Currency.

Rosenbaum, Paul. 2002. *Observational Studies*. 2nd ed. New York: Springer-Verlag.

Rosenbaum, Paul, and Donald B. Rubin. 1983. "The Central Role of the Propensity Score in Observational Studies for Causal Effects." *Biometrika* 70:41–55.

———. 1985. "Constructing a Control Group Using Matched Sampling Methods that Incorporate the Propensity." *American Statistician* 39:33–38.

Rosenstone, Steven J., and John Mark Hansen. 1993. *Mobilization, Participation, and Democracy in America*. New York: Macmillan.

Rothstein, Richard. 1998. "Charter Conundrum." *American Prospect* 9 (39), July 1–August 1.

Rubin, Donald B. 1973. "Matching to Remove Bias in Observational Studies." *Biometrics* 29: 159–83.

Rubin, Donald B. 1979. "Using Multivariate Matched Sampling and Regression Adjustment to Control Bias in Observational Studies." *Journal of the American Statistical Association* 74:318–28.

———. 1980. "Bias Reduction Using Mahalanobis-Metric Matching." *Biometrics* 36: 293–98.

———. 1987. *Multiple Imputation for Nonresponse in Surveys.* New York: John Wiley.

Saaty, Thomas L. 1986. "Axiomatic Foundation of the Analytic Hierarchy Process." *Management Science* 32:841–53.

Salganik, Laura H., and Nancy Karweit. 1982. "Voluntarism and Governance in Education." *Sociology of Education* 55 (2–3): 152–61.

Salisbury, Robert Holt. 1980. *Citizen Participation in the Public Schools.* Lexington, Mass.: Lexington Books.

Sapiro, Virginia. 1994. "Political Socialization During Adulthood: Clarifying the Political Time of Our Lives." *Research in Micropolitics* 4:197–223.

Schemo, Diana Jean. 2004. "Nation's Charter Schools Lagging Behind, U.S. Test Scores Reveal." *New York Times,* August 17.

Schneider, Anne L., and Helen M. Ingram. 1997. *Policy Design for Democracy: Studies in Government and Public Policy.* Lawrence: University Press of Kansas.

Schneider, Barbara, Kathryn S. Schiller, and James S. Coleman. 1996. "Public School Choice: Some Evidence from the National Education Longitudinal Study of 1988." *Educational Evaluation and Policy Analysis* 18 (1): 19–29.

Schneider, Mark. 1999. "Information and Choice in Educational Privatization." In *Conference on Setting the Agenda; The National Center for the Study of Privatization in Education.* New York: Teacher's College, Columbia University.

———. 2001. "Information and Choice in Educational Privatization." In *Privatizing Education,* ed. H. M. Levin. Boulder, Colo.: Westview Press.

Schneider, Mark, and Jack Buckley. 2000. "Can Modern Information Technologies Cross the Digital Divide to Enhance Choice and Build Stronger Schools?" Occasional Paper 7. National Center for the Study of Privatization in Education, Teachers College, Columbia University, New York.

———. 2002. "What Do Parents Want From Schools? Evidence from the Internet." *Educational Evaluation and Policy Analysis* 24 (2): 133–44.

———. 2003. "Making the Grade: Comparing DC Charter Schools to Other DC Public Schools." *Educational Evaluation and Policy Analysis* 25 (2): 203–15.

Schneider, Mark, Melissa Marschall, Christine Roch, and Paul Teske. 1999. "Heuristics, Low Information Rationality, and Choosing Public Goods: Broken Windows as Shortcuts to Information about School Performance." *Urban Affairs Review* 34 (5): 729–41.

Schneider, Mark, Melissa Marschall, Paul Teske, and Christine Roch. 1998. "School Choice and Culture Wars in the Classroom: What Different Parents Seek from Education." *Social Science Quarterly* 79 (3): 489–501.

Schneider, Mark, Paul Teske, and Melissa Marschall. 2000. *Choosing Schools: Consumer Choice and the Quality of American Schools.* Princeton, N.J.: Princeton University Press.

Schneider, Mark, Paul Teske, Melissa Marschall, and Christine Roch. 1998. "Shopping for Schools: In the Land of the Blind, the One-Eyed Parent May Be Enough." *American Journal of Political Science* 42 (3): 769–93.

Schneider, Mark, Paul E. Teske, and Michael Mintrom. 1995. *Public Entrepreneurs: Agents for Change in American Government.* Princeton, N.J.: Princeton University Press.

Schneider, Mark, Paul Teske, Christine Roch, and Melissa Marschall. 1997. "Networks to Nowhere: Segregation and Stratification in Networks of Information about Schools." *American Journal of Political Science* 41:1201–23.

Schuette, R. A., and Russell H. Fazio. 1995. "Attitude Accessibility and Motivation as Determinants of Biased Processing—a Test of the Mode Model." *Personality and Social Psychology Bulletin* 21:704–10.

Schwartz, Wendy. 1996. "How Well Are Charter Schools Serving Urban and Minority Students?" *ERIC/CUE Digest* 119. ERIC Clearinghouse on Urban Education, New York, http://www.ericdigests.org/1998–1/charter.htm (accessed December 15, 2005).

Sclar, Elliot D. 2000. *You Don't Always Get What You Pay For: The Economics of Privatization.* Ithaca, N.Y.: Cornell University Press.

Sexton, Robert F. 2004. *Mobilizing Citizens for Better Schools.* New York: Teachers College Press.

Shklar, Judith. 1991. *American Citizenship: The Quest for Inclusion.* Cambridge Mass.: Harvard University Press.

Simon, Herbert A. 1955. "A Behavioral Model of Rational Choice." *Quarterly Journal of Economics* 69:99–118.

Simon, Herbert A. 1957. *Models of Man.* New York: John Wiley.

———. 1978. "Rationality as Process and as Product of Thought." *American Economics Review* 68:1–16.

———. 1985. "Human Nature in Politics: The Dialogue of Psychology and Political Science." *American Political Science Review* 79:293–304.

Simpson, E. H. 1951. "The Interpretation of Interaction in Contingency Tables." *Journal of the Royal Statistical Society* B 13:238–41.

Skocpol, Theda, Marshall Ganz, and Ziad Munson. 2000. "A Nation of Organizers: The Institutional Origins of Civic Volunteerism in the United States." *American Political Science Review* 94 (3): 527–46.

Slama, Mark, and Terrell Williams. 1990. "Generalizations of the Market Maven's Information Provision Tendency across Product Categories." *Advances in Consumer Research* 17:48–53.

Slavin, Robert E. 1996. "Research on Cooperative Learning and Achievement: What We Know, What We Need to Know." *Contemporary Educational Psychology* 21 (1): 43–69.

Smith, Kevin B., and Kenneth J. Meier. 1995a. *The Case Against School Choice: Politics, Markets, and Fools.* Armonk, N.Y.: M. E. Sharpe.

———. 1995b. "Public Choice in Education: Markets and the Demand for Quality Education." *Political Research Quarterly* 48:329–43.

Smithson, Michael. 1987. *Fuzzy Set Analysis for Behavioral and Social Sciences.* New York: Springer-Verlag.

Snedecor, George W., and William G. Cochran. 1989. *Statistical Methods*. Ames: Iowa State University Press.

Sniderman, Paul M. 2000. "Taking Sides: A Fixed Choice Theory of Political Reasoning." In *Elements of Reason: Understanding and Expanding the Limits of Political Rationality*, ed. A. Lupia, M. McCubbins, and S. Popkin. London: Cambridge University Press.

Solomon, Lewis C. 2003. *Findings from the 2002 Survey of Parents with Children in Arizona Charter Schools: How Parents Grade Their Charter Schools*. Santa Monica, Calif.: Human Resources Policy Corporation.

Soss, Joe. 1999. "Lessons of Welfare: Policy Design, Political Learning, and Political Action." *American Political Science Review* 93 (2): 363–80.

SRI International. 2002. *A Decade of Public Charter Schools*. Washington, D.C.: U.S. Department of Education.

Stanley, J. Woody, and Christopher Weare. 2004. "The Effects of Internet Use on Political Participation: Evidence from an Agency Online Discussion Forum." *Administration & Society* 36:503–27.

Stein, Robert, and Kenneth Bickers. 1998. "The Micro Foundations of the Tiebout Model." *Urban Affairs Review* 34:76–93.

Steinberg, Laurence D., B. Bradford Brown, and Sanford M. Dornbusch. 1996. *Beyond the Classroom : Why School Reform Has Failed and What Parents Need to Do*. New York: Simon and Schuster.

Stewart, Abigail J., Isis H. Settles, and Nicholas J. G. Winter. 1998. "Women and the Social Movements of the 1960s: Activists, Engaged Observers, and Nonparticipants." *Political Psychology* 19:63–94.

Stimson, James. 1991. *Public Opinion in America: Moods, Cycles and Swings*. Boulder, Colo.: Westview Press.

Stockard, Jean, and Maralee Mayberry. 1992. *Effective Educational Environments*. Newbury Park, Calif.: Corwin Press.

Stone, Clarence. 1998. *Changing Urban Education*. Lawrence: University Press of Kansas.

Svenson, Ola. 1999. "Differentiation and Consolidation Theory: Decision Making Processes Before and After a Choice." In *Judgment and Decision Making: Neo-Brunswikian and Process-Tracing Approaches*, ed. P. Juslin and H. Montgomery. Mahwah, N.J.: Lawrence Erlbaum.

Tateyama-Sniezek, K. M. 1990. "CL: Does It Improve the Academic Achievement of Students with Handicaps?" *Exceptional Children* 56:426–37.

Tedin, Kent, and Gregory R. Weiher. 2004. "Education Related Social Capital, General Social Capital, and the Results of School Choice." Paper presented at the Annual Meetings of the Midwest Political Science Association, Chicago, Illinois, April.

Teske, Paul, Mark Schneider, Jack Buckley, and Sara Clark. 2001. "Can Charter Schools Change Traditional Public Schools?" In *Charters, Vouchers, and Public Education*, ed. P. E. Peterson and D. E. Campbell. Washington, D.C.: Brookings Institution Press.

Teske, Paul, Mark Schneider and Erin Cassese. 2005. "Local School Boards as Charter School Authorizers." In *Besieged: School Boards and the Future of Education Politics*, ed. W. Howell. Washington, D.C.: Brookings Institution Press.

Teske, Paul, Mark Schneider, Michael Mintrom, and Samuel Best. 1993. "Establishing the Micro Foundations of a Macro Theory: Information, Movers, and the Competitive Local Market for Public Goods." *American Political Science Review* 87:702–13.

Tetlock, Phillip E. 2000. "Coping With Trade-Offs: Psychological Constraints and Political Implications." In *Elements of Reason: Understanding and Expanding the Limits of Political Rationality*, ed. A. Lupia, M. McCubbins, and S. Popkin. London: Cambridge University Press.

Thorelli, Hans, and Jack Engledow. 1980. "Information Seekers and Information Systems: A Policy Perspective." *Journal of Marketing* 44:9–27.

Toch, Thomas. 1998. "New Education Bazaar: Charter Schools Represent the Free Market in Action—With All Its Problems." *U. S. News and World Report*, April 27.

Todd, Peter M., and Gerd Gigerenzer. 1999. *Simple Heuristics That Make Us Smart*. London: Oxford University Press.

Tolbert, Caroline, Karen Mossberger, and Ramona McNeal. 2002. "Beyond the Digital Divide: Exploring Attitudes about Information Technology, Political Participation and Electronic Government." Paper presented at the Annual Meetings of the American Political Science Association, Boston, Mass.

Tomz, Michael, Jason Wittenberg and Gary King. 2000. "CLARIFY: Software for Interpreting and Presenting Statistical Results." Harvard University, Center for Basic Research in the Social Sciences.

Torney-Purta, Judith. 1995. "Psychological Theory as a Basis for Political Socialization Research." *Perspectives on Political Science* 24:23–33.

———. 1997. "Links and Missing Links Between Education, Political Knowledge, and Citizenship." *American Journal of Education* 105 (4): 446–58.

Tversky, Amos. 1972. "Elimination by Aspects: A Theory of Choice." *Psychological Review* 79:281–99.

Tversky, Amos, and Daniel Kahneman. 1974. "Judgment Under Uncertainty: Heuristics and Biases." *Science* 185:1124–31.

Tyack, David. 2004. *Seeking Common Ground: Public Schools in a Diverse Society*. Cambridge, Mass.: Harvard University Press.

Tybout, Alice, and Nancy Artz. 1994. "Consumer Psychology." *Annual Review of Psychology* 45:131–69.

U.S. Department of Commerce. 1998. "The Emerging Digital Economy." Washington, D.C.: Secretariat on Electronic Commerce.

———. 2000. "Falling Through the Net: Toward Digital Inclusion." Washington, D.C.: National Telecommunications and Information Administration.

U.S. Department of Education. 2004. *Innovations in Education: Successful Charter Schools*. Washington, D.C.: U.S. Department of Education.

U.S. General Accounting Office. 1994. *Elementary School Children: Many Change Schools Frequently, Harming Their Education*. GAO/HEHS-94-45. Washington, D.C.: GAO.

Vallely, Richard M. 1996. "Couch-Potato Democracy?" *American Prospect* 25 (March–April): 25–26.

van Buuren, S., H. C. Boshuizen, and D. L. Knook. 1999. "Multiple Imputation of Missing Blood Pressure Covariates in Survival Analysis." *Statistics in Medicine* 18:681–94.

Van Dunk, Emily, and Anneliese Dickman. 2004. "The Power of School Choice Depends on Accountability." *Education Week* January 21:52.

Vanourek, Greg, Bruno V. Manno, and Chester E. Finn Jr. 1998. "Charter Schools as Seen by Students, Teachers, and Parents." In *Learning from School Choice*, ed. P. E. Peterson and B. C. Hassel. Washington, D.C.: Brookings Institution Press.

Verba, Sidney, Kay Lehman Schlozman, and Henry E. Brady. 1995. *Voice and Equality: Voluntarism in American Politics*. Cambridge, Mass.: Harvard University Press.

Vergari, Sandra. 2002. *The Charter School Landscape*. Pittsburgh: University of Pittsburgh Press.

Von Neumann, John, and Oskar Morgenstern. 1943. *Theory of Games and Economic Behavior*. New York: John Wiley.

Walberg, Herbert J., and Joseph L. Bast. 2003. *Education and Capitalism: How Overcoming Our Fear of Markets and Economics Can Improve America's Schools*. Stanford, Calif.: Hoover Institution Press.

Wasley, Patricia, Linda C. Powell, Esther Mosak, Sherry P. King, Nicole E. Holland, Matt Gladden, and Michelle Fine. 2000. *Small Schools: Great Strides. A Study of New Small Schools in Chicago*. New York: Bank Street College of Education. http://www.bnkst.edu/html/news/SmallSchools.pdf (accessed July 3, 2002).

Weesie, Jeroen. 1999. "sg121: Seemingly Unrelated Estimation and the Cluster-Adjusted Sandwich Estimator." *Stata Technical Bulletin* 13:19–23.

Weiher, Gregory R., and Kent L. Tedin. 2002. "Does Choice Lead to Racially Distinctive Schools? Charter Schools and Household Preferences." *Journal of Policy Analysis and Management* 21 (1): 79–92.

Weimer, David L., and Adrian R. Vining. 2004. *Policy Analysis: Concepts and Practice*. 4th ed. Englewood Cliffs, N.J.: Prentice-Hall.

Wells, Amy Stuart. 1993. "The Sociology of School Choice: Why Some Win and Others Lose in the Educational Marketplace." In *School Choice: Examining the Evidence*, ed. E. Rassell and R. Rothstein. Washington, D.C.: Economic Policy Institute.

———. 2002. "Why Public Policy Fails to Live Up to the Standard of Charter School Reform: An Introduction." In *Where Charter School Policy Fails: The Problems of Accountability and Equity*, ed. Amy Stuart Wells, 1–25. New York: Teachers College Press.

Wells, Amy Stuart L., Ligia Artiles, Sibyll Carnochan, Camille Wilson Cooper, Cynthia Grutzik, Jennifer Jellison Holme, Alejandra Lopez, Janelle Scott, Julie Slayton, and Ash Vasudeva. 1998. *Beyond the Rhetoric of Charter School Reform: A Study of Ten California Districts*. Los Angeles: University of California, Los Angeles.

Wells, Amy Stuart, Ash Vasudeva, Jennifer Jellison Holme, and Camille Wilson Cooper. 2002. "The Politics of Accountability: California School Districts and Charter School Reform." In *Where Charter School Policy Fails: The Problems of Accountability and Equity*, ed. Amy Stuart Wells, 29–53. New York: Teachers College Press.

Wenglinsky, Harold. 1997. *When Money Matters: How Educational Expenditures Improve Student Performance and How They Don't*. Princeton, N.J.: Educational Testing Service, Policy Information Center.

WestEd. 2003. "USCS: History of Charter Schools," http://www.uscharter schools.org/pub/uscs_docs/o/history.htm.

Westheimer, Joel, and Joseph Kahne. 2004. "Educating the "Good" Citizen: Political Choices and Pedagogical Goals." *PS—Political Science & Politics* 37: 241–47.

White, Halbert. 1980. "A Heteroskedasticity-Consistent Covariance Matrix Estimator and a Direct Test for Heteroskedasticity." *Econometrica* 48:817–30.

White, Halbert. 1982. "Maximum-Likelihood Estimation of Misspecified Models." *Econometrica* 50:1–25.

Wilhelm, Tony, Delia Carmen, and Megan Reynolds. 2002. *Connecting Kids to Technology*. Baltimore: Annie E. Casey Foundation.

Willms, J. Douglas. N.d. "Three Hypotheses about Community Effects," http://www.oecd.org/dataoecd/25/4/1825818.pdf (accessed June 1, 2005).

Wilson, Steven F. 1992. *Reinventing the Schools: A Radical Plan for Boston*. Boston, Mass.: Pioneer Institute.

Witte, John F., Andrea B. Bailey, and Christopher A. Thorn. 1992. "Second Year Report: Milwaukee Parental Choice Program." University of Wisconsin, Robert M. LaFollette Institute of Public Affairs, Madison.

Witte, John F., Arnold F. Shober, and Paul Manna. 2003. "Analyzing State Charter School Laws and Their Influence on the Formation of Charter Schools in the United States." Paper presented at the Annual Meetings of the American Political Science Association, Philadelphia, Pa.

Wohlstetter, Priscilla, and Noelle Griffin. 1998. *Creating and Sustaining Learning Communities: Early Lessons from Charter Schools*. Philadelphia, Pa.: Consortium for Policy Research in Education, University of Pennsylvania.

Wolf, Patrick J., and Steven Macedo. 2004. *Educating Citizens: International Perspectives on Civic Values and School Choice*. Washington, D.C.: Brookings Institution Press.

Wood, D., N. Halfon, D. Scarlata, Paul Newacheck, and S. Nessim. 1993. "Impact of Family Relocation on Children's Growth, Development, School Function, and Behavior." *Journal of the American Medical Association* 270 (11): 1334–38.

Yancey, Patty. 2000. "We Hold On to Our Kids, We Hold On Tight: Tandem Charters in Michigan." In *Inside Charter Schools: The Paradox of Radical Decentralization*, ed. Bruce Fuller, 66–97. Cambridge, Mass.: Harvard University Press.

Youniss, James, I. A. McLellan, and Miranda Yates. 1997. "What We Know about Engendering Civic Identity." *American Behavioral Scientist* 40:620–31.

Zadeh, Lofti A., King-Sun Fu, Kazau Tanaka, and Masamichi Shimura. 1975. *Fuzzy Sets and Their Applications to Cognitive and Decision Processes*. New York: Academic Press.

Zaller, John, and Stanley Feldman. 1992. "A Simple Theory of the Survey Response: Answering Questions versus Revealing Preferences." *American Journal of Political Science* 36:579–616.

Zavoina, R., and W. McElvey. 1975. "A Statistical Model for the Analysis of Ordinal Level Dependent Variables." *Journal of Mathematical Sociology* 4:103–20.

Zimmer, Ron W., and Eugenia F. Toma. 2000. "Peer Effects in Private and Public Schools across Countries." *Journal of Policy Analysis and Management* 19 (1): 75–92

Zollers, Nancy J., and Arun K. Ramanathan. 1998. "For-Profit Charter Schools and Students with Disabilities: The Sordid Side of the Business of Schooling." *Phi Delta Kappan* 80: 297–304.

INDEX

Page numbers printed in italics refer to tables or figures in the text.